Green **Line**

Basisgrammatik

von
Ellen Butzko
Rosemary Hellyer-Jones
Niamh Humphreys
Elise Köhler-Davidson
Peter Lampater
Michael Pfau
Michael Rybicki
Elizabeth Schröder

Ernst Klett Verlag
Stuttgart • Leipzig

So lernst du mit der Green Line Basisgrammatik

Wenn du Fragen zur Grammatik hast, schaust du am besten ins Inhaltsverzeichnis oder Register. So findest du die gesuchten Grammatikregeln am schnellsten. Abkürzungen wie z. B. → G20 verweisen auf eine andere bzw. ähnliche Grammatikeinheit. Jedes der 21 Kapitel hat einen anderen thematischen Kontext.

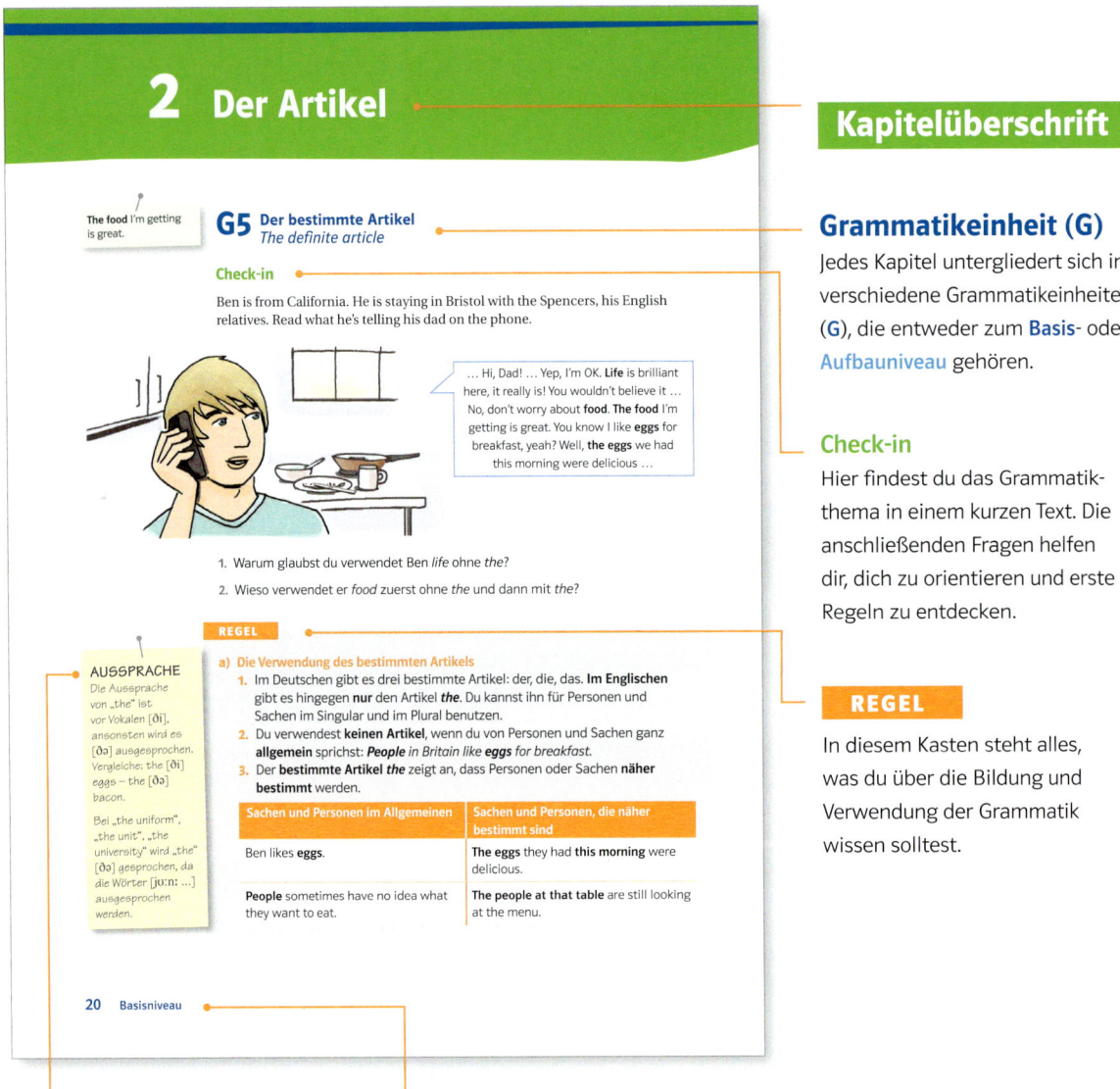

Kapitelüberschrift

Grammatikeinheit (G)

Jedes Kapitel untergliedert sich in verschiedene Grammatikeinheiten (G), die entweder zum **Basis**- oder **Aufbauniveau** gehören.

Check-in

Hier findest du das Grammatik-thema in einem kurzen Text. Die anschließenden Fragen helfen dir, dich zu orientieren und erste Regeln zu entdecken.

REGEL

In diesem Kasten steht alles, was du über die Bildung und Verwendung der Grammatik wissen solltest.

TIPPS UND MERKHILFEN

Hinweise am Rand informieren über Unterschiede im britischen und amerikanischen Englisch, die Aussprache oder bieten Eselsbrücken.

Dunkelblau kennzeichnet Regeln, die du bis zum Ende der 10. Klasse sicher anwenden können solltest.

(= **Basisniveau**)

Hellblau kennzeichnet Regeln, die dir helfen, deine Grammatikkenntnisse noch weiter auszubauen. Sie gehen über das Basisniveau hinaus.

(= **Aufbauniveau**)

2. Das *going to-future* wird gebildet aus einer **Form von** *be* + *going to* + Infinitiv des Verbs.

Aussage:	We**'re going to have** a video conference with our partner school in May.
Verneinung:	You **aren't going to work** on your own, but in groups of three.
Frage mit Fragewort:	When **is** the conference **going to be**?
Entscheidungsfrage mit Kurzantwort:	**Are** we **going to have** live presentations? – Yes, you **are**. / No, you **aren't**.

■ **Achtung!**
– Um etwas Zukünftiges auszudrücken, kannst du im Deutschen das Präsens oder das Futur verwenden. **Im Englischen** musst du jedoch **immer eine Form des Futurs** benutzen. Vergleiche:
  • *At the end of the month we***'re going to show** *each other our videos.*
  Am Ende des Monats **zeigen** wir uns unsere Videos.
  Am Ende des Monats **werden** wir uns unsere Videos **zeigen**.

■ **Schriftlicher/mündlicher Sprachgebrauch**
– In der gesprochenen Umgangssprache hörst du manchmal ***gonna*** statt *going to*. Dies ist vor allem im amerikanischen Englisch der Fall.
  • Betty: *What are you* ***gonna do***?
  Chris: *I'm* ***gonna do*** *something on cars.*
  Betty: *Really? Isn't that* ***gonna be*** *boring?*

English summary

How it works	Examples
The going to-future is made up of a form of *be* + *going to* + infinitive. You use the going to-future when … – you want to say what someone plans to do in the near future. – there are definite signs that something is sure to happen.	– Chris: I**'m going to ask** Mr Hilton a few questions about our project. – Jay: Watch out, Sir! That pile of papers **is going to fall** off your desk.

Check-out

1. Die englischen Schüler sollen ihrem Lehrer sagen, mit wem und worüber sie das Projekt machen wollen. Wie beantwortet Jay Mr Hiltons Fragen? Schreibe ganze Sätze.

a) *Who are you going to do your project with?* (Chris, Sarah)
b) *What is your project going to be about?* (cars)
c) *How long is your video going to be?* (five minutes)
d) *Where are you going to make your video?* (car factory)

■ **Achtung!**
Hier wird erklärt, wie häufig gemachte Fehler vermieden werden können.

■ **Mündlicher/schriftlicher Sprachgebrauch**
Hier findest du Hinweise zu Unterschieden im Sprachgebrauch.

English summary
Der Bereich *English summary* fasst die Regel kurz zusammen. So lernst du Grammatikregeln in englischer Sprache zu verstehen.

Check-out
Anhand der Übungen kannst du selbst kontrollieren, ob du die Grammatikregel wirklich verstanden hast. Die Lösungen findest du im Anhang der Grammatik.

Anhang

Hier findest du die **Lösungen** zu den Check-in- und Check-out-Aufgaben, **Übersichten** zu unregelmäßigen Verben, Zahlen, Datum und Uhrzeit sowie den **Lernertyptest** mit Beispielen für **Lernertypaufgaben**.

Register

Das umfangreiche Register hilft beim Auffinden einzelner Themen.

Green Line Basisgrammatik
Arbeitsheft mit Lösungsheft
978-3-12-560013-3

Arbeitsheft passend zur Green Line Basisgrammatik mit vielen weiteren Übungsmöglichkeiten und Lösungen.

Inhaltsverzeichnis

7 *Be, have* und *do* als Voll- und Hilfsverben

Thema: Zu Besuch bei Sue

8 Die Zeitformen der Gegenwart

Thema: Mode

Thema: Musikbands

9 Die Zeitformen der Vergangenheit

Thema: Straßenkriminalität

Thema: Im Museum

10 Die Zeitformen der Zukunft

Thema: Videokonferenz mit einer Partnerschule

11 Die Modalverben

Thema: Im Sportverein

12 Das Passiv

Thema: New York

13 Die indirekte Rede

Thema: Wellen, Wind und Meer

14 Der Infinitiv

Thema: Als Austauschschüler in Florida

15 Das Gerundium

Thema: Bei den Pfadfindern

16 Das Partizip

Thema: Schulbasketball

17 Das Verb und seine Ergänzungen

Thema: In der Schule

18 Die Satzarten

Thema: Eine Onlinebekanntschaft

19 Die Relativsätze

Thema: Kino

20 Die Bedingungssätze

Thema: Beziehungen

21 Satzverknüpfungen

Thema: Der amerikanische Westen

Anhang

1 Das Nomen

My **cousin** is picking me up at the airport.

G1 Nomen zur Bezeichnung von Personen
Nouns for people

Check-in

It is the middle of January, and even in Britain there has been a lot of snow. So much that a lot of flights from Heathrow Airport are now delayed.

Amy: This stupid snow! Where are you travelling to?

Maria: I'm flying back home to Berlin. What about you?

Amy: I'm flying to Malaga. I hope there won't be a long delay. My **cousin** is picking me up at the airport.

Maria: Your cousin? Does he live in Malaga?

Amy: Not he. She! Yes, my **aunt** and **uncle** have got a hotel there.

Maria: Really? That sounds great.

1. Welche der im Gespräch hervorgehobenen Personen ist männlich, welche weiblich und welche könnte sowohl männlich als auch weiblich sein?

2. Wieso glaubt Maria zuerst, dass *Amy's cousin* männlich ist?

REGEL

TIPP
In einigen wenigen Fällen haben die Bezeichnungen für weibliche Berufe die Nachsilbe „-ess":
– My friend works as a **waitress**.
– Marilyn Monroe was a famous **actress**.
Ebenso: hostess, stewardess.

1. Genau wie im Deutschen kannst du auch im Englischen am **Namen** erkennen, ob es sich um eine männliche oder weibliche Person handelt.
   - *Amy* and *Maria* are waiting at Heathrow Airport.
2. Auch bei den Bezeichnungen *aunt*, *boy*, *brother*, *father*, *girl*, *man*, *mother*, *sister*, *uncle*, *woman* etc. ist das Geschlecht eindeutig.
   - Amy's *aunt* and *uncle* have got a hotel in Malaga.
3. Die meisten **Bezeichnungen für Personen und für Berufe** können sich jedoch auf **beide Geschlechter** beziehen, z. B. *cousin, doctor, friend, neighbour, officer, teacher*. Ob es sich dabei um eine weibliche oder männliche Person handelt, ergibt sich aus dem Kontext.
   - Amy's **cousin Jane** will be at the airport to meet her.
   - A **customs officer** opened my bag. **She** took everything out.

■ **Achtung!**
   − Wenn du beispielsweise die deutschen Begriffe „Ärztin" oder „Busfahrerin" ins
   Englische übersetzen möchtest, reicht es, wenn du *doctor* bzw. *bus driver* sagst.

English summary

How it works	Examples
The name of a person usually tells you whether a boy/man or a girl/woman is meant.	− **Maria** is flying to Berlin.
Nouns like *aunt, brother, sister, uncle* also tell you whether the person is a boy/man or a girl/woman.	− Her **sister** isn't travelling with her today.
The same noun is often used for both men and women (*cousin, doctor, friend, neighbour*). You can normally tell from the context whether a girl/woman or a boy/man is meant.	− Our **neighbour** very kindly took us to the airport in **her** car.

Check-out

1. Erstelle eine Tabelle und trage ein, welche von diesen Nomen nur für männliche
   Personen, nur für weibliche Personen oder sowohl für männliche als auch für
   weibliche Personen verwendet werden können.

   *aunt • author • baby • Ben • brother • bus driver • cousin • dancer • doctor •
   Emma • film star • footballer • grandmother • lawyer • Caroline • Mr Turner •
   model • police officer • sister • tennis player • uncle • waitress*

männlich	weiblich	männlich oder weiblich
Ben, …	…	…

G2 Nomen zur Bezeichnung von Gruppen
Nouns for groups of people

The **police** are here.

Check-in

Amy is waiting at Heathrow Airport for her flight to Malaga. She's calling her
cousin Jane, who is going to pick her up. Read what she's telling her.

Yes, my flight is delayed. − Can you hear me OK, Jane? The
noise in here is terrible. So many **people** are waiting for their
flights! There is even a football **team** here now. They're so
angry − they're afraid they'll miss their match! − Oh, no! What's
up now? The **police** are here! They're just coming in … No, it's
OK, Jane, don't worry. I'll call back later. Bye!

1. Welche Personalpronomen und Possessivbegleiter gehören zu den im Telefonat hervorgehobenen Nomen?

2. Was fällt dir bei der Verbform auf, die nach *police* steht?

REGEL

1. Wenn du betonen möchtest, dass die **Gruppe als Ganzes** (*class, crowd, family, team*) gesehen wird, verwendest du wie auch im Deutschen die **Singularform des Verbs und der Pronomen**.
   • The **team has** improved a lot this year. That's because **it has** got a new manager now.
   • There **was** a huge **crowd** at the match last Saturday.

2. Wenn du betonen möchtest, dass es um die **einzelnen Mitglieder der Gruppe** (*class, crowd, family, team*) geht, verwendest du die **Pluralform des Verbs und der Pronomen bzw. Begleiter**. Diese Betrachtungsweise wird im Englischen sehr häufig gebraucht.
   • There is even a football **team** here now. Why **do they** look so angry?
     – **They're** afraid **they**'ll miss **their** match.
   • Look at the huge **crowd** at the check-in. **They've** been waiting for ages.

3. Bei den Nomen *people* („Leute", „Menschen") und *police* werden immer die einzelnen Mitglieder der Gruppe gesehen. Daher musst du sie **mit der Pluralform des Verbs und der Pronomen bzw. Begleiter** verwenden.
   • At least five hundred **people are** in the check-in area now. **Most people don't** like waiting.
   • At busy places like airports, the **police are** never far away. **They do their** best to deal with emergencies quickly.

TIPP
– Du kannst „people" mit Zahlwörtern gebrauchen: There were more than **20 people** at the counter.
– Wenn du über einzelne Polizisten sprechen willst, musst du „police officer" verwenden: There were **three police officers** at the entrance.

English summary

How it works	Examples
You can use nouns for groups of people like *class, crowd, family, team* with singular or plural verb forms, pronouns and determiners.	– Maria's **class are** doing a project on transport in London. – **Class 8 B has** Geography on Mondays and Thursdays.
People (= 'persons') and *police* can only be used with plural forms.	– **People were** making trouble in one of the airport lounges. – The **police were** called to deal with a group of crazy football fans.

Check-out

1. Einer dieser drei Sätze ist falsch. Finde und korrigiere ihn.

   a) *Maria's family were all waiting for her at the airport.*
   b) *The police has stopped the fighting.*
   c) *There was a crowd of at least a hundred people in the departure lounge.*

2. Übertrage diese beiden Sätze ins Englische.

   a) Die Polizei versucht, Menschen zu helfen.
   b) Siehst du die zwei Polizisten da drüben?

G3 Regelmäßige und unregelmäßige Pluralformen
Regular and irregular plural forms

> It's especially hard for **families** with small **children**.

Check-in

Matthew Fielding is reporting live about the chaos at Heathrow Airport, where people are still waiting for their delayed flights.

> … No change in the situation here at London's biggest airport. People are now preparing to spend the night in the airport **lounges** and **corridors**. It's especially hard for **families** with small **children**. I've spoken to two **women** who are travelling alone with their **babies**. They both say that actually the babies don't mind the noise here – they can sleep through an earthquake! But there won't be much sleep for everyone else here. People are putting their **feet** up on empty **seats** – if they can find any – or are even trying to sleep on the floor …
> Matthew Fielding , BBC News, Heathrow.

1. Wie heißen die Singularformen von *children*, *women* und *feet*?

2. Wie schreibst du die Singularformen von *families* und *babies*?

REGEL

1. Du kannst den Plural der meisten englischen Nomen bilden, indem du ein **-s** an die **Singularform** anhängst, z. B.:

Singular – Plural	Singular – Plural
a book – some boo**ks** [s]	a tree – a few tr**ees** [z]
one seat – four sea**ts** [s]	a job – some jo**bs** [z]
a cliff – the clif**fs** [s]	a nurse – two nur**ses** [ɪz]
one shop – two sho**ps** [s]	one page – ten pa**ges** [ɪz]

AUSSPRACHE
– Sprich [s] nach den stimmlosen Lauten [k], [p], [t] usw.
– Sprich [z] nach Vokalen und stimmhaften Konsonanten [b], [d], [g] usw.
– Sprich [ɪz] nach den Zischlauten [s], [z], [ʃ], [tʃ], [dʒ] und [ʒ].

TIPP

Wenn du eine einzelne Person meinst, verwendest du das Wort „person". Eine Gruppe von Menschen sind „people".

2. Allerdings gibt es auch einige **unregelmäßige Pluralformen**, die du lernen musst.

Singular – Plural	Singular – Plural
one m**a**n [mæn] – a few m**e**n [men]	a m**ouse** [maʊs] – lots of m**ice** [maɪs]
a wom**a**n [wʊmən] – two wom**e**n [wɪmɪn]	one child [tʃaɪld] – some child**ren** [tʃɪldrən]
my left f**oo**t [fʊt] – both my f**ee**t [fi:t]	one fish – millions of **fish**
a t**oo**th [tu:θ] – 32 t**ee**th [ti:θ]	a sheep – a group of **sheep**

■ **Achtung!**

– Wenn ein Nomen auf einen Konsonanten + -y endet, so wird -y zu -ies, z. B.:
   a baby – all the bab**ies**, our family – other famil**ies**, city – cit**ies**, story – stor**ies**.
   Steht jedoch vor dem -y ein Vokal, so bleibt das y erhalten, z. B.:
   a boy – lots of bo**ys**, day – da**ys**, monkey – monke**ys**.

– Bei einigen Nomen auf -o wird -es angefügt, z. B.: one potato – two potato**es**,
   a tomato – five tomato**es**. Bei disco, photo, radio und video wird jedoch nur ein -s
   angehängt, z. B.: a photo – some photo**s**.

– Nomen, die auf -f oder -fe enden, haben meist die Pluralendung -ves, z. B.:
   one scarf – two scar**ves**, a knife – a few kni**ves**, life – li**ves**. Bei roof wird jedoch
   nur ein -s angehängt: one roof – some roof**s**.

English summary

How it works	Examples
Most English nouns have -s plural forms. But they are pronounced in different ways.	– I bought two **magazines** [z] in one of the airport **shops** [s]. – This thriller has more than 400 **pages** [ɪz].
Some nouns have special plural forms, e. g. potatoes, stories, knives.	– Amy likes adventure **stories**.
A few nouns have irregular plural forms, e. g. feet, men, mice, sheep.	– Have you ever read Steinbeck's Of **Mice** and **Men**?

Check-out

1. In diese Sätze haben sich falsche Pluralformen eingeschlichen. Finde und korrigiere sie.

   a) Do more man than woman work at Heathrow Airport?
   b) I actually saw two mouses in the departure lounge.
   c) Many passengers can't brush their tooths because their toothbrushes are in their bags on the plane.
   d) It is difficult for familys to travel with small childs and babys.
   e) There are some funny photoes of sheeps in the magazine I bought.

G4 Nomen, die nur im Singular stehen und Nomen, die nur im Plural stehen *Nouns that only use the singular and nouns that only use the plural*

A child dropped her ice cream on my **jeans**.

Check-in

After all the delay Amy is now on her flight to Malaga. A Spanish businessman is sitting next to her. Read their conversation.

Man: So we're finally in the **air**! But what a night! Did you manage to sleep at all?

Amy: Not really. Some **coffee** would do me good! – But I must say, I missed my **baggage**. It was already on the plane, of course, so I only had a small piece of hand baggage with me. No problem, normally. But a child dropped her chocolate ice cream on my **jeans** and I couldn't change them. I didn't have another pair of **trousers** in my hand baggage.

Man: No, of course not. Poor you. – Well, for me the main problem was the delay. I had plans for an important business meeting today. But the **information** we got wasn't good enough. So I had no idea whether I'd make it to the meeting or not.

Amy: Will you?

Man: Yes. The good **news** is that the meeting will be tomorrow. There's **snow** in Spain, too.

1. Warum werden die Nomen *jeans* and *trousers* im Plural gebraucht? Was glaubst du?

2. Übertrage diese beiden Sätze ins Deutsche.

   a) *The information we got wasn't good enough.*
   b) *The good news is that the meeting will be tomorrow.*

REGEL

a) Nomen, die nur im Singular stehen

1. Die meisten **Stoffbezeichnungen** wie *air, bread, coffee, flour, hair, milk, rain, snow, sugar, tea* können **nur im Singular** gebraucht werden:
   • *I'd like some **coffee**, please. – Would you like some **milk** with **it**?*
   • *My **hair is** a real mess after that night. – Don't worry. **It looks** quite OK.*

2. Einige **abstrakte Begriffe** werden – anders als die deutschen Entsprechungen – immer **im Singular** verwendet:
   • *The **information** he got **wasn't** very good. **It** didn't help him at all.*
   • *Maria, however, got some good **advice** at the information desk. **It was** very useful.*

3. **Sammelbegriffe** wie *baggage, fruit* und *furniture* sind Begriffe, die eine Anzahl von Einzelteilen zusammenfassen (bei *furniture* z. B. *chair, table, cupboard*). Während für *baggage* auch im Deutschen die Singularform „Gepäck" steht, wird für *furniture* die Pluralform „Möbel" verwendet. *Fruit* kann durch „Früchte" oder „Obst" wiedergegeben werden.
   • *Maria's **baggage was** terribly heavy. But a kind woman helped her with **it**.*
   • *Amy's aunt gave her a big room in the hotel. The **furniture was** old-fashioned but **it** looked very nice.*

> **TIPP**
> Bei einigen Stoffbezeichnungen kannst du den Plural verwenden. Die Bedeutung ändert sich jedoch:
> – Can we have **two coffees**, please? (= zwei Tassen Kaffee)
> – Don't sit there. There are some dog **hairs** on the seat. (= einzelne Haare)

> **TIPP**
> Wenn du auf bestimmte Früchte hinweisen möchtest, kannst du auch die Pluralform von „fruit" verwenden: I like tropical **fruits** like bananas and oranges.

TIPP

Auch „homework"
gehört zu den
nicht zählbaren
Nomen. Vergleiche:
Ich konnte meine
Hausaufgaben nicht
machen. **Sie waren**
zu schwierig. –
I couldn't do my
homework. **It was**
too difficult.

TIPP

Wenn du von einer
Anzahl an Hosen
oder Brillen
sprechen möchtest,
verwendest du
„pair(s) of":
– Amy has bought
  herself **two** new
  pairs of jeans.
– I need a new **pair
  of glasses**.

4. **Einige Nomen** (*Maths, news, the United States, the Netherlands*) **haben** zwar die **Pluralendung -s**, werden aber **als eine Einheit gesehen** (*the USA* als ein Land) **und** deshalb **wie eine Singularform gebraucht**:
   • The **news is** very interesting this morning. (Die Nachrichten sind …) *It* **says** the **United States has** had **its** coldest winter for twenty years. (Die Vereinigten Staaten haben ihren …)

b) Nomen, die nur im Plural stehen

1. Anders als die deutschen Entsprechungen „Kleidung" bzw. „Treppe" werden *clothes* und *stairs* **nur im Plural** verwendet:
   • Amy's **clothes were** dirty. But she couldn't change **them**.
   • Where is the cafeteria? – It's upstairs. The **stairs are** that way. **They are** at the end of the corridor.

2. Paarwörter wie *glasses*, *jeans*, *pants* und *trousers* bestehen aus zwei Teilen (zwei Brillengläsern, zwei Hosenbeinen). Deshalb werden sie **nur im Plural** verwendet:
   • *Those trousers look* really good on you. *Are they* new?
     Diese **Hose steht** dir wirklich gut. **Ist sie** neu?
   • I can't find my **glasses**. Have you seen **them** anywhere?
     Ich kann meine **Brille** nicht finden. Hast du **sie** irgendwo gesehen?

■ **Achtung!**

– Du kannst vor Nomen, die nur im Singular verwendet werden, keinen unbestimmten Artikel (*a, an*) und auch kein Zahlwort (*three, twenty*) stellen, da sie nicht zählbar sind. Wenn du bei diesen Begriffen Angaben über die Menge machen möchtest, musst du Umschreibungen (**→ G18**) verwenden, z. B.:
   • *a little bit of snow*   • *a glass of water*
   • *three bottles of milk*   • *a pound of butter*
   • *a piece of baggage*

– Vor allen Nomen kannst du dagegen *some* und *any* verwenden (**→ G20**).
   • I don't know what to do. Can you give me **some advice**?
   • We didn't get **any** useful **information**.

English summary

How it works	Examples
There are some English nouns that you cannot count, e.g. *coffee*, *milk*, *advice*, *homework*, *furniture*. You can only use them in the singular.	– This **coffee smells** good. Could I have some **milk** with **it**? – The **advice** that Amy got **was** very useful.
You use *a glass of*, *a pound of*, *a piece of* etc. if you want to express an exact quantity.	– I'd like **a piece of cake** with **a cup of tea**, please.

How it works	Examples
A few nouns that end in -s can only be used in the singular, e.g. *news, the United States*.	– The **news is** on. Let's watch **it**. Listen! **The United States has** a new president.
Some nouns can only be used in the plural, e.g. *glasses, trousers*. To talk about the number of trousers, glasses etc., you use *a pair of/two pairs of*.	– I like **these jeans**. I'm going to buy **them**. – Maria has got at least **three pairs of sunglasses**.

Check-out

1. Erstelle eine Tabelle und gib an, welche dieser Nomen nur im Singular und welche im Singular und im Plural verwendet werden können. Bilde die Pluralform, wo dies möglich ist.

   advice • baggage • book • child • butter • bread • coal • foot • furniture • glass • homework • information • job • milk • mouse • tomato • tree • wife

2. Übertrage die folgenden Sätze ins Englische.

   a) Die Hausaufgaben waren zu schwierig.
   b) Danke für die guten Ratschläge. Sie werden mir sehr helfen.
   c) Ich habe eine neue Hose gekauft.
   d) Die Nachrichten sind heute nicht sehr interessant.

2 Der Artikel

The food I'm getting is great.

G5 Der bestimmte Artikel
The definite article

Check-in

Ben is from California. He is staying in Bristol with the Spencers, his English relatives. Read what he's telling his dad on the phone.

… Hi, Dad! … Yep, I'm OK. **Life** is brilliant here, it really is! You wouldn't believe it … No, don't worry about **food**. **The food** I'm getting is great. You know I like **eggs** for breakfast, yeah? Well, **the eggs** we had this morning were delicious …

1. Warum glaubst du verwendet Ben *life* ohne *the*?

2. Wieso verwendet er *food* zuerst ohne *the* und dann mit *the*?

REGEL

AUSSPRACHE
Die Aussprache von „the" ist vor Vokalen [ði], ansonsten wird es [ðə] ausgesprochen. Vergleiche: the [ði] eggs – the [ðə] bacon.

Bei „the uniform", „the unit", „the university" wird „the" [ðə] gesprochen, da die Wörter [juːnː …] ausgesprochen werden.

a) Die Verwendung des bestimmten Artikels

1. Im Deutschen gibt es drei bestimmte Artikel: der, die, das. **Im Englischen** gibt es hingegen **nur** den Artikel *the*. Du kannst ihn für Personen und Sachen im Singular und im Plural benutzen.

2. Du verwendest **keinen Artikel**, wenn du von Personen und Sachen ganz **allgemein** sprichst: *People in Britain like eggs for breakfast.*

3. Der **bestimmte Artikel *the*** zeigt an, dass Personen oder Sachen **näher bestimmt** werden.

Sachen und Personen im Allgemeinen	Sachen und Personen, die näher bestimmt sind
Ben likes **eggs**.	**The eggs** they had **this morning** were delicious.
People sometimes have no idea what they want to eat.	**The people at that table** are still looking at the menu.

b) Stoffbezeichnungen und abstrakte Begriffe

1. Wenn du **Stoffbezeichnungen** (*tea, food*) **oder abstrakte Begriffe** (*life, time*) **im allgemeinen Sinn** verwendest, steht **kein Artikel**. Dies ist auch der Fall, wenn vor dem Nomen ein Adjektiv, z. B. *British*, steht.
2. Wenn du solche Nomen **näher bestimmen** möchtest, verwendest du den **bestimmten Artikel**.

ohne *the*	mit *the*
Tea is a popular drink in Britain.	**The tea (that) Tom's aunt makes** is quite strong.
British food can taste great.	**The food (which) Ben got on his flight to London** turned out to be OK.
Time goes quickly when you're enjoying **life**.	Ben is reading a book about **the life of a soldier** in Britain at **the time of the Romans.**

> **TIPP**
> Die nähere Bestimmung erfolgt z. B. durch …
> – einen Relativsatz (→ **G108**): The tea (that) Tom's aunt makes is quite strong.
> – den of-Genitiv (→ **G16**): Ben is reading a book about the life of a soldier in Britain.

c) Institutionen und Verkehrsmittel

1. Wenn du von **Institutionen und Verkehrsmitteln im Allgemeinen** sprichst, steht **kein Artikel**. Hier steht der Zweck der Institution im Vordergrund bzw. die Verkehrsverbindung allgemein.
2. Ist jedoch ein **bestimmtes Gebäude oder Fahrzeug** gemeint, musst du den **bestimmten Artikel** verwenden.

ohne *the*	mit *the*
School in Britain usually starts at 9 o'clock.	**The school (that) Ben's cousin goes to** is in the centre of Bristol.
Die Schule (= der Unterricht) …	*Die Schule (= Gebäude) in die Bens Cousin geht, …*
A lot of students go to school by **bus**.	**The bus** was ten minutes late **this morning**.
… mit dem Bus …	*Heute morgen hatte der Bus …*

d) Monate, Wochentage und Mahlzeiten

1. **Monate, Wochentage und Mahlzeiten** werden **ohne *the*** verwendet, wenn du von ihnen **im Allgemeinen** sprichst.
2. Ist aber ein ganz **bestimmter Monat, Wochentag** oder eine bestimmte **Mahlzeit** gemeint, verwendest du den **bestimmten Artikel**.

ohne *the*	mit *the*
Ben arrived in England in **July**.	Ben's parents were in New York in **the September of 2001.**
His cousin Jack's holidays start on **Thursday**.	They will always remember **the Tuesday when the World Trade Center was attacked.**
Shall we have **lunch** at Mario's today, Ben?	**The lunch we had there last time** wasn't bad.

English summary

How it works	Examples
You don't use the definite article when you talk about people or things in general.	– It is sometimes surprising what **people** in other countries eat.
You must use the definite article when you talk about definite people or things.	– **The people** next door have got some relatives in California.
With some nouns you use the definite article differently in German and in English, e.g. with abstract nouns, institutions, transport and meals. When you think of institutions, transport and meals in general, you don't use the definite article.	– **Life** is full of suprises. – **Time** flies. – Jack doesn't like **school**. – Ben travelled to Bristol by **train**. – For Ben **breakfast** is the most important meal of the day.
When you talk about a definite building, train or meal, you use the article.	– **The school** Jack goes to was built in the 19th century. – The Spencers recognized Ben when he got off **the train**. – **The breakfast** Ben had this morning was very good.

Check-out

1. Vervollständige den Text mit dem bestimmten Artikel *the*, wo dies nötig ist.

   Jack, Ben's cousin, is a vegetarian and he doesn't eat … meat. He only eats … cereals, … vegetables and … bread his mother bakes herself. But he enjoys … life just as much as everyone else. He says that … people often have no idea about … hard life of … animals. He likes … coffee, and especially … coffee his mother makes. Jack still goes to … school. He goes to … school by … bus. He always catches … 8:30 bus. Every day he has … lunch in the school cafeteria. But this isn't always easy because Jack likes … healthy food, and … food they offer at the cafeteria is not very good.

G6 Der bestimmte Artikel bei Namen
The definite article with names

> Tomorrow we're going to **the Tower of London.**

Check-in

Ben is in London with his cousin and his uncle. Read the post that he has put on the Internet for his friends back in California.

Ben   30 minutes ago

Hey! Guess where I am now … London! Yep! I'm here for a long weekend with **Jack** (my cousin), and **Uncle David**. Poor **Aunt Chrissie** has to work, so she couldn't come with us. We saw **Buckingham Palace** today (but no Queen!), and then we went shopping in **Oxford Street**. That's where I bought this cool T-shirt with **Big Ben** on it! Tomorrow we're going to **the Tower of London** by river boat on **the Thames**! More news later. See ya!

1. Schau dir die hervorgehobenen Namen an. Nenne zwei Beispiele aus dem Eintrag, bei denen sich der Gebrauch des bestimmten Artikels im Englischen nicht vom Deutschen unterscheidet.

2. Wo würdest du im Deutschen einen Artikel verwenden, wo im Englischen kein *the* steht?

a) Personennamen und Verwandtschaftsbezeichnungen

1. **Personennamen im Singular und Verwandtschaftsbezeichnungen** die wie Namen gebraucht werden, verwendest du im Englischen **ohne** den **Artikel**. Das ist auch der Fall, wenn dem Namen ein Adjektiv vorausgeht:
   - *Poor Aunt Chrissie has to work.*
2. Im Englischen stehen **Familiennamen im Plural** immer **mit** dem **bestimmten Artikel**. Im Deutschen werden sie meistens ohne Artikel verwendet.

Personennamen im Singular ohne *the*	Familiennamen im Plural mit *the*
Ben is in London with **Jack** and **Uncle David**.	**The Spencers** live in Bristol.
Ben ist mit **Jack** und **Onkel David** in London.	**(Die) Spencers** wohnen in Bristol.
Poor Aunt Chrissie had to stay home.	
Die arme Tante Chrissie musste zu Hause bleiben.	

b) Bezeichnung von Ländern, Bergen und Gebirgen

1. Die **meisten Namen von Ländern und Bergen im Singular** stehen **ohne** den bestimmten **Artikel**. Ausnahmen sind z. B. *the United Kingdom, the Republic of Ireland, the Matterhorn, the Zugspitze.*
2. Die **im Plural** gebrauchten Namen von **Ländern und Gebirgen** stehen jedoch **mit** dem bestimmten **Artikel**.

Ländernamen, Berge im Singular ohne *the*	Ländernamen, Gebirge im Plural mit *the*
California is on the border to **Mexico**.	California is one of the most beautiful parts of **the United States**.
Mount Whitney is in California.	**The Rocky Mountains** are also known as **the Rockies**.

c) Bezeichnung von Flüssen, Seen, Meeren, Gebäuden, Straßen und Parkanlagen

1. Die Namen von **Seen, Gebäuden, Straßen** und **Parkanlagen** verwendest du normalerweise **ohne** den **Artikel**.
2. Die Namen von **Flüssen, Meeren** und alle **Namen mit einem *of*-Genitiv** werden **mit** dem **Artikel** gebraucht.

Seen, Gebäude, Straßen, Parkanlagen ohne *the*	Flüsse, Meere, Namen mit *of*-Genitiv mit *the*
Loch Lomond is the largest lake in Britain.	**The Thames** is the most famous English river.
Buckingham Palace is open to the public in the summer.	Tomorrow we're going to **the Tower of London**. (Sometimes it's just called **the Tower**.)
Ben and his cousin looked at the shops in **Oxford Street**.	Lots of ships sail through **the English Channel** to **the North Sea**.
They're staying at a hotel near **Regent's Park**.	

English summary

How it works	Examples
Names of people in the singular are used without the definite article.	– **Jack** is **Ben's** cousin. – Poor **Aunt Chrissie** couldn't go to London.

How it works	Examples
Names of people in the plural are used with the article.	– **The Spencers** and **the Carters** live in the same road.
Names of mountains, countries in the singular, buildings, lakes, parks and streets are used without the article.	– **Mount Whitney** is 4,421 metres high. – You can easily walk from **Oxford Street** to **Buckingham Palace**.
Names of mountain chains and countries in the plural and names of seas and rivers are used with the definite article.	– **The Mississippi** is the longest river in **the United States**.

Check-out

1. Bilde aus den Satzteilen vollständige Sätze bzw. Fragen mit der richtigen Wortstellung. Entscheide, wo du den bestimmten Artikel verwenden musst und wo nicht.

a) *Spencers • neighbours • Carters • are*
b) *the highest mountain • Mount Whitney • in • isn't • United States*
c) *almost fell into • poor Uncle David • Tower of London • Thames on the way to*
d) *Central Park • Hyde Park • bigger than • is • ?*
e) *on the border to • Lake Michigan • is • Canada*
f) *more famous than • Fifth Avenue • is • Oxford Street • ?*

G7 Der unbestimmte Artikel
The indefinite article

Ben's aunt works as **a** detective.

Check-in

After their trip to London Ben, his cousin and his uncle are back in Bristol. It's Monday morning. Aunt Chrissie is just leaving for work. Read their conversation.

Ben: Bye, Aunt Chrissie. Hope you have a good day. But – hey! You're **a police officer**, right? But you aren't wearing your uniform! And you're going to work without **a gun**?

Jack: Oh, Ben. No guns. This is Britain. We're not in the States here!

Aunt Chrissie: And I work as **a detective**, Ben. Detectives don't wear **a uniform**. Didn't you know that?

Ben: Oh, I'm **an idiot**. Sure. It's the same in America.

Aunt Chrissie: Well, I must fly! Bye, you two. See you later.

Jack: Bye, Mum. – There she goes – in **a hurry**, as always!

1. Schau dir die hervorgehobenen Artikel und Nomen im Gespräch an.

   a) Wann gebraucht man vor dem Nomen *a* und wann *an*?
   b) Wieso steht vor *uniform a* und nicht *an*?

2. Übertrage den folgenden Satz ins Deutsche. Was stellst du hinsichtlich des unbestimmten Artikels fest?
   You're a police officer.

REGEL

1. Im Englischen gibt es zwei **unbestimmte Artikel**: *a* und *an*. **Vor Konsonanten** benutzt du **a** (*a detective*), **vor Vokalen** *an* (*an idiot*).

2. Der unbestimmte Artikel wird im Englischen meistens genauso verwendet wie die deutschen Entsprechungen:

<table>
<tr><td>um allgemein über etwas/jemanden zu sprechen</td><td>A detective is somebody who investigates crimes and catches criminals.</td></tr>
<tr><td></td><td>Ein Kriminalpolizist ist jemand der Straftaten untersucht und Kriminelle festnimmt.</td></tr>
<tr><td>um zu sagen, dass eine Sache/Person nur einmal vorhanden ist</td><td>The Spencers have got a son.</td></tr>
<tr><td></td><td>Die Spencers haben einen Sohn.</td></tr>
<tr><td>wenn du etwas/jemanden zum ersten Mal erwähnst</td><td>Mrs Spencer has got a car. It's blue.</td></tr>
<tr><td></td><td>Frau Spencer hat ein Auto. Es ist blau.</td></tr>
<tr><td>um zu sagen, dass etwas/jemand eins von vielen ist</td><td>Take a piece of toast.</td></tr>
<tr><td></td><td>Nimm (irgend)eine Scheibe Toastbrot.</td></tr>
</table>

AUSSPRACHE
Genau wie beim bestimmten Artikel ist auch hier die Aussprache entscheidend. „Uniform" wird [ˈjʊːnɪ] gesprochen. Deshalb heißt es „a uniform".

3. Nur in einigen wenigen Fällen unterscheidet sich der Gebrauch:
   – Bei **Berufsbezeichnungen** und bei der Angabe der **Nationalität steht** im Englischen der **unbestimmte Artikel**. Das ist vor allem der Fall, wenn die Berufsbezeichnung auf das Verb *be* oder auf *as* folgt.
   – **Kein Artikel** steht, wenn man von einem **bestimmten Amt** spricht, das nur **eine einzige Person** (z. B. in einem Land) inne hat.

Berufsbezeichnungen, Nationalität mit *a/an*	Amt ohne *a/an*
Jack's mother is **a police officer**.	Ben is interested in politics and would like to be **President** of the United States.
… ist Polizistin.	… Präsident der Vereinigten Staaten.
She doesn't wear a uniform because she works as **a detective**.	Would you like to be **King** or **Queen** of England?
… als Kriminalpolizistin.	… König oder Königin von England?
Ben's father is **an American**.	
… ist Amerikaner.	

TIPP
Statt des Nomens „an American" kannst du auch ein Adjektiv verwenden: Ben's father is **American** but his mother is **English**.

■ **Achtung!**

– Der unbestimmte Artikel wird auch bei **Zeiteinheiten** und **Maßeinheiten** verwendet. Er entspricht dann dem Deutschen „je" oder „pro":
  • *My mother doesn't work full time. She only works three days **a week**.*
  • *Don't buy that water, Ben. It's £5 **a bottle**.*

– Bei bestimmten **Wendungen** wird – anders als im Deutschen – der unbestimmte Artikel verwendet:
  • *That boy was **in a hurry** to get off the train.* (… in Eile …)
  • *Maybe he was travelling **without a ticket**.* (… ohne Fahrkarte)

English summary

How it works	Examples
The indefinite article *a/an* is used when you talk about a person's job or someone's nationality.	– Mrs Spencer is **a police officer**. – Her sister married **an American**.
You don't use the article when there is only one person (e.g. in a country) who does a special job.	– Elizabeth II became **Queen** in 1952.
A/an can also be used in phrases that express units of time or measurement.	– Ben has basketball practice **four times a week**. – These crisps are cheap. They are only 50p **a bag**!
The indefinite article is also used in special phrases.	– Aunt Chrissie is always **in a hurry**. – Most British police officers work **without a gun**.

Check-out

1. Was erzählt Ben seinem Cousin über seinen Vater? Übertrage die folgenden Sätze ins Englische.

   Mein Vater ist Amerikaner. Er arbeitet als Journalist in Los Angeles. Er arbeitet fünf Tage die Woche und er ist immer in Eile. Er versucht immer perfekt zu sein. Ein Beispiel: er geht nie ohne Einkaufsliste aus dem Haus. Aber letzte Woche hat er eine Pressekonferenz verpasst und dachte: „Ich bin ein Idiot!"

> What **a** wonderful place to live!

G8 Die Stellung der Artikel
The position of the articles

Check-in

Ben is talking to his aunt and uncle about life in California. Read their conversation.

Aunt Chrissie: California must be great! Beautiful beaches! A sunny climate … **What a wonderful place** to live!

Ben: **All the people** I've met here seem to think **half the population** of California are on the beach **all the time**. It's not like that really … Too much sunshine can create problems. Actually, **quite a large part** of California is desert.

Uncle David: Yes. And I've heard water is **quite a problem**.

Ben: Especially in southern California. There's just not enough water for **all the golf courses, green gardens and swimming pools** …

1. Beantworte die folgenden Fragen auf Englisch. Verwende dabei die im Dialog hervorgehobenen Wendungen.

   a) *Who thinks that Californians spend most of the time on the beach?*
   b) *How much of California is desert?*
   c) *What is a lot of water used for?*

REGEL

1. Genau wie im Deutschen stehen der **bestimmte und der unbestimmte Artikel meistens vor einem Adjektiv und Nomen**:
   • *The sunny climate* makes California very attractive.
   • It is *a wonderful place* to live.
2. **Bei bestimmten Ausdrücken** wie *all, both, half, quite* und *what* wird jedoch der **Artikel nachgestellt**.

Nachstellung des bestimmten Artikels bei *all, both, half*	Nachstellung des unbestimmten Artikels bei *half, quite, what*
All the people Ben has met think California is fantastic.	Let's sit in the sun for **half an hour**.
Alle Leute …	… eine halbe Stunde …
Both the boys play basketball.	Water is **quite a problem** in California.
Beide Jungen …	… ein ziemliches Problem …
People think that **half the population** of California spend every day on the beach.	**What a wonderful day** we've had on the beach!
… die halbe Bevölkerung …	Was für einen wunderbaren Tag …

English summary

How it works	Examples
The normal word order in English is: article + adjective + noun.	– California is **a fantastic place**.
But with *all*, *both*, *half*, *quite* and *what* this word order is changed and the article is put after these words.	– **What a wonderful** holiday! – **Half the people** I know want to go to America. – Californians aren't on the beach **all the time.**

Check-out

1. Während Ben im Flugzeug nach Kalifornien sitzt, schreibt Tante Chrissie ihrer Schwester eine E-Mail. Übertrage die folgenden Sätze ins Englische.

Ben hatte eine tolle Zeit hier. Alle Leute, die ihn kennenlernten, mochten ihn sehr. Gestern waren wir in der Stadt. Beide Jungen haben sich das gleiche T-Shirt gekauft. Danach sind wir auf das *Bristol Kite Festival* gegangen und haben eine halbe Stunde lang den Drachen zugeschaut. Wir hatten ziemlich starken Wind. Was für ein toller Tag!

3 Pronomen und Begleiter

G9 Die Personalpronomen als Subjekt im Satz
Personal pronouns as subject

Check-in

Look at the picture of Jake and his family. They are on holiday in Scotland and have just arrived in Inverness.

Welcome to Inverness! **You**'re in the centre of our famous town!

At least **he** knows where **we** are. **I** don't. Do **you**, Dad?

1. Schau dir die hervorgehobenen Personalpronomen in den Sprechblasen an. Kennst du weitere Pronomen, die das Subjekt eines Satzes sein können?

2. Das Personalpronomen *you* wird zweimal verwendet. Wie übersetzt du es jeweils?

REGEL

1. Die **Personalpronomen** können das **Subjekt** eines Satzes sein. Obwohl sie Personalpronomen heißen, können sie sich auf Personen oder Sachen beziehen:
   * *Where are **the tourists / the brochures**? – **They**'re here.*

	Singular	Plural
1. Person	**I**'m lost.	Where are **we**?
2. Person	**You** are here.	**You** are here.
3. Person	**He/She** is looking at the map. Our hotel? **It** isn't on the map.	**They** don't know the town.

2. Die Personalpronomen *he, she, it, we* und *they* **ersetzen Nomen**, die bereits bekannt sind. So kannst du Wiederholungen vermeiden:
   * *Let's ask **that man in the café** the way. **He** may know where we are.*

3. Achte bei der Vewendung der Personalpronomen auf Folgendes:
  – Das Personalpronomen *I* wird **immer groß** geschrieben.
  – Das Personalpronomen *you* kann im Deutschen „du", „ihr" oder „Sie" heißen.
  – Die Personalpronomen *he* und *she* verwendest du **nur für Personen. Für Sachen** verwendest du das Pronomen *it*.
  – **Für Tiere**, die du gut kennst oder die einen Namen haben, verwendest du *he* oder *she*; sonst bezeichnest du Tiere mit *it*.

> **TIPP**
> „It" kannst du auch verwenden, um z. B. Angaben über die Zeit, das Wetter oder Entfernungen zu machen:
> – **It**'s ten oclock.
> – **It**'s three miles to the beach.

◼ **Achtung!**
  – Das deutsche Pronomen „**sie**" kann im Englischen durch *she* (Singular) **oder** *they* (Plural) ausgedrückt werden:
    • **They**'re all here apart from Gemma. **She**'s coming later.
      Sie sind alle hier, außer Gemma. Sie kommt später.

  – Im Deutschen wird manchmal das Personalpronomen „es" für eine Person verwendet, z. B. „das Kind" = „es". Im Englischen wird eine **Person immer** mit *he* oder *she* bezeichnet. Das richtige Personalpronomen ergibt sich dabei aus dem Zusammenhang.

  – Die Pronomen *you* und *they* verwendest du auch, um **Menschen im Allgemeinen oder eine unbestimmte Gruppe von Menschen** zu bezeichnen. Wenn du selbst Teil dieser Gruppe bist, benutzt du eher *you*:
    • **You** never know what will happen.
    Im Deutschen kannst du diese Pronomen mit „man" wiedergeben.

English summary

How it works	Examples
You can use personal pronouns as the subject of a sentence. *He, she, it, we* and *they* can be used to talk about people, animals or things that have already been mentioned.	– Do **you** mind if **I** ask a few questions? – **We** have never been to Scotland before. – **The boys** asked Lauren because **they** were lost.
It can also be used generally, e. g. to talk about time, distance, the weather.	– **It**'s raining.

Check-out

1. Ersetze die Nomen, die als Subjekt verwendet werden, durch Personalpronomen. Tipp: Nicht überall ist es sinnvoll.

Yesterday my dad and I went to Macduff. My dad and I wanted to visit the aquarium, but the aquarium was closed. Then my dad and I went into a café. A woman there told us about the ships in the harbour. The woman said that the ships were very famous. Dad said, "Let's go there," so my dad and I went to find the harbour. But my dad and I got lost. There was a large street map, but the street map was full of graffiti. So my dad and I asked two boys for help and the two boys pointed to the right street.

> Are you sure this photo is of **us**?

G10 Die Objektformen der Personalpronomen
The object forms of personal pronouns

Check-in

In a shop Jake finds a postcard of Nessie, the famous monster that lives in one of the Scottish lakes.

Are you sure this photo is of **us**?
It looks like two trees in the water to **me**!

1. Übertrage die Worte von Nessie ins Deutsche.

2. Außer den beiden hervorgehobenen Pronomen findest du zwei weitere Pronomen in der Aussage von Nessie. Welche sind es? Wie unterscheiden sie sich in ihrer Funktion von den hervorgehobenen Pronomen?

REGEL

> **TIPP**
> Frage nach dem direkten Objekt (Akkusativobjekt): „Wen oder Was?"
> Frage nach dem indirekten Objekt (Dativobjekt): „Wem?"

1. Du kannst **Personalpronomen** als Subjekt (→ G9) oder **Objekt eines Satzes** verwenden: *This photo shows **us** in the water.* Objektpronomen können auch nach Präpositionen stehen: *It's a photo of **us**.*

2. Die Pronomen *it* und *you* können sowohl **Subjekt als auch Objekt** eines Satzes sein: *It's a monster. Can you see **it**?*
   Bei allen anderen Pronomen gibt es **zwei** Formen, die **Subjektform** und die **Objektform**.

3. Die **Objektformen** entsprechen sowohl den **deutschen Akkusativformen** als auch den **Dativformen**:

object pronoun	Deutsch
Is it for **me**? Can you help **me**?	mich mir
I don't see **you** in the picture. She can show **you** the way.	dich dir

object pronoun	Deutsch
I met **him** yesterday. She bought **him** a souvenir.	ihn ihm
Do you like **her**? I'll talk to **her**.	sie ihr
He wore **it** every day. (his T-shirt / his watch / his hat) They've given **it** a new name. (the museum / the school)	es/sie/ihn ihm/ihr
She sometimes lends **us** money.	uns
I can't see **you**! We can offer **you** cheap tickets.	euch/Sie euch/Ihnen
She loves **them**. I told **them** the sad story.	sie ihnen

■ **Achtung!**

– Im Gegensatz zum Deutschen benutzt du **nach** dem Verb *be* und in Vergleichen **nach *as* und *than* die Objektform des Personalpronomens**, obwohl es sich hier nicht um das Objekt des Satzes handelt. Vergleiche:

- *Is that you in the picture, Jake? – Yes, it's **me**.*
  Bist du das auf dem Foto, Jake? – Ja, **ich** bin's.
- *Look at those tourists. I think they're as lost as **us**. (= … as we are.)*
  Schau dir diese Touristen an. Ich glaube, sie sind genauso verloren wie **wir**.
- *Dad knows more about Scottish history than **me**. (= … than I do.)*
  Papa weiß mehr über schottische Geschichte als **ich**.

English summary

How it works	Examples
In English you use the same object pronouns, both for the direct and the indirect object.	– I bought a souvenir T-shirt and wore **it** every day. – We met two nice boys and gave **them** our mobile numbers.

Check-out

1. Nach seinem Urlaub in Schottland berichtet Jake seinem Freund David über seine Erlebnisse. Übertrage den kurzen Dialog ins Englische. Achte dabei besonders auf die Verwendung der Personalpronomen.

David: Du hast das Ungeheuer gesehen? Das glaube ich dir nicht. Zeig mir ein Foto von ihm!

Jake: Das Ungeheuer war größer als ich. Es hat uns angeschaut, aber es hat uns nicht verfolgt.

2. Vervollständige den Text über Edinburgh Castle mit den richtigen Pronomen.

Edinburgh Castle is popular with everyone who visits … . Tourists are happy when guides tell … stories about the ghost. The ghost is a young boy. He plays the drums at night. Luke and Mick said to their guide, "You can't convince …! We want to listen to the boy and take a photo of … ." But the guide didn't allow … to spend the night in the castle.

Come to northwest Scotland – and prepare **yourself** for a big surprise!

G11 Die Reflexivpronomen und *each other*
Reflexive pronouns and each other

Check-in

Jake and his father are thinking of going hiking. Look at the information they've found about the Scottish Highlands.

www.northwest-scotland.co.uk

HOME | ACTIVITIES | CULTURE | NATURE | HISTORY | HOTELS

Come to northwest Scotland – and prepare **yourself** for a big surprise! You'll find that the Highlands are not just dramatic mountains. – There are also miles of coastline and lonely islands. If you want an active outdoor holiday, this is just the place for you! The region around Fort William calls **itself** "the outdoor capital of the UK". Visitors who are looking for a quieter holiday can enjoy **themselves** at some of the region's many historical and cultural attractions or relax at a luxury hotel.

1. Übertrage die folgenden beiden Sätze ins Deutsche.

   a) *Prepare yourself for a big surprise!*
   b) *Visitors can enjoy themselves at a luxury hotel.*

2. Nenne andere Wörter, die auf -*self* oder -*selves* enden.

REGEL

1. Pronomen, die auf -***self/-selves*** enden, verwendest du, wenn das **Subjekt** und das **Objekt** eines Satzes **identisch** sind: *It calls **itself** "the outdoor capital of the UK".* Das Pronomen *itself* bezieht sich hier auf das Subjekt *it* zurück.
2. Die Endung -***self*** benutzt du im **Singular**, -*selves* im **Plural**. Bei dem Subjektpronomen *you* musst du gut überlegen, ob du den Singular *yourself* oder den Plural *yourselves* brauchst.

Subjekt	Verb	Pronomen auf *-self/-selves*	Deutsch
I	can see	**myself** in the lake.	ich – mich
I	wrote	a postcard to **myself**.	ich – mir
You	should prepare	**yourself** for a long day.	du – dich
You	must buy	**yourself** a new map.	du – dir
He	taught	**himself** some Gaelic.	er – sich
She	introduced	**herself**.	sie – sich
It	calls	**itself** a restaurant!	er/sie/es – sich
We	should get	**ourselves** some food.	wir – uns
You	can allow	**yourselves** a quiet day.	ihr – euch / Sie – sich
They	hurt	**themselves** on the hike.	sie – sich

> **TIPP**
> Die Reflexivpronomen kannst du auch als verstärkendes Pronomen verwenden. Dabei wird ein Nomen oder Pronomen, meist das Subjekt, hervorgehoben: You needn't help me. I can do it **myself**. Im Deutschen benutzt du dafür das Wort „selbst".

🟧 **Achtung!**

– Im Deutschen gibt es viel mehr reflexive Verben als im Englischen. Vergewissere dich deshalb, ob du im Englischen wirklich ein *self*-Pronomen brauchst. Hier sind einige Verben, die **im Deutschen reflexiv** sind, **im Englischen** aber **nicht**:

sich (ver)ändern – *change*
sich anziehen – *get dressed*
sich beeilen – *hurry*
sich bewegen – *move*
sich entscheiden – *decide*
sich entspannen – *relax*
sich ereignen – *happen*
sich erinnern – *remember*
sich entschuldigen – *apologize*
sich fragen – *wonder*

sich freuen auf – *look forward to*
sich fühlen – *feel*
sich fürchten – *be afraid*
sich öffnen – *open*
sich (hin)setzen – *sit down*
sich treffen – *meet*
sich trennen – *split up*
sich verirren – *get lost*
sich verstecken – *hide*
sich etw. vorstellen – *imagine sth*

– Achte darauf, dass du die Reflexivpronomen nicht mit *each other* verwechselst:

*They're taking pictures of **themselves**.*

*They're taking pictures of **each other**.*

• Im ersten Bild fotografiert **jeder sich selbst**, deswegen wird das Reflexivpronomen **themselves** verwendet: *He's taking a picture of himself and she's taking a picture of herself.*

• Im zweiten Bild fotografiert das Mädchen den Jungen und umgekehrt: *He's taking a picture of her and she's taking a picture of him. = They're taking pictures of each other.* Wenn es um **Gegenseitigkeit** geht, verwendest du **each other**.

English summary

How it works	Examples
You use reflexive pronouns when the subject and the object of a sentence are the same or when you want to stress something.	– When you're hiking in the mountains, you must protect **yourself** from the cold. – Mike has bought **himself** a book about climbing. – Tina drew the map **herself**.
You use *each other* when you're talking about 'two-way' activities.	– Climbers help **each other**. They don't only think of themselves.

Check-out

1. Setze die richtige Form ein.

   *When Liam was on holiday in the mountains, he fell and hurt (him/himself/–).
   "I felt very sorry for (me/myself/–)," he said. Then two young men came along
   and introduced (themselves/each other/–) as doctors. First they talked to
   (themselves/each other/–) about my situation. Then they decided (themselves/
   each other/–) to call an ambulance. In hospital Liam was very lonely. "Nobody
   talks to (me/myself/–)," he told his brother. "Some patients can visit (them/
   themselves/each other), but I have to stay in bed!" "Well, buy (you/yourself/each
   other) a guidebook and plan your next holiday!" his brother answered.*

This place here looks nice.

G12 Die Demonstrativbegleiter und -pronomen
Demonstrative determiners and pronouns

Check-in

On Friday it rained all afternoon, so Jake decided to go on with his book *Under
the tropical sun*.

> #### CHAPTER 2
>
> It was early afternoon when they arrived at the market place. "What about
> a drink?" Dean suggested. "**This** place here looks nice."
>
> "No," Emily answered, "let's go to **that** café over there. Just look at all
> **those** young people. It must be a nice place."
>
> "**That**'s a good idea," Dean said. They went in and sat down.
>
> "When does the festival start?" Dean asked.
>
> "At seven o'clock **this** evening," Emily answered. She remembered it
> from their first day in the town. – **That** Tuesday morning she had seen
> a poster for the festival at the tourist office. They ordered drinks and
> something to eat.
>
> "Mmm," Emily said, "I like **these** little chocolate things. What are they?"
>
> "No idea. Insects, maybe?"

1. Auf welche Wortart beziehen sich die hervorgehobenen Wörter in Jakes Buch? Gibt es eine Ausnahme im Text?

2. Schau dir den Text noch einmal genau an. Formuliere dann Regeln zur Verwendung von *this/these* und *that/those*.

REGEL

1. Du verwendest ***this/these***, um auf Personen und Sachen hinzuweisen, die relativ **nah** sind, entweder räumlich oder zeitlich. Mit *this place here* bezeichnet Dean das Lokal direkt vor ihm; *these little chocolate things* liegen vor Emily auf dem Teller. Mit *this evening* ist der Abend desselben Tages gemeint.

2. Mit ***that/those*** weist du auf Personen und Sachen hin, die **weiter weg** liegen, entweder räumlich oder zeitlich. Emily schaut hinüber zu *that café* und *those young people*.

3. Die **Demonstrativbegleiter** *this/that* (Singular) und *these/those* (Plural) stehen **vor einem Nomen bzw. vor dem zum Nomen gehörigen Adjektiv**:
   • *Let's go to **that café** over there.*
   • *Just look at all **those** young people.*

4. Als **Demonstrativpronomen** stehen *this/that* und *these/those* **ohne nachfolgendes Nomen**:
   Waiter: *Is **this** your first visit to our town?*
   Emily: *Yes, it is.*
   Waiter: *There's a big festival party here at ten o'clock.*
   Dean: *Really? I didn't know **that**.*

5. Die **Demonstrativpronomen im Singular** (*this/that*) **beziehen sich meist auf Sachen**, nicht auf Personen. Ausnahme: wenn Personen z. B. am Telefon identifiziert werden:
   • *Hello, **this** is Jenny. Is **that** Mrs Morton?*

TIPP
– Achte auf deine Aussprache! Unterscheide deutlich zwischen „this" [ðɪs] und „these" [ðiːz].
– Signalwörter für die Verwendung der Demonstrativbegleiter und -pronomen sind: this/these – here that/those – over there.

TIPP
Du kannst „this" und „that" benutzen, um zwei Sachen miteinander zu vergleichen: **This** picture is OK, but I don't like **that** one.

English summary

How it works	Examples
You use the demonstrative determiners *this/these* to talk about people or things near to you in time or space.	– Do you like **these** sweets? I bought them **this** morning.
You use the demonstrative determiners *that/those* to talk about people or things further away from you in space – or in the past.	– Look at **that** old café over there. It opened in 1910, and in **those** days it was very popular.
You can use the demonstratives as pronouns (without a following noun) in the same way: *this/these* = near to you; *that/those* = further away.	– **This** is a nice café. Let's go in. – Look at all the cakes. **These** look good – better than **those** over there.

Check-out

1. Was fehlt in den folgenden Sätzen: *this, that, these* oder *those*?

   a) *… festival is great! I'm enjoying myself so much!*
   b) *Did you see the big show? … dancers were fantastic!*
   c) *I think we're lost. Come and look at … map here.*
   d) *Let's go and ask … police officer over there.*
   e) *I'd like to eat something. … cakes here look nice.*
   f) *Sorry, the shop isn't open on Sundays. I didn't know … .*

2. Übertrage das Gespräch ins Englische. Verwende *this, that, these* und *those*.

Martin:	Hallo, Steve! Schau dir dieses T-Shirt an!
Steve:	Es ist toll! Hast du es in dem Laden dort drüben gekauft?
Martin:	Nein, mein Bruder hat es mir heute Morgen geschenkt.
Steve:	Das ist eine Überraschung! Warum?
Martin:	Er hat es in einem von diesen kleinen Läden auf dem Markt gekauft. Und es ist ihm zu klein.

We had a few little accidents in **our** family.

G13 Die Possessivbegleiter
Possessive determiners

Check-in

Read the e-mail Jake sent to his girlfriend Alison after a visit to the Isle of Harris.

| Subject: | Hello! |

Hi Alison!
Our trip to the Isle of Harris was good fun, but we had a few little accidents in **our** family. When we were getting off the ferry at Tarbert, **my** stupid sister threw **her** heavy backpack down and it landed on **my** foot. Typical!
It was even worse for Dad. He fell down some steps and hurt **his** arm.
But **our** holiday home was nice. – We had **our own** garden! We all loved the island with **its** wild coastline – and that strange language. Did you know? They have all **their** road signs in English and in Gaelic!
"Mar sin leat" for now!
J.

1. Übertrage den folgenden Satz ins Deutsche. Es gibt zwei Möglichkeiten.
   He hurt his arm.

1. Mit den **Possessivbegleitern** gibst du an, **(zu) wem etwas gehört**: der Rucksack gehört Jakes Schwester = *her backpack*; die Küste gehört zur Insel = *its coastline*.

2. Die Possessivbegleiter stehen **vor einem Nomen**. Zwischen dem Possessiv-begleiter und dem Nomen können ein oder mehrere Adjektive stehen:
   - *She threw **her backpack** down.*
   - *I loved the island with **its wild coastline.***

3. Im Gegensatz zum Deutschen hat **jeder Possessivbegleiter** im Englischen **nur eine Form**.

Subjekt	Possessivbegleiter	Deutsch
I I	hurt **my** foot. can tell you stories about **my** family.	meinen Fuß meine Familie
Did you Do you	find **your** mobile? want to give me **your** backpack?	dein Handy deinen Rucksack
Dad Jake	hurt **his** arm. was angry with **his** sister.	seinen Arm seine Schwester
My sister She	threw **her** backpack down. took off **her** shoes on the hike.	ihren Rucksack ihre Schuhe
The island Scotland	is cool with **its** wild coastline. is very attractive with **its** many lakes.	ihrer Küste seinen Seen
We We	loved **our** trip. couldn't find the way to **our** holiday home.	unseren Ausflug unserer Ferienwohnung
Did you You	like **your** holiday home? mustn't park **your** car here.	eure/Ihre Ferienwohnung eurer/Ihr Auto
They They	have **their** road signs in Gaelic. didn't find **their** way.	ihre Straßenschilder ihren Weg

■ **Achtung!**

– Die Possessivbegleiter werden im Englischen ähnlich verwendet wie im Deutschen. Es gibt aber einige Fälle, in denen im Deutschen der bestimmte Artikel statt des Possessivbegleiters stehen kann, im Englischen aber nicht. Vergleiche diese Sätze:

Deutsch	Englisch
Zieh dir bitte die Schuhe aus.	Take **your** shoes off, please.
Tinas Bruder hat sich das Bein gebrochen.	Tina's brother has broken **his** leg.
Du gehst mir auf die Nerven!	You're getting on **my** nerves!
Viele Menschen kamen ums Leben.	Many people lost **their** lives.

– Die folgenden Wörter klingen ähnlich. Achte deshalb darauf, dass du sie nicht miteinander verwechselst:
- *your – you're (= you are)*
- *his – he's (= he is)*
- *its – it's (= it is)*
- *their – they're (= they are)*

> **TIPP**
>
> Mit „of my/your/ his/… own" betonst du noch stärker, dass jemandem etwas gehört: He's got a room **of his own**.

– Vorsicht bei dem Wort *own* („eigen")! **Vor *own* muss** im Englischen immer ein **Possessivbegleiter** stehen:
- *We had **our own** garden.*
  Wir hatten unseren eigenen Garten.

Deutsche Sätze wie „Er hat ein/kein eigenes Zimmer." kannst du nicht wörtlich ins Englische übertragen. Richtig heißt es:
- *He has got **his own** room.*
- *He hasn't got **his own** room.*

English summary

How it works	Examples
You use possessive determiners before nouns to show what belongs together.	– The teenagers enjoyed **their** trip although Jake hurt **his** foot.
You can use the possessive determiners with the word *own* to stress their meaning.	– They had **their own** TV. – Linda would like a dog **of her own**.

Check-out

1. Vervollständige das Interview zwischen einem Lokalreporter und einem jungen Touristen. Verwende dabei die richtigen Possessivbegleiter.

   my • your • his • her • its • our • their

   Reporter: *You're on holiday here with • class, right?*
   Boy: *Yes, we arrived here with • teacher yesterday.*
   Reporter: *And how do you like this region with • old castles and wild mountains?*
   Boy: *I love it. But some of • friends think they're wasting • time here.*
   Reporter: *That's a pity. Most tourists love • landscape.*
   Boy: *Yes, it's fantastic. • friend Tess thinks mountains are boring, but I'm sure she'll change • opinion soon.*
   Reporter: *I hope so. Enjoy • holiday!*

G14 Die Possessivpronomen
Possessive pronouns

Is that your car? –
Yes, it's **ours**.

Check-in

Look at Jake's holiday scenes.

1. Die hervorgehobenen Wörter sind Possessivpronomen. Versuche, sie durch Possessivbegleiter + Nomen zu ersetzen, z. B. *Yes, it's our car*.

REGEL

1. Du benutzt **Possessivpronomen**, **um Besitzverhältnisse anzuzeigen** und um die **Wiederholung von Nomen** zu **vermeiden**. Vergleiche: *Why does she borrow your camera? – Because mine is better than hers.* ist stilistisch besser als *Because my camera is better than her camera.*
2. Du verwendest ein Possessivpronomen oft **als Antwort auf eine Frage mit** *whose*:
   • *Whose is that dog? – Mine.*
3. Du kannst ein **Possessivpronomen in Verbindung mit** *of* verwenden, wenn du über eine Gruppe von Personen oder Sachen sprichst:
   • *The Smiths know Jake quite well. He is a friend of theirs. (= one of their friends.)*

Possessivbegleiter + Nomen	Possessivpronomen
That's **my ice cream**.	That's **mine**.
Is that **your camera**?	Is it **yours**?
This is **his dog**.	It's **his**.
These aren't **her bags**.	They aren't **hers**.
Look at **our car**.	It's **ours**.
Come on, kids, take **your tickets**.	They're **yours**.
These are **their books**.	They're **theirs**.

TIPP
– Auf eine Frage mit „Whose …?" kannst du auch mit dem **s-Genitiv** (→ **G15**) antworten: Whose camera is that? – Jake's. / My brother's.
– Anstatt eines Ausdrucks „**of**" + **Possessivpronomen** kannst du auch einen Ausdruck mit s-Genitiv verwenden: a friend of Jake's.

English summary

How it works	Example
You use a possessive pronoun to show what belongs together if you don't want to repeat a noun.	– Whose are those backpacks over there? They aren't **ours** (= our backpacks).

Check-out

1. Setze die richtige Form ein.

   a) *Yesterday Kelly introduced (my/mine/me) to Martin. He's a friend of (her/hers/she) from Bristol.*

   b) *Martin is a great swimmer; sailing is a hobby of (his/him/he) too!*

   c) *Is that Martin's boat over there? – No, (his/him/he) is blue and white.*

   d) *May I borrow your mobile? I've left (my/mine/me) at home. – Ask Kim or Laura. They never forget (their/theirs/they).*

   e) *There are lots of dogs on the beach. Is it OK if we take (our/ours/us), too?*

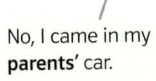

No, I came in my **parents**' car.

G15 Der s-Genitiv
The s-genitive

Check-in

When Jake and his family went to the Glencoe Visitor Centre, he met a group of young hikers from Edinburgh. Read their conversation.

Boris: Did you walk here from the village?

Jake: No, I came in my **parents**' car. We drove over from Oban.

Boris: That's a nice town. I'm Boris, by the way, and this is Tommy, my **sister's** boyfriend.

Jake: I'm Jake. Are you staying in the village?

Tommy: No, we're on our way to meet some friends in Kinlochleven. That's a bigger place. The little shop here in Glencoe village is OK, but there isn't a **baker's** or a supermarket.

Jake: We've just had a sandwich in the café. My sister's looking at the **children's** toys in the shop over there. – She's too old for all that really.

Amy: Hi there, I'm **Boris's** sister Amy. Sorry to interrupt, but we must get to our **friends'** place by six o'clock. Come on, Boris!

1. Schau dir diese Ausdrücke aus dem Dialog an: *my parents' car, my sister's boyfriend, the children's toys*. Wann steht der Apostroph (') vor und wann nach dem Buchstaben „s"? Vervollständige die folgenden Regeln:

   a) Apostroph vor „s" wenn … oder wenn …
   b) Apostroph nach „s" wenn …

2. Was ist hier anders?
   She's too old.

> **REGEL**

1. Wenn du sagen willst, dass **jemandem etwas gehört**, hängst du im **Singular** einen **Apostroph** und ein **-s** an das Nomen: *Boris's*. Bei **Pluralformen, die mit -s enden**, fügst du **nur** einen **Apostroph** hinzu: *friends'*. Bei **Pluralformen**, die **nicht mit -s enden** (→ G3), **hängst du zuerst einen Apostroph** an und **dann ein -s** (wie im Singular): *children's*.

einer Person gehörend	mehreren Personen gehörend
This is **my sister's** boyfriend.	I came in **my parents'** car.
Das ist der Freund **meiner Schwester**.	Ich kam im Auto **meiner Eltern**.
I'm **Boris's** sister.	We must get to **our friends'** place.
Ich bin die Schwester **von Boris**.	Wir müssen zum Haus **unserer Freunde** kommen.
There isn't a **baker's** (shop).	She's looking at the **children's** toys.
Es gibt keine **Bäckerei**.	Sie schaut sich das **Kinderspielzeug** an.

■ **Achtung!**
- Bei manchen Wendungen fehlt das Bezugswort:
  - *There isn't a **baker's**.* (shop)
  - *I must go to the **doctor's**.* (surgery, office)
  - *You can book a flight at the **travel agent's**.* (shop)
  - *We want to go to **Luigi's**.* (restaurant)
  Dasselbe gilt oft für die Eigennamen von Geschäften (*I got it at **Sainsbury's**.*) und auch für Privatwohnungen (*Let's meet at **Patrick's** this evening.*).

- Bei Lebewesen benutzt du meistens den s-Genitiv. Bei Sachen verwendest du einen Ausdruck mit *of* (→ G16). Zu dieser Regel gibt es aber auch Ausnahmen. So wird der s-Genitiv oft bei Ortsnamen und Zeitbezeichnungen verwendet:
  - ***Barcelona's** oldest market*
  - *last **year's** model*

- Außer beim s-Genitiv benutzt du einen Apostroph bei Kurzformen, um zu zeigen, dass Buchstaben fehlen. Wenn du im Text einen Apostroph plus -s siehst, könnte es sich auch um einen von diesen beiden Fällen handeln:
  - *Sandra's (= is) a great cook.*
  - *Mike's (= has) just come back from Spain.*

AUSSPRACHE
Die Aussprache des Buchstaben „s" hängt von dem Laut davor ab:
- Nach stimmlosen Lauten wird [s] gesprochen, z. B. *parents'*.
- Nach stimmhaften Lauten wird [z] gesprochen, z. B. *baker's*.
- Nach Zischlauten wird [iz] gesprochen; das Wort wird um eine Silbe länger, z. B. *Boris's*.

TIPP
Das Nomen nach dem s-Genitiv kannst du weglassen, wenn aus dem Zusammenhang deutlich wird, wem etwas gehört: *Is that your camera? – No, it's Michael's.*

English summary

How it works	Examples
You add 's to a noun to show that something "belongs" to one person.	– This is my **brother's** mobile. – I've just met **Boris's** sister.
You add an apostrophe (') to a plural noun which ends in s.	– Where is your **parents'** car? – Susie is in the **kids'** playground.
You add 's to a plural noun which does not end in s.	– Ricardo designs **children's** toys. – This store sells **women's** clothes.

Check-out

1. Was hat Amy unter ihre Urlaubsfotos geschrieben? Übertrage die Bildunterschriften ins Englische.

    a) Das Hotel meines Onkels
    b) Der Hund meiner Freundin am Strand
    c) Das Lieblingscafé der Teenager
    d) Alex' Fahrrad nach dem Unfall
    e) Charlotte beim Arzt

> You will get to know the old quarter **of** this exciting city.

G16 Der Genitiv mit *of*
The of-genitive

Check-in

While Jake and his family are in Edinburgh, they decide to go on a walking tour of the city. Read this text from their travel guide.

On this part **of** your Edinburgh walking tour you will get to know the old quarter **of** this exciting city. You begin your tour in the High Street near St Giles.
  On your way you will discover the building **of** the "Old Town Guard", which later became the Edinburgh Police. Your tour leaves the High Street and goes over South Bridge to the old part **of** the University. Soon you will arrive at the scene **of** a famous murder: Lord Darnley was killed here in 1567. He was the second husband **of** Mary Queen of Scots, Elizabeth I's enemy.

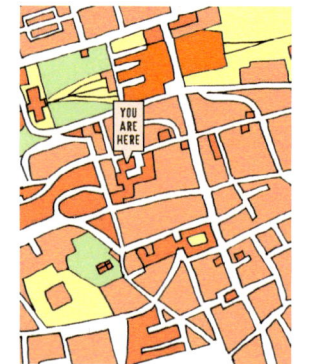

1. Schau dir die Ausdrücke mit *of* in der Wegbeschreibung noch einmal genau an.

    a) Beziehen sie sich eher auf Menschen oder auf Sachen?

    b) Kannst du einen Ausdruck mit *of* finden, der sich auf eine Person bezieht?

REGEL

1. Wenn du sagen willst, **dass etwas einer Sache zugeordnet wird** (oder dazu „gehört"), verwendest du *of*: *the scene **of** a famous murder; the old part **of** the University*. Bei Lebewesen benutzt du normalerweise den s-Genitiv (→ **G15**).

Menschen und Tiere	Sachen
Put those old toys in the **dog's** bed.	We've taken some photos **of the town**.
Have you seen the **girls'** photos?	South Bridge is at the end **of the street**.
I can't remember the **men's** names.	This book describes the history **of the city**.

Achtung!

– Zu dieser Regel gibt es eine Ausnahme: Man verwendet einen Ausdruck mit *of* auch bei Personen, wenn die Person ausführlicher beschrieben wird: *Lord Darnley was the second husband **of** Mary Queen of Scots, who was Elizabeth I's enemy.*

– Denk daran, dass das deutsche Wort „von" nicht immer dem englischen Wort *from* entspricht. Vergleiche: *a postcard **of** London* (darauf ist London abgebildet); *a postcard **from** London* (sie wurde in London abgeschickt).

– Im Deutschen spricht man vom „höchsten Gebäude der Welt" oder vom „besten Restaurant in der Stadt". Im Englischen sagt man *the highest building **in** the world* und *the best restaurant **in** the town*.

English summary

How it works	Examples
There are different ways of showing that somebody/something belongs to somebody or is connected with something. You usually use a phrase with *of* for things.	– The tour starts in the centre **of the town**. – At the end **of the tour** everybody felt tired.
You usually use the s-genitive for people.	– You can see **tourists'** photos on the Internet. – I've just sent a photo to **my friend's** mobile.

Check-out

1. Vervollständige die Sätze, indem du einen passenden Satzteil mit *of* anschließt.

   *the dark sea at night • all the people in her group • the school holidays •
   the Scottish coast*

   a) *Last year Louisa decided to go on a trip at the beginning …*
   b) *She went on a guided tour …*
   c) *She took funny photos …*
   d) *She loved the sight …*

2. Welche ist die richtige Ergänzung?

   a) *Let me tell you about (Marcus's trip/the trip of Marcus) to London.*
   b) *He stayed in (a friend's flat/the flat of a friend) who works for a TV company.*
   c) *At the British Museum he bought (a Roman soldier's model/a model of a Roman soldier).*
   d) *Marcus sent his parents (a postcard of the royal family/a postcard from the royal family).*
   e) *He thinks London is (the most famous city of the world/the most famous city in the world).*

4 Die Mengenwörter

G17 Die Mengenwörter *much / many, a lot of / lots of*
The quantifiers much / many, a lot of / lots of

> We haven't got **many** bananas or kiwis for the fruit salad.

Check-in

Nick and Jill want to give a party for their friends on Saturday. They are talking about what things they still need. Read their conversation.

Nick: For the pizza, we still have **a lot of** vegetables, but we haven't got **many** bananas or kiwis for the fruit salad. So how **many** should we buy? Er, have we got ketchup for the chips? And how **much** milk do we need for the cake? I'm getting nervous …

Jill: Hey, keep cool! It's not our first party! There's still **lots of** milk. But ketchup? Oh no, there isn't **much**. So let's add six bananas, eight kiwis and some ketchup to our shopping list.

1. Welche der folgenden Dinge sind zählbar? Woran erkennst du das?

   a) *vegetables*   b) *bananas*   c) *milk*   d) *kiwis*   e) *ketchup*

REGEL

1. Um zu sagen, **wie viel oder wie wenig von etwas vorhanden ist**, verwendest du *much*, *many* oder *a lot of/lots of*. Dabei gibt es zwei wichtige Regeln, auf die du achten musst.
2. Du musst unterscheiden, ob die Dinge zählbar sind oder nicht:
   - *many* steht **vor zählbaren Dingen oder Personen**, also bei Nomen im Plural wie z. B. *vegetables*, *bananas*, *kiwis*, *friends*.
   - *much* steht **vor nicht zählbaren Dingen**, also bei Nomen, die immer im Singular stehen wie z. B. *milk* und *ketchup*.
   - *a lot of* oder *lots of* kann sowohl **vor zählbaren** als auch vor **nicht zählbaren Dingen** stehen.
3. Du musst nach Satzarten unterscheiden:
   - *much* und *many* stehen hauptsächlich **in Fragen** (*how much, how many*) **und verneinten Sätzen** (*not much, not many*).
   - *a lot of* und *lots of* stehen **am häufigsten in bejahten Sätzen**, manchmal aber auch in Fragen oder verneinten Sätzen.

MERKHILFE

„Much" hat wie das Deutsche „viel" eine Silbe. Ebenso hat „many" wie das Deutsche „viele" zwei Silben. Zur Unterstützung kannst du die Silben auch klatschen: much – viel (Ketchup); ma-ny – vie-le (Bananen).

TIPP

Es gibt keinen Unterschied zwischen „a lot of" und „lots of". Beachte aber: Wenn kein Nomen folgt, fällt „of" weg, z. B.: How much flour do we need? – **A lot.**

much oder many in Fragen und verneinten Sätzen	
many (zählbare Dinge)	**much** (nicht zählbare Dinge)
We haven't got **many** potatoes for the chips. So how **many** should we buy?	How **much** ketchup do we need? Ice cream? Oh no, there isn't **much** left.

a lot of / lots of in bejahten Sätzen (zählbare und nicht zählbare Dinge)
We need **a lot of/lots of** kiwis and bananas for the fruit salad. I think there's still **a lot of/lots of** coke in the cupboard.

■ Achtung!

– *Much* und *many* können auch **ohne nachfolgendes Nomen** stehen, d.h. sie können dieses ersetzen. Im Gespräch mit Nick sagt Jenny: *Oh no! There isn't much.* Mit *much* meint sie *ketchup.*

– Achte darauf, dass es im Englischen Wörter gibt, die im Gegensatz zum Deutschen nicht zählbar sind, z. B.:
  • *This book doesn't give **much information** on party food.*
  • *Have you got **much homework** over the weekend?*

English summary

How it works	Examples
You can use *much* and *many* to define quantities. You use *much* with singular nouns (uncountable) and *many* with plural nouns (countable) mostly in negative statements and questions.	– How **much bread** have we still got? – We haven't got **much time** to do the shopping. – How **many sandwiches** do we need? – There aren't **many vegetables** for the Indian salad.
A lot of / lots of can be used with countable and uncountable nouns in positive statements.	– We still have **a lot of/lots of cheese** for the pizza. – Jill needs **a lot of/lots of kiwis** for the fruit salad.

Check-out

1. Nick macht sich Gedanken, ob für die Party alles vorbereitet ist. Vervollständige sie mit *much, many* oder *a lot of/lots of.*

   a) *How … flour do we need for the cake?*
   b) *We haven't got … apples for the fruit salad.*
   c) *There are … chocolate crispies next to the microwave.*
   d) *We haven't got … iced tea.*
   e) *Jane and Amanda usually drink … coke.*

G18 Mengenangaben mit *of*
Expressions of quantity with of

We need three pounds **of** potatoes and a bottle **of** ketchup.

Check-in

Here's part of Nick and Jill's party shopping list.

> SHOPPING LIST
>
> – fruit salad: 6 bananas, 8 kiwis
>
> – chips: 3 pounds **of** potatoes,
>   a bottle **of** ketchup
>
> – pizza: 600 grams **of** cheese, a bag **of** flour
>
> – drinks: 4 packets **of** iced tea

1. Übertrage die Einkaufsliste von Nick und Jill ins Deutsche. Was fällt dir bezüglich des Worts *of* auf?

REGEL

1. Die genaue **Menge von zählbaren Dingen** (*bananas, kiwis*) kannst du näher bestimmen, indem du einfach eine **Zahl** (*6, 8*) **davor** setzt.
2. Bei **nicht zählbaren Dingen** musst du dir **Mengenwörter** zu Hilfe nehmen, d.h. Behältnisse, Verpackungen, Maßangaben und Gewichte wie z.B. ***bottle***, ***packet***, ***litre***, ***gram***, um diese Dinge zählbar zu machen. Vergiss dabei nicht, dass im Englischen **zwischen** dem **Mengenwort und** dem **zu bestimmenden Nomen** das Wort ***of*** steht:
   • *a bag of sweets* („eine Tüte von Süßigkeiten")
3. Natürlich kannst du mit diesen Mengenwörtern auch die Menge von zählbaren Dingen bestimmen:
   • *3 pounds of potatoes*

Mengenwort +	*of* +	Nomen	Deutsch
four litres	of	water	vier Liter Wasser
a bottle	of	milk	eine Flasche Milch
a glass	of	apple juice	ein Glas Apfelsaft
ten grams	of	sugar	10 Gramm Zucker
a pound	of	oranges	ein Pfund Orangen
three tins	of	coke	drei Dosen Cola
a bag	of	sweets	eine Tüte Bonbons
a box	of	chocolates	eine Schachtel Pralinen

TIPP
Beachte, dass die Mengenwörter in den Plural gesetzt werden, z.B.: **one litre** of water – **four litres** of water.

English summary

How it works	Examples
If you want to 'count' things like *flour, tea*, etc., you use words like *bag of, glass of*, etc.	– Jill needs **a bag of flour**. – Let's buy **four packets of iced tea**.

Check-out

1. Übertrage weitere Teile der Einkaufsliste von Nick und Jill ins Englische.

    a) 5 Flaschen Wasser   c) 1 Päckchen Tee
    b) 3 Pfund Äpfel   d) 2 Schachteln Eier

You're giving a party for **a few** friends?

G19 Die Mengenwörter *a little* und *a few*
The quantifiers a little *and* a few

Check-in

At home, Nick and Jill are watching the following advertisement on TV.

You're giving a party for **a few** friends? You need **a little** help with the food? Then go to Hyperfood, Britain's number one in food and drinks. This week's special offer: MaPiMi – Magic Pizza Mix – you just need **a little** water for the mix and **a few** people to come around and join you. Buy three packets of MaPiMi and get one free!

1. Ordne die Wörter, die im Werbetext nach *a little* und *a few* stehen, in die Kategorien „zählbar" und „nicht zählbar" ein. Was stellst du fest?

1. Mit *a little* („ein wenig", „ein bisschen") und *a few* („einige", „ein paar") drückst du aus, dass etwas nur **in kleinen Mengen oder geringer Anzahl vorhanden** ist.
2. Du unterscheidest ebenso wie bei *much* und *many* zwischen zählbar und nicht zählbar:
   - *a little* steht nur **vor nicht zählbaren Dingen**, d.h. bei Nomen die immer im Singular stehen wie z.B. *help* und *water*.
   - *a few* verwendet man **vor zählbaren Dingen oder Personen**, d.h. bei Nomen im Plural wie z.B. *friends* und *things*.

a little (nicht zählbare Dinge)	*a few* (zählbare Dinge)
You just need **a little** time to prepare the pizza.	There are still **a few** things on our shopping list.
Sie brauchen nur **ein wenig** Zeit, um die Pizza zuzubereiten.	Es gibt noch **ein paar** Dinge auf unserer Einkaufsliste.

English summary

How it works	Examples
You use *a little* with singular nouns (uncountable) and *a few* with plural nouns (countable).	– I still have **a little water** in my glass. – Let's buy **a few oranges**.

Check-out

1. Ordne den folgenden Wörtern die Mengenangabe *a little* oder *a few* zu.

milk • bagels • noodles • tea • coffee • apples • kiwis • coke

a little	a few

Could I have **some** more chips?

G20 Die Verwendung von *some* und *any*
Using some *and* any

Check-in

It's Saturday evening. Nick, Jill and their friends are enjoying the party.
Read their conversation.

Michael: Could I have **some** more chips? They're delicious.

Jill: I'm glad you like them. Nick's just making **some** more in the kitchen.
Would you like to try **some** Indian salad? It's really tasty.

Michael: No, thanks. I never eat **any** salads.

Amanda: Is there **any** more iced tea, Jill?

Jill: Yes, sure. Would you like **some** more? I can get you **some**.

Amanda: Oh, yes please. – But what's that strange smell? … I think it's coming
from the kitchen.

Jill: Oh no, Nick! What have you done? The pizza …!

Nick: Er, we'll have to make another pizza. This one's black.

Amanda: I'll help you. Is there still enough flour?

Jill: We don't need **any**. We only have to open another packet of *Magic Pizza Mix*!

1. Finde im Gespräch …

   a) einen bejahten Aussagesatz.
   b) einen verneinten Aussagesatz.
   c) einen Satz, in dem eine höfliche Bitte oder Frage gestellt wird.
   d) einen einfachen Fragesatz.

   In all den Sätzen muss entweder *some* oder *any* stehen.

2. Übertrage Amandas erste Frage ins Deutsche. Was fällt dir in Bezug auf das
   Wort *any* auf?

1. Die Mengenwörter *some* und *any* verwendest du vor nicht zählbaren Nomen und den Pluralformen zählbarer Nomen.
2. *Some* verwendest du **in bejahten Aussagesätzen** sowie in **höflichen Bitten, Angeboten oder Vorschlägen**, bei denen du eine **positive Antwort** erwartest und die nur der Form nach Fragen sind.
3. *Any* wird **in verneinten Aussagesätzen** und **echten Fragen** verwendet.
4. Wenn ein Nomen bereits genannt wurde, kann es im folgenden Satz weggelassen werden und so stehen *some* oder *any* allein:
   • *Have you got **any flour**? – No, we don't need **any** (= any flour).*

bejahte Aussagen:	Jill can use **some** *Magic Pizza Mix*. Michael had **some** chips on his plate.
höfliche Bitten, Angebote, Vorschläge:	Could you get me **some** iced tea? Would you like **some** chips with your pizza?
verneinte Aussagen:	There isn't **any** bread on the table. I never eat **any** vegetables.
Fragen:	Have we got **any** cheese? Are there **any** potatoes in the cupboard?

■ **Achtung!**
– Obwohl *some* und *any* den deutschen Wörtern „etwas", „einige" bzw. „ein paar" entsprechen, brauchst du sie oft nicht zu übersetzen. Zum Beispiel kannst du Amandas erste Frage einfach übertragen mit „Gibt es noch Eistee?".

English summary

How it works	Examples
Some is used in positive statements or polite requests.	– We'll make **some** more pizza. – Would you like **some** iced tea?
Any is used in negative statements and questions.	– I'm afraid we haven't got **any** apples. – Is there **any** chocolate in the kitchen?

Check-out

1. Übertrage die folgenden Sätze ins Englische. Denke daran, dass im Englischen Mengenangaben gebraucht werden, auch wenn im Deutschen keine stehen.

   a) Haben wir Kerzen für den Geburtstagskuchen?
   b) Möchtest du Pommes?
   c) Es ist keine Milch mehr in der Flasche.
   d) Sind Teller auf dem Tisch?

There is **no** curry in the food.

G21 Die Verwendung von *no* und *none*
Using no *and* none

Check-in

At 11 pm the friends are still enjoying the party at Nick and Jill's house. But something seems to be wrong with Amanda. Read their conversation.

Amanda: I feel terribly hot.

Jill: Why? Theres **no** reason for that. It isn't hot in here. Have you drunk much alcohol?

Amanda: No, **none** at all! Really!

Jill: But your face is all red!

Amanda: Oh! Could it be curry? I'm allergic to curry, you know. But that can't be it – Nick said that there was **no** curry in the food.

Jill: Oh no! He didn't tell me! I put a lot of it in the Indian salad!

Nick: I told you, Jill! But if you don't listen to what I say, **none of** our friends will ever want to come here again!

1. Welche Unterschiede im Gebrauch zwischen *no, none* und *none of* kannst du im Gespräch oben erkennen? Tipp: Schau dir an, ob andere Wörter auf *no, none (of)* folgen und um welche Art von Wörtern es sich dabei handelt.

> **REGEL**

1. Wenn du eine Nullmenge angeben möchtest, d.h. wenn **jemand** (*friend*) **oder etwas** (*curry, alcohol*) **nicht vorhanden** ist, so kannst du *no* bzw. *none* („kein/keine/keines") verwenden.

2. *No* kann nur **direkt vor** einem **Nomen** stehen:
   • *There's **no reason** for that.*
   • *There's **no curry** in the food.*

3. Möchtest du ein **Nomen** in einem Satz **nicht** noch einmal **wiederholen**, so kannst du manchmal *none* verwenden:
   • *Have you drunk **any alcohol**? – No, **none** at all.*

4. *None of* verwendest du, wenn *the* oder **ein Pronomen** folgt:
   • ***None of our** friends will ever want to come here again.*
   Keiner unserer Freunde wird wieder herkommen wollen.

no + Nomen im Singular oder Plural	*none* als Ersatz eines Nomens oder vor *the* oder einem Pronomen
There's **no curry** in the salad.	Are there any clean glasses? There are **none** in this cupboard.
There are **no chocolate cakes** in the kitchen.	**None of my classmates** is allergic to flour.

🟧 **Achtung!**

– Das deutsche „**kein**" übersetzt du **bei Nomen im Singular** mit *no* bzw. *not a(n)*.
Vergleiche:

  • Ich bin kein Sänger. = *I'm **no** singer.* / *I'm **not a** singer.*

  Bei Nomen im Plural, **Sammelbegriffen und abstrakten Dingen** verwendest du
  no bzw. *not any*. Vergleiche:

  • Ich habe keine Vorschläge. = *I have **no** suggestions./I have**n't** got **any** suggestions.*

  • Er hat kein Geld. = *He has **no** money./He has**n't got** any money.*

English summary

How it works	Examples
You can use *no* or *none* if you want to say that someone or something isn't here. *No* is followed by a plural or singular noun; *none* replaces a noun.	– There are **no sweets** on the shelf. – Are there any vegetables? – No, there are **none**!
You use *none of* before *the* or a pronoun.	– **None of my party recipes** is difficult to prepare.

Check-out

1. Vervollständige die folgenden Sätze. Verwende dabei jeweils einmal *no, none*
und *none of*.

   a) *… my friends can sing.*

   b) *No, there is … sugar in the tea.*

   c) *Have you got any apples? There are … on the table.*

> Let me know if there's **something** I can do.

G22 Zusammensetzungen mit *some* und *any*
The compounds of some *and* any

Check-in

It's the morning after the party. Read what Nick and Jenny's friends have written on the Internet.

Amanda

Hi there, thanks for a great party! Oh, I nearly forgot. I can't find the scarf I had on last night. Maybe it's **somewhere** in your living-room. Have you seen it **anywhere**? I could come round and look – I'm sure you need **someone** to tidy up, anyway. Let me know if there's **something** I can do. OK? C U

Michael

Hi guys, I tried to call you but there wasn't **anyone** at home. The party was cool. I hope your parents didn't say **anything** about all the mess we made! Has **anyone** come round yet to help you with the washing up? – And Jill, you promised to look for the article on how to organise a good party. Have you found it **anywhere**? Could you please look if there is **something** in it about costume parties? Let me know, bye!

1. Schau dir die Sätze in den Chateinträgen oben genau an und ordne dann **1)** und **2)** den Satzarten **a)** bis **d)** zu.

1) *someone, something, somewhere*

2) *anyone, anything, anywhere*

a) Fragen
b) verneinte Aussagen
c) bejahte Aussagen
d) höfliche Bitten, Vorschläge

REGEL

1. Für *some* und *any* gibt es **Zusammensetzungen mit -one** bzw. **-body** („jemand", „irgendjemand"), **-thing** („etwas", „irgendetwas") und **-where** („irgendwo").
2. Du verwendest die Zusammensetzungen in den verschiedenen Satzarten in der gleichen Weise wie *some* und *any* (→ **G20**):

> **TIPP**
> „Anybody" bzw. „anyone" kann auch jeder x-beliebige bedeuten: Anybody can organise a party.

bejahte Aussagen:	Nick and Jenny need **someone** to do the washing up. I saw some crisps **somewhere** under the sofa.
höfliche Bitten, Angebote, Vorschläge:	Could I do **something** to help you?
verneinte Aussagen:	What a mess! Nick can't find **anything** the morning after the party. Your CD? I can't see it **anywhere**.
Fragen:	Has **anyone** found my scarf?

English summary

How it works	Examples
You use the compounds of *some* in positive statements and polite requests and offers.	– **Someone** has left their bag in the hall. – Would you like **something** to drink?
The compounds of *any* are used in negative statements and questions.	– I can't find Michael's CDs **anywhere**. – Is there **anything** I can help you with?

Check-out

1. Amanda berichtet über die Party. Vervollständige ihren Blog mit einer passenden Zusammensetzung von *some* oder *any*.

"Would you like something/anything to eat?" That was Jill's favourite question! The food was really good! Mmm! I also liked the music, but there wasn't somebody/anybody who wanted to dance with me. So I talked a lot to someone/anyone from the United States. It was Nick's cousin. We had a lot of fun! This morning the living-room and the kitchen were a mess! Jill couldn't find something/anything. She called me and asked: "Do you know somebody / anybody who can help us?"

G23 Zusammensetzungen mit *every* und *no*
The compounds of every *and* no

> Choose some music
> that **everybody** likes.

Check-in

Read part of the article Jill has cut out for her friend.

HOW TO HAVE A PARTY TO REMEMBER

✔ Choose some music that **everybody** likes. **Everything** will be fine if you have a room to dance in!
✔ Make sure your guests know what to wear – **nobody** wants to put on the wrong clothes, so tell your friends if you have a dress code or not!
✔ Don't let your guests go **everywhere** in the house. (Your parents won´t want people in their bedroom!)
✔ You should prepare your party well: **nothing** is more embarrassing than running out of food or drinks!
✔ And your parents? If they have **nowhere** to go, advise them to see a late-night film at the cinema.

1. Finde im Artikel die englischen Wörter für die Gegensatzpaare:

    a) jeder • niemand   b) alles • nichts   c) überall • nirgendwo

TIPP
Beachte die Rechtschreibung von „no one" – es sind zwei getrennte Wörter!

REGEL

1. Neben *some* und *any* können auch **no** und **every** mit *-one* bzw. *-body*, *-thing* und *-where* **zusammengesetzt** werden.
2. Die **Zusammensetzungen mit *no*** drücken aus, dass **jemand oder etwas nicht vorhanden** ist: *nobody/no one* („niemand"), *nothing* („nichts") und *nowhere* („nirgendwo", „nirgends").
3. Im Gegensatz dazu drücken **Zusammensetzungen mit *every*** aus, dass **jemand oder etwas komplett vorhanden bzw. vollständig** ist: *everyone/everybody* („jeder", „alle"), *everything* („alles"), *everywhere* („überall").

no one/-body/-thing/-where (Nichtvorhandensein)	*everyone/-body/-thing/-where* (Vollständigkeit)
Nobody wants to dance if the music isn't good.	**Everybody** enjoyed the party.
The food was OK, but there was **nothing** for vegetarians.	**Everything** went well.
Where is my CD? – No idea! It's **nowhere** here.	We opened all the doors so you could hear the music **everywhere**.

English summary

How it works	Examples
The compounds of *no* are used to express that something or someone isn't there.	– You didn't write invitations for your party? **Nobody** is perfect! – There is **nothing** worse than the wrong music.
You use the compounds of *every* to show completeness.	– Ask your guests to help you tidy up **everywhere** after the party. – **Everybody** should enjoy the atmosphere.

Check-out

1. Vervollständige die folgenden Sätze mit der passenden Form. Wenn du alles richtig machst, kommt ein Lösungswort heraus.

   everybody (E) • *everywhere (R)* • *nothing (L)* • *nobody (U)*

   a) *There is music … in the house.*
   b) *I'm so sad: … came to my birthday party!*
   c) *She tried to turn on the music, but … happened.*
   d) *Ice cream is something that … likes.*

5 Das Adjektiv

G24 Die Verwendung von Adjektiven
The use of adjectives

> My parents and I are having a **hard** time together.

Check-in

Read what two teenagers have posted on the Internet forum of their favourite teenage magazine *Millennium Teen*.

An_thony@98

My parents and I are having a **hard** time together. I've got a **nice** family but I've been arguing with my mum a lot for a **long** time. She thinks that I'm **lazy** and **impolite**, but I think that she's just not **relaxed**.

fashion.girl@99

I haven't got any **cool** clothes. I've seen two **trendy new** skirts that I really want to buy but my parents are **strict**. They won't give me the money. I'm **young** and I like **modern** clothes so I'll have to get a job.

---

1. Schau dir die hervorgehobenen Adjektive im Forum einmal genau an. Welche Eigenschaften haben sie? Wähle aus.

   Adjektive beziehen sich auf … .   **a)** Verben   **b)** Nomen
   Sie sind … .   **a)** veränderlich **b)** unveränderlich

2. Vergleiche die Stellung der Adjektive in den folgenden beiden Sätzen. Was fällt dir auf? Tipp: Was folgt dem Adjektiv bzw. was geht voran?

   a) *I've got a **nice** family.*
   b) *My parents are **strict**.*

REGEL

1. Mit **Adjektiven** beschreibst du **Eigenschaften von Nomen**. Sie geben also an, wie eine Person (*I'm young*) oder eine Sache (*cool clothes, a hard time*) ist.
2. Adjektive sind **unveränderlich**, d. h. du gleichst sie in Geschlecht und Zahl nicht an das Nomen an (wie etwa im Deutschen oder Französischen). Vergleiche:
   • ein schön**er** Rock – schön**e** Röcke
   • une joli**e** jupe – des joli**es** jupes
   • a nice skirt – nice skirts
3. **Adjektive stehen vor** dem **Nomen** auf das sie sich beziehen (*a nice family, modern clothes*) **oder nach einer Form des Verbs *be*** (*I'm young, she's not relaxed*).

> **TIPP**
> Einige Adjektive stehen nur nach bestimmten Verben, d.h. nicht vor einem Nomen, z. B.: afraid, alive, alone, asleep, ill.
> – The boy is alive. (Nicht: the alive boy!)

TIPP
Zwei Farbadjektive verknüpfst du mit „and", z.B.: a **red and white** T-shirt.

4. Möchtest du einmal **mehrere Adjektive** verwenden, um ein Nomen zu beschreiben, dann kann dir folgende **Reihenfolge** helfen:

Gefühl / Meinung	Größe / Länge	Alter	Form / Breite	Farbe	Ursprung	Material
friendly	short	young	thin	yellow	European	wooden

Zum Beispiel: *Ann is the **friendly young** girl with a **short yellow** T-shirt on.*

English summary

How it works	Examples
Adjectives describe nouns (people and things). They don't change in form.	– She is a **nice** girl with **blue** eyes. – Teenagers like **trendy** clothes.
Adjectives are used before a noun but after a form of *be*.	– Anthony prefers **relaxed parents**, but his mother **is strict.**
If you want to describe a noun with more than one adjective, use the following order: opinion/feeling – size/length – age – shape/width – colour – origin – material.	– He is wearing a **large green** T-shirt. – *Millennium Teen* has an **interesting new** website.

Check-out

1. Schau dir das Bild von fashion.girl@99 an. Vervollständige dann die Sätze mit einem Adjektiv aus der Liste, sodass wahre Aussagen über sie entstehen. Tipp: Zwei Adjektive bleiben übrig.

early • great • pink • dark • strict • attractive • blue • white

Fashion.girl@99 is wearing … boots and … trousers. She has got … eyes and … hair. She is … . At the moment, she is dreaming of a guy. His name is Brian. She wants to go out with him, but her parents are …, so she has to stay at home.

2. Bilde vollständige Sätze, indem du die Adjektive in die richtige Reihenfolge bringst.

a) *Wendy is a(n) young / American / happy teenager.*
b) *She likes to wear her yellow / nice jacket.*

G25 Das Adjektiv nach bestimmten Verben
Verbs followed by an adjective

> A good friend wants to **make** you **happy**.

Check-in

You'd like to find out what this week is going to be like for you. In *Millennium Teen* you find these horoscopes.

LEO (July 23-August 23)
LIFE: You'll get an invitation – a good friend wants to make you **happy**. But keep **quiet**, don't tell anyone about it!
LOVE: An old friend finds you **attractive**. Don't miss this chance!
MONEY: Watch out! You feel **great** when you go shopping but you are spending too much!

VIRGO (August 24-September 23)
LIFE: You are **lazy** at the moment. Do some sport and get **fit**.
LOVE: On Monday, your partner might turn **nasty**. Stay **calm**!
MONEY: Everything seems **fine** for you on Friday, but don't spend any money from Monday to Thursday!

1. Wo stehen die im Horoskop hervorgehobenen Adjektive in den meisten Beispielsätzen?

   a) vor dem Nomen   b) nach dem Nomen   c) nach dem Verb

2. Ordne die Verben, die zu den hervorgehobenen Adjektiven gehören, den folgenden Kategorien zu:

   a) Eigenschaften/Zustände des Nomens werden beschrieben
   b) im Deutschen würde man „werden" sagen
   c) Sinneswahrnehmungen/Gefühle werden ausgedrückt
   d) vor dem Adjektiv steht ein Objekt, Eigenschaften werden beschrieben

REGEL

1. Manche Verben stehen in Verbindung mit einem Adjektiv. Dies trifft zu auf …

Verben, die auf einen Zustand oder eine Eigenschaft des Nomens verweisen: *be, seem, remain, stay, keep*	Your friends **are helpful** this week.
	You should **stay calm** if your date goes out with another girl.
	Keep cool if you don't have enough money for new clothes.
Verben, die dem deutschen Wort „werden" entsprechen: *become, grow, get, go, turn*	You can **become popular** if you take part in a TV competition.
	This week you'll **grow impatient**.
Verben der Sinneswahrnehmung, wenn sie einen Zustand (keine Tätigkeit!) beschreiben: *feel, look, sound, taste, smell*	You'll **feel great** tomorrow.
	It's time for new clothes next week: all the old T-shirts and trousers **don't look nice** on you!

> **TIPP**
> Beschreiben „feel", „look", „taste", „smell" und „sound" einen Zustand folgt ihnen ein Adjektiv, z. B.: She looked **angry**. (= Sie sah wütend aus.) Beschreiben sie aber eine **Tätigkeit**, so muss ihnen ein **Adverb** folgen, z. B.: She looked at me **angrily**. (= Sie sah mich wütend an.)

Verben wie *find, like, see, call, keep, make,* denen ein Objekt und ein Adjektiv folgt. Das ist ähnlich wie im Deutschen!	Your best friend will **find your reaction stupid**.
	If you go out on Saturday, try to **keep your make-up fresh**.
	You can **make your friends happy** with an invitation to a party.

English summary

How it works	Examples
Certain verbs are followed by an adjective. This goes for … – verbs describing the state or quality of a noun, – verbs referring to a future state (German 'werden'), – verbs of perception (state, not action), – certain verbs (e. g.: *call, find, see, keep, make, like*) used with an object + adjective.	– This week, everything **seems fine** for you. You can **stay relaxed**. – It's your first date? Don't **get nervous**! – I **feel good** when I read horoscopes – they **sound positive**! – Your friends hate to **see you unhappy**.

Check-out

1. Warum gibt es Horoskope? Bilde logische Sätze.

Horoscopes		seem		glad to have them.
Many boys and girls	➕	get	➕	nervous without advice.
A lot of teens		feel		safe when they read them.
Readers		can be		helpful.

2. Übertrage die folgenden beiden Sätze ins Englische.

   a) Meine Mutter findet Horoskope peinlich.
   b) Paul macht seine Eltern nicht glücklich.

G26 Die Steigerung der Adjektive
Comparison of adjectives

> I don't know which of the two is **nicer**, **funnier** or **more attractive**.

Check-in

Gwendella is *Millenium Teen's* agony aunt. Here's one of the typical e-mails she gets every week.

From:	jason@greenmail.co.uk
To:	gwendella@millennium-teen.co.uk
Subject:	Two girls want to go out with me!

Dear Gwendella,

I can't believe anyone out there has a **bigger** problem: two girls want to go out with me! I don't know which of the two is **nicer**, **funnier** or **more attractive**. I was thinking about going out with each of them on two different nights to find out who is **the sweetest** and **the friendliest**. What would be **simpler**? But they know each other, and if they find out what's going on, I'll be in **the most embarrassing** situation you can imagine. Can you think of a **better** way to sort this out? The situation is getting **worse** and I don't want to be **the most heartless** person in the world. Please help me!

Jason

1. Ergänze die fehlenden Formen mit Hilfe von Jasons E-Mail.

    a) *nice • … • the nicest*   **c)** *attractive • … • the most attractive*
    b) *sweet • sweeter • …*   **d)** *heartless • more heartless • …*

2. Vergleiche nun **a)** und **b)** mit **c)** und **d)**. Was fällt dir bezüglich der Steigerungsregeln auf? Tipp: Achte auf die Anzahl der Silben!

REGEL

1. Bei Adjektiven gibt es **zwei Möglichkeiten der Steigerung**. Welche du benötigst, hängt davon ab, **wie viele Silben** die **Grundform** des Adjektivs hat.

2. Viele Adjektive steigerst du im Englischen, indem du **-er** (1. Steigerung) bzw. **-est** (2. Steigerung) **an die Grundform** des Adjektivs **anhängst**. Das machst du so bei …

    a) allen einsilbigen Adjektiven:
      • *I can't believe anyone out there has a **bigger** problem.*

> **TIPP**
> Für die Steigerungsstufen werden auch folgende Bezeichnungen verwendet:
> – Grundform = Positiv
> – 1. Steigerung = Komparativ
> – 2. Steigerung = Superlativ.

Grundform	1. Steigerung	2. Steigerung	Besonderheiten
sweet	sweet**er**	the sweet**est**	–
big fit	bi**gger** fi**tter**	the bi**ggest** the fi**ttest**	Endkonsonant nach kurzem Vokal wird verdoppelt
nic**e**	nic**er**	the nic**est**	stummes -e am Ende des Adjektivs fällt weg

b) allen zweisilbigen Adjektiven, die auf **-y, -le, -ow** oder **-er** enden:
- *I don't know which of the two girls is **funnier**.*

Grundform	1. Steigerung	2. Steigerung	Besonderheiten
funn**y**	funn**ier**	the funn**iest**	-y wird zu i, wenn Adjektiv auf Konsonant + -y endet
simp**le**	simp**ler**	the simp**lest**	-e am Ende des Adjektivs fällt weg
narrow	narrow**er**	the narrow**est**	–
clever	clever**er**	the clever**est**	–

3. Bei allen **zweisilbigen Adjektiven**, die **nicht auf -y, -le, -ow** oder **-er** enden, sowie bei allen **Adjektiven**, die **mehr als zwei Silben** haben, setzt du **more** (1. Steigerung) bzw. **most** (2. Steigerung) vor die Grundform. Das **Adjektiv** selbst bleibt **unverändert**:
- *I don't want to be **the most heartless** person in the world.*

Grundform	1. Steigerung	2. Steigerung
heartless	**more** heartless	the **most** heartless
attractive	**more** attractive	the **most** attractive
embarrassing	**more** embarrassing	the **most** embarrassing

4. Einige **wenige Adjektive** werden **unregelmäßig** gesteigert. Diese musst du auswendig lernen:
- *Can you think of a **better** way to sort this out?*

Grundform	1. Steigerung	2. Steigerung
good	better	the best
bad	worse	the worst
much/many	more	the most
little (= wenig)	less	the least

■ **Achtung!**
- Das Adjektiv *little* in der Bedeutung von „klein" kann zwar gesteigert werden, aber den Formen *littler* und *littlest* begegnest du nicht sehr oft. Häufiger werden *smaller* (1. Steigerung) und *the smallest* (2. Steigerung) verwendet, z. B.:
  - *Your problem is **smaller than** mine.*

- „Nächste/r/s" hat im Englischen zwei Entsprechungen:
  1. räumlich: *the nearest supermarket* (der nächste Supermarkt),
  2. Reihenfolge: *the next meeting* (das nächste Treffen).

English summary

How it works	Examples
You use the comparison with *-er/-est* with adjectives of one syllable and adjectives of two syllables ending in *-y, -le, -ow* or *-er*.	– Jason is a **happy** boy. But he would be **happier** if he didn't have the **biggest** teenage problem.
The comparison with *more/most* is used with adjectives of more than two syllables and adjectives of two syllables not ending in *-y, -le, -ow* or *–er*.	– Jason is in an **embarrassing** situation. It will be even **more embarrassing** if the two girls find out about it. – They might think he's **the most heartless** boy they've ever met.
There are adjectives (*good, bad, much/many, little*) with irregular forms of comparison.	– **Good** advice is hard to find. – His friend's advice could have been **better**. – Gwendella gave him **the best** piece of advice.

Check-out

1. Bilde die erste und zweite Steigerungsstufe folgender Adjektive:

   dirty • disappointing • clean • silly • realistic • wet • dry • shocking

2. Ergänze Jasons Gedanken. Verwende dazu die erste (+) oder zweite (++) Steigerungsstufe des Adjektivs in Klammern.

   a) *Lisa is … (+ friendly), but Julia is (+ ambitious).*
   b) *Julia's parents have got … (++ big) house in our street, but Lisa's dad has got … (++ expensive) car in town.*
   c) *But who is … (+ funny), … (+ polite) and … (+ helpful)? I don't really know. Finding … (++ good) girlfriend isn't … (++ easy) task in the world!*

Five years ago e-mails were **not as important as** social networks and text messages.

G27 Vergleiche mit Adjektiven
Making comparisons

Check-in

Millennium Teen presents interesting facts for its readers every week:

Did you know?
British teenagers

	Pocket money per week	Communication	First girl-/boyfriend at the age of …
five years ago	£7.90	e-mails	12
today	£9.15	social networks / text messages	12

★ 12- to 16-year-olds get more pocket money: £9.15 per week, so they are **richer than** teens five years ago!
★ In terms of communication, e-mails are **not as important as** social networks and text messages today.
★ One thing hasn't changed: 12 is the age at which they meet their first girl-/boyfriend, so they are **as old as** five years ago.

1. Welcher der Beispielsätze aus der Zeitschrift drückt Gleichheit aus, welche Ungleichheit?

> **REGEL**

1. Es gibt verschiedene Möglichkeiten, wie du mit Hilfe von Adjektiven Personen oder Sachen in einem Satz vergleichen kannst.
   Wenn die **Personen oder Sachen gleich** sind, verwendest du *as + Grundform + as*:
   • *The boys are **as old as** the girls.* (… genauso alt wie …)
   • *Alcohol is **as dangerous as** cigarettes.* (… genauso gefährlich wie …)
2. Wenn die **Personen oder Sachen ungleich** sind, hast du zwei Möglichkeiten, dies auszudrücken:
   a) **1. Steigerung +** *than*
   • *Teenagers nowadays are **richer than** teenagers five years ago.*
     (… reicher als …)
   • *Lots of young people think that school life is **more boring than** free time activities.*
     (… langweiliger als …)
   b) *not as* **+ Grundform +** *as*
   • *Classical music is **not as trendy as** rap music.*
     (… nicht so angesagt wie …)
   • *E-mails are **not as important as** text messages.*
     (… nicht so wichtig wie …)

TIPP
„less" + Grundform + „than" ist ähnlich in der Bedeutung wie „not as" + Grundform + „as", z. B.: E-mails are **less trendy than** text messages.

3. Mit *the ...* , *the ...* (jeweils mit 1. Steigerung) kannst du im Englischen „**je ...** ,
  desto ..." wiedergeben:
  • *The older* teenagers are, *the more independent* they become.
     (Je älter ..., desto unabhängiger, ...)

■ **Achtung!**
 – Verwechsle *th**a**n* (Vergleichswort „als") nicht mit *th**e**n* (Zeitadverb „dann").
   Vergleiche:
   • *Some teenagers get more pocket money **than** others.*
   • *The reporters interviewed about one thousand teenagers and **then** wrote an
     article about the results.*

English summary

How it works	Examples
There are different ways to compare people or things with the help of adjectives: – If there is no difference between the people or things compared, you use *as* + positive + *as*. – If there is a difference between the people or things compared, you can use either comparative + *than* or *not as* + positive + *as*.	– Sometimes girls are **as aggressive as** boys. – Do you think that girls **are more jealous than** boys? – For most teens, books are **not as interesting as** films.
You can also use *the ...*, *the ...* + comparative to make comparisons.	– **The younger** the children are, **the less** pocket money they get.

Check-out

1. Beim Besuch der Website von *Millennium Teen* blinkt folgende Werbung für eine
   neue Fast-Food-Kette auf. Vergleiche die Artikel auf der Speisekarte. Verwende
   dazu die Adjektive in Klammern.

Cheeseburger £2.15	*Giant doubleburger £3.99*	
Green salad £1.99	*Doughnut £0.99*	
Coke small £0.99 large £1.79		

a) *cheeseburger / giant doubleburger*   *(cheap)*
    A cheeseburger is cheaper ...
b) *green salad / doughnut*   *(healthy)*
c) *giant doubleburger / cheeseburger*   *(big)*
d) *small coke / doughnut*   *(expensive)*
e) *cheeseburger / green salad*   *(tasty → your own choice)*

Which dress should I wear? The black **one** or the red **one**?

G28 Das Stützwort *one/ones* nach Adjektiven
The prop-word one/ones *after adjectives*

Check-in

Every week *Millennium Teen* presents a typical teenage topic as a comic.
This week Ann and Susan are discussing party clothes.

A hard choice ...

Oh, Susan, please help me! Which dress should I wear? The black **one** or the red **one**?

Right. And what about the earrings? The small **ones** or the big **ones**?

The big **ones**. They're trendier than the small **ones**.

I'd wear the red **one**. Black is too formal for a birthday party, isn't it?

1. Schau dir die Aussagen von Ann und Susan einmal genau an. Welches Wort wird durch *one* ersetzt?

   a) *Susan*   **b)** *wear*   **c)** *dress*   **d)** *help*

2. Welches Wort wird durch ***ones*** ersetzt?

REGEL

1. Wenn du ein **zählbares Nomen** nicht noch einmal wiederholen möchtest, kannst du es **durch *one/ones*** ersetzen.
2. Mit *one* ersetzt du **Nomen im Singular**, mit *ones* Nomen im Plural.
3. Anders als im Deutschen darf **im Englischen das Adjektiv nicht allein** stehen – es muss **durch *one/ones* „unterstützt"** werden. Darum werden *one/ones* auch Stützwörter genannt.

Satz mit Nomen	Ersetzung durch *one/ones*	Deutsch
Which **dress** should I wear?	Should I wear the black **one** or the red **one**?	Soll ich das schwarze oder das rote anziehen?
Ann has got lots of **earrings**.	The big **ones** are trendier than the small **ones**.	Die großen sind moderner als die kleinen.

English summary

How it works	Examples

If you don't want to use the same countable noun again, you can use the prop-word *one* for nouns in the singular and *ones* for nouns in the plural.	– Is this your **jacket**?
	   – No, I've got a blue **one**.
	– These **shoes** are great!
	   – Yes, but I like the other **ones** better.

Check-out

1. Susan und Ann diskutieren noch immer. Vervollständige ihren Dialog, indem du das Nomen jeweils durch *one* oder *ones* ersetzt. Verwende die Adjektive in Klammern.

Ann: *Which boots are trendier, the … (black) or the … (white)?*

Susan: *The … (white). They are really nice.*

Ann: *What do you think of my handbag?*

Susan: *You mean the … (new)? Oh no, it doesn't go with your red dress. Take the … (old) that you bought in London last year.*

G29 Adjektive als Nomen
Adjectives used as nouns

You will soon enter the world of **the rich** and **the famous**!

Check-in

In *Millennium Teen* you find this advert for a casting show.

❂ *STARMANIAC* ❂

ARE YOU **A YOUNG GIRL** BETWEEN 14 AND 17? DO YOU WANT TO BE FAMOUS? ARE YOU **A TALENTED PERFORMER**? ❂ *STARMANIAC* ❂, ONE OF BRITAIN'S MOST POPULAR TALENT SHOWS, IS WAITING FOR YOU! DON'T MISS THIS CHANCE: SEND US AN E-MAIL AND YOU WILL SOON ENTER THE WORLD OF **THE RICH** AND **THE FAMOUS**! BCD BROADCASTING CORP.
CONTACT: STARMANIAC@BCD.CO.UK

BCD We offer a great future for **the young**.

----

1. Ordne die in der Anzeige hervorgehobenen Wörter in die folgende Übersicht ein:

bezieht sich auf eine Gesamtgruppe von Personen	bezieht sich auf eine bestimmte Person

---

REGEL

1. Anders als im Deutschen kannst du **im Englischen Adjektive nur in bestimmten Fällen als Nomen** verwenden.
2. Wenn das Adjektiv als Nomen verwendet wird, **bezieht** es **sich auf eine Gesamtgruppe** von Personen: *the young* bezeichnet die Jugendlichen bzw. junge Menschen allgemein, also die Jugend.
3. Das **Adjektiv** wird in dem Fall **wie eine Pluralform verwendet**, obwohl es keine Pluralendung hat. Es muss mit Verben und Pronomen im Plural stehen:
   - *The rich have their own problems.*
4. Sprichst du aber von **einzelnen Personen oder** von bestimmten **Gruppen einzelner Personen**, dann musst du das **Adjektiv durch ein Nomen** (z. B. *girl, person*) **ergänzen**. Das Adjektiv kann nicht wie im Deutschen allein stehen:
   - die Kleine = *the little girl* (Nicht: *the little!*)

the + Adjektiv = gesamte Gruppe von Personen	(*the/a(n)* +) Adjektiv + Nomen = einzelne Personen/bestimmte Gruppen
Do you want to live like **the rich**?	Do you think many **famous people** watch casting shows?
… die Reichen?	… berühmte Leute …
With STARMANIAC, **the young** have their future in their own hands.	**A young man** wrote an e-mail to starmaniac@bcd.co.uk.
… die Jugendlichen …	Ein junger Mann …

English summary

How it works	Examples
You use *the* + adjective for a whole group of people.	– Casting shows are often a chance for **the young**.
You use (*the/a(n)* +) adjective + noun for individual people or certain groups of individual people.	– **The young girl** wanted to take part in STARMANIAC, but she couldn't really sing.

Check-out

1. Der Manager von STARMANIAC berichtet über ein paar seltsame Ereignisse während der letzten Staffel. Vervollständige die Sätze mit *the* + Adjektiv oder *a/an* + Adjektiv + Nomen. Wähle Adjektive und Nomen aus der Liste aus.

   homeless • old • man • rich • poor • woman

   a) *"… wanted to be like Robin Hood – he thought that he could rob … and give to … . But the police caught him and took him to prison."*
   b) *"Some people will do anything to take part in our show. Once, … said on the phone that she was just 17 years old. In fact, she was 65!"*

6 Adverbien und adverbiale Bestimmungen

G30 Adverbien der Art und Weise
Adverbs of manner

> Do you talk to your friends **openly**?

Check-in

Jenny has found this test on friendships in a magazine.

Are you a good friend?

		Yes	No	Sometimes
1.	Do you talk to your friends **openly**?	○	○	○
2.	Do you answer their questions **honestly**?	○	○	○
3.	Do you take their problems **seriously**?	○	○	○
4.	Do you give advice **gently**?	○	○	○
5.	Do you think about their problems **realistically**?	○	○	○
6.	Can you deal with it if your friends react **emotionally**?	○	○	○

How many times have you marked ...   __ __ __

☞ Turn to the next page to find out more about yourself.

---

1. Schau dir den Test einmal genau an. Nenne das Wort auf das sich das hervorgehobene Adverb jeweils bezieht. Um welche Wortart handelt es sich dabei?

2. Schau dir die hervorgehobenen Adverbien in den Fragen 1–3, 4, 5 und 6 an. Von welchen Adjektiven stammen sie ab? Wie unterscheiden sie sich in der Bildung?

REGEL

1. Du verwendest **Adverbien**, um eine Tätigkeit, also ein **Verb**, **näher zu beschreiben**, z. B. *talk openly*, *take seriously*. Damit sagst du, wie etwas getan wird. Diese Art von Adverbien nennt man Adverbien der Art und Weise.
2. **Viele** von ihnen werden aus Adjektiven gebildet und **enden auf -ly**. Die nachfolgende Tabelle zeigt dir die Grundregeln bei der Bildung von Adverbien aus Adjektiven.

Bildung	Adjektiv	Adverb der Art und Weise
Adjektiv + -ly	Jenny is an **open** person.	She **talks** to friends **openly**.
	Her answers are always **serious**.	She **takes** their problems **seriously**.
Adjektiv auf -ic + -ally	She is **realistic**.	She always **looks at** things **realistically**.
Adjektiv auf -al endet als Adverb auf -ally	She has a **logical** way of thinking.	She **thinks** about problems **logically**.

■ **Achtung!**
– Beachte folgende Rechtschreibregeln:

Regel	Adjektiv	Adverb
Adjektiv endet auf -y → Adverb auf -ily	Jenny is happ**y**.	She is reading the magazine happ**ily**.
Ausnahme: shy	She is a sh**y** girl.	She smiles sh**yly**.
Adjektiv endet auf -le → Adverb auf -ly	Larry feels terrib**le** at home.	He misses his friends terrib**ly** .
Adjektiv endet auf -l → Adverb auf -lly-	Jenny is carefu**l**.	She does the test carefu**lly**.
Adjektiv endet auf stummem -e → -e bleibt erhalten	Larry is always polit**e** to people.	He always speaks to people polit**ely**.

– Merke dir, dass *well* das **Adverb des Adjektivs** *good* ist. Vergleiche:
  • *Jenny is a **good** friend.* (Adjektiv)
  • *She understands her friends' problems **well**.* (Adverb)
  Es gibt aber auch das Adjektiv ***well***. Es bedeutet „gesund".
  • *I'm not **well**.*
    Ich bin nicht **gesund**. / Mir geht es nicht **gut**.

– Von einigen wenigen Adjektiven, z. B. ***friendly*** und ***difficult***, kann **kein Adverb** gebildet werden. Um dennoch ein Verb näher bestimmen zu können, musst du eine **Umschreibung verwenden**. Eine solche Umschreibungen nennt man adverbiale Bestimmung.
  • *He is **friendly**.* (Adjektiv)
    Er ist freundlich.
  • *He smiles **in a friendly way**.* (adverbiale Bestimmung)
    Er lächelt freundlich.
  • *Her work is **difficult**.* (Adjektiv)
    Ihre Arbeit ist schwierig.
  • *She finished the work **with great difficulty**.* (adverbiale Bestimmung)
    Sie erledigte die Arbeit unter großen Schwierigkeiten.

■ **Schriftlicher/mündlicher Sprachgebrauch**
  – In der Umgangssprache wird manchmal die Endung -ly bei kurzen Adverbien weggelassen, z. B. *bad, easy, normal, quick, real, slow*. In geschriebenen Texten solltest du jedoch auch bei kurzen Adverbien immer die eigentlich korrekte Form verwenden.

English summary

How it works	Examples
Adverbs describe how something is done. For most adverbs you use the adjective + -ly or -ally.	– You can make friends **quickly**. – She answers letters person**ally**.
If an adjective ends in –y, you must change the -y to i, e.g. *angry – angrily*, *easy – easily, noisy – noisily*.	– You react angr**ily** when somebody lies to you.
Well is the adverb of *good*.	– As Tina's friend, Jenny always talks **well** of her.
For just a few adjectives (e.g. *friendly*, *difficult*) you need to find another expression when you want to describe the verb.	– It's nice if people talk to you **in a friendly way**.
In spoken English, people often drop -ly when they use short adverbs.	– Take it **easy**! – Come **quick**!

Check-out

1. Vervollständige die Testauswertung mit einem Adjektiv oder Adverb.

   Which did you tick most often: yes, no, or sometimes?
   Mostly 'yes':
   What a good friend! You are always (helpful/helpfully). You listen to your friends (careful/carefully) and give good advice. We all need friends like you!
   Mostly 'no':
   Oh dear. You don't take friendships (serious/seriously). Maybe you behave (friendly/in a friendly way) but when people really need you, you aren't there.
   Mostly 'sometimes':
   (True/Truly) friendships are the best, so try to be open with your friends all the time and make sure they can always speak (open/openly) to you!

> I talk to everyone openly but I talk **most openly** to you.

G31 Die Steigerung der Adverbien
The comparison of adverbs

Check-in

Jenny often thinks of her friend Tina, who has recently moved to another city. While she is shopping, she comes across this postcard:

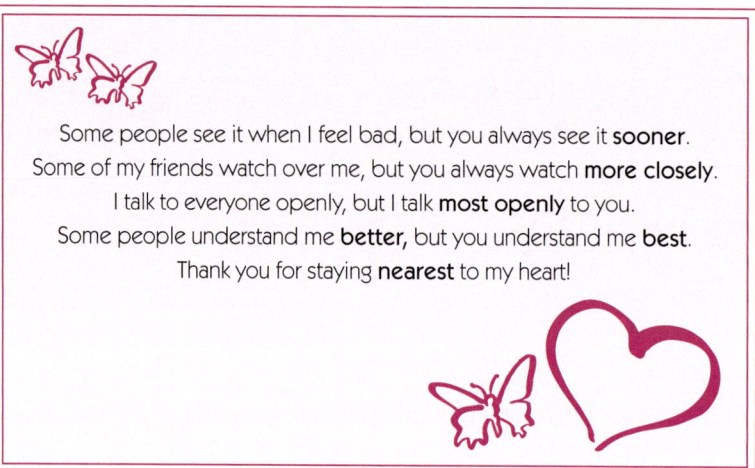

Some people see it when I feel bad, but you always see it **sooner**.
Some of my friends watch over me, but you always watch **more closely**.
I talk to everyone openly, but I talk **most openly** to you.
Some people understand me **better,** but you understand me **best**.
Thank you for staying **nearest** to my heart!

1. Schau dir die Botschaft auf der Postkarte genau an und vervollständige diese Tabelle.

Grundform	1. Steigerung	2. Steigerung
soon		*soonest*
closely		*most closely*
openly	*more openly*	
well		
near	*nearer*	

2. Übertrage die folgenden beiden Sätze ins Deutsche. Achte dabei auf die gesteigerten Adverbien.

a) *Friends stay nearest to your heart.*
b) *I talk most openly to you.*

REGEL

1. Die **Steigerungsformen der Adverbien** verwendest du, um auszudrücken, dass z. B. jemand etwas genau**er** oder **am** genau**sten** bzw. **besser** oder **am besten** gemacht hat:
   • *Jenny looked at the cards **more closely**.*
   • *She liked this card **best**.*
2. Im Englischen gibt es genau wie im Deutschen neben der Grundform **zwei Steigerungsstufen**. **Bei der Bildung** musst du **auf die Anzahl der Silben** des Adverbs **achten**:

a) **Einsilbige Adverbien** steigerst du mit **-er/-est**:
   • *Thank you for staying **nearest** to my heart!*

Grundform	1. Steigerung	2. Steigerung
run **fast**	fast**er**	fast**est**
work **hard**	hard**er**	hard**est**
stay up **late**	lat**er**	lat**est**
speak **loud**	loud**er**	loud**est**
sit **near**	near**er**	near**est**
come **soon**	soon**er**	soon**est**

Beachte, dass *early* mit *-er/-est* gesteigert wird, obwohl es zwei Silben hat:

wake up **early**	earl**ier**	earl**iest**

b) Alle **Adverbien**, die **auf -ly** (außer *early*) enden **oder mehrsilbig** sind, steigerst du mit **more/most**; das Adverb selbst bleibt unverändert:
   • *They watch over me, but you watch **more closely**. I talk **most openly** to you.*

Grundform	1. Steigerung	2. Steigerung
listen **closely**	**more** closely	**most** closely
answer **personally**	**more** personally	**most** personally
meet **often**	**more** often	**most** often

c) Bei einigen Adverbien ist die **Steigerung unregelmäßig**:
   • *Some people understand me **better**, but you understand me **best**.*

Grundform	1. Steigerung	2. Steigerung
drive **badly**	worse	worst
go **far**	further	furthest
drink **little**	less	least
eat **much**	more	most
swim **well**	better	best

> **TIPP**
> Für die Steigerungs-
> stufen werden auch
> folgende Bezeich-
> nungen verwendet:
> – Grundform = Positiv
> – 1. Steigerung
>   = Komparativ
> – 2. Steigerung
>   = Superlativ.

> **TIPP**
> Die unregelmäßigen
> Formen der
> Steigerung musst du
> auswendig lernen.

English summary

How it works	Examples
To form the comparative and the superlative forms of one-syllable adverbs you add -er/-est.	– Jenny thought she had arrived home **late**, but her sister arrived **later**. Then their mother arrived **latest** of them all.
You use *more* and *most* for adverbs with the ending -*ly* or those with two or more syllables.	– Can you explain the way to the post office **more simply**? – What do you send **most often**: postcards, e-mails or text messages?
You have to learn the irregular forms like *much – more – most* by heart.	– She misses Tina **most** at weekends. – I hope she doesn't move **further** away.

Check-out

1. Larry, Jenny und Brenda treffen sich in einem Fastfood-Restaurant.
   Vervollständige die Sätze mit der korrekten Form des Adverbs.
   (0 = Grundform, + = 1. Steigerung, ++ = 2. Steigerung)

   fast (++) • *easy* (0) • *serious* (+) • *careful* (+) • *quick* (0)

   a) *They walk … towards the last free table.*
   b) *Jenny and Brenda can find food that they like … .*
   c) *Larry has got an allergy and has to check the menu … .*
   d) *When they met last week they laughed a lot, but this week they talk … .*
   e) *Larry and Brenda eat fast, but Jenny eats … .*

G32 Vergleiche mit Adverbien
Comparisons with adverbs

> Go back to your favorite ride with your friend **as often as** you like.

Check-in

Larry wants to go to a theme park with his friends. He's looking at the website and notices a competition.

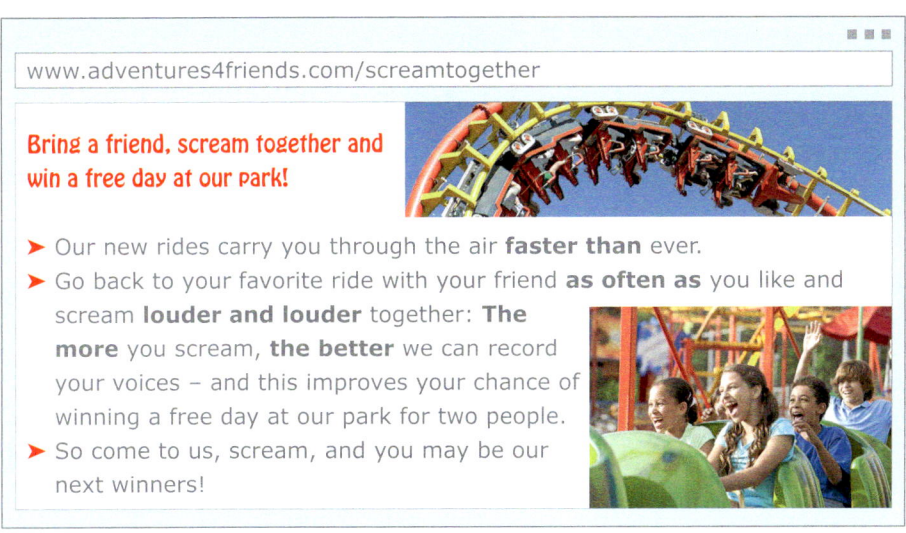

www.adventures4friends.com/screamtogether

Bring a friend, scream together and win a free day at our park!

➤ Our new rides carry you through the air **faster than** ever.
➤ Go back to your favorite ride with your friend **as often as** you like and scream **louder and louder** together: **The more** you scream, **the better** we can record your voices – and this improves your chance of winning a free day at our park for two people.
➤ So come to us, scream, and you may be our next winners!

1. Schau dir die Website einmal genau an. Welche Steigerungsstufe verwendest du …

   a) bei Vergleichen mit *than*?
      Grundform   1. Steigerung   2. Steigerung
   b) bei Vergleichen mit *as … as*?
      Grundform   1. Steigerung   2. Steigerung

2. Übertrage den folgenden Satz ins Deutsche. Wie gibst du *The …, the …* wieder?
   The more you scream, the better we can record your voices.

REGEL

1. Um Vergleiche mit Adverbien anzustellen, kannst du diese Formulierungen verwenden:

	Beispiel	Deutsch
as + Grundform + *as*	Nobody smiles **as happily as** visitors to our park.	… **so** glücklich **wie** …
1. Steigerung + *than*	Our rides carry you through the air **faster than** you can imagine.	… schnell**er als** …
	Our visitors return **more regularly than** visitors to other parks.	… regelmäßig**er als** …

TIPP

Die 1. Steigerung (=Komparativ) bildest du bei einsilbigen Adverbien aus Adverb + „er". Bei Adverbien auf „-ly" oder mit mehr Silben verwendest du „more" + Adverb. (→ G31)

	Beispiel	Deutsch
the + 1. Steigerung ..., *the* + 1. Steigerung	The louder you scream, **the better** we can record your voices.	Je lauter ..., **desto besser** ...
	The earlier you arrive at the park, **the more quickly** you'll get in.	Je früher ..., **desto** schnell**er** ...
1. Steigerung + *and* + 1. Steigerung bzw. *more and more* + Grundform	Our visitors have started screaming **louder and louder** to win a free ticket.	... **immer** lauter ...
	They are trying **more and more excitedly** to win the prize.	... **immer** aufgeregt**er** ...

English summary

How it works	Examples
To make comparisons with adverbs use *as* + adverb + *as*.	– Come back to your favorite rides **as often as** you like.
You can also use the comparative form + *than*.	– The rides carry you much **faster than** you think. – The lines got longer **more quickly than** we had expected.
Another way to make comparisons is to use *the* + comparative form, *the* + comparative form.	– **The louder** you scream, **the better** we can hear you.
You can also use comparative form + *and* + comparative form or *more and more* + positive.	– The rides go **faster and faster**. – The visitors are taking part in the competition **more and more actively**.

Check-out

1. Der Freizeitpark macht eine kleine Umfrage unter den Besuchern. Übertrage die folgenden Sätze ins Deutsche.

   a) *I go back to the park as often as I can.*
   b) *I ride the ferris wheel more than once each time I visit the park.*
   c) *I prefer to watch animal shows. I like them better than other attractions.*

2. Welche Aussage aus Aufgabe 1 trifft auf dich zu?

3. Jenny und Larry haben einen Tag im Freizeitpark verbracht und eine Rundmail an ihre Freunde geschickt. Vervollständige die E-Mail mit geeigneten Vergleichen.

Dear all,
Our day at the theme park was really brilliant. We almost won a day at the park for free. We screamed (loud) we could on all the rides, but there were these two guys who got back in line so much (quick) than we did that we really had no chance. The animal shows were good, too. In fact, they were so good that we went back to see them (often) than we had planned. It was a really hot day, and (high) the temperatures went up, (fast) we went back to the restaurants for more cold drinks.

G33 Gradadverbien
Adverbs of degree

> Friends sometimes hurt each others' feelings **quite** badly.

Check-in

Larry has had an argument with a friend. He is unhappy about it and has asked Tim, the agony uncle for his favorite teen magazine, for help.

The problem with mates
Recently, I had an argument with my best mate. Now he has been lying to me and keeps talking about me behind my back. I don't know what to do – help!

TIM SAYS:
Friends sometimes hurt each others' feelings **quite** badly. Afterwards they feel **extremely** sorry. Now it is **very** important to talk to your friend if you want to solve your problem. If you **really** want to get on well with him again, then it is **absolutely** necessary to be **truly** open with each other.

1. Finde in Tims Antwort drei Beispiele für Wörter, die andere Wörter in ihrer Aussage verstärken, z. B.: **extremely** *sorry*.

2. Schau dir die hervorgehobenen Gradadverbien in Tims Antwort genau an. Vor welchen Wortarten können sie stehen?

REGEL

1. **Gradadverbien verstärken** die Aussage eines Wortes, **schwächen** sie **ab oder schränken** sie **ein**. Zu ihnen gehören: *absolutely, almost, completely, especially, extremely, much, only, perfectly, pretty, quite, really, terribly, truly, very* und *wholly*.
2. Gradadverbien können **vor** einem **Adjektiv, Adverb oder Verb** stehen:
   - *It was a **very good** idea to ask Tim for help.* (vor Adjektiv)
   - *Friends sometimes hurt each others' feelings **quite badly**.* (vor Adverb)
   - *Be honest if you **really want** to get on well with each other.* (vor Verb)
3. Nur das Gradadverb **enough** wird dem Wort, das es erläutert, **nachgestellt**:
   - *He is **old enough** to decide for himself.*

TIPP
Wenn „enough" sich auf ein Nomen bezieht, steht es als Adjektiv vor diesem Nomen, z. B.: enough money, enough time.

English summary

How it works	Examples
Adverbs of degree (e.g. *absolutely, completely, extremely, much, pretty, quite, really, terribly, very*) help to modify the meaning of the following adjective, adverb or verb.	– Larry is **extremely unhappy**. – Tim answered his letter **very quickly**. – Tim **quite understands** how he feels.
Only *enough* follows the word it refers to.	– Is Tim's advice **good enough**?

Check-out

1. Mit welchen Problemen haben sich Jugendliche noch an Tim gewandt?
   Finde Überschriften indem du die Wörter in die richtige Reihenfolge bringst.

   a) *drives • absolutely • my friend • me • crazy*
   b) *completely • me • they • ignore*
   c) *others • really • my mate • treats • badly*
   d) *pocket money • I • enough • don't get*
   e) *she • my birthday • forgot • almost*

> I spend **nearly** all my free time with my best friend.

G34 Adverbien mit der gleichen Form wie Adjektive und Adverbien mit und ohne *-ly*   *Adverbs with the same form as adjectives and adverbs with and without* -ly

Check-in

This month the school paper has a special section on best friends. Read what Brenda has written about Jenny.

I think a best friend should be someone you really want to spend time with, and also someone you admire. I spend **nearly** all my free time with my best friend Jenny: we meet up **daily**. **Lately** we have been going swimming **fairly** often after school – sometimes until **late** in the evening. Why? Both of us are **fast** swimmers and we enjoy this **daily** routine. She swims so **well**. In the **near** future she is even going to take part in a school contest. And I **deeply** admire her, too, because she always plays **fair** with everyone. That's why she is so **highly** respected at school. I'm lucky to have such a great best friend!

1. Ordne die im Text hervorgehobenen Wörter ihrer deutschen Entsprechung zu.

   täglich • in letzter Zeit • spät • fast • nahe • ziemlich • gut • fair • zu tiefst • höchst • schnell

REGEL

1. Manche **Adverbien** haben **dieselbe Form wie Adjektive**. Dazu gehören z. B. die Zeit- und Häufigkeitsadverbien *early, daily, weekly, yearly* sowie die Adjektive *fast, long* und *low*. Diese Adjektive und Adverbien haben dieselbe Bedeutung.

	Adjektiv	Adverb
early (zeitig, früh)	Let's take the **early** train.	We will arrive **early**.
daily (täglich)	I'll tell you something about my **daily** life.	She meets her friends **daily**.
weekly (wöchentlich)	They have two **weekly** meetings.	They meet twice **weekly**.
fast (schnell)	They are **fast** swimmers.	They swim **fast**.
long (lang)	We still have a **long** way to go.	Will it take **long**?
low (leise)	She spoke to him in a **low** voice.	They turned the music down **low**.

2. Manche **Adverbien** haben zwar **dieselbe Form wie** ihre **Adjektive**, jedoch haben sie **zusätzlich eine Form auf -*ly* mit unterschiedlicher Bedeutung** zum Adverb ohne -*ly*. Dazu gehören z. B. *deep, fair, hard, high, late, near* und *pretty*.

Adjektiv	Adverb	Deutsch
The water is **deep**.	a) He kept his hands **deep** in his pockets. b) She **deeply** respects her friends.	a) tief b) zutiefst
Hey! That's not **fair**!	a) She plays **fair**. b) She plays **fairly** well.	a) fair b) ziemlich
Their daily routine is **hard**.	a) The friends work **hard** every day. b) He **hardly** does any work for school.	a) hart, schwer b) kaum
She has **high** hopes of winning.	a) The kite is flying **high**. b) The love story was **highly** emotional.	a) hoch b) höchst
She is **late**.	a) The train arrived **late**. b) They have asked a lot of questions **lately**.	a) (zu) spät b) in letzter Zeit
We're going to see them in the **near** future.	a) Please do not stand so **near**. b) He is here **nearly** all the time.	a) nahe b) fast, beinahe

Beachte, dass bei *pretty* das unveränderte Adverb eine andere Bedeutung hat als das Adjektiv („hübsch"):

She is a **pretty** girl.	a) This is a **pretty** difficult game. b) She dresses **prettily**.	a) ziemlich b) hübsch

■ **Achtung!**

– Das **Adverb** *well* hat zwar dieselbe Form wie das **Adjektiv** *well*, jedoch hat es eine andere Bedeutung. Vergleiche:

• *She is not well.* (Adjektiv)
  Sie ist nicht **gesund**. / Sie fühlt sich nicht **wohl**.

• *She has not eaten well today.* (Adverb)
  Sie hat heute nicht **gut** gegessen.

■ **Schriftlicher/mündlicher Sprachgebrauch**

– Die Adverbien *fairly* und *pretty* bedeuten beide „ziemlich". *Pretty* gehört jedoch der Umgangssprache an.

English summary

How it works	Examples

Some adverbs have the same form as their adjectives. They also share the same meaning.	– The train is **fast**. (adj.)
	  The girl swims **fast**. (adv.)
	– Do you get a **daily** paper? (adj.)
	  She calls him **daily**. (adv.)

Some adjectives have two adverbs with two different meanings (e.g. *fair/fairly, hard/hardly, late/lately*).	– The bus was **late**. (adj.)
	  They got up **late**. (adv.)
	  Have you seen her **lately**? (adv.)

Some adverbs have the same form as their adjectives but their meaning is different (e.g. *pretty, well*).	– He is **well**. (adj.) – He cooks **well**. (adv.)

Check-out

1. Was erzählt Jenny dem Reporter von *Sports Daily* nach dem Schwimmwett-kampf? Vervollständige ihre Aussagen.

a) *I practised* (täglich) *with my friend for eight weeks before the contest.*

b) *We stayed in the water for* (beinahe) *two hours every day.*

c) *But* (in letzter Zeit) *I've been* (ziemlich) *nervous.*

d) *My coach says that this is* (ziemlich) *normal.*

e) *When the race was over, the crowd cheered for a* (lange) *time.*

f) *I can* (kaum) *believe that I've made it!*

g) *Everything went very* (gut).

h) *And I'm* (höchst) *satisfied with the results.*

G35 Adverbien und adverbiale Bestimmungen der bestimmten Zeit und Häufigkeit *Adverbs of definite time and frequency*

Have you got any plans for **this evening**?

Check-in

It's Friday. Brenda is calling Jenny to find out whether she's got any plans for the evening.

Brenda: Hi, Jenny. It's Brenda. What's up? Sorry I missed you **yesterday**. Have you got any plans for **this evening**?

Jenny: Um … yes , I'm pretty busy **today**. Later **this afternoon** I'm meeting Kelly and Mike. We want to go to Luigi's restaurant. **Every second Friday between 5 and 7** they have this special offer for students. The food there is so good – I like to go there at least **once a month**.

Brenda: I went there **twice last month** with my parents. It's so cool. Are you going to that dance **tonight**, too?

Jenny: Definitely. Everyone is going.

Brenda: OK. See you later.

Jenny: Sure. Bye.

1. Schau dir die im Gespräch hervorgehobenen Adverbien und adverbialen Bestimmungen der bestimmten Zeit und Häufigkeit einmal genau an. Sortiere sie in eine Tabelle ein.

bestimmte Zeit	bestimmte Häufigkeit
yesterday	*every second Friday*

2. Übertrage drei der Sätze mit einer bestimmten Zeitangabe ins Deutsche. Du wirst merken, dass die Angaben an einer anderen Stelle im Satz stehen als im Englischen. Welche Unterschiede kannst du feststellen?

REGEL

1. Zu den **Adverbien und adverbialen Bestimmungen der bestimmten Zeit** („Wann?") gehören z.B. *last week, yesterday, today, this morning, tonight, tomorrow* und *next month*. Sie stehen entweder in der **Anfangsstellung**, das heißt vor dem Subjekt, **oder** in der **Endstellung**, also nach dem Vollverb oder nach dem Objekt:
   - *Today Jenny is meeting her friends.*
   - *They are going to a dance tonight.*
2. **Adverbien und adverbiale Bestimmungen der bestimmten Häufigkeit** („Wie oft?") sind z.B. *once, twice, three times, every day/week/year, daily, weekly* und *yearly*. Sie stehen in der **Endstellung**:
   - *Last month I went there twice.*

TIPP
Adverbien und adverbiale Bestimmungen der bestimmten Zeit und Häufigkeit stehen **nie** in der **Binnenstellung**.

6 | Adverbien und adverbiale Bestimmungen | G35

Anfangsstellung	Binnenstellung			Endstellung
	Subjekt	Verb	Objekt	
	Brenda	missed	Jenny	**yesterday**.
Today	she	phoned	her.	
Last month	Brenda	ate	pizza	**twice**.

English summary

How it works	Examples
To express a definite time you use words or expressions like *last week*, *yesterday*, *today*, *this morning*, *tomorrow*, *next month*. You find them in front position or in end position.	– **Last month** Brenda went to an Italian restaurant with her parents. – Brenda phoned Jenny **this afternoon**.
Adverbials of definite frequency (e.g. *once*, *twice*, *three times*, *every day*, *daily*, *weekly*) are found in end position.	– The two friends talk to each other **every day**. – They go to a dance **twice a month**.

Check-out

1. Bei einem Sportevent an dem beide Mädchen teilnehmen, lernen sich Brendas Vater und Jennys deutsche Tante kennen. Jennys Tante spricht kein Englisch. Du vermittelst zwischen Vater und Tante.

Tante: Schön, Sie kennenzulernen. Wie ich hörte, machen Brenda und Jenny fast jeden Tag etwas zusammen.
Du: *Nice to meet you. She's heard Jenny and Brenda …*
Vater: *Well, that's right, but they don't see each other every weekend.*
Du: Das stimmt, aber sie sehen sich …
Vater: *I think Jenny is staying at home this weekend.*
Du: Er glaubt, …
Tante: Stimmt. Ich bin diese Woche zu Besuch da, also geht Jenny gerade nicht so viel weg.
Du: *That's right. Jenny is not going out so much right now because …*
Tante: So weit ich weiß, geht sie aber heute Abend noch zu Ihnen.
Du: *But as far as Jenny's aunt knows, Jenny …*
Vater: *Really? We might see her later, then.*
Du: Vielleicht …

G36 Adverbien der unbestimmten Zeit und Häufigkeit
Adverbs of indefinite time and frequency

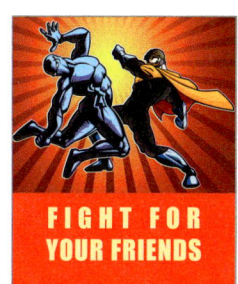

LAN parties with friends are **always** great fun.

Check-in

Larry and his friends are planning a LAN party. They're looking for new games and have found this review about *Fight for your Friends* in a computer magazine.

REVIEW: **FIGHT FOR YOUR FRIENDS**

LAN parties with friends are **always** great fun. To add to this fun, there is a new multiplayer game on the market, *Fight for your Friends*, which we think you simply must have. Why?

Multiplayer games **normally** get you to play against the other people at your LAN party, so it's **usually** every player for him- or herself. *Fight for your Friends* is different: The game **regularly** asks friends to form a team and put all their skills together to defeat the enemy. You can **sometimes** go up one or even two levels when playing on your own, but you will **often** find that you'll get into trouble without your friends' help.
Our opinion: We've **never** played a game that does so much for your social skills!

---

1. Finde in der Rezension einen Satz mit einem Adverb der unbestimmten Zeit oder Häufigkeit und …

   a) mit dem Verb *be*.
   b) mit Modalverb + Vollverb.
   c) mit Vollverb.
   d) mit Hilfsverb + Vollverb.

2. Was kannst du für die Fälle a)–d) aus Aufgabe 1 jeweils bezüglich der Satzstellung von Adverbien der unbestimmten Zeit und Häufigkeit feststellen?

REGEL

1. Die **Adverbien der unbestimmten Zeit und der unbestimmten Häufigkeit** umfassen Wörter und Wortgruppen wie *already, almost never, always, hardly ever, just, mostly, never, now, often, regularly, sometimes, soon* und *usually*.
2. Du findest diese Adverbien meist in der Binnenstellung, also …

vor dem Vollverb, wenn der Satz kein Hilfsverb enthält	The friends **sometimes organize** LAN parties.
zwischen Modal- und Vollverb	They **can usually use** the youth club for their parties.
nach dem ersten Hilfsverb (wenn es aus mehreren Teilen besteht, dann nach dem ersten Teil)	Larry's team **will always** remember their first game.
	They **have already been** playing this game for half an hour.

TIPP

Die Adverbien „normally", „often", „sometimes", „soon" und „usually" kannst du auch in der Anfangs- oder Endstellung verwenden, wenn du die Information betonen möchtest, z. B.:
– **Sometimes** I go to LAN parties.
– I'll buy a new game **soon**.

3. **In verneinten Sätzen** steht das **Häufigkeitsadverb nach *not***:
   - They **don't always** have their LAN parties at the youth club.
   - They **can't always** use the room.

   Außer bei *sometimes*:
   - They **sometimes don't** use the youth club for their parties.

4. Verwendest du eine Form von ***be* als Vollverb**, wird das **Adverb der unbestimmten Zeit bzw. Häufigkeit nachgestellt**:
   - LAN parties **are always** great fun.

   Außer bei *sometimes* in verneinten Sätzen:
   - The friends **sometimes aren't** fair when they play against each other.

English summary

How it works	Examples
You usually put adverbs of indefinite time and frequency (e.g. *always*, *already*, *just*, *mostly*, *now*, *usually*) in mid position.	– John **always** tries hard to win. – He should **now** ask his friend for help. – They have **just** gone up one level.
If you use a form of *be* as a main verb, the adverb of indefinite time and frequency comes after the form of *be*.	– Games aren't **always** exciting.
You sometimes find adverbs of indefinite time and frequency in front position or in end position to add emphasis.	– **Often** Larry gets angry when he loses.

Check-out

1. Vervollständige die folgenden Sätze mit den Adverbien in Klammern ohne ihnen eine besondere Betonung zu verleihen.

   a) Larry and John have played this game before. (never)
   b) The friends order some pizzas for their LAN parties. (usually)
   c) The pizzas don't arrive on time. (sometimes)
   d) The parties became a big success. (soon)
   e) You should play fair. (always)
   f) John is late. (hardly ever)

G37 Adverbien des Orts und der Richtung
Adverbs of place and direction

We can either stay **at home** or go **downtown**.

Check-in

Jenny's friend Tina has moved to another city recently. Jenny is visiting her for the weekend. They aren't sure what to do tonight. Read their conversation.

Jenny: So, what shall we do tonight?

Tina: Well, we can either stay **at home** or go **downtown**.

Jenny: What's on **downtown**?

Tina: I've heard there's a good dance party **at the New City Palace**, **upstairs in the large forum**.

Jenny: OK, let's go **there**.

Tina: We can park the car **around the corner** and walk **to the disco** – it isn't far.

1. Lies dir den Dialog zwischen den beiden Freundinnen noch einmal genau durch und beantworte die folgenden Fragen nach dem „Wo" bzw. „Wohin" in ganzen Sätzen.

   a) *Where are Tina and Jenny?*
   b) *If they don't stay at home, where can they go?*
   c) *Where can they park the car?*
   d) *After parking the car, where are they going to walk?*

2. Schau dir deine Antworten aus Aufgabe 1 an und vervollständige die Regel zur Satzstellung:
   Adverbien des Orts und der Richtung stehen … .

REGEL

1. **Ob** es sich um ein **Orts- oder** ein **Richtungsadverb** handelt, **hängt von der Bedeutung des Verbs ab**. Häufige Adverbien des Orts und der Richtung sind …

Wörter wie *here / there, up / down, in front of / behind, left / right, inside / outside, upstairs / downstairs*	Let's drive **there**. (Wohin?) The music is really good **there**. (Wo?)
Zusammensetzungen wie *somewhere, everywhere, nowhere, anywhere*	Let's go **somewhere** in town. (Wohin?) I can't find the car keys **anywhere**. (Wo?)
Wortgruppen (z.T. mit Präposition) wie *at home* (Ort) / *home* (Richtung), *in town* (Ort) / *into town* (Richtung), *at the station* (Ort) / *to the station* (Richtung), *to Miami* (Richtung) / *in Miami* (Ort)	They drove **home**. (Wohin?) They are **at home**. (Wo?)

2. Orts- und Richtungsadverbien findest du üblicherweise **in der Endstellung**.

			Endstellung
Subjekt	Verb	Objekt	Ort/Richtung
Tina	wants to take	her friend	**to the disco.**
They	are driving		**downtown.**
They	can park	the car	**around the corner.**

English summary

How it works	Examples
Adverbs of place or direction are words like *here, there, inside, upstairs, everywhere, (at) home, in/to the US.*	– The DJ is playing their favorite song **upstairs**. (place) – They go **downstairs** to buy some drinks. (direction)
Whether a word is used as an adverb of place or as an adverb of direction depends on the verb.	– Lots of people **are waiting outside the disco**. (place) – They want to **go inside**. (direction)
You mostly find adverbs of place and adverbs of direction in end position, but before other adverbial phrases and adverbs of time.	– People are dancing **everywhere**. (place) – Lots of people have come **to the disco** tonight. (direction)

Check-out

1. Jenny und Tina machen sich für die Disco fertig. Vervollständige die Sätze mit einem passenden Adverb des Orts oder der Richtung.

   *anywhere • to a dance • behind the sofa • upstairs in the bathroom •
   everywhere • somewhere*

   a) *The girls want to go … .*
   b) *Tina is … . She's looking for her make-up … . It must be … .*
   c) *Jenny has finally found her scarf. It had fallen … . But now she can't find her
      handbag … .*

2. Bestimme, ob es sich bei den Sätzen in Aufgabe 1 jeweils um ein Adverb des Orts oder der Richtung handelt.

G38 Die Reihenfolge mehrerer adverbialer Bestimmungen
Sequence of adverbials at the end of a sentence

> You were dancing **wildly near the DJ all evening**!

Check-in

Yesterday Jenny and Brenda went to a dance together. Now it's Sunday evening and they are chatting online.

Jenny16   September 4, 9:05 pm

That was a cool weekend, but now I'm really tired!

Brenda_J   September 4, 9:08 pm

I'm not surprised. You were dancing **wildly near the DJ all evening**!
You didn't notice that Larry was there.

Jenny16   September 4, 9:10 pm

Oh! Why didn't you tell me?

Brenda_J   September 4, 9:14 pm

I wanted to but he went **home by train quite early**.

Jenny16   September 4, 9:16 pm

What about you? You and that boy were talking **enthusiastically for hours**.
Who was he?

Brenda_J   September 4, 9:18 pm

Just my cousin Henry. He was asking about you! He's been studying **hard
at college this year**. We phone **on weekends** but I hardly ever see him.

Jenny16   September 4, 9:20 pm

Oh. Hey, it's really time for bed. See you **in school tomorrow**.

---

1. Schau dir die adverbialen Bestimmungen im Chat genau an und trage sie entsprechend ihrer Funktion in eine Tabelle ein. Welche Regelmäßigkeit kannst du feststellen?

Art und Weise (Wie?)	Ort (Wo?)	Mittel (Womit?)	Zeit (Wann?)
wildly	*near the DJ*	–	*all evening*
...			

REGEL

1. Stehen mehrere adverbiale Bestimmungen am Satzende, folgen sie gewöhnlich diesem Muster: **Art und Weise** vor **Ort bzw. Richtung** vor **Zeit**.

	Art und Weise	Ort/Richtung	Zeit
She was dancing	**wildy**	**near the stage**	**most of the time.**
She was talking	**excitedly**		**for ages.**
He went		**home**	**early.**
He is studying	**hard**		**at the moment.**

MERKHILFE

Du kannst dir die Reihenfolge ganz einfach mit Hilfe des Alphabets merken:
A vor **O** vor **Z**.
Diese Merkhilfe funktioniert auch auf Englisch: **m**anner – **p**lace – **t**ime.

2. Du kannst von dieser Reihenfolge abweichen, wenn du die Zeit oder den Ort besonders betonen willst:
   - *The friends will see each other again **at school on Monday**.*
   - ***On Monday** the friends will see each other again **at school**.*
   - ***At school on Monday** the friends will see each other again.*
3. Willst du darauf hinweisen, womit etwas getan wird, steht diese **adverbiale Bestimmung des Mittels** (z. B. *by car, by bus, by bike, by train, by plane, on foot*) **zwischen der Richtungs- und der Zeitangabe**.

	Richtung	Mittel	Zeit
They went	to the disco	**by car**	last Saturday.

■ **Achtung!**
  – Bei mehreren Zeitangaben steht die exaktere vor der allgemeineren:
    - *He's meeting his friends at **9 am next Sunday**.*

English summary

How it works	Examples
If you use more than one adverbial in end position, then the rule is **m**anner – **p**lace – **t**ime.	– The friends talked **excitedly at the party last Saturday.**
If you want to stress the time or the place, you can put the adverbial at the beginning of the sentence.	– **Last Saturday** the friends talked excitedly at the party. – **At the party last Saturday** the friends talked excitedly.
An adverbial of means is normally placed between an adverbial of direction and an adverbial of time.	– They go to school **by bus** every day.

Check-out

1. Bilde Sätze aus den folgenden Bestandteilen mit der gewöhnlichen Satzstellung, d.h. ohne den adverbialen Bestimmungen eine besondere Betonung zu verleihen.

   a) *him • happily • at the youth club • talked to • she • yesterday evening*
   b) *tomorrow • they • about the disco • will chat • online*
   c) *last night • your friend • did you miss • at the party • ?*
   d) *by bus • to school • every morning • at 8 • go • they*
   e) *at my friend's house • the weekend • enjoyed • I • last month*

2. Gib den adverbialen Bestimmungen eine besondere Betonung, indem du die Sätze umstellst.

   a) *Tariq and Rhona were dancing happily on the stage all the time.*
   b) *Her cousin talked excitedly in the college canteen the next day.*
   c) *The girls discuss their plans at school every morning.*

G39 Satzverknüpfende und kommentierende Adverbien
Linking adverbs and adverbs of comment

> **Luckily**, many songs deal with friendship.

Check-in

While Brenda is watching her favorite music show, the presenter announces a competition.

> And remember that you can still take part in our competition 'Songs for Friends': You write the lyrics for a new song about friends for your favorite star, and if you're lucky, your song will be chosen and recorded for our big show. **Luckily**, many songs deal with friendship, so there is a lot of material you can listen to. **Obviously**, you need to be quick because **unfortunately** time is running out. **In fact**, you should send us your ideas within the next three days! And then **hopefully**, we will meet you here on stage next month. But now let's welcome a good friend of mine. **Actually**, he's my very best friend …

1. Schau dir die hervorgehobenen Wörter in der Ansage genau an. An welcher Stelle stehen sie zumeist im Satz?

   a) Anfangsstellung   b) Binnenstellung   c) Endstellung

2. Ordne die folgenden Adverbien ihrer Funktion zu.

actually	Bedauern
in fact	Hoffnung
hopefully	Betonung
unfortunately	Erläuterung

REGEL

> **TIPP**
>
> Kommentierende und satzverknüpfende Adverbien werden oft durch ein Komma abgetrennt, sodass der Sprecher eine kurze Pause macht.

REGEL

1. **Satzverknüpfende Adverbien** verbinden die Gedanken zweier Sätze und **stellen** eine **logische Beziehung her**. Sie stehen meist **am Satzanfang**.

Funktion	Beispiel
Schlussfolgerung (deshalb, darum, deswegen)	There isn't much time left for you to write your song text. **Therefore**, you need to be quick.
Betonung , Erläuterung (sogar, eigentlich)	**Actually**, it would be a good idea to enter your lyrics fast.
Erläuterung (und zwar)	**In fact**, you should send us your ideas as soon as possible.
Gegensätzlichkeit (jedoch, allerdings)	I thought it would be easy to write a song text. **However**, it was more difficult than I had expected.

2. **Kommentierende Adverbien leiten** den folgenden **Gedanken ein und kommentieren diesen** zugleich. Sie können Erleichterung (*fortunately, luckily*), Bestätigung (*of course*), Hoffnung (*hopefully*), Bedauern (*unfortunately, unluckily*), Wahrscheinlichkeit (*apparently, obviously, probably*) u.ä. ausdrücken.

Funktion	Beispiel
Erleichterung (glücklicherweise)	**Luckily,** many songs deal with friendship.
Bestätigung (natürlich)	**Of course,** you'll want to try and write something new.
Hoffnung (hoffentlich, wenn alles gut geht)	**Hopefully,** your friends will be able to see you on TV next month.
Bedauern (leider)	**Unfortunately,** you can only bring along two friends.
Wahrscheinlichkeit/ Vermutung (vielleicht, wahrscheinlich, anscheinend, offenbar)	**Apparently,** we've received more than 400 e-mails with lyrics.

> **TIPP**
>
> Binnenstellung (→ **G36**) heißt, das Adverb steht …
> – vor dem Vollverb (außer bei „be"),
> – nach dem ersten Hilfsverb,
> – nach dem Modalverb.

3. Kommentierende **Adverbien, die eine Wahrscheinlichkeit oder Vermutung ausdrücken**, können auch in der **Binnenstellung** auftreten:
   • *Her song **apparently** has the best chances.*
   • *She has **obviously** written the best song.*
   • *She will **probably** win first prize.*

4. **Kommentierende Adverbien** treten mitunter auch **als Nachgedanke** in der **Endstellung** auf. Sie werden **durch Komma vom Hauptsatz abgetrennt**:
   • *You know so many songs, **of course**.*

English summary

How it works	Examples
Linking adverbs connect sentences logically. They usually appear in front position. You use them to draw a conclusion, make a contrast or give an explanation.	– Your lyrics are the best of all. **Therefore**, you are the winner tonight. – **However**, your star is not here now. **In fact**, she's giving a concert a thousand miles away!
Adverbs of comment can often be found in front position, sometimes in mid position, and sometimes in end position.	– **Luckily**, your lyrics have convinced the jury. – She will **probably** win the contest. – She'll meet her star in the big show, **of course**.

Check-out

1. Übertrage die folgenden Sätze ins Englische.

   a) Unsere Gewinnerin war offensichtlich nicht erfahren im Lieder schreiben.
   b) Deshalb glaubte sie nicht, dass sie gewinnen würde.
   c) Als sie dann gewann, war sie natürlich sehr glücklich.
   d) Wahrscheinlich werden wir sie nächstes Jahr wieder hier sehen.

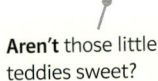

Aren't those little teddies sweet?

G40 *Be* als Voll- und Hilfsverb
Be used as main verb and auxiliary verb

Check-in

Sue has just moved house. Her friends Kim and Ben are in a shop to buy a present for her. Read the dialogue.

Shop assistant: Can I help?

Kim: It's OK, thanks. We're just **looking**.

Ben: What about a T-shirt? These blue ones **are** nice.

Kim: You're right. But they're expensive, Ben. – Oh, look.
Aren't those little teddies sweet?

Ben: Teddies??? You're **joking**!

Kim: Sue collects them. Really, Ben!

Ben: But look. They're **made** in China.

Kim: I don't care. That pink one **is** cool. It **can be** from both of us.
I'm sure she'll like it.

1. Nenne jeweils drei Formen von *be*, die allein (ohne ein anderes Verb) und in zusammengesetzten Formen (mit einem anderen Verb) verwendet werden.

2. Für welche Zeitformen oder grammatischen Strukturen werden die Formen von *be* in Aufgabe 1 verwendet?

REGEL

1. Bei dem Verb *be* findest du die folgenden Formen:

a) *simple present*

Langformen	Kurzformen
I **am** (not) sure. You **are** (not) right. He / She / It **is** (not) OK. We / You / They **are** (not) nice.	I'm ('m not) sure. You're (aren't) right. He / She / It's (isn't) OK. We / You / They're (aren't) nice.

b) *simple past*

Langformen	Kurzformen
I **was** (not) in the shop. You **were** (not) with me. He / She / It **was** (not) right. We / You / They **were** (not) together.	I **wasn't** in the shop. You **weren't** with me. He / She / It **wasn't** right. We / You / They **weren't** together.

c) **Infinitiv:** *The present can **be** from both of us.*

d) *present participle* oder Gerundium: *Kim enjoys **being** with Ben.*

e) *past participle: Have you **been** to Sue's house yet?*

2. Wenn *be* als **Vollverb** gebraucht wird, drückt es einen **Zustand** oder eine **Eigenschaft** aus. In diesem Fall folgt der Form von *be* immer eine Ergänzung. Diese kann sein:
  - ein Nomen: *Kim and Sue are* **friends***.*
  - ein Adjektiv: *These blue T-shirts are* **nice***.*
  - eine Zeit- oder Ortsangabe: *Kim and Ben are* **in a shop***.*

3. Du kannst die Formen von *be* auch als **Hilfsverb** zusammen mit dem *present participle* eines Vollverbs (*looking*) verwenden, um die *progressive* Form zu bilden, z. B.: *I'm looking for a present.* (→ **G44**, **G47**, **G50**)

4. Außerdem kannst du die Formen von *be* zusammen mit dem *past participle* eines Vollverbs (*made, invited*) verwenden, um das Passiv (→ **G69**, **G71**) zu bilden, z. B.: *The teddies* **are made** *in China.*

■ **Achtung!**
  – In Fragen und in verneinten Sätzen wird die Form von *be* nicht mit dem Hilfsverb *do* umschrieben.
    • *I think I saw you yesterday.* **Were** *you at the shop with Ben?* (Nicht: *Did you be at the shop with Ben?*)
    • *Sarah* **isn't** *friends with Sue any longer. Don't tell her that we're going to Sue's house.*

English summary

How it works	Examples
In the simple present the forms of *be* are: *(I) am*, *(he, she, it) is* and *(we, you, they) are*. In the past tense there are only two forms: *(I, you, he, she, it) was* and *(we, you, they) were*.	– They **are** friends. – The blue T-shirt **was** nice.
As a main verb *be* expresses a state or a quality.	– Ben **is** in the shop with Kim. – The teddies **weren't** expensive.
As an auxiliary verb *be* is used to form the progressive forms and the passive.	– We**'re looking** for a present. – The T-shirts **are made** in Germany.

Check-out

1. Bestimme, ob *be* in den folgenden Sätzen als Voll- oder Hilfsverb verwendet wird.

  a) *Kim and Ben are in the shop.*
  b) *They're looking at all the things.*
  c) *Where was this T-shirt made?*
  d) *The teddies have been in the shop for only a short time.*

2. Forme diese Aussagen in Ja-/Nein-Fragen um.

  a) *Kim and Ben are both invited to Sue's house.*
  b) *The T-shirts were hanging in the shop window.*

I'm so glad you**'ve come**. **Have** a drink.

G41 *Have* als Voll- und Hilfsverb
Have *used as main verb and auxiliary verb*

Check-in

Kim and Ben have just arrived at Sue's house. Read what they say.

Sue: Hi, you two! I'm so glad you**'ve come**. **Have** a drink.
Kim: We**'ve brought** you a little present. – Here you are …
Sue: Thanks! Ooh, let me open it right away.
Ben: We **had** no idea what to get. But then Kim saw this –
Sue: Oh! A teddy! How funny! – Oh, it's great, Kim, I just love your pink teddy.
    It **has** beautiful blue eyes. But Fiona **has given** me the same one.
Kim: No problem, they can be brother and sister.

1. Fertige eine Tabelle an. Trage die Formen von *have* ein, die allein (ohne ein anderes Verb) und in zusammengesetzten Formen (mit einem anderen Verb) stehen.

2. Zur Bildung welcher Zeitform wird das Hilfsverb *have* in den folgenden beiden Sätzen verwendet?

I'm so glad you've come.
We've brought you a little present.

> **REGEL**

1. Bei dem Verb *have* findest du die folgenden Formen:

a) *simple present*

nur Langformen	
I / You **have**	
He / She / It **has**	blue eyes.
We / You / They **have**	

b) *simple past*

nur Langformen	
I / You **had**	
He / She / It **had**	some water.
We / You / They **had**	

c) *present perfect*

Langformen		Kurzformen	
I / You **have**		I**'ve** / You**'ve** (**haven't**)	
He / She / It **has**	come.	He**'s** / She**'s** / It**'s** (**hasn't**)	come.
We / You / They **have**		We**'ve** / You**'ve** / They**'ve** (**haven't**)	

d) *past perfect*

Langformen		Kurzformen	
I / You **had**		I**'d** / You**'d** (**hadn't**)	
He / She / It **had**	arrived.	He**'d** / She**'d** / It**'d** (**hadn't**)	arrived.
We / You / They **had**		We**'d** / You**'d** / They**'d** (**hadn't**)	

e) **Infinitiv**: *I want to **have** a party.*
f) ***present participle* oder Gerundium**: *What about **having** a second piece of cake?*
g) ***past participle**: I've **had** three pieces already.*

2. Wie das deutsche „haben" kann *have* als **Vollverb** ausdrücken, dass jemandem etwas gehört oder dass etwas zu jemandem gehört:
- *She has **her own room**.*
- *She has **a sister**.*

3. Häufig wird das Vollverb *have* **in festen Verbindungen** mit bestimmten Nomen gebraucht, z. B.: *have a party, have breakfast, have fun*. In diesen Wendungen kann *have* auch in der *progressive* Form verwendet werden:
- *Sue **is having** a party.*

4. Du kannst die Formen von *have* auch als **Hilfsverb** zusammen mit dem *past participle* eines Vollverbs (*arrived, bought*) verwenden, um die *perfect tenses* zu bilden: ***have/has arrived*** (*present perfect simple* → G46), ***have/has been living*** (*present perfect progressive* → G47), ***had started*** (*past perfect simple* → G54), ***had been working*** (*past perfect progressive* → G55), ***will have done*** (*future perfect* → G61).

5. Vor allem im britischen Englisch wird im *simple present* häufig auch **have got** anstelle von *have* verwendet. Es wird in Fragesätzen und Verneinungen nicht mit *do* umschrieben.

Aussage:	Sue **has got** a very nice room in the new house.
Verneinung:	I'm afraid we **haven't got** enough glasses. They are still in one of the boxes.
Frage:	**Have** you **got** any ice cream?
Kurzantwort:	Yes, I **have**. / No, I **haven't**.

◼ **Achtung!**
- In Fragen und in verneinten Sätzen musst du zwischen *have* als Voll- und als Hilfsverb unterscheiden:
  - Für das Vollverb *have* verwendest du die Umschreibung mit *do*:
  ***Does** Sue **have** a sister?*
  ***Did** you **have** a good time?*
  *Their old flat **didn't have** a garden.*
  - Das Hilfsverb *have* wird dagegen nicht mit *do* umschrieben:
  ***Have** you **given** her a drink?* (Nicht: *Do you have given …?*)
  *She **hasn't opened** her present yet.*

- Sei vorsichtig bei den Kurzformen *'s* und *'d*. Sie können zweierlei bedeuten:
  - *She's* kann für *she **is*** und *she **has*** stehen:
  She's coming back. (*present progressive*)
  She's come back. (*present perfect*)
  - Ganz ähnlich ist es bei der Kurzform *'d*. Sie kann eine Abkürzung von **had** oder von **would** sein:
  He'd bought a present. (*past perfect*)
  He'd buy a present. (*conditional*)

English summary

How it works	Examples
In the present tense the forms of *have* are (*I, you, we, you, they*) *have* and (*he, she, it*) *has*. In the past tense there is only one form: *had*.	– Sue **has** a lot of friends. – Sue's teddies **have** blue eyes. – She **had** a small room at their old house.
As a main verb *have* expresses that something belongs to someone. You can also use *have* together with a number of nouns, e.g. *party, breakfast*.	– Her new room **has** a nice view. – We**'re** just **having** a party. – Oh, great. **Have** fun!
As an auxiliary verb *have* is used to form the perfect tenses.	– The party **has** just **started**.
In British English *have got* is often used in the simple present.	– Sue **has got** two pink teddies now.

Check-out

1. Forme die folgenden Aussagesätze in Ja-/Nein-Fragen um.

   a) *Ben has been invited to Sue's party.*
   b) *Kim had a good time at the party last Saturday.*

2. Verneine die folgenden Aussagesätze.

   a) *The house has a large garden.*
   b) *The Brooks have bought a new house.*

> My mum always **does** everything in the kitchen.

G42 *Do* als Voll- und Hilfsverb
Do *used as main verb and auxiliary verb*

Check-in

Kim and Sue are looking at a teen magazine together.

WHAT TYPE ARE YOU?	Yes, a lot.	Sometimes.	Not often.	Never.
1. **Do** you **help** at home?				
2. **Do** you **sit down** with your family for meals?				

Kim: Let's fill this in. Just for fun. – OK. No, I **don't** often **help** at home. **Do** you **do** much, Sue?

Sue: No, I **don't**. Well, actually I **did** the cooking yesterday! Amazingly.

Kim: Wow! What **did** you **cook**?

Sue: I made a vegetable soup. It **didn't taste** too bad.

Kim: I**'ve** never **done** anything like that. My mum always **does** everything in the kitchen.

1. Fertige eine Tabelle an. Trage die Formen von *do* ein, die allein (ohne ein anderes Verb) und in einer zusammengesetzten Form (mit einem anderen Verb) stehen.

2. In welchem Satz erscheint *do* sowohl als Hilfsverb als auch als Vollverb?

REGEL

1. Bei dem Verb *do* findest du die folgenden Formen:

    a) *simple present*

Langformen		verneinte Kurzformen	
I / You **do**		I / You **don't**	
He / She / It **does**	the job.	He / She / It **doesn't**	help.
We / You / They **do**		We / You / They **don't**	

    b) *simple past*

Langformen		verneinte Kurzformen	
I / You **did**		I / You **didn't**	
He / She / It **did**	the job.	He / She / It **didn't**	help.
We / You / They **did**		We / You / They **didn't**	

    c) **Infinitiv**: *Can you **do** something for me, please?*
    d) ***present participle*** oder **Gerundium**: *I don't like **doing** the cooking.*
    e) ***past participle***: *Have you **done** your homework yet?*

2. Als **Vollverb** beschreibt *do* eine **Tätigkeit**. Es wird häufig im *simple past* und in der *progressive* Form gebraucht:
    *   *I **did** the cooking yesterday.*
    *   *What **are** the girls **doing**?*

3. Wenn du kein anderes Hilfsverb hast, musst du in **Fragen** und **Verneinungen** das **Vollverb** *do* mit dem Hilfsverb *do* umschreiben.

    #### *do* als Vollverb

    What **is** Sue **doing**? **Is** she **doing** her homework?
    – No, she**'s doing** the cooking now.

    What **do** you **do** at the weekends?
    Kim goes out with her friends on Saturdays, but she **doesn't do** much on Sundays.
    Did you **do** anything special last night?
    Mum **didn't do** the shopping yesterday.

TIPP
Manchmal wird im Englischen „do" verwendet, wo du im Deutschen „machen" sagst: Have you **done** your homework? – Hast du deine Hausaufgaben **gemacht**?

4. Wenn du **Fragen** und **Verneinungen** bilden möchtest, verwendest du das **Hilfsverb** *do* zusammen mit einem Vollverb (*like, taste*).

do als Hilfsverb

Do you **like** vegetables? – Yes, I **don't eat** much meat.
This bread **doesn't taste** bad.
Did you **make** the soup? – Yes, it **didn't take** long.

■ **Achtung!**
– Denke daran, dass die **Verneinung** und die **Fragebildung** im Englischen sich von der im Deutschen unterscheidet. Während du im Deutschen einen Fragesatz mit dem Vollverb beginnen und ein Vollverb mit „nicht" verneinen kannst, ist das im Englischen nicht möglich. Vergleiche:
- **Hilfst du** oft zu Hause? – *Do you often help at home?*
- Kim **wohnt nicht** in der Stadtmitte. – *Kim doesn't live in the town centre.*

English summary

How it works	Examples
In the simple present the forms of *do* are (*I, you, we, they*) *do* und (*he, she, it*) *does*. In the past tense there is only one form: *did*.	– Her mum **does** the cooking. – Sue's dad **did** the shopping for the weekend.
You often use the main verb *do* in the progressive form to describe activities.	– What **is** Kim **doing**? – She **isn't doing** anything special at the moment.
You use the auxiliary verb *do* to form questions and negative statements.	– **Does** the soup taste good? – **Did** Sue make it? – I **don't** like vegetables much.

Check-out

1. Bestimme, ob *do* in den folgenden Sätzen als Voll- oder Hilfsverb verwendet wird.

a) *My father usually does the shopping.*
b) *Yesterday I did my homework late at night.*
c) *When they moved house, Sue didn't see her friends very often.*
d) *Do you want to make a chicken curry with me?*

2. Bilde Ja-/Nein-Fragen mit den vorgegebenen Elementen.

a) *often • meet • your friends • you*
b) *like • their new house • Sue*
c) *do • their homework • Kim and Ben • yesterday*

8 Die Zeitformen der Gegenwart

G43 Die einfache Gegenwart
The simple present

> I **buy** new clothes once a month.

Check-in

Caroline has just answered these questions about fashion she found in a teen magazine. Now she wants to find out her results.

Which sentences are true for you?		points
I **buy** new clothes once a month or more.		3
My best friend **wears** exactly the same type of clothes as me.		3
I sometimes **go** shopping with friends and we **have** a lot of fun.	✔	2
I **don't want** to wear clothes that look old.	✔	2
I never **think** about my clothes in the mornings. I **wear** the first thing I find!		1

7–10 points	4–6 points	1–3 points
You **love** fashion! **Do** you **have** time for other interests? Remember, some things are more important than new clothes. They **look** nice but fashion isn't everything!	You **like** nice clothes but they **don't mean** everything to you.	You aren't interested in fashion. That is unusual for a teenager, but it's perfectly OK!

1. Schau dir die Verbform in dem Satz *We have a lot of fun.* an und vervollständige die folgende Regel:
   Das *simple present* wird mit dem … des Verbs gebildet.

2. Die Verbform *wears* unterscheidet sich von den anderen Verbformen im Test. Warum musst du hier ein *-s* anhängen?

REGEL

1. Das *simple present* verwendest du, …
   a) um auszudrücken, dass etwas häufig, regelmäßig, selten oder nie passiert:
      • *I often **buy** new clothes.*
   b) um Tatsachen auszudrücken:
      • *Most young people **like** nice clothes.*
2. Bei *I*, *you*, *we* und *they* hat das Verb im *simple present* dieselbe Form wie der Infinitiv.
3. Bei *he*, *she* und *it* hängst du ein **-s** an den Infinitiv des Verbs an. Wenn der Infinitiv auf einen **Zischlaut** endet, wie bei *watch* oder *push,* brauchst du **-es**.

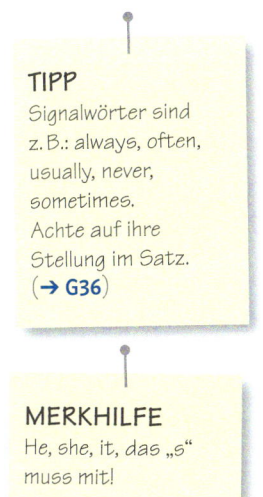

TIPP
Signalwörter sind z. B.: always, often, usually, never, sometimes. Achte auf ihre Stellung im Satz.
(→ G36)

MERKHILFE
He, she, it, das „s" muss mit!

TIPP
Für Modalverben wie „can", „should", „must" (→ **G62**) gibt es im simple present nur eine Form. Du brauchst auch kein „do" oder „does", um sie zu verneinen oder um eine Frage zu stellen: Paul **shouldn't** wear such old clothes.

4. Zur Verneinung stellst du **don't** (bei **I**, **you**, **we**, **they**) oder **doesn't** (bei **he**, **she**, **it**) vor das Vollverb.
5. Um eine Frage im *simple present* zu bilden, brauchst du **do** (bei **I**, **you**, **we**, **they**) oder **does** (bei **he**, **she**, **it**).

Aussage:	I **wear** the first thing I find. Susie never **wears** jeans. She **watches** fashion shows online.
Verneinung:	I **don't wear** old clothes. Robby **doesn't read** fashion magazines.
Frage mit Fragewort:	Why **does** he always **wear** black?
Entscheidungsfrage mit Kurzantwort:	**Do** you **wear** earrings? – Yes, I **do**. **Does** Serena **like** fashion shows? – No, she **doesn't**.

6. Das **Verb be** hat im *simple present* mehr als zwei Formen (→ **40**) und braucht kein *do* oder *does* bei Fragen und Verneinungen:
   • *I **am** interested in fashion.*
   • *Fashion **isn't** important to me.*
   • ***Are** you interested in new styles?*

■ **Achtung!**
   – Wenn ein Verb auf **-y** endet, schreibst du es in der 3. Person Singular mit *ie*: *carry* → *carr**ies***. Das *-y* wird aber **nicht** durch *-ie* ersetzt, **wenn davor ein Vokal** kommt: *play* → *pl**ays***.
      • *My dad **says** that my sister **worries** too much about clothes.*

   – Manchmal verwendest du das *simple present*, obwohl die Handlung in der Vergangenheit liegt, z. B. wenn du den Inhalt eines Films oder eines Buchs zusammenfasst:
      • *One day, Fiona **goes** into town and **meets** George …*
      Auch bei der Live-Übertragung von Sportveranstaltungen wird das *simple present* verwendet:
      • *He **kicks** the ball past Romney …*

■ **Mündlicher/schriftlicher Sprachgebrauch**
   – Die Langformen *do not* und *does not* werden meist im formellen schriftlichen Sprachgebrauch verwendet. Die Kurzformen *don't* und *doesn't* gehören eher dem mündlichen Sprachgebrauch an.

English summary

How it works	Examples
You use the simple present to talk about regular activities and facts. You use the infinitive form of the verb for *I, you, we* and *they*, and you add *-s* or *-es* in the third person singular.	– I usually **wear** jeans at the weekend. – Monty **watches** all the TV shows about fashion and models.

How it works	Examples
To make questions and negative sentences, you need a form of the auxiliary verb *do* (*do, don't, does* or *doesn't*).	– **Does** Karen **want** to be a model? – We **don't think** clothes and fashion are important.

Check-out

1. Verneine die folgenden Sätze.

   a) *I enjoy TV shows about fashion.*
   b) *Josie works in a clothes shop.*
   c) *Models earn too much money.*

2. Schreibe die Fragen zu den Antworten.

   a) *(you / like / jewellery?) – Yes, I do. I love it!*
   b) *(Where / Tony / get his T-shirts?) – He gets them at a shop called H & A.*
   c) *(When / most people / go shopping for clothes?) – They go on Saturdays.*

G44 Die Verlaufsform der Gegenwart
The present progressive

> She**'s wearing** a long green dress.

Check-in

Fashion designer Frederico Fry has just arrived at the Fashion Awards. The TV presenter gets the chance to talk to him. Read what they say.

> And now we can see fashion designer Frederico Fry and his new girlfriend, model Lena Bow. They**'re getting** out of the car. She**'s wearing** a long green dress by Gabino and … oh! **Are** they **wearing** rings?

> Because my best friend is jewellery designer Lars Love, and we want to show the world the beautiful things he makes.

> Frederico and Lena, why **are** you both **wearing** a ring of the same style?

> I'm sure people **are wondering** if you have another reason!

1. Schau dir die hervorgehobenen Formen in den Aussagen und Fragen der Moderatorin an und vervollständige die folgende Regel:
Das *present progressive* wird mit einer Form von … und dem *present participle* gebildet.

2. Warum sagt die Moderatorin *She's wearing a long green dress* und nicht *She wears a long green dress*?

REGEL

1. Das *present progressive* verwendest du, …
   a) um auszudrücken, dass jemand etwas in diesem Moment tut oder dass eine Handlung über einen längeren Zeitraum hinweg abläuft:
      • She **is wearing** a green dress.
   b) um über Entwicklungen und Tendenzen zu sprechen:
      • It **is getting** easier to buy designer clothes.
   c) wenn eine länger andauernde Handlung im Augenblick des Sprechens gerade unterbrochen ist, aber später wieder aufgenommen wird:
      • I**'m doing** a lot of shopping these days.
2. Das *present progressive* bildest du mit einer **Form von be** (*am/is/are*) + **present participle**.
3. Zur **Verneinung** setzt du *not* zwischen die **Form von be** und das *present participle*.
4. Um eine **Frage** zu bilden, stellst du die **Form von be** an den **Satzanfang oder bei Fragen mit Fragewort hinter das Fragewort**.

Aussage:	Lena **is wearing** a beautiful dress. People **are asking** questions about Frederico and Lena.
Verneinung:	The presenter **is not getting** the information that she wants. You **aren't telling** me what I want to know.
Frage mit Fragewort:	Why **are** they **wearing** rings?
Entscheidungs-frage mit Kurzantwort:	**Is** Lena **wearing** earrings? – Yes, she **is**. **Are** Lena and Frederico **talking** about their plans? – No, they **aren't**.

■ **Achtung!**
– Wenn ein Verb auf einen kurzen, betonten Vokal gefolgt von einem Konsonanten endet (*win, put,* usw.), verdoppelst du den Konsonanten bei der Bildung des *present participle*: wi**nn**ing, pu**tt**ing.
Wenn das Verb auf ein stummes *-e* endet (*dance, write,* usw.), entfällt das *-e* im *present participle*: dan**c**ing, wri**t**ing.

- Es gibt Verben, die du normalerweise nicht in der Verlaufsform verwendest, die so genannten **Zustandsverben**. Dazu gehören Verben wie *be, believe, belong to, hear, hope, know, look, notice, remember, see, seem, smell, taste, think, understand, want* und *wish*. Viele von ihnen drücken Meinungen, Sinneswahrnehmungen oder Wünsche aus.
  - *I **think** she **looks** fantastic today.*
  - *The presenter **believes** that Frederico is going to marry Lena.*

■ **Mündlicher/schriftlicher Sprachgebrauch**
- Wenn du das *present progressive* verwendest, musst du entscheiden, ob du das Hilfsverb *be* in seiner Lang- oder Kurzform benutzt:
  - *I **am** wearing my new shoes today.*
  - *I**'m** wearing my new shoes today.*
  Die Langform ist förmlicher und sollte daher in der Schriftsprache verwendet werden. Beim Sprechen verwendet man fast immer die Kurzform.

English summary

How it works	Examples
You use the present progressive to talk about things that are happening now or around now. It is formed with the verb *be* and the present participle.	- I**'m buying** something new to wear to the party.
To make negative sentences, you put *not* between the form of *be* and the present participle.	- Carl **is not wearing** a coat today.
To make yes/no questions, you put the correct form of *be* before the subject of the sentence.	- **Is** Frederico **smiling** at Lena?
In questions with question words the form of *be* comes after the question word.	- What **is** Lena **wearing?**

Check-out

1. Übertrage die folgenden Sätze ins Englische. Verwende dabei das Verb, das in Klammern steht.

   a) Lisa redet gerade mit einem Journalisten. (*talk*)
   b) Wir tragen heute unsere Winterkleidung nicht. (*wear*)
   c) Sieht Tim gerade seine Lieblingssendung? (*watch*)
   d) Ich lese gerade eine Modezeitschrift. (*read*)
   e) Gefällt dir die Show? (*enjoy*)

I **love** my job.
At the moment I'**m designing** some shirts and trousers.

G45 Gegenüberstellung von *simple present* und *present progressive*   *Comparing the simple present and the present progressive*

Check-in

Fashion designer Frederico Fry has been invited to a TV talk show. Read what he tells the presenter of the show.

Presenter: **Do** you **enjoy** your work, Frederico?
Frederico: Oh yes. I **love** my job. The most beautiful film stars and models **buy** my clothes and they **look** fantastic. I'm so lucky!
Presenter: But most people **don't have** enough money for your designs.
Frederico: Well, at the moment I'**m designing** some shirts, trousers and dresses for the inexpensive clothes store C & M. I'**m working** with a team of young designers and we'**re creating** clothes that anyone can buy. It'**s getting** easier for normal people to wear fantastic clothes, and I **want** to be part of that!

1. Vervollständige die Sätze mit der richtigen Form.

   a) Frederico hat (normalerweise / zur Zeit) Spaß an seiner Arbeit.
   b) Er entwirft (normalerweise / zur Zeit) Kleidung für Menschen, die keine Stars oder Models sind.

2. Welche Zeitform verwendest du, um Gewohnheiten auszudrücken und welche für Handlungen, die momentan passieren oder sich über einen längeren Zeitraum erstrecken?

REGEL

1. Das *simple present* (→ G43) verwendest du, um auszudrücken, dass etwas häufig, regelmäßig, selten oder nie passiert:
   • *Famous people often **buy** Frederico's designs.*
   Du verwendest es auch, um Tatsachen auszudrücken:
   • *I **love** my job.*
2. Das *present progressive* (→ G44) verwendest du, um auszudrücken, dass jemand gerade dabei ist, etwas zu tun, oder für Handlungen, die sich über einen längeren Zeitraum erstrecken:
   • *Frederico **is designing** some clothes for an inexpensive store.*
   Du benutzt es auch, um über Entwicklungen und Tendenzen zu sprechen:
   • *It **is getting** easier to buy designer clothes.*

simple present	present progressive
Actors often **wear** my clothes to their film premieres.	Look! This evening Angela Monita **is wearing** a dress that I designed.
Students **don't** usually **buy** expensive clothes.	Marie **isn't buying** clothes today. She'**s** just **looking**.
Do you **design** costumes for films, too?	What kind of clothes **are** you **designing** at the moment?

■ **Achtung!**
– Du kannst sowohl das *simple present* (→ **G59**) als auch das *present progressive* (→ **G60**) verwenden, um über die Zukunft zu sprechen. Der Kontext und die Verwendung von Zeitangaben helfen dir zu erkennen, ob über die Gegenwart oder die Zukunft gesprochen wird.
  • *The train **never arrives** on time.* (Gegenwart)
  • *The train **arrives** at six **tomorrow morning**.* (Zukunft)
  • *The train **is just leaving**.* (Gegenwart)
  • *We'**re leaving tomorrow**.* (Zukunft)

English summary

How it works	Examples
You use the simple present to talk about regular events and facts.	– Zoe **likes** nice clothes but she **doesn't** often **wear** jewellery. – Top models **spend** a lot of money on clothes.
You use the present progressive to talk about things that are happening now or around now.	– I'm a journalist and today, for example, I'**m writing** a story about the life of a model.

Check-out

1. Vervollständige den Text mit der richtigen Form des Verbs.

Richard is a fashion photographer and he ... (love) his job. He usually ... (travel) a lot. He regularly ... (go) to fashion shows in a lot of different countries. At the moment, he ... (not travel) so much. He ... (write) a book about the people who he meets in his job. He often ... (meet) famous designers and models but they ... (not talk) to him very much. Richard says they sometimes ... (forget) that the photographer is a very important person for their success!

> Our next guests on the show **have won** awards for their music worldwide.

G46 Die einfache Form des Perfekts
The present perfect simple

Check-in

Read how the TV host introduces *Manmade*, a popular UK band, to the show:

> Our next guests on the show **have won** awards for their music worldwide. So far, they**'ve had** five number one hits in the UK, and their latest album **has** already **sold** more than two million copies. And they**'ve** just **finished** their tour of the US. Please give them a very warm welcome. It's *Manmade*.

1. Schau dir die hervorgehobenen Verbformen in der Ankündigung der Moderatorin an und vervollständige die folgende Regel:
Das *present perfect simple* wird mit … oder … und dem *past participle* gebildet.

2. Welche der beiden Aussagen trifft zu?
Das *present perfect simple* verwendest du oft in Verbindung mit …

   a) Angaben der unbestimmten Zeit wie *already, so far, just.*
   b) Angaben der bestimmten Zeit wie *yesterday, two hours ago, last week.*

REGEL

> **TIPP**
> Signalwörter sind z. B.: already (schon in Aussagen), ever (schon in Fragen), just (gerade), never (noch nie), so far (bis jetzt), recently (in letzter Zeit), yet (schon), not … yet, (noch nicht), this week.

1. Mit dem *present perfect simple* kannst du ausdrücken, dass …
   a) eine **Handlung irgendwann in der Vergangenheit stattgefunden** hat und das **Ergebnis** dieser Handlung **bis in die Gegenwart spürbar** ist:
      • *Their latest album **has** already **sold** more than two million copies.*
      Ihr letztes Album hat sich schon mehr als zwei Millionen Mal verkauft.
   b) eine **Handlung gerade erst abgeschlossen** wurde:
      • *They**'ve** just **finished** their tour of the US.*
      Sie haben gerade ihre Tour durch die USA beendet.
   c) eine **Handlung bis jetzt einmal, mehrmals, noch nicht oder nie stattge-funden** hat:
      • ***Have** you ever **won** the MTV Music Award? – Yes, we**'ve won** it twice.*
      Habt ihr je den MTV Music Award gewonnen? – Ja, wir haben ihn schon zweimal gewonnen.
   d) ein **Zustand in der Vergangenheit begonnen hat und bis in die Gegenwart andauert**:
      • *She **has known** Manmade since their first concert.*
      Sie kennt *Manmade* schon seit ihrem ersten Konzert.

2. Das *present perfect simple* bildest du mit ***have*** oder ***has*** (für die 3. Person Singular) **und** dem ***past participle***.

Aussage:	*Manmade* **have** just **come back** from their tour of the US.
Verneinung:	I **haven't bought** their new single yet.
Frage mit Fragewort:	Where **have** you **bought** the ticktes?
Entscheidungs-frage mit Kurzantwort:	**Have** they already **started** to sell tickets for their next tour? – Yes, they **have**. / No, they **haven't**. **Has** their single sold well in the US? – Yes, it **has**. / No, it **hasn't**.

■ **Achtung!**
– Das *present perfect simple* bildest du im Englischen immer mit *has/have + past participle*, auch wenn es sich um Verben der Fortbewegung handelt. Vergleiche:
  • They ***have*** just ***come back*** from their tour of the US.
    Sie **sind** gerade erst von ihrer US-Tournee **zurückgekehrt**.

– Die Stellung der Signalwörter im Satz ist unterschiedlich (➜ **G36**):
  • *just, already, ever, never, always* und *often* stehen direkt **nach *have* bzw. *has***:
    I have **always** wanted to be a singer.
  • *yet* steht am **Satzende**: *Have you found a manager **yet**?*
  • *so far, today, this week* stehen entweder am **Satzanfang oder am Satzende**:
    ***So far**, I haven't had much luck. / I haven't had much luck **so far**.*

■ **Schriftlicher/mündlicher Sprachgebrauch**
– Beim Sprechen und in informellen Texten verwendest du meist die Kurzform:
  *I**'ve** played, he**'s** made, you **haven't** done*, usw. Beim Schreiben von formellen Texten verwendest du hingegen die Langform: *I **have** played, he **has** made, you **have not** done*.

English summary

How it works	Examples
The present perfect simple is made up of *have* or *has* and the past participle.	– The band **has had** some great reviews this year.
You use the present perfect simple … – to stress the result of an activity that happened at an indefinite time in the past. – to say how often an activity has happened or not happened so far. – to express that states began in the past and have continued up to the present.	– They **have** just **finished** their new album. – My brother **has won** his school's music award three times. – I**'ve been** a fan of the band all my life.

Check-out

1. Vervollständige den Auszug aus einem Interview mit der richtigen Form des Verbs.

This year (be) really fantastic for you, hasn't it? Your latest single (just/land) at number one in the UK charts and your album (already/sell) more than four million copies. You (win) platinum discs worldwide. In the last four weeks you (give) ten concerts and you (have) some fantastic reviews. (your success/change) you in any way? (you/ever/wish) you weren't quite so famous?

Tell us what you**'ve been doing**.

G47 Die Verlaufsform des Perfekts
The present perfect progressive

Check-in

This week our reporter Selina Adams has been talking to Harry. He is a member of *One-way*, one of the UK's most successful bands.

INTERVIEW WITH HARRY

from One-way

Hello! It's nice to see you again. Now, you**'ve been working** quite hard recently, haven't you? So tell us what you**'ve been doing** since we last met.

Well, we**'ve been touring** the UK for the past ten months, so, yeah, that's right, we **have been working** really hard. But we **have been enjoying** ourselves, too! Everything **has been going** brilliantly! And we**'ve been getting** the most amazing support from all our fans. So thanks for that, everybody.

1. Schau dir die hervorgehobenen Formen in dem Interview an und vervollständige die folgende Regel:
   Das *present perfect progressive* wird mit … oder … + … und dem *present participle* gebildet.

2. Selina fragt Harry: *What have you been doing since we last met?*
   Harry antwortet: *We've been touring the UK for the past ten months.*
   Worin liegt der Unterschied in der Verwendung von *since* und *for*?

REGEL

1. Mit dem *present perfect progessive* kannst du ausdrücken, dass eine **Handlung in der Vergangenheit begann und bis in die Gegenwart andauert**. Häufig verwendest du dabei eine Zeitangabe, die angibt, **seit wann** (*since*) oder **wie lange** (*for, recently, …*) die Handlung schon andauert:

- *The boys **have been working** very hard since January.*
  Die Jungs arbeiten seit Januar sehr hart.
- *They **have been touring** the UK for the past ten months.*
  Sie sind seit zehn Monaten auf Tour in Großbritannien.

> **TIPP**
> Signalwörter sind z. B.: since (seit), for (seit), recently (in letzter Zeit), all year (das ganze Jahr), all the time (die ganze Zeit).

past	present
They started filming their music video on Monday, 9th April.	Now it is Friday, 13th April. They are still filming their music video.

Monday ————————————————————→ Friday

They **have been filming** their music video all week.

> **MERKHILFE**
> „since" = Zeit**punkt**
> since January, since 3 o'clock, since yesterday, since last week, since 2010
>
> „foR" = Zeit**R**aum
> for five hours, for three days, for ages, for a long time, for as long as I can remember

2. Das *present perfect progressive* bildest du mit **have** oder **has** + **been** und dem *present participle*.

Aussage:	Harry **has been chatting** to the reporter since 9 am.
Verneinung:	He **hasn't** only **been answering** questions about their tour.
Frage mit Fragewort:	What **have** you **been doing** since we last met?
Entscheidungsfrage mit Kurzantwort:	**Has** Selina **been asking about** their private lives, too? – Yes, she **has**. / No, she **hasn't**.

■ Achtung!

– Das *present perfect progressive* kannst du wie alle Verlaufsformen **nur bei Tätigkeitsverben** verwenden, z. B. *run, work, live*. Bei Verben, die keine Tätigkeit sondern einen **Zustand** darstellen (z. B. *be, believe, belong to, hear, hope, know, look, notice, remember, see, seem, smell, taste, think, understand, want, wish*), steht normalerweise **nur das *present perfect simple*** (→ G46):

- *We've **been** pretty busy recently.*
  In letzter Zeit haben wir viel zu tun gehabt.

– Um auszudrücken, wie lange etwas dauert, verwendest du im Deutschen meist das Präsens + „schon". Vergleiche:

- *Pete **has been listening** to music all day long.*
  Pete **hört schon** den ganzen Tag Musik.

English summary

How it works	Examples
The present perfect progressive is made up of *have* or *has* + *been* and the present participle.	– The fans **have been trying** to get tickets for the concert since the early morning.
You use the present perfect progressive to express that an activity began in the past and has been going on until now.	– Harry **has been talking** to Selina for half an hour.

Check-out

1. Bei welchen Zeitangaben verwendest du *since* und bei welchen *for*? Vervollständige die Tabelle.
   The boys have been talking about songs for their new album …

   weeks • last week • ages • 2011 • a long time • half an hour • yesterday • the beginning of the year • August • a few months

for	since
weeks, …	2011, …

2. Bilde Sätze mit dem *present perfect progressive* und *since* oder *for*.

   a) *The boys • chat with • fans • two hours.*
   b) *They • answer • fans' questions • 11 am.*
   c) *Jason • play • the drums • as long as he can remember.*
   d) *The boys • make music together • they met on a TV talent show.*

3. Was machen diese Menschen und wie lange schon? Schau dir das Beispiel an und bilde ähnliche Sätze.

   a) *The band **have been practising** for their concert **all morning**.*

What?	Started when?	Time now
a) *The band are practising for their concert.*	*at 9 am*	*lunchtime*
b) *They are touring France.*	*on 1st May*	*31st May*
c) *Harry is signing autographs.*	*at 2 pm*	*3.30 pm*
d) *Jason is answering fan mail.*	*at 6 pm*	*10 pm*
e) *They are working hard.*	*in January*	*December*

G48 Gegenüberstellung von *present perfect simple* und *present perfect progressive*   *Comparing the present perfect simple and the present perfect progressive*

> How long **have** you **been playing** together? – For about six years, but we**'ve known** each other since school.

Check-in

Harry from the band *One-way* is chatting on an Internet forum to Dave, one of their fans. Read their conversation.

Dave | 2:26 pm
Have you **written** any new songs recently?

Harry | 2:31 pm
We**'ve written** two new songs! We're going to play them at the concert in Birmingham tonight.

Dave | 2:33 pm
Great. I can't wait to hear them. You **haven't played** here for a while, have you?

Harry | 2:34 pm
No, it**'s been** about two years now since our last concert here. So we're really excited about it.

Dave | 2:38 pm
How long **have** you **been playing** together now?

Harry | 2:40 pm
For about six years, but we**'ve been performing** together for a lot longer. We**'ve known** each other since school.

---

1. Beantworte die folgenden Fragen auf Deutsch.

   a) Wie oft hat die Band in den letzten zwei Jahren in Birmingham gespielt?
   b) Wie lange machen sie schon zusammen Musik?

REGEL

1. Mit dem *present perfect simple* (→ G46) drückst du aus, dass …
   a) eine **Handlung irgendwann in der Vergangenheit stattgefunden** hat und das **Ergebnis** dieser Handlung **bis in die Gegenwart spürbar** ist:
      • *We've written two new songs.*
   b) Du verwendest es auch, wenn du sagen willst, **wie oft etwas bis jetzt schon geschehen ist**:
      • *Some fans have gone to their concerts three times this year.*
      Hierzu zählen auch Handlungen, die bis zum Moment des Sprechens **kein Mal** geschehen sind:
      • *We haven't given a concert in Liverpool yet.*
   c) Auch für einen **Zustand, der in der Vergangenheit begann und bis in die Gegenwart andauert**, verwendest du das *present perfect simple*:
      • *We've known each other since school.*

> **TIPP**
> Das present perfect simple verwendest du für Handlungen, die bereits stattgefunden haben. Das Ergebnis ist spürbar. Das present perfect progressive benutzt du für Handlungen, die in der Gegenwart noch andauern.

2. Mit dem *present perfect progressive* (→ **G47**) drückst du aus, dass eine **Handlung in der Vergangenheit begann und bis heute andauert**. Häufig verwendest du hier eine Zeitangabe, die angibt, seit wann oder wie lange die Handlung schon andauert:

• *The boys **have been playing** together for six years now.*

present perfect simple	present perfect progressive
We**'ve written** twenty songs this year.	We**'ve been writing** our own songs for about ten years now.
They **haven't made** a new album recently.	They **haven't been working** on their new album for very long.
How long **have** you **known** each other?	How long **have** you **been touring** together?

English summary

How it works	Examples
You use the present perfect simple to stress the result of an activity that happened at some time in the past.	– They **haven't won** any prizes this year.
You use the present perfect progressive to say that an activity started in the past and has been going on until now.	– Harry **has been playing** the drums since he was ten.

Check-out

1. Übertrage die folgenden Sätze ins Englische.

   a) Wie lange arbeitet ihr schon an eurem neuen Album?
   b) Wie lange kennt ihr euch schon?
   c) Die Band hat noch nie in Deutschland gespielt.
   d) Ich versuche schon seit letzter Woche Karten für ihr Konzert zu bekommen.

9 Die Zeitformen der Vergangenheit

G49 Die einfache Vergangenheit
The simple past

> When I **was** 14 years old, I **joined** a gang.

Check-in

17-year-old Rob is talking about his life as a 14-year-old criminal. Read what he says.

> Three years ago, when I **was** 14 years old, I **joined** a gang and **had** my first fight. After that, things quickly **got** worse and my mates and I **were** always in trouble with the police. We **stole** from shops, we **broke into** cars and we **painted** graffiti all over the town. But we never **carried** knives and we **didn't** ever **hurt** anyone. The police often **stopped** us, but **did** we **care**? No, we **didn't**. We **did** whatever we **wanted**. We **weren't** afraid of anything or anyone.

1. Schau dir die *simple past*-Formen der Verben *join, have, get, steal, paint, carry, hurt* und *stop* in der Aussage oben an und vervollständige die Tabelle.

Infinitiv	Aussagesatz	Verneinung	Frage
join	*joined*	*didn't join*	*did (he) join*
have	…	…	…

2. Warum erzählt Rob seine Geschichte im *simple past*?

REGEL

1. Du verwendest das *simple past*, um ausdrücken, dass …

eine Handlung oder ein Ereignis zu einem bestimmten Zeitpunkt in der Vergangenheit stattfand und abgeschlossen ist:	Rob **joined** a gang **three years ago**. **Vor drei Jahren schloss** sich Rob einer Bande **an**.
eine Handlung oder ein Ereignis immer, manchmal oder nie (*always, often, sometimes, never*) in der Vergangenheit stattfand:	They **were always** in trouble with the police. Sie **hatten ständig** Schwierigkeiten mit der Polizei. They **never carried** knives. Sie **trugen nie** Messer bei sich.
Handlungen oder Ereignisse nacheinander (*first, then, after that, next, finally, suddenly*) stattfanden:	**After that**, things quickly **got** worse. **Danach verschlechterten** sich die Dinge schnell.

TIPP

Bei „in (2010)",
„yesterday", „(a few
weeks) ago" und
„last (year)" folgt
das simple past.
Die Zeitangaben
können zu Beginn
eines Satzes oder
am Satzende
stehen. Auch „when"
im Sinne von „als"
oder „wann", „on
Friday" und „the
day before" können
den Gebrauch
des simple past
signalisieren.

2. Bei der Bildung des *simple past* unterscheidet man zwischen zwei Verbarten:
   - **regelmäßige Verben** bilden das *simple past* aus dem **Infinitiv** + **-ed**, z. B.: *join – joined, paint – painted, want – wanted*.
   - **unregelmäßige Verben** haben **eigene Formen**, die du auswendig lernen musst, z. B.: *have – had, steal – stole, break – broke, do – did*. (siehe Anhang)
3. Das *simple past* ist in allen Personen gleich (außer: *be – was/were*).
4. Die **Verneinung** bildest du **mit** *didn't* und **Entscheidungs- und Objektfragen mit** *did*. Für das Verb *be* gelten andere Regeln (siehe Achtung!).

Aussagesatz:	Three years ago Rob **joined** a gang. He **had** his first fight at the age of 14.
Verneinung:	But he **didn't** ever **hurt** anyone with a knife.
Frage mit Fragewort:	Why **did** they **steal** from shops?
Entscheidungsfrage mit Kurzantwort:	**Did** the police **stop** his gang? – Yes, they **did**. / No, they **didn't**.

■ **Achtung!**
   - Achte auf die Besonderheiten bei der Rechtschreibung. Bei Konsonant + -*y* wird das *y* zu *i*: *carry – carried, copy – copied*.
   Bei kurzem betonten Vokal + Konsonant wird der Konsonant verdoppelt: *stop – stopped, chat – chatted*.

   - Im *simple past* gibt es zwei Formen von *be*, nämlich *I/he/she/it* **was** und *we/you/they* **were**. Enthält die Frage oder Verneinung eine Form von *be*, wird nicht mit *did* umschrieben:

Aussage:	Rob **was** the youngest member of the gang. His mates **were** all older.
Verneinung:	Rob **wasn't** scared of the police. He and his mates **weren't** scared of anyone.
Frage mit Fragewort:	Who **was** the youngest member of the gang?
Entscheidungsfrage mit Kurzantwort:	**Were** they often in trouble with the police? – Yes, they **were**. / No, they **weren't**.

■ **Mündlicher/schriftlicher Sprachgebrauch**
   - Beim Sprechen verwendest du meist die Kurzform: *I* **didn't**, *he* **wasn't**, *they* **weren't**. In der formellen Schriftsprache benutzt du jedoch die Langform: *I* **did not**, *he* **was not**, *they* **were not**.

   - Das *simple past* findest du oft in Berichten, Geschichten und Märchen.
     • *Once upon a time there* **was** *a beautiful princess who* **had** *a golden ball. She* **lived** *in a palace with her father, the King.*

English summary

How it works	Examples
You use the simple past to describe an activity or event that was completed at a definite time in the past. It is often used in stories and reports about past events.	– **Last week** a 30-year-old man **attacked** a woman at the bus stop.
Regular verbs end in -ed.	– In an interview Rob **talked** about his life as a criminal.
Irregular verbs have their own form.	– Yesterday somebody **broke into** our house.
In object questions and negative statements you use did/didn't and the infinitive of the verb.	– What **did** they **steal**? – They **didn't take** much.
The simple past forms of be are I/he/she/ it was and you/we/they were. You use wasn't/weren't for negative statements.	– Where **were** you when it happened? – I **wasn't** at home. I **was** at the library.

Check-out

1. Im Gitter sind die *simple past*-Formen von neun unregelmäßigen Verben versteckt. Finde sie und schreibe sie gemeinsam mit ihrer Infinitivform auf.

a	m	b	u	i	l	t	s
t	a	u	g	h	t	p	a
e	d	i	d	f	l	e	w
w	e	n	t	w	e	r	e

2. Die 16-jährige Kelly erzählt aus ihrem Leben als 14-jähriges Mädchen. Lies ihre Geschichte und setze die fehlenden Verben in der richtigen Form ein.

be (3x) • not believe • stop • paint • not do • pick • steal • have • put • find • call • not be allowed to • join

Kelly … 14 years old when she … a gang. They often … graffiti around town, and some of the girls … from shops, too, but Kelly … that. Then one day when they … at the supermarket, one of the girls … up some make-up and … it into Kelly's pocket. Kelly … no idea. So she … surprised when the store detective … her and … the make-up. The store manager … her story and … the police. After that she … enter his shop again.

3. Ein Reporter möchte einen Bericht über Kelly schreiben. Schau dir, nachdem du Aufgabe 2 erledigt hast, Kellys Antworten an. Schreibe dann die Fragen des Reporters auf.

   a) *I was 14 years old when I joined the gang.*
   b) *No, I didn't, but some of the other girls in my gang did.*
   c) *Because he didn't believe what I said.*

Just as I **was going** past house number 20, a woman stopped me.

G50 Die Verlaufsform der Vergangenheit
The past progressive

Check-in

Last Friday a boy stole Leonie's handbag. A short time later, Leonie spoke to a police officer at the police station. Read their conversation.

Police officer: So, at half past one, you **were walking** down Ash Street, right?

Leonie: Yes, that's right. And just as I **was going** past house number 20, a woman stopped me. She **was looking for** her dog.

Police officer: And while you **were talking** to her, a boy, about 15 years old with dark hair, ran off with your handbag. You say he **was carrying** a bag.

Leonie: No, he **wasn't carrying** a bag. He **was carrying** a bat.

Police officer: Oh sorry, a bat. And what **was** he **wearing**?

Leonie: Um, jeans, a dark blue T-shirt and large black sunglasses.

1. Schau dir die im Gespräch hervorgehobenen Verbformen an und vervollständige die folgende Regel:
   Das *past progressive* wird mit … oder … und dem … gebildet.

2. Warum wurde bei den hervorgehobenen Formen nicht das *simple past* verwendet?

REGEL

1. Das *past progressive* verwendest du, um die Dauer einer Handlung zu betonen. Dabei gibt es folgende Varianten:

Eine Handlung fand gerade zu einem bestimmten Zeitpunkt in der Vergangenheit statt und war noch nicht zu Ende.	**At half past one**, Leonie **was walking** down Ash Street.
Zwei Handlungen liefen gleichzeitig ab.	While she **was going** past house number 20, a woman **was looking for** her dog.
Eine Handlung war noch im Verlauf, als eine neue Handlung bzw. ein neues Ereignis einsetzte.	While Leonie **was talking** to a woman, a boy stole her handbag.

TIPP

Mit dem past progressive antwortest du auf die Frage „Was lief gerade ab?"

While Leonie was talking to a woman, …
(ablaufende Handlung)
past progressive

simple past
a boy stole her bag.
(neues Ereignis)

2. Das *past progressive* bildest du mit **was**/**were** + **present participle**.

Aussage:	The boy **was wearing** jeans when Leonie saw him.
Verneinung:	He **wasn't carrying** a bag.
Frage mit Fragewort:	What **was** he **wearing**?
Entscheidungsfrage mit Kurzantwort:	**Were** the police **looking for** a 15-year-old boy? – Yes, they **were**. / No, they **weren't**.

TIPP
Signalwörter sind: while (während), just (gerade dabei), just as (gerade als), still, this time last (week).

■ Achtung!

– Die *progressive*-Form kann **nur bei** den **Verben** verwendet werden, **die eine Tätigkeit bzw. Hintergrundhandlung ausdrücken**, z. B. *carry, look for, walk, wear*. Verben wie *be, believe, belong to, hear, hope, know, look, notice, remember, see, seem, smell, taste, understand, want, wish* die keine Tätigkeit, sondern einen **Zustand** beschreiben, stehen normalerweise nur in der *simple*-Form.

English summary

How it works	Examples
You use the past progressive (*was/were* + present participle) to describe an unfinished action or activity in the past. It is often used together with a point in time.	– **At 7 o'clock**, the police officer **was going** to work. – It **was raining**, when he left the house.
It is also used to talk about two events going on at the same time.	– **While** he **was interviewing** Leonie, he **was taking** some notes.
The past progessive often describes something that was going on at a time when a new action or event happened.	– **Just as** he **was talking** to Leonie, his phone rang.

Check-out

1. Lies dir das Gespräch im Check-in noch einmal durch und beschreibe den Dieb, damit ein Phantombild erstellt werden kann. Wie sah er aus? Was hatte er an? Was hielt er in der Hand?

2. Gestern Abend wurde der Bahnhof mit Graffiti besprüht. Die Polizei verdächtigt einige Jugendliche und fragt sie nach ihrem Alibi. Schau dir die Bilder an. Wie beantworten sie jeweils die Frage der Polizistin?

What were you doing between 9 and 11 o'clock last night?

Dan **was sitting** on the train when two boys **got on**.

G51 Gegenüberstellung von *simple past* und *past progressive*
Comparing the simple past and the past progressive

Check-in

Yesterday Dan was on his way home from a friend's house when two boys stole his money and his mobile. Read what he posted on the Internet.

Dan

I **was sitting** on the train when two boys **got on** and **sat down** opposite me. Almost at once they **began** to fight. While they **were pushing** and **pulling** each other, one of them suddenly **fell** onto my rucksack. To my surprise, the boy **apologized** and after that they **moved away**. It **was** only later when I **was unpacking** my rucksack that I **discovered** that my mobile and my money were no longer there.

1. Welche der hervorgehobenen Formen in Dans Eintrag beschreiben kurze abgeschlossene Handlungen? Bei welchen dauerte die Handlung länger an?

2. Welche Signalwörter findest du in dem Eintrag für das *simple past* und welche für das *past progressive*?

REGEL

1. Das *past tense* hat, wie alle anderen englischen Zeitformen auch, eine **simple-Form** und eine *progressive*-**Form**, die unterschiedliche Funktionen haben.

   a) Das *simple past* (→ **G49**) verwendest du für …

TIPP
Signalwörter für das simple past sind: first, then, later, after that, suddenly, immediately, yesterday, last (year), (four days) ago, in (2010), when.

Handlungen, die sich zu einem bestimmten Zeitpunkt in der Vergangenheit ereignet haben und abgeschlossen sind:	**Last week** two boys **stole** Dan's money and his mobile.
Handlungen, die nacheinander stattfanden:	Two boys **got** on the train and **sat down** opposite him.
Zustandsverben wie *be* und *know*, die normalerweise keine Verlaufsform haben:	Dan **didn't know** them. They **weren't** friends of his.

   b) Das *past progressive* (→ **G50**) verwendest du für …

TIPP
Signalwörter für das past progressive sind: while, still, just (gerade dabei), just as (gerade als), this time last (week), when.

Handlungen, die zu einem bestimmten Zeitpunkt in der Vergangenheit gerade abliefen und somit noch nicht abgeschlossen waren:	At 4 o'clock Dan **was sitting** on the train home from school.
Handlungen, die bereits im Verlauf waren, als etwas Neues geschah:	Dan **was unpacking** his rucksack when he noticed that his money and his mobile were no longer there.

■ **Achtung!**

– *When* wird manchmal im Sinne von *while* („während") verwendet. In diesem Fall steht die nachfolgende Handlung im *past progressive*.

  • ***When*** *(= while) Dan **was unpacking** his rucksack, he noticed that his mobile and his money were no longer there.*

– Das englische Wort *just* hat verschiedene Bedeutungen und kommt deswegen auch in Kombination mit anderen Zeitformen vor. Vergleiche:

  • ***present progressive:*** *Look! Tom is just **getting** off the train. (just = jetzt gerade)*
  • ***simple past***: *Tom just **got** off the train without even saying goodbye. (just = einfach)*
  • ***past progressive***: *Tom **was** just **getting** off the train when he remembered that he had forgotten his rucksack. (just = gerade dabei)*
  • ***present perfect***: *Tom **has** just **got** off the train. (just = gerade eben)*

English summary

How it works	Examples
You use the simple past to describe a finished action or a number of finished actions which happened at a definite time in the past.	– **Yesterday** Dan **had** a horrible experience on the train. – A boy **fell** onto his rucksack and **stole** his mobile.
You use the past progressive to describe an unfinished action in the past. Very often it is used to describe an action which started before a new event in the past and possibly also continued after it.	– At half past five Dan **was leaving** the police station. – It **was raining** when he left the building.

Check-out

1. Diese Geschichte passierte vor ein paar Tagen. Vervollständige den Text, indem du das Verb in Klammern in die richtigen Zeitform setzt.

   Alan (wait) for his train when he first (see) the two boys. They (kick) a plastic bottle around the platform. While he (watch) them, they suddenly (notice) him and they (shout) something at him angrily. A few moments later the train (arrive) and Alan (get on). Just as the doors (close), the two boys (jump on), too. They (be) still angry and Alan (be) scared. But then some teenagers who (stand) near the door (come) over to help. As soon as the two boys (see) how much taller and stronger they were, they quickly (move) away.

2. Lies dir den Text in Aufgabe 1 noch einmal durch. Beantworte dann die folgenden beiden Fragen.

   a) *What were the two boys doing when Alan first saw them?*
   b) *What did the two boys do when they noticed Alan?*

   Erkläre nun den Unterschied in der Bedeutung zwischen den beiden Fragen.

> I've just **told** my mum what **happened**.

G52 Gegenüberstellung von *simple past* und *present perfect*
Comparing the simple past and the present perfect

Check-in

Last week Emily needed some expert advice. Read her e-mail to Laura, the agony aunt for her favourite teen magazine.

From:	e4u@mail.com
To:	laura@agonyaunt.co.uk
Subject:	My friend steals

Dear Laura,
Please help me. Last Saturday, my best friend and I **were** in our favourite shop when suddenly she **picked up** an expensive watch, **put** it in her bag and calmly **walked** out of the store. I **was** shocked. I'**ve known** Holly for years and she **has** never **done** anything like that before. When I **asked** her why, she just **said** she **didn't have** enough money to pay for it. Her parents **have** always **given** her lots of pocket money, so that can't be the real reason. I'**ve** just **told** my mum what **happened** and she thinks I should tell her parents, but I don't want to lose a friend.
Emily

1. Welche Zeitform verwendet Emily, um über die Ereignisse zu berichten, die am letzten Samstag geschehen sind?

2. Welche Zeitform verwendet sie, um über Sachverhalte zu berichten, die bis in die Gegenwart hineinreichen?

REGEL

1. Sowohl das *simple past* als auch das *present perfect simple* beschreiben **Handlungen, die bereits stattgefunden haben**. Du kannst sie jedoch nicht beliebig verwenden.

   a) Das *simple past* (→ G49) verwendest du für …

Handlungen, die sich zu einem bestimmten Zeitpunkt in der Vergangenheit ereignet haben und abgeschlossen sind:	**A few days ago**, Emily and her best friend Holly **went** into their favourite shop.
Handlungen, die nacheinander stattfanden:	Suddenly Holly **picked up** an expensive watch, **put** it in her bag and calmly **walked** out of the store.

b) Das *present perfect simple* (→ G46) verwendest du wenn …

das Ergebnis einer vergangenen Handlung in der Gegenwart noch sichtbar oder spürbar ist:	Emily **has told** an agony aunt about her problem.
die Handlung gerade erst (*just*) oder bereits (*already*) abgeschlossen wurde:	Emily **has just told** her mum. She **has already sent** an e-mail to Laura.
die Handlung in einem Zeitraum liegt, der von der Vergangenheit bis in die Gegenwart (und vielleicht auch darüber hinaus) andauert:	Holly's parents **have always given** her a lot of pocket money.

TIPP
Das present perfect verbindet die Vergangenheit mit der Gegenwart.

Last week Holly **stole** *a watch from a shop.*

→

past   present perfect   now

Holly **has** never **done** anything like that before. (bis heute)

■ **Achtung!**
– Signalwörter können hilfreich sein, aber wichtiger ist immer der Zeitraum, in dem etwas geschieht. Vergleiche:
  • **Did** you ever **do** anything silly when you were a small child? (abgeschlossen)
  • **Have** you ever **done** anything silly? (bis heute)

English summary

How it works	Examples
You use the simple past when you talk about a finished action or a number of finished actions which happened at a definite time in the past.	– **A few days ago** I **met** my best friend in town. – First we **had** a meal in a snack bar, and then we **went** to our favourite shop.
You use the present perfect simple when you talk about a period of time which began in the past and continues until the present, or when you talk about a recent action which is connected with the present (or has a result in present time).	– We**'ve been** close friends **for ages**. – Emily **has just written** an e-mail. Look! You can read it.

Check-out

1. Vervollständige den Text über Robin Hood. Wähle die richtige Lösung.

Have you ever heard of Robin Hood? Maybe you (read / have read) stories about him. Or maybe you (saw / have seen) a Hollywood film about his life. In the 13th century, he (was / has been) a hero because he (stole / has stolen) money from the rich and (gave / has given) it to the poor. For many Britons today he is still a hero, although nobody actually knows if he (ever really lived / has ever really lived).

> Trains don't seem to be as safe now as they **used to** be.

G53 Die Verwendung von *used to* (früher)
Used to

Check-in

Luke has been invited to Emily's party on Saturday. He wants to catch the train home but his dad would prefer to collect him in the car. Read their conversation.

Luke: Oh Dad! You don't need to pick me up from Emily's party. I can catch the last train home.

Dad: I'd rather you didn't.

Luke: Why not? You never **used to** mind.

Dad: No, but there have been a few problems on the trains recently. They just don't seem to be as safe now as they **used to** be.

Luke: Oh Dad. You shouldn't believe everything you read in the newspaper. Anyway, I won't be on my own. I can come home with Dave.

Dad: I can drive Dave home, too.

Luke: Oh, come on, Dad. **Did** your parents **use to** pick you up from parties when you were my age?

Dad: No, they didn't, but I **didn't use to** stay out as late as you do. I always **used to** be home by ten.

1. Lies dir das Gespräch noch einmal durch und übertrage alle Sätze, die eine Form von *used to* enthalten ins Deutsche.

2. In welcher Form steht das Verb nach *used to*?

REGEL

1. Mit *used to* + **Infinitiv** berichtest du über **Gewohnheiten oder Tatsachen**, die **in der Vergangenheit** liegen und heute nicht mehr zutreffen. Im Deutschen kannst du *used to* mit „früher" oder „damals" wiedergeben.
   • *I always **used to** be home by ten.*
     Ich war früher immer vor 22 Uhr zu Hause.
2. Von *used to* gibt es **nur** die *simple past*-Form.
3. Es gibt zwei Möglichkeiten der **Verneinung**.
   a) *didn't use to* + **Infinitiv**: *I **didn't use to stay** out as late as you do.*
   b) *never used to* + **Infinitiv**: *You **never used to** mind.*
4. **Fragen** bildest du mit *did ... use to* + **Infinitiv**:
   • ***Did** your parents **use to pick** you up from parties?*
     Haben dich deine Eltern (damals) von Partys abgeholt?

■ Achtung!

– Verwechsele *used to* nicht mit *be used to* („etwas gewohnt sein") oder *get used to* („sich an etwas gewöhnen")! Vergleiche:

used to	My dad **used to** drive a lot. But now he prefers to travel by train.
	Mein Vater ist **früher** öfters mit dem Auto gefahren. Aber jetzt fährt er lieber mit dem Zug.
be used to	He**'s used to** travelling by train.
	Er **ist es gewohnt**, mit dem Zug zu fahren.
get used to	He**'s got used to** travelling by train. It's so much faster.
	Er **hat sich daran gewöhnt**, mit dem Zug zu fahren. Es ist viel schneller.

English summary

How it works	Examples
Used to expresses that … – something happened regularly in the past but no longer happens now. – a situation which existed in the past is no longer true now.	– We **used to** leave our garage door unlocked at night (but we don't now). – There **used to** be a police station in the High Street (but there isn't one now).

Check-out

1. Schreibe die folgenden Sätze um. Verwende dabei *used to* oder *didn't use to*.

   a) *This was a safe neighbourhood but it isn't now.*
   b) *There was never much crime in the area when I was a kid.*
   c) *It certainly wasn't as bad as it is today.*
   d) *We always left our doors open but you can't do that now.*

2. Übertrage die folgenden Sätze ins Englische.

   a) Früher sind wir immer mit dem Bus in die Stadt gefahren.
   b) Unsere Eltern haben uns damals nirgendwohin gefahren.
   c) Es war damals nie ein Problem.
   d) Haben dich deine Eltern früher von der Disko abgeholt?

> In 43 AD the Romans arrived in Britain. But, of course, they **had been** here before.

G54 Das Plusquamperfekt
The past perfect simple

Check-in

You are visiting the British Museum in London. Here is what a guide tells you about early Roman history.

> In 43 AD the Romans arrived in Britain and began to take over the lands which we now call England and Wales. Of course, this was not the first time that the Romans **had come** to Britain. As I'm sure you will all know, they **had been** here before under Julius Caesar in 55 BC and again in 54 BC. But both times they **had not stayed** for very long. And it was only in the first century AD that Britain actually became part of the Roman Empire.

1. Schau dir die hervorgehobenen Zeitformen in der Sprechblase oben an und vervollständige die folgende Regel:
   Das *past perfect simple* wird mit … und dem … gebildet.

2. In welcher Zeitform stehen alle Ereignisse, die **a)** nach und **b)** vor Ankunft der Römer im Jahre 43 n. Chr. geschehen sind?

REGEL

> **TIPP**
> Vor allem im gesprochenen American English wird oft das simple past statt des past perfect verwendet.

1. Mit dem *past perfect simple* drückst du aus, dass ein **Ereignis bereits vor einem anderen Ereignis in der Vergangenheit stattfand und abgeschlossen** ist.

simple past (einfache Vergangenheit)	*past perfect* (Vorvergangenheit)
In 43 AD the Romans **arrived** in Britain.	Roman soldiers **had** already **come** to Britain a hundred years earlier in 55 BC and 54 BC, but they **had not stayed** for very long.
Ausgangspunkt	davor

2. Das *past perfect simple* spielt vor allem in Erzählungen und Berichten eine Rolle. Dort wird es **häufig in Nebensätzen mit *after* oder *when*** („nachdem") verwendet, um die **Vorzeitigkeit einer Handlung** zu **betonen**.

past perfect (Vorvergangenheit)	*simple past* (einfache Vergangenheit)
After Caesar **had left** Britain in 54 BC,	Roman soldiers **did not come back** again until the first century.
davor	danach

3. Du verwendest das *past perfect simple* auch, um auszudrücken, dass eine **Handlung bis zu einem bestimmten Zeitpunkt in der Vergangenheit noch nie geschehen war**:
- *Yesterday was Carl's first day at the museum. He **had** never **worked** as a museum guide before.*

4. Das *past perfect simple* wird mit **had** und dem **past participle** (= 3. Verbform) gebildet. Es ist für alle Personen gleich.

Aussage:	Roman soldiers **had been** to Britain before 43 AD.
Verneinung:	They **had not stayed** for very long.
Entscheidungsfrage mit Kurzantwort:	**Had** they **liked** the climate? – Yes, they **had**. / No, they **hadn't**.

TIPP
- Adverbien wie „already", „always", „just", „never", „often", „recently" stehen nach „had": Roman soldiers had **already** come to Britain in 55 BC.
- Beachte den Unterschied:
  • I had been to London many times **before**. (zuvor)
  • They had been to Britain **before** 2008. (vor)

◼ **Achtung!**
- Wenn mehrere Ereignisse in einer Erzählung oder in einem Bericht der Reihe nach berichtet werden, benutzt du das *simple past*.

simple past	simple past
In 43 AD the Romans **arrived** in Britain	and **began** to take over the lands which we now call England and Wales.
Ausgangspunkt	danach

- Im Deutschen bildest du die Vorvergangenheitsform mit **hatte/hattest/hatten/hattet** oder **war/warst/waren/wart** + **Partizip Perfekt**. Im Englischen verwendest du jedoch immer **had (not)** + **past participle**:
  • *The Romans **had** first **come** to Britain in 55 BC.*
    Die Römer **waren** schon im Jahre 55 v. Chr. das erste Mal nach Britannien **gekommen**.

- Vorsicht bei der **Kurzform 'd**.
  • **would** + **infinitive**: *I**'d visit** the British Museum if I were you.*
    An deiner Stelle **würde** ich das British Museum **besuchen**.
  • **had** + **past participle**: *I**'d visited** the British Museum before.*
    Ich **hatte** das British Museum zuvor schon einmal **besucht**.

English summary

How it works	Examples
You use the past perfect simple (*had* + past participle) to talk about actions and situations that happened before a given time in the past.	- Before we visited the British Museum, we **had** already **learned** a lot about Roman Britain at school. - After we **had seen** everything, we all went to the cafeteria.
You can also use the past perfect simple to talk about an action that did not happen before the given time in the past.	- I **had** never **been** to an exhibition on Romans before.

Check-out

1. Setze die richtige Form ein. Überlege, ob die Handlung in Klammern weiter zurückliegt oder nicht.

   a) *When Peter arrived at school on Monday morning, the first lesson (already started/had already started).*
   b) *It was History and Peter (didn't like/hadn't liked) History because his teacher (was/had been) too strict.*
   c) *Peter apologized because he was late and then he (sat down/had sat down) quickly at his desk.*
   d) *When the teacher wanted to see his homework, he suddenly (remembered/ had remembered) that he (left/had left) it on the kitchen table.*

2. Setze die richtigen Formen des *simple past* oder des *past perfect simple* ein.

   The Romans arrived in Britain in 43 AD and (stay) for almost 400 years. Although Roman soldiers (already/come) to Britain about a hundred years before, it wasn't until the first century that Britain (become) part of the Roman Empire. By the time they (leave) again in the early 5th century, Britain (change) completely: the Romans (build) roads, towns, baths and palaces, and they (also/introduce) a new language as well as the calendar that we still use today.

The Celts **had been living** in Britain for hundreds of years.

G55 Die Verlaufsform des Plusquamperfekts
The past perfect progressive

Check-in

While you are visiting the British Museum, you do this quiz to win the book prize.

A QUIZ ABOUT ROMAN HISTORY

To win the book prize answer the questions below.

I When the Romans arrived in Britain in 43 AD, people known as the Celts **had** already **been living** there for ... .

☐ hundreds of years   ☐ fifty years   ☐ ten years

2 The Celtic Britons **had been keeping** farm animals and they **had** also **been growing** their own food for a long time before ... came.

☐ the Romans   ☐ the Vikings   ☐ the Normans

3 At the beginning of the ... century, the Romans had to leave Britannia to fight against tribes who **had been attacking** other parts of their Empire.

☐ 3rd   ☐ 4th   ☐ 5th

---

1. Schau dir die im Quiz hervorgehobenen Zeitformen an und vervollständige die folgende Regel:
   Das *past perfect progressive* wird mit … und dem … gebildet.

2. Beantworte die folgende Frage.
   How long had Celtic tribes been living in Britain before the Romans came?

REGEL

1. Mit dem *past perfect progressive* betonst du, dass eine **Handlung oder Situation vor einem bestimmten Zeitpunkt der Vergangenheit begonnen hatte und** zu diesem Zeitpunkt …
   a) **noch andauerte:**

simple past	past perfect progressive
When the Romans **arrived** in Britain in 43 AD,	the Celts **had** already **been living** there for hundreds of years.
Ausgangspunkt in der Vergangenheit	andauernde Handlung bis dahin und ggf. darüber hinaus

> **TIPP**
> Signalwörter sind z. B.: since, for, all (day), all the time, how long, already.

   b) **sich mehrfach wiederholt hatte (immer wieder):**

simple past	past perfect progressive
In the early 400s the Romans **left** Britain to fight against tribes	who **had been attacking** other parts of their Empire in Europe.
Ausgangspunkt in der Vergangenheit	sich wiederholende Handlung bis dahin und ggf. noch darüber hinaus

2. Das *past perfect progressive* bildest du mit **had been** und dem **present participle**.

Aussage:	The Celts **had been living** in houses for a long time before the Romans arrived.
Verneinung:	They **hadn't been living** in caves.
Entscheidungsfrage: mit Kurzantwort:	**Had** they **been growing** their own food? – Yes, they **had**. / No, they **hadn't**.

■ **Achtung!**
 – Beachte den Unterschied zum *past progressive*! Mit dem *past progressive* beschreibst du einen **Vorgang, der noch im Verlauf war als etwas Neues eintrat**.
   • *The Celts **were** already **living** in Britain when the Romans came.*
     Die Kelten lebten bereits in Britannien als die Römer kamen.
   Mit dem *past perfect progressive* betonst du, **wie lange ein Vorgang schon angedauert hatte** (z. B. jahrelang, seit 500 v. Chr., den ganzen Tag usw.), **bevor eine neue Handlung begann**.
   • *The Celts **had** already **been living** in Britain for hundreds of years before the Romans came.*
     Die Kelten hatten schon seit Jahrhunderten in Britannien gelebt, bevor die Römer kamen.

– Denk daran, dass die *progressive form* nur **bei Tätigkeitsverben** verwendet werden kann, z. B. *grow, keep, live*. **Zustandsverben** wie *be, believe, belong to, hear, hope, know, look, notice, remember, see, seem, smell, taste, understand, want, wish* usw. stehen normalerweise nur **in der *simple form***:

- *Our History teacher **had been** at the school for 15 years when he left.*

English summary

How it works	Examples
You use the past perfect progressive to stress how long an activity had continued before another event in the past happened. It is often used with an expression of time such as *since* or *for*.	– The Celts **had been farming** the land **for a long time** before the Romans came.
The past perfect progressive is also used for actions that happened repeatedly up to a point in the past (and continued after that point).	– John **had been talking** about going to the British Museum **since they began to learn about Roman history at school**.

Check-out

1. Setze die richtige Form ein. Überlege, ob sich die Handlung auf die Gegenwart oder auf einen Zeitpunkt in der Vergangenheit bezieht.

   a) *Is there a test tomorrow? But we (have only been learning/had only been learning) about Roman Britain for two weeks.*

   b) *The students (have only been learning/had only been learning) about Roman Britain for two weeks before the test last Monday.*

2. Übertrage die Lösung zu Aufgabe 1 ins Deutsche.

3. Vervollständige den Text mit der passenden Verbform. Verwende dabei das *past perfect simple* oder das *past perfect progressive*.

   When Tom got home from school, he was very tired because he (work) hard all day. He was also very hungry because he (forget) to take his sandwiches with him that day. They were still on the kitchen table, just where he (leave) them that morning. After he (eat) them, he decided to turn the TV on. He (only/watch) for a few minutes when he fell fast asleep.

10 Die Zeitformen der Zukunft

G56 Das Futur mit *going to*
The going to-future

Check-in

> I'm going to give you some information about our video conference now.

Mr Hilton is giving his class some information about the project with their Australian partner school. Read what he says.

Can I have your attention, everybody! I'**m going to give** you some information about our video conference with our Australian partner school now, so please listen carefully. First, you'**re going to find** a topic. Then, we'**re going to make** videos and at the end of the month we'**re going to show** each other our videos. We **aren't going to have** live presentations.

Why not, Sir?

That would be too difficult. And the next few weeks **are going to be** hard enough!

1. Schau dir die hervorgehobenen Zeitformen in den Sprechblasen oben an und trage die fehlenden Formen in eine Tabelle ein.

Subjekt	Form von *be*	*going to*	Infinitiv	restlicher Satz
I	*'m*	*going to*	*give*	*you some information.*
You	…	…	…	*a topic.*

2. Übertrage den folgenden Satz ins Deutsche. Wie machst du das Futur kenntlich?
   At the end of the month we're going to show each other our videos.

REGEL

1. Das *going to-future* verwendest du für …

(feststehende) Pläne und Absichten für die nahe Zukunft:	I'**m going to give** you some information about our video project now.
	At the end of the month we'**re going to show** each other our videos.
zukünftige Ereignisse, die sich in der Gegenwart schon abzeichnen:	There are topics to choose and videos to make. So the next few weeks **are going to be** hard enough!

2. Das *going to-future* wird gebildet aus einer **Form von** *be* + *going to* + **Infinitiv des Verbs**.

Aussage:	We**'re going to have** a video conference with our partner school in May.
Verneinung:	You **aren't going to work** on your own, but in groups of three.
Frage mit Fragewort:	When **is** the conference **going to be**?
Entscheidungsfrage mit Kurzantwort:	**Are** we **going to have** live presentations? – Yes, you **are**. / No, you **aren't**.

■ **Achtung!**
  – Um etwas Zukünftiges auszudrücken, kannst du im Deutschen das Präsens oder das Futur verwenden. **Im Englischen** musst du jedoch **immer eine Form des Futurs** benutzen. Vergleiche:
    • *At the end of the month we**'re going to show** each other our videos.*
      Am Ende des Monats **zeigen** wir uns unsere Videos.
      Am Ende des Monats **werden** wir uns unsere Videos **zeigen**.

■ **Schriftlicher/mündlicher Sprachgebrauch**
  – In der gesprochenen Umgangssprache hörst du manchmal ***gonna*** statt *going to*. Dies ist vor allem im amerikanischen Englisch der Fall.
    • Betty: *What are you **gonna do**?*
      Chris: *I'm **gonna do** something on cars.*
      Betty: *Really? Isn't that **gonna be** boring?*

English summary

How it works	Examples
The going to-future is made up of a form of *be + going to* + infinitive. You use the going to-future when … – you want to say what someone plans to do in the near future. – there are definite signs that something is sure to happen.	– Chris: I**'m going to ask** Mr Hilton a few questions about our project. – Jay: Watch out, Sir! That pile of papers **is going to fall** off your desk.

Check-out

1. Die englischen Schüler sollen ihrem Lehrer sagen, mit wem und worüber sie das Projekt machen wollen. Wie beantwortet Jay Mr Hiltons Fragen? Schreibe ganze Sätze.

  a) *Who are you going to do your project with?*   (Chris, Sarah)
  b) *What is your project going to be about?*   (cars)
  c) *How long is your video going to be?*   (five minutes)
  d) *Where are you going to make your video?*   (car factory)

I'll **interview** a British car maker.

G57 Das Futur mit *will*
The will-future

Check-in

Jay, Sarah and Chris have decided to work on the project together.
Read their conversation.

Jay: Why don't we do a project about cars?

Sarah: Good idea. How about: What kind of cars **will** we **have** 50 years from now?

Chris: Yeah, great. **I'll interview** a British car maker. I think that **will be** interesting for Australians.

Jay: Great, and **I'll be** the cameraman! Sarah, **will** you **write** an introduction for the interview?

Sarah: OK. But promise me that you **won't play** around with the camera!

1. Schau dir Sätze mit dem *will-future* genau an. Finde …

   a) eine Frage.
   b) die Kurzform von *will*.
   c) eine Aussage.
   d) eine verneinte Aussage.

2. Chris sagt: *I think that will be interesting for Australians.*
   Was drückt er damit aus?

   a) einen Plan, wie das Projekt bei den Australiern ankommen wird
   b) eine Vorhersage, wie das Projekt (wahrscheinlich) bei den Australiern ankommen wird
   c) ein Versprechen, wie das Projekt bei den Australiern ankommen wird

REGEL

1. Du verwendest das *will-future* um …

Vorhersagen über die Zukunft zu machen, die wahrscheinlich sind bzw. auf Vermutungen basieren:	In 50 years' time we **will have** safer and more environmentally friendly cars.
eine spontane Entscheidung auszudrücken:	**I'll interview** a British car maker.
eine persönliche Ansicht oder Hoffnung über die Zukunft zu äußern:	I'm sure that **will be** interesting for Australians.
ein Versprechen zu machen:	I promise that I **won't play** around with the camera.
zu sagen, dass etwas ganz sicher eintreten wird und nicht vom Sprecher beeinflusst werden kann:	Chris **will be** 16 next March.

TIPP
Das Futur mit „will"
kannst du auch
verwenden, um eine
Bitte auszudrücken,
z. B.: **Will** you **write**
an introduction?
(Schreibst du bitte
eine Einleitung?)

TIPP
Das Futur mit „will"
wird oft mit Wendungen
wie „I hope", „I'm sure",
„I think", „I expect"
oder Adverbien wie
„certainly", „definitely",
„maybe", „probably"
verwendet.

2. Das Futur mit *will* wird gebildet aus ***will*** (Kurzform: *'ll*) + **Infinitiv ohne** *to*. Die Verneinung lautet ***will not*** (Kurzform: ***won't***).

Aussagesatz:	I hope we**'ll find** enough information.
Verneinung:	There definitely **won't be** much time to prepare the project.
Frage mit Fragewort:	When **will** you **have** the interview with the car maker?
Entscheidungsfrage mit Kurzantwort:	**Will** we **have** safer cars in the future? – Yes, we **will**. / No, we **won't**.

◼ **Achtung!**
– Verwechsle nicht „Ich will" und *I will*! Vergleiche:
  • **Ich will** das Interview machen. = *I want to do the interview*. (= Wunsch)
  • *I will do the interview*. = **Ich werde** das Interview machen.
    (= spontane Entscheidung)

◼ **Schriftlicher/mündlicher Sprachgebrauch**
– In der mündlichen Sprache wird sehr häufig die **Kurzform von** *will* verwendet;
  fast immer nach Personalpronomen:
  • Jay: ***It'll*** *be interesting to find out more about the future of cars.*
  • Chris: *I think* ***you'll*** *do a good job with the camera, Jay.*

English summary

How it works	Examples
The will-future is made up of a form of *will* + infinitive without *to*. You use the will-future when … – you want to express a prediction about the future. – you have just made a spontaneous decision. – you say what you personally think or hope about a future event. – you promise something for the future. – you know something will happen that you can't change.	– 80 years from now we **won't have** cars any more. – Are you looking for more information? I**'ll help** you! – I hope these people **will have** time for an interview. – I promise that I**'ll be** a good cameraman. – Sarah **will be** 16 in November.

Check-out

1. Schreibe das Gespräch um, indem du Kurzformen verwendest.

Chris: *I phoned Royal Cars yesterday. They will have time for an interview on Monday.*
Jay: *I will come with you.*
Chris: *Good idea, we will both ask them questions.*

2. Vervollständige die folgenden Sätze mit dem *will-future.*

a) *I think a project about cars ... for students.*   (be interesting)
b) *In 80 years' time the world ... .*   (not have cars)

G58 Gegenüberstellung des Futurs mit *will* und *going to*
Comparing the will-future and the going to-future

> It**'s going to be** a great project. I**'ll help** you with it.

Check-in

Jay, Chris and Sarah meet in a chatroom to talk about their video project. Read what they say.

Jay
Sarah, I have already made three practice videos. (They are really quite good.) It**'s going to be** a great project – thanks to your fantastic expert cameraman! You**'re going to be** very happy with my work!!!

Chris
I**'m going to try** and interview two or three people. My dad knows a university professor and he**'s going to contact** him tomorrow. :)

Sarah
I have a maths test next week, which is too bad because I **won't have** a lot of time to work on the project. :(

Jay
I've just read your message, Sarah. I**'ll help** you with your maths test, don't worry. I**'ll meet** you after school tomorrow, how about that???

1. Ordne die folgenden Sätze aus den Einträgen oben ihrer Sprechabsicht zu.

a) *The practice videos are really good. You're going to be happy with my work.*
b) *My dad is going to contact the professor tomorrow.*
c) *I won't have a lot of time to work on the project.*
d) *I've just read your message. I'll help you with your maths test.*

   feststehender Plan

   spontane Entscheidung

➕ Vorhersage über die wahrscheinliche Zukunft

   Zukünftiges, das sich schon in der Gegenwart abzeichnet

2. Schau dir die Sätze in Aufgabe 1 noch einmal an. Formuliere dann eine Regel: Wann verwendest du das *going to-future*, wann das *will-future?*

REGEL

1. Ob du das Futur mit *going to* (→ **G56**) oder *will* (→ **G57**) verwenden musst, hängt davon ab, was genau du ausdrücken möchtest.

going to-future	Beispiel
a) Du möchtest ausdrücken, dass jemand einen (feststehenden) **Plan** oder eine bestimmte **Absicht für** die (nahe) **Zukunft** hat.	My dad **is going to contact** the professor tomorrow.
b) Du möchtest ausdrücken, dass es **in der Gegenwart** schon deutliche **Anzeichen** dafür gibt, **wie die Zukunft werden wird**.	The practice videos are really good. You**'re going to be** happy with my work.

will-future	Beispiel
c) Du möchtest eine **Vorhersage über die Zukunft** machen, die wahrscheinlich ist bzw. auf Vermutungen basiert.	I **won't have** a lot of time to work on the project because I have a maths test next week.
d) Du möchtest eine **spontane Entscheidung** ausdrücken.	I've just read your message. I**'ll help** you with your maths test.

English summary

How it works	Examples
Use the going-to-future when … – you want to say what someone plans to do in the near future. – there are definite signs that something is sure to happen.	– My dad has his telephone number. He**'s going to give** him a call tomorrow. – I've made three good practice videos. You**'re going to get** good pictures from me!
Use the will-future when … – you want to express a hope or prediction about the future, i.e. say something is likely to happen. – you make a spontaneous decision.	– I probably **won't have** time to collect any information for the introduction tomorrow. – Sarah: I don't understand this maths exercise! Jay: I**'ll come** over to your house and explain it to you.

Check-out

1. Vervollständige die Gedanken der Jugendlichen. Verwende das Futur mit *will* oder *going to*.

Sarah is a clever girl. With my help I'm sure she … (get) a good mark in her maths test.

I hope my maths test … (not be) too difficult.

I … (prepare) the questions now, and then I … (send) them to the people.

G59 Die einfache Gegenwart mit Futurbedeutung
The simple present with future meaning

My last lesson **finishes** at 3:30.

Check-in

Sarah and Chris need to arrange a meeting to work on their project. Here's what they say.

Chris: Sarah, we need to work on the introduction for our video. When have you got time?

Sarah: How about after school on Tuesday? My last lesson **finishes** at 3:30.

Chris: No, sorry. I'm busy on Tuesday afternoon. My guitar lesson **starts** at four. How about Tuesday evening?

Sarah: That's fine with me.

Chris: Great, I'll catch a bus to your house. There's one that **goes** at seven. But we must finish in time. The last bus **leaves** at 8:50.

Sarah: Oh I'm sure that will give us enough time.

1. Chris und Sarah unterhalten sich über einen Tag in der Zukunft. Welche Zeitform verwendet Sarah, um über ihre letzte Schulstunde zu sprechen?

2. Wie würde Chris auf Englisch sagen, dass seine Gitarrenstunde um 17 Uhr endet?

TIPP

Das simple present wird für feststehende Termine in der Zukunft verwendet. Deshalb wird es auch timetable future genannt.

1. Wenn du **über feststehende Termine in der Zukunft** wie z. B. den Anfang oder das Ende vom Unterricht oder von Veranstaltungen bzw. Zeiten in Fahrplänen sprechen möchtest, verwendest du das *simple present*.
2. Es wird häufig mit folgenden Verben verwendet: *arrive, begin, come, depart, end, finish, get (there / in), go, leave, start*.

Subjekt	simple present	Zeitangabe
The last lesson	**finishes**	at 3:30 pm.
The guitar class	**starts**	at 4 pm.
The bus	**goes**	at 7 pm.

◼ **Achtung!**

– Denk daran, dass du im Englischen eine Form des Futurs – z. B. das **will-future**, um eine Hoffnung auszudrücken – verwenden musst, wenn du über dich selbst und deine zukünftigen Handlungen sprechen willst.
  • *I hope I'll make it for the last bus.*
    Ich hoffe, ich **erwische** den letzten Bus.

– Das *simple present* wird auch **in Nebensätzen mit *if, when, as soon as*** verwendet, wenn der Hauptsatz Zukünftiges ausdrückt.
  • Sarah: *If we **work** quickly enough, you**'ll make** it for the last bus. We**'ll start** working **as soon as** you **arrive**.*

English summary

How it works	Examples
Use the simple present when you talk about times when events begin and end or public transport arrives and leaves.	– What time **does** the bus **arrive**? – It **arrives** at 7:15 pm.

Check-out

1. Jay und Chris wollen sich verabreden. Vervollständige ihren Dialog.
   Tipp: Achte auf das *timetable future* und das *will-future*.

18 Wednesday	**18** Wednesday
3:30–5 pm football practice (at stadium)	4–5:30 pm basketball training (at town centre)
Jay's diary	Chris's diary

Bus # 181

Stadium	5:00	5:15	5:30
Train station	5:05	5:20	5:35
Cathedral	5:15	5:30	5:45
Town centre	5:20	5:35	5:50

Jay: *Can we meet on Wednesday? Football practice … at five.*
Chris: *That's difficult. My basketball training … .*
Jay: *I can catch the bus to the town centre. There's a bus that … at 5:15.
So I … in the town centre shortly after 5:30.*
Chris: *I hope our trainer … on time.*

G60 Die Verlaufsform der Gegenwart mit Futurbedeutung
The present progressive with future meaning

> We **are meeting** in the computer room at 7 pm on Friday.

Check-in

Read the information that Mr McLaren from the Australian partner school has put on the school's intranet.

Re: Video conference with British partner school

Tim McLaren   May 12, 3:45 pm
Dear students,
This is to let you know the arrangements for our video conference in two weeks' time. We **are meeting** in the computer room at 7 pm on Friday, May 26. The video conference won't begin before 7:30, but we must get the computers and the projector started first.

Amanda Smith   May 12, 9:15 pm
Is the headmaster **coming** to the conference, too?

Tim McLaren   May 14, 10:22 am
No, he isn't. But some parents **are coming** because they are interested in our project.

---

1. Woher weißt du, dass es sich bei dem folgenden Satz um ein zukünftiges Ereignis handelt?
   We are meeting in the computer room at 7 pm on Friday.

2. Die Form *are meeting* oder *is coming* kennst du schon. Wie heißt diese Zeitform?

REGEL

1. Wenn du darüber reden möchtest, welche **festen Vereinbarungen oder Pläne** du **für die Zukunft** getroffen hast, verwendest du das *present progressive*.
2. Du benutzt es **in Verbindung mit einer Zeitangabe**, um deutlich zu machen, dass du nicht über die Gegenwart sprichst.

Subjekt	*present progressive*	Zeitangabe
We	**are meeting**	at 7 pm on May 26.
Some parents	**are coming** to the meeting	on Friday.

English summary

How it works	Examples
Use the present progressive when you talk about something that has already been arranged for the future.	– Mr McLaren **is giving** a short welcome speech at 7:30 pm. – Sarah's group **are presenting** their video at 7:40 pm Australian time.

Check-out

1. Chris erzählt Sarah aus seiner Arbeitsgruppe von dem Interviewtermin, den er vereinbart hat. Vervollständige die Sätze mit dem *present progressive*.

   On Monday morning I … (interview) someone from Royal Cars. We … (meet) in his office. Jay … (come) with me as our cameraman.

G61 Das Futur Perfekt (vollendete Zukunft)
The future perfect

> We **will have run** out of oil by 2060.

Check-in

During the conference Sarah, Chris and Jay are presenting their video "A world without oil". Read Chris's interview with a car maker.

Chris: We **will have run** out of oil by 2060 – that's what some experts say. That means **we will have run** out of fuel for our cars, too. And what will happen then? **Will** we **have found** alternative energy sources for our cars?

Car maker: I think we will. I'm optimistic. Car makers **will have built** cheap electric cars by then and we **won't have used** up all our oil by 2060. I'm pretty sure about that.

Chris: Thank you very much. Let's hear what oil expert Professor Cole from London University has to say …

1. Wenn es nach einigen pessimistischen Experten geht, was wird bis zum Jahre 2060 eingetreten sein? Formuliere deine Antwort in einem deutschen Satz.

2. Schau dir die hervorgehobenen Formen im Interview einmal genau an. Wie wird das *future perfect* gebildet?

REGEL

1. Wenn du sagen willst, dass eine **Handlung oder ein Vorgang zu** einem **bestimmten Zeitpunkt in der Zukunft abgeschlossen sein wird**, verwendest du das *future perfect*. Um diesen Zeitpunkt anzugeben, benutzt du eine Formulierung wie *by then*, *by 2060*, *in 50 years' time*, *within 50 years*.
2. Das *future perfect* setzt sich zusammen aus *will/won't + have + past participle*.

Aussage:	Some experts say we **will have run** out of oil by 2060.
Verneinung:	I'm optimistic that we **won't have used up** all our oil by then.
Entscheidungsfrage mit Kurzantwort:	**Will** we **have found** alternative energy sources for our cars by then? – Yes, we **will**. / No, we **won't**.

English summary

How it works	Examples
Use the future perfect if you want to say that at a given time in the future an action or an event has come to an end. You often use it together with adverbials like *by 2060, in 50 years' time* etc.	Chris: **Will** cars **have disappeared** by 2060? Car maker: I'm sure they **won't**. Companies **will have come** up with totally new ideas by then.

Check-out

1. Setze die folgenden Sätze, die mit dem *will-future* gebildet sind, in das *future perfect.*

   a) *Oil companies will discover new oil fields.*
      Professor Cole expects that … by 2060.
   b) *Scientists will invent new ways to produce energy.*
      He is sure that … in 30 years' time.
   c) *People will save a lot of energy.*
      He hopes that … by 2050.
   d) *The world will understand the importance of energy.*
      He thinks that … within the next 25 years.

11 Die Modalverben

G62 Die Merkmale von Modalverben
Characteristics of modal auxiliaries

You **must** fill in a form with details about your fitness.

Check-in

Paul wants to join a sports club. Look at the website he has found.

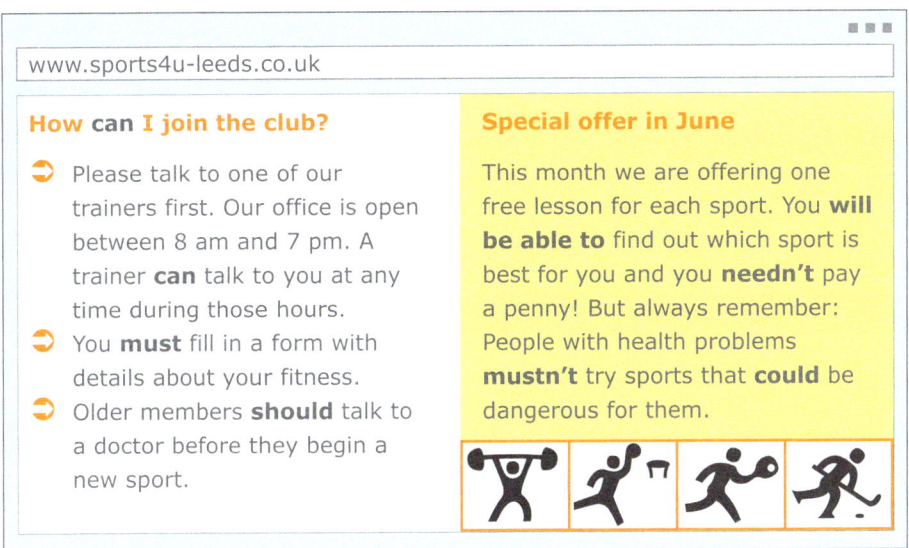

www.sports4u-leeds.co.uk

How can I join the club?

- Please talk to one of our trainers first. Our office is open between 8 am and 7 pm. A trainer **can** talk to you at any time during those hours.
- You **must** fill in a form with details about your fitness.
- Older members **should** talk to a doctor before they begin a new sport.

Special offer in June

This month we are offering one free lesson for each sport. You **will be able to** find out which sport is best for you and you **needn't** pay a penny! But always remember: People with health problems **mustn't** try sports that **could** be dangerous for them.

1. Die im Text hervorgehobenen Verben sind Modalverben. Schau sie dir noch einmal genau an und beantworte die folgenden Fragen.

   a) Welche Verbform folgt einem Modalverb?
   b) Wie werden Modalverben verneint?

REGEL

1. Die Modalverben *can, could, may, might, shall, should* und *must* haben **nur eine Form**:
   - *You can talk to a trainer today.*
   - *He can talk to you between 8 am and 7 pm.*
   Es gibt auch keine *-ing* und keine *-ed* Form.
2. Nach einem Modalverb verwendest du den **Infinitiv ohne *to***:
   - *You should talk to a doctor before you begin a new sport.*
3. Um Modalverben zu **verneinen oder** mit ihnen eine **Frage** zu stellen, brauchst du **kein zusätzliches Hilfsverb**:
   - *You needn't pay for your first lesson.*
   - *How can I join the club?*

4. Die meisten **Modalverben** werden nur **im *simple present*** verwendet. Für **alle anderen Zeitformen** benutzt du die Ersatzform ***have to**, **be able to*** bzw. ***be allowed to***:

• *You **will be able to** find out which sport is best for you.*

Die häufigsten Modalverben		
I	**can** help	you to find the best sport for you.
	Ich **kann** dir helfen, die beste Sportart für dich zu finden.	
Club members	**must** pay	at the beginning of each month.
	Klubmitglieder **müssen** zu Beginn jeden Monats bezahlen.	
	Shall I fill in	the form with you?
	Soll ich das Formular mit dir zusammen ausfüllen?	
You	**mustn't** spend	all your time at the sports club.
	Du **darfst nicht** deine ganze Zeit im Sportklub verbringen.	
You	**needn't** pay	for the first lesson.
	Du **brauchst** für die erste Stunde **nicht** zu bezahlen.	

Die Ersatzformen		
The trainer	**had to** answer	all my questions about fitness.
	Der Trainer **musste** alle meine Fragen zum Thema Fitness beantworten.	
I	**'ll be able to** go	to the yoga class tomorrow.
	Ich **werde** morgen zum Yogaunterricht gehen **können**.	
Katie	**wasn't allowed to** go	swimming because she had a cold.
	Katie **durfte nicht** schwimmen gehen, weil sie erkältet war.	

■ **Achtung!**
– Das Vollverb steht direkt nach dem Modalverb und nicht wie im Deutschen am Satzende. Vergleiche:
  • *The trainer **can talk** to you now.*
    Der Trainer **kann** jetzt mit dir **sprechen**.

■ **Mündlicher/schriftlicher Sprachgebrauch**
– **Wenn du dich unterhältst**, verwendest du bei der Verneinung der Modalverben meist die **Kurzform**, z. B. ***mustn't, shouldn't***. Im schriftlichen Englisch werden dir aber manchmal die **Langformen** begegnen, z. B. ***must not, should not***. Das ist der Fall, wenn der **Text förmlich** ist oder das **Modalverb betont** werden soll.

English summary

How it works	Examples
In the simple present modal verbs have only one form. They are followed by the infinitive of another verb without *to*.	− Paul **must tell** the trainer if he doesn't feel fit. − You **should try** a new sport.
You don't need another auxiliary verb (e.g. *do*) to form questions.	− **Can** you **come** to the tennis lesson next week?
Negative sentences are formed simply with *not* or *n't*.	− I've got a cold so I **can't** go to the club today.
Use the substitute forms (*have to, be able to, be allowed to*) for other tenses.	− He **was able to find** some useful information on the Internet.

Check-out

1. Verbinde die Satzteile mit einem passenden Modalverb.

can • can't • must • should • able to • allowed to

I can play football but I	swim.
Sports club members	join the club because I was too young.
My back hurts. Maybe I	pay at the beginning of each month.
The trainer wants to know if you	see you tomorrow morning.
I wasn't	play rugby.
The doctor will be	see a doctor before I start rugby training.

G63 Eine Fähigkeit mit *can*, *could* und *be able to* ausdrücken
Can, could *and* be able to *to talk about ability*

I **can** jog for nearly an hour.

Check-in

Paul is joining a sports club. Here's part of the form he is filling in.

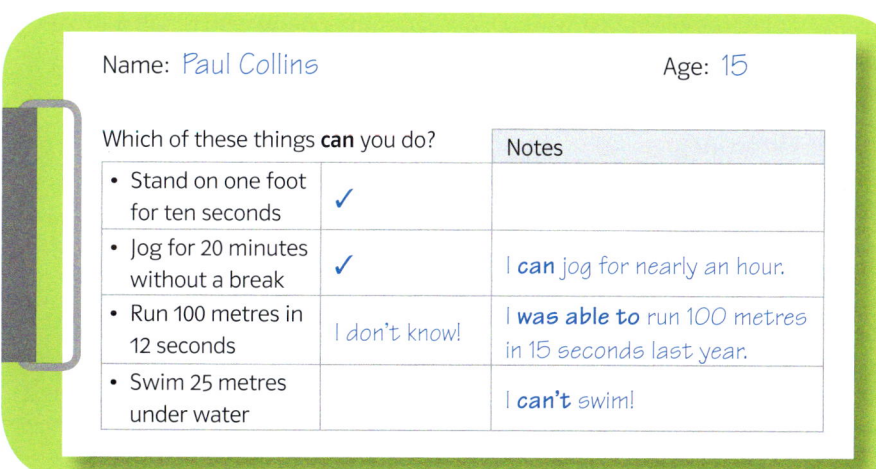

Name: Paul Collins   Age: 15

Which of these things **can** you do?		Notes
• Stand on one foot for ten seconds	✓	
• Jog for 20 minutes without a break	✓	I **can** jog for nearly an hour.
• Run 100 metres in 12 seconds	I don't know!	I **was able to** run 100 metres in 15 seconds last year.
• Swim 25 metres under water		I **can't** swim!

1. Beantworte die folgenden Fragen mit der Kurzantwort *Yes, he can.* oder *No, he can't.*

a) *Can Paul jog for 20 minutes without a break?*
b) *Can he swim under water?*

2. Schau dir die rechte Spalte auf dem Formular noch einmal genau an und vervollständige die folgende Regel:

Nach dem Verb *can* folgt immer der ... ohne ... .

TIPP

Manchmal wird die Ersatzform „be able to" auch im simple present verwendet, z. B.: Paul **isn't able to** walk on his hands.

REGEL

1. Mit dem Modalverb *can* drückst du aus, dass jemand **etwas kann**. Die verneinte **Form lautet *can't***:
  • *Paul **can't** swim.*
2. Im *simple past* verwendest du die Formen *could* und *couldn't* oder die Ersatzform *be able to*:
  • *I **couldn't** go / **wasn't able to** go to my swimming lesson yesterday.*
3. Die **Ersatzform** verwendest du auch für alle übrigen **Zeitformen der Vergangenheit und der Zukunft**:

can, could und *be able to* (können)		
simple present	I **can** play	tennis.
	Carlo **can't** run	very fast.
simple past	He **could** swim	when he was very young.
	I **was able to** go ice skating	every day last winter.
present perfect	Lucy **has been able to** play	in every important hockey match this year.
past perfect	Mike **had been able to** swim	for years before he had swimming lessons at school.
will-future	She **'ll be able to** play	on the national volleyball team next year.

■ **Achtung!**
  – Die Verneinung *can't* wird von Briten und Amerikanern unterschiedlich ausgesprochen: Im britischen Englisch hört man [kɑːnt] und im amerikanischen [kænt]. Letzteres klingt fast wie *can*, der Zusammenhang wird dir aber helfen, die beiden Formen zu unterscheiden.

English summary

How it works	Examples
You use the modal verb *can* to talk about ability in the simple present tense.	– Caroline **can** play volleyball.
You normally use *could* in the simple past. You can use *be able to* in all tenses, but you must use it for the future, the present perfect and past perfect tense.	– I **could** ride a pony when I was four years old. – We**'ll be able to** use the new gym next month.

Check-out

1. Setze *can, can't, could, couldn't* oder *be able to* in der richtigen Zeitform ein.

I'm not very fit. I … run very far and I'm not very fast. But I'm good at some sports. I … swim better than most people my age. I think that's because I … swim when I was very young. It has always been easy for me. My friend Monica … swim when she was a small child and it's very hard for her to learn now. I want to get fitter and be good at other sports, too. I hope I … learn some new sports when I join the sports club next month.

G64 Eine Erlaubnis oder ein Verbot mit *can, may, mustn't* und *be allowed to* ausdrücken   Can, may, mustn't *and* be allowed to *to say what is (not) allowed*

You**'re not allowed** to hold your stick so high!

Check-in

Paul is playing hockey for the first time. He doesn't know all the rules yet. Read what his trainer tells him.

Trainer: Stop! You**'re not allowed to** hold your stick so high! You **mustn't** do that!

Paul: Why not?

Trainer: It's dangerous. You **can** hold the stick below your shoulder, not higher.

Paul: But the ball was flying high up in the air!

Trainer: That's dangerous, of course. You **may** stop the ball when it's in the air but you **mustn't** hit it. It's not tennis!

1. Vervollständige die beiden Sätze.

a) Den Hockeyschläger über Schulterhöhe zu halten ist (erlaubt/nicht erlaubt).

b) Einen durch die Luft fliegenden Hockeyball zu schlagen ist (erlaubt/nicht erlaubt).

REGEL

1. Mit den Modalverben *can, may* und der Ersatzform *be allowed to* kannst du ausdrücken, dass jemand **etwas tun darf**:
   • *You **may** stop the ball when it's flying.*

2. Wenn du ausdrücken möchtest, dass jemand **etwas nicht tun darf**, verwendest du die verneinten Formen *can't, may not, not be allowed to* oder *mustn't*:
   • *You**'re not allowed to** hold your stick so high!*

3. Die Modalverben *can, may* und *mustn't* kannst du nur **im *simple present*** verwenden. Die **Ersatzform *be allowed to*** verwendest du an Stelle des Modalverbs, wenn du über die **Zukunft** oder die **Vergangenheit** sprechen möchtest:

can, may, be allowed to (können, dürfen) und mustn't (nicht dürfen)		
simple present	He **can** stop	the ball with his stick.
	Can I throw the ball?	I throw the ball?
	All players **may** try	to score a goal.
	A player **may not** hit	another player.
	They **mustn't** hit	the ball in the air.
	May I play	in goal now?
	Are you **allowed to** hold	the ball in your hands?
	Paul **isn't allowed to** play	hockey on school days.
simple past	We **were allowed to** play	every day during the holidays.
present perfect	I **haven't been allowed to** run	since I broke my leg.
past perfect	After Paul **had been allowed to** join	the club, he became a member of the hockey team.
will-future	They **won't be allowed to** watch	all the matches when school starts again.

■ **Achtung!**
– Mit dem Modalverb *could* kannst du auch höflich um Erlaubnis bitten. Du verwendest es allerdings nur, um zu fragen, ob du etwas **Bestimmtes** tun darfst. Wenn du fragen willst, ob etwas **im Allgemeinen** erlaubt ist, verwende lieber *can*. Vergleiche:
  • *This game is hard! Could I have a little break?* (= bestimmt, in diesem Spiel) Das Spiel ist hart. **Könnte** ich eine kleine Pause machen?
  • *I'm not sure about the rules. Can I catch the ball?* (= allgemein, in allen Spielen) Ich bin mir nicht sicher wie die Regeln sind. **Darf** ich den Ball fangen?

■ **Mündlicher/schriftlicher Sprachgebrauch**
– Das Modalverb *may* ist viel **förmlicher als** *can* und wird daher öfter in der Schriftsprache verwendet. Wenn du zum Beispiel Spielregeln durchliest, wirst du oft Sätze wie diesen finden:
  • *Players **may not** use their hands to stop the ball.*

English summary

How it works	Examples
You use *can*, *may* and *be allowed to* if you want to say that someone is allowed to do something.	– You **can** borrow a hockey stick from the sports club.
You use *can't*, *may not*, *mustn't* and *not be allowed to* if you want to say that someone is not allowed to do something.	– The game starts at two and you **mustn't** be late.
The verbs *can*, *may* and *mustn't* can only be used in the simple present. *Be allowed to* can be used in all tenses.	– We **will not be allowed to** use the swimming pool next Saturday because there is a competition in the pool then.

Check-out

1. Vervollständige die Sätze mit *can*, *can't* oder einer Form von *be allowed to*.

   a) *We don't have a school uniform for sports. I … wear anything I want.*
   b) *In my last school I … choose between hockey, rugby and tennis.*
   c) *Next year I … join the school hockey team.*
   d) *Now that we've got a new gym, we … play tennis there after school.*

G65 **Mit *must*, *needn't* und *have to* ausdrücken, was (nicht) notwendig ist** Must, needn't *and* have to *to talk about what is (not) necessary*

You **must** wear the correct sports shoes for all sports.

Check-in

Paul has joined the sports club now. Here are some of the rules.

Club rules

1. You **must** wear the correct sports shoes for all sports.
2. Don't wear shoes in the area around the swimming pool.
3. Please keep the changing rooms clean. Remember, you **have to** share them with a lot of other people.
4. You **needn't** bring your own racket. You can borrow one at the club.
5. No chewing gum, please!

1. Im Text steht *You must wear the correct sports shoes.* Könnte man auch sagen *You have to wear the correct sports shoes*?

2. Wie übersetzt du *needn't* in der Vereinsregel 4 ins Deutsche?

REGEL

1. Mit *must* und der Ersatzform *have to* drückst du aus, dass **etwas notwendig** ist. Wenn du sagen möchtest, dass **etwas nicht notwendig** ist, verwendest du *needn't* oder *not have to* („nicht müssen", „nicht brauchen"):
   • *You **must** wear sport shoes.*
2. Die Modalverben *must* und *needn't* stehen nur **im *simple present*, *have to*** kannst du **in allen Zeiten** verwenden:
   • *He **had to** clean the changing rooms.*
3. Da *have to* ein Vollverb ist, brauchst du **bei Fragen und Verneinungen** das **Hilfsverb *do***:
   • ***Do** you **have to** buy special shoes for hockey?*
   • *He **didn't have to** buy a hockey stick.*

TIPP
Manchmal wird auch „can't" benutzt um ein Verbot auszudrücken: You **can't** wear those shoes for tennis.

must, have to (müssen, brauchen) und needn't (nicht müssen, nicht brauchen)		
simple present	You	**must** wear	the correct shoes.
		Must we follow	all these rules?
	You	**needn't** bring	your own racket.
	You	**don't have to** do	any sports that you don't like.
	Paul	**has to** learn	how to swim.
simple past	We	**had to** share	the pool with a group of children.
	She	**didn't have to** go	to training yesterday.
present perfect	He	**has had to** buy	new football boots because his old ones were too small.
past perfect	If he	**had had to** go	to school every afternoon, he couldn't have played football for our team.
will-future	Club members	**won't have to** pay	more next year.
		Will we **have to** clean	the changing rooms ourselves?

■ **Achtung!**

– Mit *must* und *have to* kannst du ausdrücken, dass etwas notwendig ist. Die Verneinungen dieser Modalverben – *mustn't* und *don't have to* (bzw. *needn't*) – werden aber unterschiedlich verwendet. ***Mustn't*** bedeutet nicht „nicht müssen", sondern „**nicht dürfen**". Vergleiche:
  • *You **mustn't** wear football boots in the fitness room.*
    Du **darfst** im Fitnessraum keine Fußballschuhe tragen.
  • *You **don't have to**/**needn't** buy your own hockey stick.*
    Du **musst**/**brauchst keinen** Hockeyschläger kaufen.

English summary

How it works	Examples
You use *must* and *have to* to say that something is necessary.	– Everybody **has to** read the club rules.
You use *needn't* and *not have to* to say that something is not necessary.	– You **don't have to** do sports that you don't enjoy.
Must and *needn't* can only be used in the simple present. *Have to* can be used in all tenses.	– We **will have to** practise more often.

Check-out

1. Übertrage die folgenden Sätze ins Deutsche.

   a) *I must buy some good football boots.*
   b) *We don't have to clean the changing rooms.*
   c) *Frank is tired. He needn't go to training.*
   d) *Did you have to buy expensive tennis shoes?*
   e) *They didn't have to pay for the swimming lessons.*

G66 Mit *shall* und *should* etwas vorschlagen oder raten
Shall *and* should *to make suggestions or give advice*

Should I eat more before I play?

Check-in

Paul has joined the hockey team, but he feels that he is not playing well enough. He talks to another person on the team. Read their conversation.

Paul: I don't have enough energy to play for the whole match. **Should** I eat more before I play?

Leo: No. You **shouldn't** eat too much before a hockey match. But you **should** do more for your fitness. Do you go jogging?

Paul: No. I think jogging is boring.

Leo: Well, it's more fun if you do it with a friend. Let's go together. **Shall** I come to your house on Saturday morning? We could jog in the park near where you live.

Paul: OK, let's do that. Thanks!

1. Übertrage die folgenden beiden Fragen ins Deutsche.

   a) *Should I eat more?*
   b) *Shall I come to your house on Saturday?*

2. Welche der beiden Fragen aus Aufgabe 1 bezieht sich auf eine einmalige Situation und welche bittet allgemein um Rat?

REGEL

1. Mit *should* kannst du ausdrücken, dass jemand **etwas tun sollte**. Du kannst damit einen **Rat geben** oder **um Rat fragen**:
   - *You **should** go jogging.*
   - ***Should** I go jogging more often?*
2. Mit *shouldn't* kannst du ausdrücken, dass jemand **etwas nicht tun sollte**:
   - *You **shouldn't** eat too much.*
3. Mit der Frage ***Shall I ...?*** bzw. ***Shall we ...?*** kannst du etwas **vorschlagen oder anbieten**.

should und *shall* (sollen)		
You	**should** do	a sport regularly.
Paul	**shouldn't** drink	fizzy drinks before a hockey game.
	Should we wear	jogging shoes when we play hockey?
Where	**should** I buy	my sports shoes?
	Shall I help	you to improve your fitness?
	Shall we ask	our trainer for help?

English summary

How it works	Examples
You can use *should* to say that something is a good idea and to give advice.	– School children **should** get some exercise every day.
You can use *shouldn't* to say that you don't think something is a good idea.	– You **shouldn't** eat so many sweets.
You can use *shall* in questions to make a suggestion or an offer.	– You need a hockey stick. **Shall** I go with you to buy one?

Check-out

1. Vervollständige den Dialog mit *should*, *shouldn't* oder *shall*.

   Paul: *I need a new hockey stick. What do you think? ... I buy it online or go to a shop?*

   Leo: *I think you ... go to a shop. You ... buy it online because it's better to hold it in your hands before you buy it. You have to know if it feels right.*

   Paul: *OK. Which shop ... I go to?*

   Leo: *The big sports shop in the centre of town is the best. ... I go with you?*

   Paul: *Oh yes, that would be great. Thanks!*

G67 Mit *could*, *may* und *might* sagen, was möglich ist
Could, may *and* might *to express possibilities*

> We **could** play on Thursday and Friday evening, for example.

Check-in

Paul's hockey team is playing an important match next week. Read the chat.

Paul M
I'm so excited about the match next week! We're playing against a good team, but I think we **might** win!

Tony Q
Let's do some extra training before the match. We **could** play on Thursday and Friday evening, for example.

Paul M
I think that **might** be too much. We don't want to get tired before the match.

Tony Q
OK, you're right.

Karen S
Hi you two. I'm really looking forward to the match. I **may** be a bit late but I'll definitely see the second half. Good luck!

---

1. Wie lautet die richtige Antwort?

   a) Wird Pauls Mannschaft das Spiel gewinnen?   ja / nein / vielleicht
   b) Wird Karen zu spät zum Spiel kommen?   ja / nein / vielleicht

TIPP
Die Wahrscheinlich-
keit ist bei „might"
geringer als bei
„may":
– It **may** rain on
Saturday.
– It **might** even
snow.

1. Mit den Modalverben *could, may* und *might*, drückst du aus, dass **etwas möglich ist** oder **vielleicht passieren wird**:
   • *Paul's hockey team **could/may/might** win the match.*
2. Wenn du fragen willst, **ob etwas vielleicht passieren wird**, benutzt du *could* oder *might*, nicht *may*:
   • ***Could/Might** they win the match?*

could, may und *might* (könnten)		
We	**could** lose **Could** we win	the match if Tom and Jim don't play. against such a good team?
Paul's friends	**may** watch	the match.
Karen	**might** arrive **Might** they cancel	a little bit late. the match if it rains?

■ **Achtung!**
  – Das Modalverb *could* hat verschiedene Bedeutungen:
  a) Du kannst *could* („könnte") verwenden, um auszudrücken, dass etwas **möglich** ist.
     • *We want to play on Saturday, but the weather **could** be too bad.*
       Wir wollen am Samstag spielen, aber das Wetter **könnte** zu schlecht sein.
  b) *Could* („konnte") gibt es aber auch als die **simple past-Form von** *can*.
     • *It rained a bit last Saturday, but we **could** play anyway.*
       Es hat letzten Samstag geregnet, aber wir **konnten** trotzdem spielen.
  c) Du benutzt *could* auch, um eine **höfliche Frage** einzuleiten.
     • ***Could** you help me?*
       Könntest du mir helfen?

English summary

How it works	Example
Could, *may* and *might* are modal verbs that you use to say that something is possible and maybe it will happen in the future.	– England **may** become the world champion next year.

Check-out

1. Übertrage die folgenden Sätze ins Deutsche bzw. Englische.

   a) *Carl could join our sports club next month.*
   b) *I might learn to play rugby.*
   c) *Lisa may become the best player on the team.*
   d) Könnten wir nächsten Sonntag spielen?
   e) Ich werde vielleicht das Spiel im Fernsehen anschauen.
   f) Die Mannschaft könnte das Spiel verlieren.

G68 Modalverben mit dem Infinitiv Perfekt
Modal auxiliaries with the perfect infinitive

Well, it **could have been** worse.

Check-in

Paul hurt his leg while he was playing hockey. His friend Leo went to visit him. Read their conversation.

Paul: The ball hit me on the leg. Hockey balls are really hard!

Leo: Oh, that **must have hurt** a lot.

Paul: Well, it **could have been** worse. At least it didn't hit me on the head!

Leo: Well, sports are dangerous. You **should have stayed** at home on Saturday and watched TV.

1. Beantworte die folgenden Fragen auf Deutsch.

   a) Weiß Leo genau, wie schmerzhaft Pauls Verletzung war?
   b) Ist Paul letzten Samstag zu Hause vorm Fernseher geblieben?

2. Schau dir die hervorgehobenen Verbformen im Gespräch oben noch einmal genau an und vervollständige die folgende Regel:

   Um über Dinge zu reden, die in der Vergangenheit hätten geschehen können, sollen oder müssen, verwendest du ein Modalverb + … + *past participle*.

REGEL

1. Du kannst **Modalverben** zusammen **mit** dem **Infinitiv Perfekt** benutzen, **wenn du sagen möchtest**, **was in der Vergangenheit hätte geschehen müssen**, **können oder sollen**.
2. Du bildest den Infinitiv Perfekt mit *must, might, could, should(n't)* oder *needn't + have + past participle*.

Beispiel	Deutsch
He can't walk. He **must have broken** his leg.	Er kann nicht gehen. Er muss sich sein Bein gebrochen haben.
He **might have had** a sports accident.	Er könnte vielleicht einen Sportunfall gehabt haben.
Why didn't you ask me? I **could have driven** you to hospital.	Warum hast du mich nicht gefragt? Ich hätte dich ins Krankenhaus fahren können.
He **should have asked** me for help.	Er hätte mich um Hilfe bitten sollen.
The hockey team **shouldn't have played** so aggressively.	Die Hockeymannschaft hätte nicht so aggressiv spielen sollen.
He **needn't have gone** to hospital alone.	Er hätte nicht allein ins Krankenhaus gehen müssen.

■ **Achtung!**

– **Needn't have** und **didn't need to** haben unterschiedliche Bedeutungen. Vergleiche:

- He **needn't have** gone to hospital.
  Er **hätte nicht** ins Krankenhaus gehen **brauchen/müssen**.
  (Er ist aber gegangen.)
- He **didn't need to** go to hospital.
  Er **brauchte nicht** ins Krankenhaus zu gehen.
  (Er ist auch nicht da hingegangen.)

English summary

How it works	Examples
You can use modal auxiliaries and the perfect infinitive (*have* + past participle) to say that maybe something happened in the past, or that it might have been different.	– Our goalkeeper isn't here. He **must have forgotten** about the match. – You've got a bad cold. You **shouldn't have gone** ice skating yesterday.

Check-out

1. Vervollständige die Sätze mit *must, needn't, should* oder *shouldn't* und dem *past participle* der folgenden Verben: *be, wear, win, worry*.

a) *Kath looks happy. She … have … the tennis match.*

b) *Serkan … have … his glasses while he was playing volleyball.*

c) *You … have … more careful!*

d) *I … have … about winning this race. Nobody is faster than me!*

12 Das Passiv

G69 Die Bildung und Verwendung des Passivs
Forming and using the passive voice

Emma Perry **was driven** to the opening of the new Broadway show.

Check-in

You are in New York on vacation. Yesterday you saw how two celebrities arrived at a Broadway theater.

1. Welcher Satz gehört zu welchem Bild?

   a) *Kate Smith drove to the opening of the new Broadway show.*
   b) *Emma Perry was driven to the opening of the new Broadway show.*

REGEL

1. In Abbildung 1 **wurde** der Star zur Eröffnung der neuen Broadway-Show **gefahren**: *Emma Perry **was driven** to the new Broadway show*. Wenn du **betonen** willst, **was mit einer Person oder einer Sache geschieht**, verwendest du das **Passiv**. Dabei bleibt der **Verursacher** der Handlung (hier: der Chauffeur) **meist unerwähnt**, weil er unwichtig oder unbekannt ist.
2. Das Passiv wird im Englischen aus einer **Form von *be* + *past participle*** gebildet, z. B. *are driven, was photographed, have been cut, will be shown*. Eine Liste der unregelmäßigen Verben und ihrer *past participles* findest du ab Seite 261.
3. In der nachfolgenden Tabelle stehen die vier häufigsten Zeitformen des Passivs. Eine Liste aller Zeitformen findest du im Abschnitt G71.

	Passiv
simple present	Celebrities **are** usually **driven** to special events.
simple past	The actress was **photographed** when she arrived at the theater last night.
present perfect	Ben Johnson's hair **has been cut** for his new role.
will-future	The new film **will be shown** in cinemas in April.

TIPP
Aktiv bedeutet tatkräftig. Daher verwendest du das Aktiv, wenn dir wichtig ist zu sagen, **wer etwas tut**, also aktiv ist und handelt: She **drove** to the opening of the new Broadway show.

Passiv heißt soviel wie untätig. Folglich verwendest du das Passiv, um auszudrücken, dass **etwas mit einer Person oder einer Sache getan wird**.

■ **Achtung!**

– Im Deutschen verwendest du eine Form von „werden" für das Passiv, im Englischen dagegen eine Form von *be*. Vergleiche:
  • *The actress **is admired** worldwide.*
    Die Schauspielerin **wird** weltweit **bewundert**.

– Im Deutschen wird eine Form von „werden" nicht nur zur Bildung des Passivs, sondern auch zur Bildung der Zukunftsform verwendet. Vergleiche:
  • Zukunft: Ich **werde** morgen zur Eröffnung **kommen**.
    *I **will come** to the opening tomorrow.*
  • Passiv: Die Schauspielerin **wird** oft **interviewt**.
    *The actress **is** often **interviewed**.*

– Verb und Präposition sind im Englischen eng miteinander verbunden. Deshalb darfst du sie auch im Passivsatz nicht trennen:
  • *For big premieres, the streets around the theater **are** always **closed off** so you can't get too near the stars.*

■ **Schriftlicher/mündlicher Sprachgebrauch**

– Das Passiv wird häufig in Beschreibungen von Experimenten, in Nachrichten, Protokollen, Zeitungsberichten oder Regeln verwendet:
  • *The audience **were asked** to turn off their cell phones before the show.*
    Das Publikum wurde vor Beginn der Aufführung gebeten, die Handys auszuschalten.

– In Zeitungsüberschriften wird die Form von *be* oft ausgelassen, z. B. *New musical theater **opened***. Um welche Zeitform es sich handelt, wird im Bericht deutlich.

English summary

How it works	Example
You use the passive voice to express what happens to a person or thing. You form the passive with a form of *be* and the past participle of the verb.	– Emma Perry **has been named** *Best Musical Actress of the Year*.

Check-out

1. Was wird in einem Theater gemacht? Schreibe vollständige Sätze und verwende dabei das *simple present* des Passivs.

   a) *sell tickets*   c) *offer backstage tours*
   b) *perform musicals* d) *make costumes*

2. Was geschah nach der Uraufführung des Musicals? Vervollständige die Sätze mit dem *simple past* des Passivs.

   a) *A number of speeches (make).*
   b) *All the actors (thank) for their hard work.*
   c) *Five fans (invite) to the after-show party.*
   d) *The main stars of the evening (interview) for television.*

G70 Der *by-agent*
The by-agent

> The original story was written **by William Shakespeare**.

Check-in

You'd like to see a musical in New York. At the tourist information you pick up this flyer.

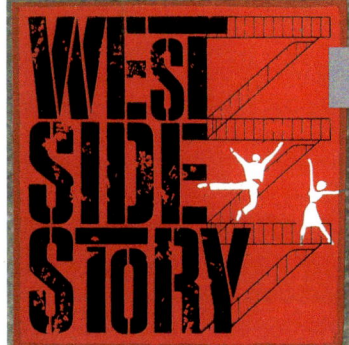

West Side Story

NOW PLAYING AT THE PALACE THEATER

West Side Story is a world-famous musical. The story is set in New York. It is about the Jets and the Sharks, two teenage street gangs. The original story *Romeo and Juliet* was written **by William Shakespeare** between 1591 and 1595. In the 1950s the words of the songs were written **by Stephen Sondheim** and the music was composed **by Leonard Bernstein**.
Since its first performance in 1957 the musical has been translated into other languages and has been enjoyed **by audiences all over the world**.

1. Beantworte die folgenden Fragen auf Deutsch.

   a) Von wem wurden die Songtexte des Musicals geschrieben?
   b) Steht im Text, von wem das Musical in andere Sprachen übersetzt wurde?

REGEL

1. Wenn du in einem englischen **Passivsatz** erwähnen möchtest, wer der **Verursacher der Handlung** (= Agens) ist, verwendest du den so genannten *by-agent*: ... **by** *William Shakespeare*, ... **by** *Leonard Bernstein*.
2. Du kannst den *by-agent* weglassen, wenn es unwichtig ist zu sagen, von wem etwas getan wird, z.B. von wem das Musical übersetzt wurde. Du entscheidest im Einzelfall, ob der *by-agent* eine wichtige Zusatzinformation ist oder nicht.
3. Bei der Umwandlung eines Aktivsatzes in einen Passivsatz wird das **Objekt des Aktivsatzes** (*the music*) zum **Subjekt des Passivsatzes**. Das **Subjekt des Aktivsatzes wird zum Agens** im Passivsatz, dem die Präposition *by* vorangestellt wird. Vergleiche:

	Subjekt	Verb	Objekt
Aktivsatz	**Leonard Bernstein**	composed	**the music.**

	Subjekt	Verb	Objekt
Passivsatz	**The music**	was composed	**by Leonard Bernstein.**

English summary

How it works	Examples
If it is important to mention who does or did something in a passive sentence, you use the *by-agent*.	– *Romeo and Juliet* **was written** by Shakespeare. Tonight the part of Juliet **will be played** by Susan Lee.

Check-out

1. Schreibe einen kurzen Artikel für die Kulturzeitung. Vervollständige dazu die Sätze mit dem *simple present, simple past* oder *present perfect* des Passivs und dem *by-agent*, wo nötig.

   Perry presented with award
   Yesterday the new musical season opened at the River Theater with a performance of Alice, the musical which (love / children and adults) everywhere. Since it (first perform) in London in 2005, it (enjoy / audiences) all over the world. The River Theater (design / architects from Florida) and (build) in the late 1990s. Last night the show (attend / 1,740 people). At the after-show party Emma Perry (present) with the Award for Best Musical Actress of the Year. Perry (discover / Alan Smith) three years ago. After the presentation of the award a delicious meal (enjoy / the party guests), who celebrated until the early hours of the morning.

> The Empire State Building Run-up **is being held** at the moment.

G71 Das Passiv in den verschiedenen Zeiten
The different tenses of the passive voice

Check-in

While you're in New York, you'd like to find out more about the Empire State Building. This is what you find on its website.

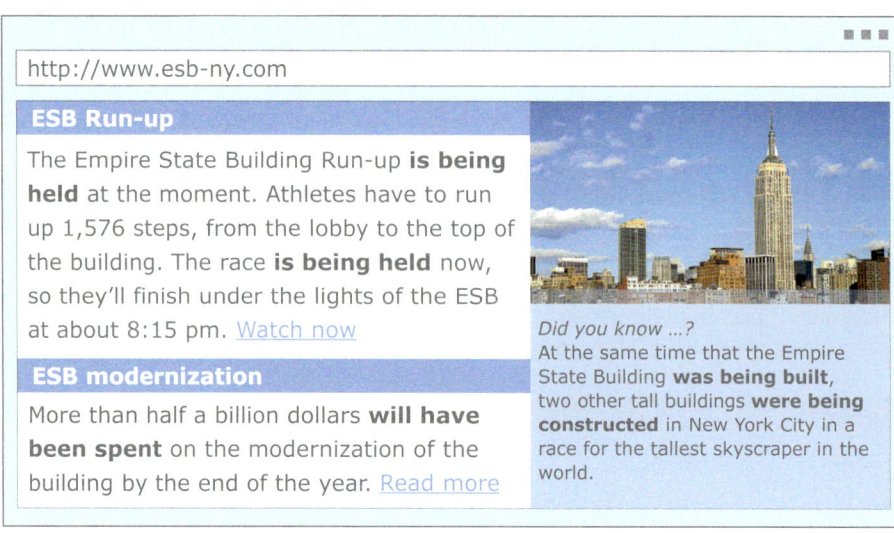

http://www.esb-ny.com

ESB Run-up

The Empire State Building Run-up **is being held** at the moment. Athletes have to run up 1,576 steps, from the lobby to the top of the building. The race **is being held** now, so they'll finish under the lights of the ESB at about 8:15 pm. Watch now

ESB modernization

More than half a billion dollars **will have been spent** on the modernization of the building by the end of the year. Read more

Did you know ...?
At the same time that the Empire State Building **was being built**, two other tall buildings **were being constructed** in New York City in a race for the tallest skyscraper in the world.

1. Bestimme die hervorgehobenen Zeitformen in den folgenden Passivsätzen.

   a) The ESB Run-up **is being held** at the moment.
   b) At the time same that the Empire State Building **was being built**, two other tall buildings **were being constructed** in New York City.
   c) More than half a billion dollars **will have been spent** on the modernization of the building by the end of the year.

REGEL

1. Das Passiv wird, wie du in ➔ **G69** gelernt hast, in allen Zeiten aus einer **Form von *be* + *past participle*** gebildet. Für den Gebrauch der einzelnen Zeitformen im Passiv gelten dieselben Regeln wie im Aktiv.

	Passiv
simple present ➔ G43, G59	The Empire State Building Run-up **is held** every year.
present progressive ➔ G44, G60	The Empire State Building Run-up **is being held** at the moment.
present perfect ➔ G46	The Empire State Building Run-up **has been held** every year since 1978.
past perfect ➔ G54	After it **had been completed**, the Empire State Building became a great tourist attraction.
simple past ➔ G49	The Empire State Building **was** officially **opened** in 1931.
past progressive ➔ G50	At the same time that the Empire State Building **was being built**, two other tall buildings **were being constructed** in New York City in a race for the tallest skyscraper in the world.
going to-future ➔ G56	The Empire State Building **is going to be shown** in the colors red, orange and yellow for Thanksgiving.
will-future ➔ G57	The last tickets for the observation deck **will be sold** at 1:15 am.
future perfect ➔ G61	More than half a billion dollars **will have been spent** on the modernization of the building by the end of the year.
conditional	The lights at the top of the ESB can change color. For example, if it was Easter today, green, pink and yellow lights **would be used**.
conditional perfect	If things hadn't gone so unexpectedly well, the ESB **would** never **have been completed** so quickly. In fact, it was finished in only 15 months.

TIPP
Im Passiv gibt es nur zwei progressive-Formen, das present progressive und das past progressive.

English summary

How it works	Examples
The rules for the use of the different tenses in the passive (form of *be* + past participle) are the same as the rules for the use of the active forms. There are two progressive forms – the present progressive and the past progressive.	– Since the Empire State Building opened, lots of tickets **have been sold** to visitors from all over the world. – While we were in New York a new skyscraper **was being built**.

Check-out

1. Bilde Passivsätze mit den Angaben in Klammern.

   a) *In the Empire State Building newsletter you … about all events.*
      (inform + will-future)
   b) *Invitations to the Empire State Building Run-up … to athletes worldwide.*
      (send + present perfect)
   c) *If you tried to take a skateboard into the Empire State Building, you … to leave it outside. (ask + conditional)*
   d) *The top of the Empire State Building …by a film crew all next week.*
      (use + going to-future)

> A lot of young actors should **be warned** about Broadway.

G72 Der Infinitiv des Passivs
The passive infinitive

Check-in

You're watching a talk show. Today's topic is 'Rich and famous on Broadway'.

Actor: Young actors should **be warned** about Broadway.
TV host: Why is that?
Actor: A lot of actors that are new to Broadway expect **to be chosen** for a big role right away. When I first started, I hoped **to be welcomed** with open arms! But I'm afraid I was very disappointed because I earned so little. It wasn't even enough to live on. In the end I had to look for a second job. And luckily I was accepted as a waiter at a diner.
TV host: What do you think can **be done** to improve the situation for actors?
Actor: Well, I'm afraid it must **be said** quite openly – very, very little.

1. Beantworte die Fragen. Bleibe dabei möglichst nah am Text.

   a) *What do new actors on Broadway often expect?*
   b) *What did the young actor on the show hope for when he first started.*

2. Schau dir das Interview noch einmal genau an. Nach welchen Verben verwendest du …

   a) den Infinitiv des Passivs ohne *to*?
   b) den Infinitiv des Passivs mit *to*?

1. Wie im Aktiv gibt es auch im **Passiv** einen **Infinitiv mit und ohne** *to*. Er wird mit **(*to*) *be* + *past participle*** gebildet.

2. Nach **Verben** wie *agree, choose, decide, hope, expect, seem, want, would like* wird der **Infinitiv mit** *to* verwendet:
   • *A lot of actors **expect to be chosen** for a big role right away.*
     Viele Schauspieler erwarten, dass sie sofort für eine große Rolle ausgewählt werden.

3. Bei den meisten **Modalverben** (*can, must, may, might, should*) wird der **Infinitiv ohne** *to* verwendet:
   • *Young actors **should be warned** about Broadway.*
     Junge Schauspieler sollten vor dem Broadway gewarnt werden.

English summary

How it works	Examples
The passive infinitive *(be + past participle)* with *to* is used with verbs like *agree, choose, decide, hope, expect, seem, want, would like*.	– Many young actors **would like to be invited** to a casting at one of the Broadway theaters. They **hope to be discovered** by one of the casting directors there.
The passive infinitive without *to* is used with most modal auxiliaries.	– Jobs in the entertainment industry **can be found** on special websites.

Check-out

1. Was darf nicht, sollte, muss oder kann in einem Musicaltheater gemacht werden?

mustn't • use   should • wash   must • prepare   can • buy

2. Als Rick seinen Nebenjob als Kellner begann, gab ihm sein strenger Chef ein paar Anweisungen. Vervollständige die Sätze mit dem Infinitiv des Passivs.

   a) *"Our customers expect (serve) right away."*
   b) *"Most people want (treat) like royals."*
   c) *"All tables and chairs must (clean) before the next guest sits down."*
   d) *"All cooked food should (put) on hot plates."*

He was given a job in a factory.

G73 Das Passiv bei Verben mit zwei Objekten
The passive of verbs with two objects

Check-in

While you're in New York you're doing a sightseeing tour by bus to get a first impression of the city.

Do you want to be a millionaire? Nobody says no to this question. Let's find out how Andrew Carnegie did it. He was fantastically rich – and the man whose name **was given** to Carnegie Hall. As a little boy he **was given** a job in a factory. He **was paid** very little money at first. But that changed. Soon he **was offered** better jobs and more money. When he got the chance to start his own company, he was ready for it and soon made his first million.

1. Übertrage den folgenden Satz ins Deutsche. Versuche zwei oder sogar drei Übersetzungsmöglichkeiten dafür zu finden.
   He was given a job.

2. Forme den Satz *He was given a job.* in einen Aktivsatz um.
   Somebody … .

REGEL

1. Einige Verben können ein **Dativobjekt** („Wem?") **und** ein **Akkusativobjekt** („Wen oder was?") nach sich ziehen, z.B. *give, lend, offer, pay, promise, send, show, teach* und *tell*.
   • *They offered **the young man the job**.*

2. Beide Objekte des Aktivsatzes können zum Subjekt des Passivsatzes werden:

TIPP
Beachte, dass sich die Verbform immer nach dem Subjekt am Satzanfang richtet.

	Dativobjekt (= Person)	Akkusativobjekt (= Sache)
Aktiv	They offered **the young man**	**the job**.
Passiv	a) **The young man** was offered the job.	b) **The job** was offered to the young man.

3. Im Beispielsatz a) wird das Objekt, das meistens eine Person beschreibt, zum Subjekt im Passivsatz. Deshalb wird diese Konstruktion auch „persönliches Passiv" genannt. Es ist die gebräuchlichere der beiden Passivkonstruktionen.
4. Die Passivkonstruktion mit *to* wie im Beispielsatz b) wird vor allem dann verwendet, wenn das Objekt besonders lang ist oder betont werden soll:
   • *The job was given **to the person with the best qualifications**.*

■ **Achtung!**

– Im Deutschen gibt es diese Passivkonstruktionen nicht. Häufig verwendet werden …

a) „man"-Konstruktionen:

Man bot Andrew Carnegie eine bessere Stelle an.

b) Sätze, bei denen das Dativobjekt am Anfang des Passivsatzes steht:

Andrew Carnegie (Ihm) wurde eine bessere Stelle angeboten.

c) Sätze, die mit „jemand" beginnen:

Jemand hat Andrew Carnegie eine bessere Stelle angeboten.

English summary

How it works	Examples
Verbs like *give, lend, offer, pay, promise, send, show, teach, tell* can have a direct and an indirect object. They are often used in the passive.	– We **were given** information about Andrew Carnegie. – We **were offered** cheap tickets for a concert at Carnegie Hall.
The ‚personal passive' construction starts with the person who is given or offered something.	– **The tourists were promised** a fantastic trip to New York.
The construction with *to* is mainly used when the object is very long, or if you want to stress it.	– The best seats were given **to the people who arrived first**. – I'm afraid you can't take those programs. They were given **to us**!

Check-out

1. Was passierte als Tinos Familie in New York war? Forme die Sätze um. Beginne mit dem Wort in Klammern. (Nenne keinen *by-agent*.)

a) *The lady in the hotel gave them a map of New York. (A map)*

b) *The tour guide showed them the city. (The city)*

c) *We sent grandma a postcard from New York. (She)*

d) *Someone taught Tino words in American English. (Tino)*

> **Have** your own film **made** in Times Square!

G74 Die Verwendung von *have something done*
Have something done

Check-in

While you are walking around downtown, somebody gives you this flyer.

Do you want to have your photo taken professionally?

ArtExperts will make your vacation in New York City unforgettable!

📷 You can **have** your photo **taken** in front of the Statue of Liberty or on Fifth Avenue.

📷 **Have** your portrait **painted** in watercolor or even in oils.

📷 **Have** your own film **made** in Times Square, Central Park or even Harlem.

Phone us at (0800) 1 23 12 31 23 for more information.

1. Wer macht die Bilder und Filme für die Touristen?

2. Was macht der Tourist, wenn es heißt *Have your portrait painted* … ?

REGEL

1. Um auszudrücken, dass man **etwas** nicht selber macht, sondern **von jemand anderem machen lässt**, verwendet man die Konstruktion *have something done*.

Subjekt	Form von *have*	Objekt	*past participle*	Ergänzung
Many tourists	have	their pictures	taken	on Fifth Avenue.

Viele Touristen **lassen** sich auf der Fifth Avenue fotografieren.

Subjekt	Form von *have*	Objekt	*past participle*	Ergänzung
You	can have	your portrait	painted	in oils.

Sie können ein Ölportrait von sich malen **lassen**.

Subjekt	Form von *have*	Objekt	*past participle*	Ergänzung
Some tourists	are having	their film	made	in Central Park at the moment.

Einige Touristen **lassen** sich gerade im Central Park filmen.

■ **Achtung!**
– Verwechsle die Konstruktion *have sth done* nicht mit dem *present perfect.* Vergleiche:
• *My sister **has drawn** her own portrait.* (*present perfect*)
Meine Schwester **hat** ihr eigenes Porträt **gezeichnet**.
• *The Queen always **has** her portrait **drawn** by a real artist.* (*have sth done*)
Die Queen **lässt** ihr Porträt immer von einem echten Künstler **zeichnen**.

– Du darfst „lassen" in diesen Sätzen nicht mit *let* („jemandem erlauben etwas zu tun") übersetzen (→ **G87**). Vergleiche:
  • *My mom **had** her portrait **drawn**.*
    Meine Mutter **ließ** ein Portrait von sich zeichnen.
  • *My sister **let** me use her camera.*
    Meine Schwester **erlaubte** mir, ihre Kamera zu benutzen.

English summary

How it works	Example
You can use *have something done* to say that you don't do things yourself, but that other people do them for you.	– We **had** our photos **taken** in front of the Statue of Liberty yesterday.

Check-out

1. Was lässt der Multimillionär von anderen erledigen? Forme die Sätze um, sodass sie eine Konstruktion mit *have something done* enthalten.

   a) *He doesn't take his letters to the post office himself.*
   b) *He doesn't answer the door himself.*
   c) *He never cleans the swimming pool himself.*
   d) *He never washes his clothes himself.*

G75 Passivsätze mit Verben des Sagens und Meinens
Passive sentences with verbs of saying and thinking

New York **is said to be** the city that never sleeps.

Check-in

While you're looking for information about New York, you find this blog.

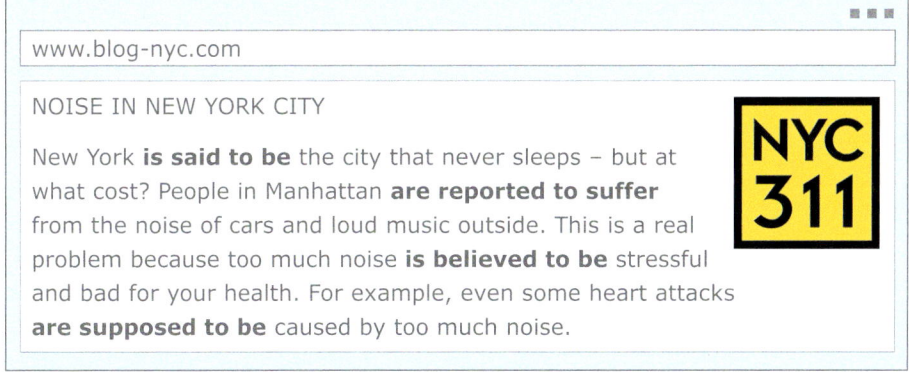

www.blog-nyc.com

NOISE IN NEW YORK CITY

New York **is said to be** the city that never sleeps – but at what cost? People in Manhattan **are reported to suffer** from the noise of cars and loud music outside. This is a real problem because too much noise **is believed to be** stressful and bad for your health. For example, even some heart attacks **are supposed to be** caused by too much noise.

NYC 311

1. Übertrage den folgenden Satz ins Deutsche. Beginne mit „Man …".
   New York is said to be the city that never sleeps.

1. Nach den **Passivformen der Verben des Sagens und Meinens** (*say, believe, report, suppose, think*) kann im Englischen der **Infinitiv mit *to*** stehen. Solche Sätze entsprechen im Aktiv Wendungen wie *People say that …* .
2. Im Deutschen können solche Passivsätze mit „Man nimmt an / denkt / sagt / berichtet, dass …", dem Verb „sollen" oder den Adverbien „vermutlich" und „angeblich" wiedergegeben werden.

Subjekt	Passiv	Infinitiv mit *to*	Ergänzung
Some people in Manhattan	**are said**	to suffer	from street noise.

In Manhattan leiden **angeblich** einige Menschen unter Straßenlärm.

Too much noise	**is believed**	to be	unhealthy.

Man nimmt an, **dass** zu viel Lärm ungesund ist.

Even some heart problems	**are supposed**	to be caused	by too much noise.

Selbst manche Herzprobleme **sollen** durch Lärmbelästigung verursacht werden.

English summary

How it works	Example
The passive form of verbs like *say, believe, report, suppose, think* can be followed by an infinitive with *to*.	– Over eight million people **are said to live** in New York City.

Check-out

1. Du bist Reporter für ein Promi-Magazin und hast leider nur Gerüchte über einen Star gehört. Forme diese Sätze für deinen TV-Beitrag um.

   be said to • be believed to • be thought to

   a) *Len Marconi earns millions of dollars a month.*
   Len Marconi is said to …
   b) *He spends his vacations on his own private island.*
   c) *He has a holiday home in Dubai.*

G76 Die indirekte Rede mit Einführungssatz im Präsens
Indirect speech with the reporting verb in the present

It says that there will be storms.

Check-in

Paul and Greg like surfing, but they have to watch the weather carefully.
Read their conversation.

Greg: What does it say about the weather tomorrow?

Paul: **It says that** there **will be** storms – that's normal for this time of year.

Greg: What else?

Paul: **They say** it **will be** stormy for the next two or three days. And **they warn surfers that** they **should read** the weather warnings.

Greg: Oh, what a shame! **My dad always tells me that** I **shouldn't go** surfing in stormy weather.

Paul: And **my mom says that** she **worries** about me when the sea is rough.

Greg: But strong winds are just perfect for surfing!

1. Paul und Greg benutzen sehr oft das Verb *say*. In welcher Zeitform verwenden sie es in ihrem Gespräch?

2. Was sagt Gregs Vater, wenn das Wetter zu stürmisch ist? Vervollständige diesen Satz: *"Greg, you … ."*

REGEL

1. Es gibt Situationen, in denen du **wiedergeben** möchtest, **was eine andere Person oft zu dir sagt** oder **was du gerade gelesen hast**, z. B. in der Zeitung, auf Schildern oder in einer E-Mail. Dazu brauchst du die indirekte Rede.

2. Du beginnst sie mit einem **Einleitungssatz**, in dem das **Verb im *simple present*** steht, z. B. *My dad tells me …* . Im anschließenden Nebensatz mit *that …*, also in der indirekten Rede, übernimmst du die Zeitform der direkten Rede:

direkte Rede	indirekte Rede
"You **shouldn't go** surfing in stormy weather."	**My dad always tells me that** I **shouldn't go** surfing in stormy weather.
"It **will be** stormy for the next two or three days."	**The weather report says that** it **will be** stormy for the next two or three days.
"Strong winds **are** just perfect for surfing!"	**Greg says** strong winds **are** just perfect for surfing.

TIPP

Beachte den Unterschied in der Verwendung von „say" und „tell"!
– say + that: My mom **says that** …
– tell + Objekt + that: My dad **tells me that** …

„That" kannst du auch weglassen: My mom says (that) she worries too much about me.

■ **Achtung!**
- Im Gegensatz zum Deutschen steht im Englischen **zwischen dem Einleitungssatz und der indirekten Rede kein Komma**. Vergleiche:
  • *The weather report says that it will be stormy tomorrow.*
    Der Wetterbericht sagt, dass es morgen stürmisch wird.

- Wenn du die Worte eines anderen wiedergibst, musst du, wie im Deutschen auch, darauf achten, dass du die Pronomen und Begleiter anpasst. Vergleiche:
  • *Paul talking to Greg:* **My** *mom worries too much about* **me**.
  • *Greg talking to his mother: Paul says that* **his** *mom worries too much about* **him**.

English summary

How it works	Examples
If you report what someone (often) says or what you have just read, you use indirect speech. You start with a sentence in the simple present. What you report is in the same tense as in direct speech.	- Greg's dad: "It**'s** too dangerous to go surfing in bad weather." → Greg talking to Paul: **My dad says that** it**'s** too dangerous to go surfing in bad weather. - Warning sign: Surfers **should read** the weather warnings before they go out. → Paul talking to Greg: **The sign says** we **should read** the weather warnings before we go out.

Check-out

1. Was erzählen sich Paul und Greg noch? Wandle die folgenden Sätze in indirekte Rede um.

   a) *Paul's girlfriend often says, "I worry about you when the weather is bad."*
      My girlfriend …
   b) *Greg's older sister often says, "You and Paul should be more careful."*
   c) *Greg's dad often says, "I always listened to my father when I was younger."*

2. Was steht auf den Hinweisschildern am Strand? Leite deine Sätze so ein:
   The sign says … .

   a) *The beach is closed in winter.*
   b) *Dogs are not allowed on the beach.*
   c) *You mustn't go surfing when the red flag is up.*

G77 Die indirekte Rede mit Zeitverschiebung
Indirect speech with tense shift

They said that Australia **was** brilliant for big waves.

Check-in

Read what Greg is telling Paul about a documentary he saw on TV last night.

Greg: I watched this cool documentary about surfing last night, Paul. **They said that** Australia **was** brilliant for big waves. And they interviewed some professional surfers.

Paul: And what did they say?

Greg: Well, **a lot of them said** they **had come** from around the world. **One guy said** he **would risk** anything for a big wave. And **he told the journalist that** you **had to start** quite young. And then **he added that** one day he **might** be a rich and famous surfer.

Paul: If we keep practising, we might be rich and famous, too.

1. Greg benutzt öfter das Wort *say*, um von der tollen Fernsehdokumentation zu erzählen. In welcher Zeitform verwendet er dieses Verb?

2. Wie würdest du den folgenden Satz ins Deutsche übertragen?
"They said that Australia was brilliant for big waves."

   a) Sie sagten, Australien war toll für hohe Wellen.
   b) Sie sagten, Australien sei toll für hohe Wellen.

TIPP
Häufig verwendete Verben sind: add, admit, explain, mention, say, tell sb und think.

REGEL

1. Wenn du **wiedergeben** willst, **was jemand** zuvor **gesagt hat**, verwendest du im **Einleitungssatz** ein **Verb** im *simple past*, z. B. *One guy said* ....

2. In der indirekten Rede musst du die Zeiten folgendermaßen verändern:

direkte Rede	indirekte Rede
"Australia **is** brilliant for big waves." simple present →	They **said** on TV that Australia **was** brilliant for big waves. simple past
"We **are waiting** for a really big wave." present progressive →	The surfers **told** journalists that they **were waiting** for a really big wave. past progressive
"I **have come** here from California." present perfect →	One guy **said** he **had come** from California. past perfect
"I **started** surfing at the age of ten." simple past →	A surfer **told** the press that he **had started** surfing at the age of ten. past perfect
"I **will risk** anything for a big wave." will-future →	He **admitted** that he **would risk** anything for a big wave. would
"You **can** get rich as a professional surfer." can →	He also **mentioned** that you **could** get rich as a professional surfer. could

direkte Rede	indirekte Rede
"You **must** start young."	He **added** that you **had to start** young.
must →	had to

- **Achtung!**
  - Das *past perfect* und die Modalverben *would, could, should* und *might* bleiben in der indirekten Rede unverändert.
    - *past perfect:* "I **had had** a lot of training before I went out on the big waves."
      → One surfer said that he **had had** a lot of training before he had gone out on the big waves.
    - *would, could, should, might:* "I **might** be rich and famous one day."
      → He said he **might** be rich and famous one day.
  - Auch wenn du deine eigenen Gedanken zu einem späteren Zeitpunkt wiedergeben möchtest, verwendest du im Einleitungssatz ein Verb im *simple past*. In der indirekten Rede musst du die Zeiten im Gegensatz zum Deutschen ändern. Vergleiche:

I'm **flying** over the water!

„Ich fliege übers Wasser."

I thought I **was flying** over the water.

„Ich dachte, ich fliege übers Wasser."

English summary

How it works	Examples
If you want to report something that a person said earlier, you use a verb in the simple past to introduce the sentence that you report. The verb in the indirect speech usually moves into the past, i.e. you put the verb back one tense. (The past perfect, *would, could, should* and *might* do not change in indirect speech.)	- "A big wave **doesn't happen** every day." (simple present) → On TV the surfers **said** that a big wave **didn't happen** every day. (simple past) - "Surfing **has become** my life." (present perfect) → One surfer **explained** that surfing **had become** his life. (past perfect) - "I **will** never **forget** my first trip to Hawaii!" (will-future) → He told me that he **would** never **forget** his first trip to Hawaii. (would)

Check-out

1. Greg möchte Paul noch mehr von der Fernsehdokumentation erzählen, die er neulich gesehen hat. Setze die Aussagen der Surfer in die indirekte Rede.

"I feel excited when I'm riding on top of a wave."

"One day I'll be the best surfer in the world."

"You can hurt yourself very badly if you go out in stormy weather."

"I have learnt a lot from my father."

G78 Zeit- und Ortsangaben in der indirekte Rede
Expressions of time and place in indirect speech

He told me that there had been storm warnings **that day**.

Check-in

Read the article Greg has found in a surfer magazine.

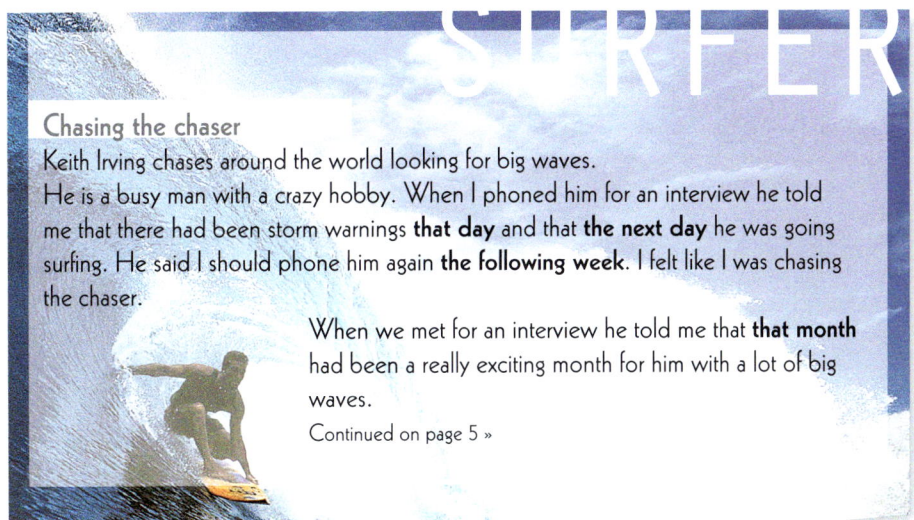

Chasing the chaser

Keith Irving chases around the world looking for big waves.
He is a busy man with a crazy hobby. When I phoned him for an interview he told me that there had been storm warnings **that day** and that **the next day** he was going surfing. He said I should phone him again **the following week**. I felt like I was chasing the chaser.

When we met for an interview he told me that **that month** had been a really exciting month for him with a lot of big waves.

Continued on page 5 »

1. Was hat Keith Irving dem Journalisten am Telefon erzählt?

a) *"I am going surfing today."*
b) *"I am going surfing tomorrow."*
c) *"I am going surfing the day after tomorrow."*

2. Wann hat das Interview stattgefunden?

   a) in derselben Woche wie das Telefongespräch
   b) im selben Monat, in dem Keith auf den hohen Wellen gesurft ist
   c) im selben Monat wie das Telefongespräch

REGEL

1. Wenn jemand **Zeitangaben wie *today*** oder ***tomorrow*** in der direkten Rede benutzt und du das Gesagte zu einem späteren Zeitpunkt wiedergeben möchtest, musst du folgende Regeln beachten, damit es nicht zu Missverständnissen kommt:

direkte Rede	indirekte Rede
Am Telefon sagt Keith:	Später schreibt der Journalist:
"There has been a storm warning … **today/ this morning/ this afternoon**."	He told me there had been a storm warning … **that day/ that morning/ that afternoon**.
"I am going surfing … **tomorrow/ next week**."	He said he was going surfing … **the next day/ the following week**.
"There were a lot of big waves **yesterday/last month/two months ago**."	He said that there had been a lot of big waves **the day before/the month before/two months before**.

2. Auch bei **Ortsangaben** (*here*) und den **Demonstrativpronomen** (*this/these*) musst du manchmal Veränderungen vornehmen, wenn sich der Standpunkt des Sprechers geändert hat:

direkte Rede	indirekte Rede

This place is perfect for surfers.
These waves are fantastic!
I really love it **here**.

Keith told me that **L. A.** was perfect for surfers. He said **the** waves were fantastic and that he really loved it **there**.

English summary

How it works	Examples
If you report somebody else's sentences some time after that person said them, you must change the adverbials of time.	– Keith says on the phone: "There was a storm warning **yesterday / the day before yesterday / earlier today.**" → Later the journalist writes in his article: He told me there had been a storm warning **the day before / two days before / earlier that day**. – Keith says in the interview: "I am going to Australia **this evening / next month.**" → Later the journalist writes in his article: He said he was going to Australia **that evening / the following month.**
Expressions of place may change too in indirect speech, e.g. *this* → *that, these* → *those, here* → *there*.	– "Surfers should come **here**. The beaches in **this** part of the country are great." → Later a journalist in New York writes the following: When I talked to Keith in Los Angeles, he said surfers should go **there**. The beaches in **that** part of the country were great.

Check-out

1. Setze Keith Irvings Sätze für einen Zeitungsartikel in die indirekte Rede, achte auf die Zeit- und Ortsangaben. Beginne die Sätze mit *Keith told me that …/Keith said that … .*

a) *"I don't have time for an interview this evening."*
b) *"There will be a lot of big waves next week. "*
c) *"Two weeks ago I rode a 10m wave on this beach here in Los Angeles."*
d) *"Someone else has asked me for an interview for tomorrow."*

> When I came home my dad wanted to know **whether** we **had been** to the beach.

G79 Indirekte Fragen
Indirect questions

Check-in

Greg and Paul had an accident while surfing when they shouldn't have.
Read their telephone conversation.

Paul: We're in trouble, Greg. We shouldn't have gone surfing in such stormy weather.

Greg: Of course not. When I came home my dad wanted to know **whether** we **had been** to the beach and **how** high the waves **had been**. And, of course, he asked me **whether** we **had checked** the storm warnings. He got really mad and asked me **if** I ever **listened** to him.

Paul: I hope you didn't tell him the whole story. When I went to the doctor, he asked me **where** the accident **had happened** and **how** I **felt**. He also asked **who** the other surfers **had been**.

Greg: But you didn't say a word, did you?

Paul: Of course I didn't.

1. Welche Frage stellte der Vater seinem Sohn Greg?

   a) *"How high are the waves?"*
   b) *"How high were the waves?"*
   c) *"How high had the waves been?"*

2. Übertrage den folgenden Satz ins Deutsche.
   He asked me whether we had checked the storm warnings before.
   Wie hast du *whether* übersetzt?

REGEL

> **TIPP**
> Verben, die eine Frage in der indirekten Rede einleiten sind: ask, want to know, wonder.

1. Wenn du Fragen in der indirekten Rede wiedergeben willst, verwendest du …
   a) das **Fragewort** der direkten Rede, z. B. **who, where, how**.
   b) **if / whether** („ob"), wenn in der direkten Rede kein Fragewort steht (= Entscheidungsfrage).
2. Die Zeitenfolge ist dieselbe wie bei Aussagesätzen, die in indirekte Rede umgewandelt werden (→ G77).

direkte Rede mit Fragewort	indirekte Rede mit Fragewort
"**Where did** the accident **happen**?"	He asked me **where** the accident **had happened**.
"**How do** you **feel**?"	He wanted to know **how** I **felt**.
direkte Rede ohne Fragewort	**indirekte Rede ohne Fragewort**
"Did you **check** the storm warnings?"	He asked me **whether** we **had checked** the storm warnings.
"Do you ever **listen** to me?"	He wanted to know **if** I ever **listened** to him.

Achtung!

– Das **Hilfsverb** *do* aus der direkten Frage erscheint nicht in der indirekten Frage. Vergleiche:
  - Dad: *Do you know how dangerous surfing is?*
    → *Greg's dad wondered if Greg knew how dangerous surfing was.*

– Achte auf die Wortstellung im indirekten Fragesatz. Vergleiche:
  - Doctor: *Who were the other surfers?*
    → *He wanted to know who the other surfers had been.*
  - Doctor: *Where did the accident happen?*
    → *He asked me where the accident had happened.*

English summary

How it works	Examples
If you want to report someone else's questions, you use *ask, want to know* or *wonder* to introduce the indirect question. If the question has a question word, you use that question word in indirect speech.	– "**How** high were the waves?" → My dad **asked me how** high the waves had been.
If the question has no question word, you use *if* or *whether*.	– "Did you say anything?" → Greg **wondered if** I had said anything.

Check-out

1. Eine Woche nach dem Unfall beim Surfen erzählen sich Greg und Paul gegenseitig, was sie alles von wem gefragt wurden. Setze die folgenden Fragen in die indirekte Rede.

   a) Greg's mom: *"Are you OK?"*
      My mom wanted to know …
   b) Greg's girlfriend: *"Does your hand hurt badly?"*
   c) Greg's older sister: *"Did you see a doctor?"*
   d) Paul's dad: *"Who was with you?"*
   e) Paul's best friend: *"Why didn't you ask me for help?"*

The governor **asked** people **to stay** off the streets.

G80 Indirekte Aufforderungssätze
Indirect commands

Check-in

Greg and his dad are listening to the news on the radio.

Listen to me, Greg. Don't leave the house today. Stay inside. Do you hear me? Find some useful work.

The weather bureau gave out a storm warning for the west coast. The governor **asked** people **to stay** off the streets. He **advised** them **not to use** their cars and he also **told** them **to follow** police orders. Most importantly, he **warned** them **not to panic**.

1. Worum handelt es sich bei dem folgenden Satz?
   The governor told people to follow police orders.

   a) einen Befehl   b) einen Ratschlag   c) eine Bitte

2. Worum handelt es sich bei dem folgenden Satz?
   He advised them not to use their cars.

   a) einen Befehl   b) einen Ratschlag   c) eine Bitte

REGEL

1. Wenn du Aufforderungssätze in der indirekten Rede wiedergeben möchtest, verwendest du ein **einleitendes Verb** wie *tell* (für Befehle und Aufforderungen), *ask* (für Bitten) oder *advise* und *warn* (für Empfehlungen, Ratschläge und Warnungen).
2. Dem **einleitenden Verb** folgt ein **Objekt und der Infinitiv mit** *to*.

TIPP
Du kannst Aufforderungen in indirekter Rede auch so formulieren:
- The governor said that people should stay off the streets.
- He said that people shouldn't panic.

direkte Rede	indirekter Aufforderungssatz			
		Verb	Objekt	Infinitiv mit *to*	
"Please stay off the streets."	The governor	**asked**	people	**to stay**	off the streets.
"Follow police orders."	He	**told**	them	**to follow**	police orders.
"Stay inside."	Greg's dad	**told**	his son	**to stay**	inside.
"Listen to me, Greg."	He	**advised**	Greg	**to listen**	to him.

■ **Achtung!**

– Beachte die Wortstellung beim verneinten Infinitiv:
  - *He warned them **not to panic**.*
  - *He advised them **not to use** their cars.*

English summary

How it works	Examples
If you want to report someone else's commands, requests, warnings or advice, you use a verb like *tell, ask, warn* or *advise* followed by an object and the infinitive with *to* or *not to*.	– "Stay at home." → The governor **told** people **to stay** at home. – "Don't use the subway." → He **advised** them **not to use** the subway.

Check-out

1. Setze die folgenden Empfehlungen des Wetterzentrums in indirekte Rede. Beginne jeden Satz mit *The weather bureau … .*

   a) *"Park your car in the garage."*
   b) *"Buy enough food for two days."*
   c) *"Don't go near the beaches."*

2. Welche Befehle bzw. Ratschläge erteilte Gregs Vater seinem Sohn als das Unwetter losbrach. Setze sie in indirekte Rede. Beginne jeden Satz mit *Greg's dad … .*

   a) *"Don't leave the house."*
   b) *"Close all the windows."*
   c) *"Bring your bike inside."*
   d) *"Don't let the cat out."*

14 Der Infinitiv

I'll **try to help** you as much as I can.

G81 Der Infinitiv mit *to* nach bestimmten Verben
The infinitive with to *after certain verbs*

Check-in

Jonas is spending a semester at Miami High School in Florida. Lynn, one of the students there, offers to help him. Read their conversation.

Lynn: Hi, I'm Lynn. Welcome to Miami High, Jonas. I guess you're feeling a little nervous right now. But don't worry, I'm here, and I'll **try to help** you as much as I can.

Jonas: That sounds great. Thanks, Lynn.

Lynn: Is there anything that you especially **want to do** while you're here?

Jonas: Um, I**'d love to watch** some good basketball games.

Lynn: Well, the first game of the season is on Saturday and it should be very exciting. I'm going. **Would** you **like to come** with me?

1. Schau dir die hervorgehobenen Formen im Dialog oben an. Nach welchen Verben steht ein Infinitiv mit *to*. Fertige eine Liste an.

REGEL

1. Den **Infinitiv mit *to*** kannst du **nach zahlreichen Verben** verwenden, die u. a. in folgende Gruppen unterteilt werden können:

TIPP

Der Infinitiv des Passivs (→ G72) wird aus „be" + past participle gebildet. Er kann mit oder ohne „to" verwendet werden:
- Jonas **wants to be told** more about Miami High.
- He **must be told** the school rules.

Wünsche und Absichten, z. B. *want, would like, hope, decide, expect, offer, plan, promise, wish*	Jonas **doesn't want to speak** any German while he's in Miami.
Vorlieben, z. B. *choose, prefer*	He **chose to go** to the US.
Versuche oder Bemühungen, z. B. *try, learn, manage*	Did he **manage to get** to the airport in time?
Anfang und Fortlauf einer Handlung, z. B. *begin, start, continue*	Lynn **started to explain** the rules at Miami High.

English summary

How it works	Examples
The infinitive with *to* is used after a large number of verbs in English, especially after verbs that express hopes, wishes and plans, as well as others like *manage, try, learn, begin, start* and *continue*.	– Jonas **plans to see and do** as much as he can in the US. – Lynn **has offered to show** him around the school. – On Saturday they **want to watch** a basketball game together.

Check-out

1. Jonas möchte bei den Basketballspielen nicht nur zuschauen, sondern auch selbst spielen. Vervollständige die folgenden Sätze mit den Verben in Klammern. Tipp: Achte auf die Zeitformen.

   a) *Jonas … the school basketball classes. (would like/join)*
   b) *Lynn has … him to Mr. Miller, the school coach. (offer/introduce)*
   c) *Jonas … him this afternoon. (want/meet)*
   d) *He … play a lot of basketball while he's in America. (hope/be able to)*

G82 Der Infinitiv mit *to* nach Verb + Objekt
The infinitive with to *after verb + object*

> The principal's secretary **asked me to give** you these forms.

Check-in

On his first day at Miami High, Ms. Carter gives Jonas some forms. Read what she says.

> The principal's secretary **asked me to give** you these forms, Jonas. She **would like you to fill** them **out** as soon as possible. Of course, she **doesn't expect you to give** them **back** to her today, but please be sure that she gets them before the end of the week.

1. Schau dir Ms. Carters Aussage eimal genau an. Welches Satzglied steht vor dem Infinitiv mit *to*?

2. Worum hat die Schulsekretärin Ms. Carter gebeten? Vervollständige diesen Satz auf Deutsch.
   Die Sekretärin …

REGEL

1. **Auf einige Verben** wie z. B. *ask, advise, expect, help, invite, prefer, teach, tell, want, warn* und *would like* **kann ein direktes Objekt + Infinitiv mit *to* folgen**.
2. Das **Objekt steht** entweder **als Nomen oder als Personalpronomen in der Objektform** (*me, you, him, her, it, us, them*).

	Verb	Objekt	Infinitiv mit *to*	
The secretary	asked	Ms. Carter	to give	Jonas some forms.
	Die Sekretärin **bat Ms. Carter**, Jonas einige Formulare **zu geben**.			
She	would like	him	to fill	them out.

Sie **möchte**, dass **er** sie **ausfüllt**.

3. Die **Verneinung** bildest du, indem du *not* **vor** den **Infinitiv mit *to*** setzt:
   • *Ms. Carter tells the students **not to be** late for class.*

■ **Achtung!**
   – Nach *want* („wollen, dass") und *would like* („möchten, dass") darfst du **keinen Nebensatz mit *that*** anschließen (→ **G80**):
   • *Ms. Carter **wants** the students **to listen** carefully.*
     Ms. Carter **will**, **dass** die Schüler aufmerksam **zuhören**.
   • *She **would like** them **to be** quiet.*
     Sie **möchte**, **dass** sie leise **sind**.

English summary

How it works	Example
Some English verbs can be followed by an object + infinitive with *to*.	– Jonas **asked Lynn to correct** his English.

Check-out

1. Letzten Samstag fand an der Miami High School der Herbstball statt. Übertrage die folgenden Sätze ins Englische.

   a) Jonas wollte, dass Lynn mit ihm zum Herbstball geht.
   b) Lynn hatte nicht erwartet, dass er sie einladen würde.
   c) Sie bat ihn, sie um 19 Uhr in der Schule zu treffen.
   d) Lynns Eltern sagten ihr, dass sie nicht zu spät nach Hause kommen soll.

G83 Der Infinitiv mit *to* nach Adjektiven und Nomen
The infinitive with to *after adjectives and nouns*

> Right now isn't the **best time to visit** the Everglades. It's **better to go** when it's a bit cooler.

Check-in

Jonas is talking to Jim, his host father, at breakfast. Read their conversation.

Jim: How are you enjoying your stay in Florida, Jonas?

Jonas: Oh, it's great, Jim. It's just **fantastic to be** here in the Sunshine State.

Jim: That's really **good to hear**. You know, you've definitely chosen a **great place to come** to.

Jonas: Yes, I know. There are so many **interesting things to do** here. It's amazing. Um … I'd really love to see the alligators in the Everglades while I'm here. Is it **difficult to get** there from here?

Jim: Oh no, it's **easy to drive** down to the Everglades. And I'll be very **happy to take** you. But right now isn't really the **best time to visit**. It's **better to go** when it's a bit cooler and there aren't so many mosquitoes about. But, don't worry, we'll definitely have a **chance to visit** before you leave.

1. Beantworte die folgenden beiden Fragen in vollständigen Sätzen auf Englisch.

   a) Was gefällt Jonas besonders gut in Florida?
   b) Was sagt Jim über die Everglades?

REGEL

1. **Nach** vielen **Adjektiven** wie z. B. *difficult, easy, fantastic, good, happy, terrible, wonderful* **und deren Steigerungen** (*better/best, more/most difficult, easier/easiest, …*) kannst du den **Infinitiv mit *to*** verwenden.

Beispiel	Deutsch
Jonas is **happy to be** in Florida.	Jonas ist **glücklich** (darüber), in Florida **zu sein**.
It's **better to visit** the Everglades when it's a bit cooler.	Es ist **besser**, die Everglades **zu besuchen**, wenn es etwas kühler ist.

2. Auch **nach Nomen** wie *chance, decision, freedom, thing, time, place* und *way* oder nach Adjektiv + Nomen-Verbindungen kann der **Infinitiv mit *to*** stehen.

Beispiel	Deutsch
Jonas will have a **chance to visit** the Everglades later.	Jonas wird **Gelegenheit** haben, die Everglades später **zu besuchen**.
The summer isn't **a good time/the best time to visit**.	Der Sommer ist keine **gute**/nicht die **beste Zeit für einen Besuch**.

- ◼ **Achtung!**
  - Nach *chance of* folgt das Gerundium (→ G91).
    - • *What is the **chance of being** bitten by an alligator?*
      Wie wahrscheinlich ist es, dass man von einem Alligator gebissen wird?

English summary

How it works	Examples
You can use the infinitive with *to* after a large number of adjectives, as well as after some nouns.	– Jonas's host parents are always **happy to help** him. – Jonas thinks it was a **good decision to spend** some time in the US. He says it's the **best way to learn** English.

Check-out

1. Jonas findet Florida spannend. Vervollständige die folgenden Sätze.

   place/spend • happy/take • chance/see • things/do

   a) *Jonas thinks that Florida is a great … a year.*
   b) *There are so many … there.*
   c) *Jim will be … Jonas to the Everglades when it's a bit cooler.*
   d) *Jonas hopes that he will have a … the alligators there soon.*

I wasn't sure **who to ask** for help.

G84 Der Infinitiv mit *to* nach Fragewörtern
The infinitive with to *after question words*

Check-in

While Jonas is spending a semester at Miami High, he decides to write an Internet blog. Lynn offers to help him write it in English. Read his first blog.

---

www.myblog_Jonas.com

MONDAY

I arrived in Florida four weeks ago and the school semester at Miami High started just three days after I got here. On my first day I was pretty nervous; I didn't really know **what to do**, I wasn't sure **where to go** or even **who to ask** for help. Then I met Lynn. She showed me **how to get around** and **how to use** the lockers. She also told me **when to go** to the cafeteria and just about everything else I needed to know. Now I'm having so much fun here; I'm wondering **whether to stay** for the whole year!

---

1. Schau dir die hervorgehobenen Wörter in dem Blogeintrag an. Nach welchen Verben oder Wendungen kannst du ein Fragewort + Infinitiv mit *to* verwenden? Fertige eine Liste an.

REGEL

1. **Nach** den **Fragewörtern** *how, what, which, when, where, how much, how many* und *whether* („ob") kann der **Infinitiv mit *to*** Nebensätze mit Modalverb (*can, must, should, …*) ersetzen. Das Modalverb entfällt dann. Diese Konstruktion ist kürzer und gebräuchlicher als Nebensätze mit Modalverb.
2. Die Konstruktion Fragewort + Infinitiv mit *to* steht häufig **nach den Verben** *decide, (not) know, show, tell* und *wonder* und **nach Wendungen** wie *have an/ no idea* oder *(not) to be sure*.

	Fragewort	Infinitiv mit *to* / Nebensatz
Jonas is wondering	**what** **what**	**to do**. (Infinitiv mit „to") **he should do**. (Nebensatz)
		Jonas fragt sich, was er tun soll.
He isn't sure	**whether** **whether**	**to stay** for a whole year. **he should stay** for a whole year.
		Er ist sich nicht sicher, ob er ein ganzes Jahr bleiben soll.

Achtung!
- Im Deutschen gibt es diese Konstruktion nicht. Du verwendest stattdessen einen Nebensatz mit Modalverb. Vergleiche:
  - *Jonas has no idea **where to go**.*
 Jonas hat keine Ahnung, **wo er hingehen soll**.

English summary

How it works	Examples
You can often use an infinitive with *to* after a question word (*how, what, when, where, whether, …*) in place of a subordinate clause.	– Jonas didn't know **where to go**. (= where he should go.) – He wasn't sure **who to ask** for help. (= who he could ask for help.)

Check-out

1. Jonas ist krank und möchte einen Arzt aufsuchen. Vervollständige die Sätze mit einem passenden Fragewort und dem Infinitiv mit *to*.

a) *Jonas looks for the names of doctors in the phone book. He finds so many that he can't decide … first. (phone)*

b) *Finally, he phones one whose office is a few blocks away. Now he isn't sure … there or … the bus. (walk/catch)*

c) *He decides to walk but on his way he gets lost. So he has to ask a man on the street … there. (get)*

I came to Miami High **to improve** my English.

G85 Der Infinitiv mit *to* zum Ausdruck einer Absicht
The infinitive with to *to express an intention*

Check-in

Jonas is filling out the forms that he has to hand in to the school secretary the next day. Read the first question and the answers that Jonas has ticked.

Exchange students

First name: Jonas

Family name: Schulze

Date of birth: 11/12/1997

Nationality: German

1. What is the purpose of your stay at Miami High School?
    - ☑ **To improve** your English.
    - ☑ **To learn** more about American schools.
    - ☑ **To experience** American culture.
    - ☐ Other:

Miami High School

---

1. Warum ist Jonas an die Miami High gekommen? Nenne seine Gründe auf Deutsch.

REGEL

1. Wie im Deutschen kannst du im Englischen einen **Infinitiv (mit *to*)** verwenden, **um eine Absicht auszudrücken**. Solche Nebensätze werden **im Deutschen** meist **mit „um … zu" wiedergegeben**.

Beispiel	Deutsch
Jonas has come to Florida **to improve** his English.	Jonas ist nach Florida gekommen, **um** sein Englisch **zu** verbessern.
He is writing a blog **to tell** his friends about his experiences in Florida.	Er schreibt einen Blog, **um** seinen Freunden von seinen Erlebnissen in Florida **zu** berichten.

English summary

How it works	Example
The infinitive with *to* is often used to express an intention.	– Jonas went to America **to learn** more about American culture.

Check-out

1. Was tat Jonas gestern nach der Schule und warum? Vervollständige die folgenden Sätze mit einem passenden Verb und dem Infinitiv mit *to*.

   tell • get • listen to • ask • watch

   a) *Yesterday afternoon Jonas stayed at school … a basketball game.*
   b) *After the game he and some friends went to a fast food restaurant … something to eat.*
   c) *He phoned his host parents … them that he would be late.*
   d) *On his way to the bus stop Jonas stopped … a street musician and forgot the time.*
   e) *Jonas missed his bus home, so he phoned his host parents again … them if they could pick him up.*

G86 Der Infinitiv mit *to* nach *the first, the last, the only one*
The infinitive with to *after* the first, the last, the only one

> I was **the last to get out** of the water.

Check-in

Read Jonas's blog, which he wrote with a little help from his host mom.

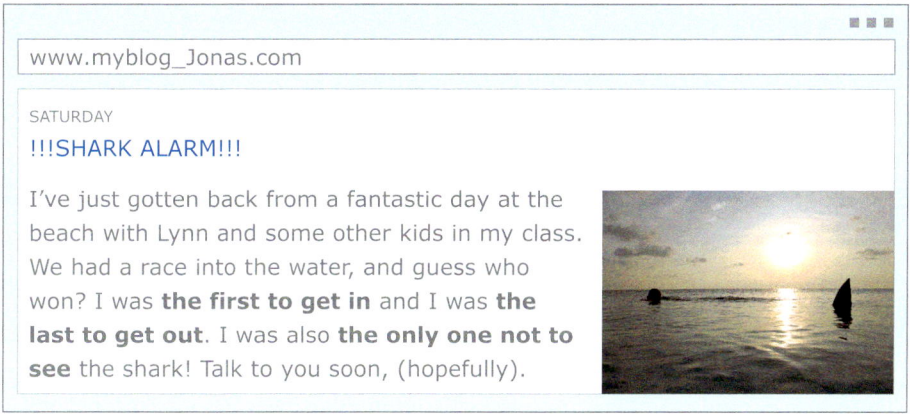

www.myblog_Jonas.com

SATURDAY
!!!SHARK ALARM!!!

I've just gotten back from a fantastic day at the beach with Lynn and some other kids in my class. We had a race into the water, and guess who won? I was **the first to get in** and I was **the last to get out**. I was also **the only one not to see** the shark! Talk to you soon, (hopefully).

1. Erkläre auf Deutsch, wer das Wettrennen gewonnen hat.

2. Vervollständige diesen Satz: Jonas war der Einzige, … .

1. **Nach** Wendungen wie *the first, the last* und *the only one* kannst du den **Infinitiv mit** *to* anstelle eines Relativsatzes verwenden.
2. *The first* und *the last* kannst du **mit oder ohne Nomen** verwenden. **Nach** *the only* muss jedoch ein **Nomen oder** das **Stützwort** *one/ones* stehen.

the first, the last, the only one	Infinitiv mit *to* / Relativsatz
Jonas was **the first (person)**	**to get** into the water. (Infinitiv mit „to") **who got** into the water. (Relativsatz)
He was **the only person/one**	**not to see** the shark. **who didn't see** the shark.

English summary

How it works	Examples
You can use the infinitive with *to* after *the first, the last* and *the only one* in place of a relative clause.	– Who was **the first (person) to get out** of the water? – Florida is **the only state to border** both the Gulf of Mexico and the Atlantic Ocean.

Check-out

1. Schreibe die folgenden Sätze um. Verwende dabei eine Infinitivkonstruktion statt des Relativsatzes.

   a) *Jonas was the first German student who went to Miami High School.*
   b) *But he won't be the last German who will spend a year there.*
   c) *Jonas is not the only person who writes an Internet blog about her/his experiences.*

G87 Der Infinitiv ohne *to* nach *make* und *let* und einem Objekt
The infinitive without to *after* make *or* let *and an object*

The coach **makes the girls train** four times a week.

Check-in

Sophie is a French exchange student at Miami High. She's at a football game with Lynn. Read their conversation.

Lynn: What a great game!

Sophie: Yes, and I loved the cheerleading. It all looks so easy.

Lynn: Yes, but it isn't easy really! Their coach, Mr. Wallis, **makes the girls train** four times a week. He **makes them work** really hard.

Sophie: I'd love to be a cheerleader. Do you think Mr. Wallis would **let me join** his class? I don't mind hard work.

Lynn: I really don't know. Look, he's over there now. Why don't we ask him?

1. Schau dir die hervorgehobenen Konstruktionen noch einmal genau an. Welches der beiden Verben *let* und *make* drückt einen Zwang und welches eine Erlaubnis aus?

REGEL

1. **Nach *make*** („lassen", „veranlassen, dass etwas geschieht", „dazu bringen", „zwingen") und ***let*** („erlauben", „zulassen") **+ Objekt** steht der **Infinitiv ohne *to*.**
2. Das direkte Objekt kann als Nomen (*the cheerleaders*) oder als Pronomen in der Objektform (*me, you, him, her, it, us, them*) stehen.

	make/let	Objekt	Infinitiv ohne *to*	
The coach	**makes**	**the girls (them)**	**train**	very hard.
Will Mr. Wallis	**let**	**Holly (her)**	**join**	the team?

TIPP
„Let's" + Infinitiv ohne „to" kannst du auch verwenden, um einen Vorschlag auszudrücken, z. B.: **Let's ask** the coach. – Lass(t) uns den Trainer fragen. / Wollen wir den Trainer fragen?

■ **Achtung!**
– Das deutsche „lassen" im Sinne von „zurücklassen", „belassen" oder „sein lassen" lässt sich im Englischen **nicht** mit *make* oder *let* wiedergeben. Hier musst du *leave* verwenden:

leave	lassen
I **left** my book on the bus.	Ich habe mein Buch im Bus **liegen lassen**.
Leave me alone.	**Lass** mich in Ruhe!
Who **left** the door open?	Wer hat die Tür offen **gelassen**?

– Auch die Wendung *have sth done* wird im Deutschen mit „lassen" wiedergegeben. Damit wird ausgedrückt, dass man etwas nicht selbst macht, sondern von jemandem machen lässt (→ **G74**):
  • *The cheerleaders **have their clothes washed** after every game.*
    Die Cheerleader **lassen** ihre Kleidung nach jedem Spiel **waschen**.

English summary

How it works	Examples
The English verbs *make* and *let* are followed by an object and an infinitive without *to*. *Make* often means the same as the verb *force*, while *let* has the same meaning as *allow*.	– How often does Mr. Wallis **make the girls train**? – Will Mr. Wallis **let Holly join** his class?

Check-out

1. Was lässt der Trainer die Cheerleader machen? Vervollständige diese beiden Sätze mit *lets* oder *makes*.

   a) *He … them train four times a week, but he … them train more often if they want.*

   b) *He … them wear normal gym clothes to practice, but he … them wear a uniform to matches.*

> Just as I was passing the shop, I **heard a woman scream**.

G88 Der Infinitiv ohne *to* nach Verben der Wahrnehmung und einem Objekt   *The infinitive without* to *after verbs of perception and an object*

Check-in

It's Jonas's last week as an exchange student in Miami. Read his final blog.

---

www.myblog_Jonas.com

THURSDAY

Yesterday I was walking down the street when I **noticed a large black car stop** outside a jeweler's shop. I **saw two men get out and hurry** inside. Just as I was passing the shop, I **heard a woman scream**. I was terrified. Then I **heard a man shout**, "Cut!" So if you just happen to see this scene on CSI Miami, look out for me!

---

1. Was drücken Verben wie *notice*, *see* und *hear* aus?

2. Beschreiben die hervorgehobenen Konstruktionen eine komplette Handlungen oder nur den Teil einer erlebten Handlung?

REGEL

1. Den **Infinitiv ohne** *to* kannst du **nach Verben der Wahrnehmung** wie *feel, hear, notice, see, watch* + **Objekt** verwenden. Damit drückst du aus, dass du die **Handlung als Ganzes** vom Beginn bis zum Ende **wahrgenommen** hast.

Verb der Wahrnehmung	Objekt	Infinitiv ohne *to*
Jonas **saw**	two men	**get out** of the car.
He **heard**	a woman	**scream**.

2. Häufig handelt es sich dabei um Handlungen von kurzer Dauer (*scream, shout, stop*) oder um eine Folge von Handlungen (*get out and hurry*).
3. Der Infinitiv entspricht hier dem *simple past*:
 • *Two men got out of the car.*
 • *The woman screamed.*

> **TIPP**
> Auch das Partizip Präsens kann nach Verben der Wahrnehmung stehen (→ **G98**). Damit drückst du aus, dass du nur einen Teil der Handlung erlebt hast, z. B.: I saw Jonas **writing** his blog.

English summary

How it works	Example
You can use the infinitive without *to* after verbs of perception, e.g. *feel, hear, notice, see* and *watch* + object to describe a completed action.	– Jonas **watched the film crew shoot** a scene for *CSI Miami*.

Check-out

1. Was hat Jonas nicht gemerkt, als er fest schlief? Bringe die Wörter in die richtigen Reihenfolge und finde es heraus.

a) *the dog • didn't • bark • hear • he*
b) *open • hear • he • anybody • and • didn't • the window • climb in*
c) *notice • his wallet • the man • he • pick up • didn't*
d) *didn't • he • take • him • see • his money*
e) *leave • he • didn't • him • see*

15 Das Gerundium

Joining the Boy Scouts is the best thing that I have ever done.

G89 Das Gerundium als Subjekt des Satzes
The gerund as subject of the sentence

Check-in

Read what Sam wrote about the Boy Scouts on their UK website.

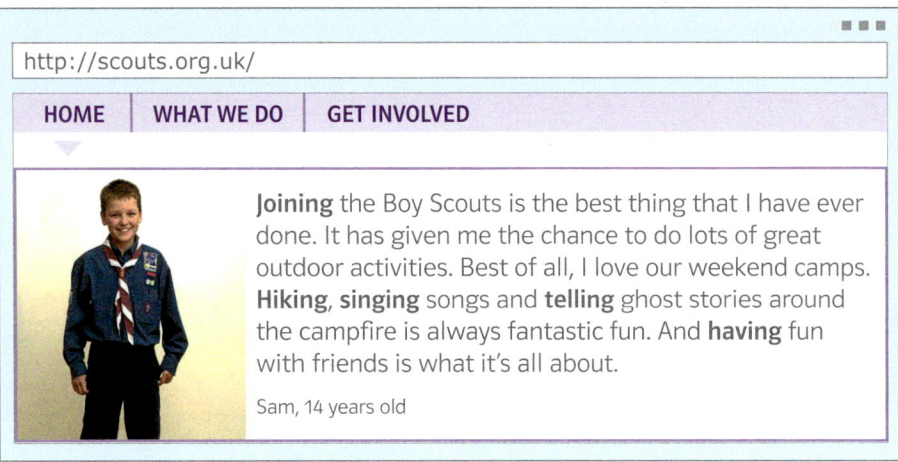

http://scouts.org.uk/

| HOME | WHAT WE DO | GET INVOLVED |

Joining the Boy Scouts is the best thing that I have ever done. It has given me the chance to do lots of great outdoor activities. Best of all, I love our weekend camps. **Hiking**, **singing** songs and **telling** ghost stories around the campfire is always fantastic fun. And **having** fun with friends is what it's all about.

Sam, 14 years old

1. Schau dir die hervorgehobenen Formen auf der Website oben an und vervollständige die Regel zur Bildung:
   Das *gerund* wird aus dem … des Verbs ohne *to* + … gebildet.

2. Welche Funktion hat das *gerund* in den Sätzen oben?

TIPP

Im Deutschen wird das Gerundium meist durch ein Nomen oder den Infinitiv mit „zu" wiedergegeben. Hier musst du eine Formulierung finden, die im Deutschen idiomatisch ist.

REGEL

1. Das Gerundium bildest du mit dem **Infinitiv des Verbs + *ing*** (*join* → *joining*). Dabei gelten die gleichen Regeln für die Rechtschreibung wie beim *present participle* (*run* → *running*; *take* → *taking*; *tie* → *tying*).
2. Das Gerundium (und seine Ergänzung) kann Subjekt des Satzes sein.

Subjekt (+ Ergänzung)	Verb	
Camping	is	something everyone enjoys.
		Zelten ist etwas, das jeder mag.
Telling ghost stories	can be	quite scary.
		Es kann ziemlich gruselig sein, Geistergeschichten zu erzählen.
But **singing** songs around the campfire	is	always great fun.
		Aber Lieder am Lagerfeuer zu singen, macht immer viel Spaß.

English summary

How it works	Examples
The gerund has the same form as the present participle: *walking, running, taking* etc. It can be used as the subject of the sentence.	– **Hiking** is always a great activity. – **Having** fun with friends is what it's all about.

Check-out

1. Bilde das *gerund* aus den folgenden Verben:

    a) *work*   b) *sit*   c) *give*   d) *lie*

2. Übertrage die folgenden Sätze ins Deutsche.

    a) *Camping with the scouts is always fun.*
    b) *Raising money for charities is just one of the many activities that scouts do.*

G90 Das Gerundium als Objekt nach bestimmten Verben
The gerund as object after certain verbs

Do you like **making** new friends?

Check-in

Read this advertisement from a newspaper.

Become A Scout Today

▶ Are you between the ages of 6 and 25?
▶ Do you like **making** new friends?
▶ Do you enjoy **being** outdoors?
▶ Can you imagine **helping** in your community and **learning** new skills?

scouts
be prepared . . .

If so, the Scouts are definitely for you.
So why not contact us and become a scout today?

1. Schau dir die Werbeanzeige genau an. Welche Verben stehen vor dem *gerund*?

2. Welche weiteren Verben kennst du, nach denen das *gerund* steht?
    Fertige eine Liste an.

TIPP

Nach den Verben „begin", „continue", „hate", „love", „prefer" und „start" kann auch der Infinitiv mit „to" stehen, ohne dass ein Bedeutungsunterschied entsteht.

1. Das Gerundium steht oft als Objekt **nach Verben, die Vorliebe oder Abneigung ausdrücken**, wie z.B. *enjoy, hate, like, love* und *can't stand*.
2. **Weitere Verben**, nach denen das Gerundium stehen kann, sind z.B.: *begin, continue, finish, imagine, keep* („etwas weiter/immer wieder tun"), *(not) mind, practise, risk, start* und *stop*.

Subjekt	Verb	Objekt
Scouts	love	**going** on adventure trips.
They	enjoy	**discovering** new things.
Sam	doesn't mind	**being** away from home for a few days.

3. Im Deutschen wird das Gerundium und seine Ergänzung oft mit dem Infinitiv mit „zu" wiedergegeben, z.B.: Pfadfinder mögen es, neue Dinge **zu entdecken**.

■ **Achtung!**
– Nach *would like, would love* und *would hate* ist nur der Infinitiv mit *to* möglich:
  • **Would** you **like to join** the Scouts? – Oh yes, I**'d love to be** a scout.

English summary

How it works	Examples
You can use the gerund as an object after verbs such as *enjoy, finish, hate, imagine, like* etc.	– Can you imagine **joining** the Scouts? – I like **hiking** with my friends.

Check-out

1. Verbinde die folgenden Sätze wie im Beispiel.

   a) *Could you wait for me? Would you mind?*
   Would you mind waiting for me?
   b) *My dad was a scout when he was a boy. He loved it.*
   c) *What do you do in your free time? What do you enjoy?*
   d) *The boys didn't climb the mountain in the fog. They didn't want to risk it.*

2. Übertrage die Lösungen aus Aufgabe 1 ins Deutsche.

G91 Das Gerundium nach Verben, Adjektiven oder Nomen + Präposition   *The gerund after verbs, adjectives or nouns + prepositions*

> I'm really looking forward to **going** on our canoe trip tomorrow.

Check-in

Sam and Chris are spending a week at Boy Scout camp. They are talking about a canoe trip down the river the next day. Read their conversation.

Chris: I'm really looking forward to **going** on our canoe trip tomorrow. What about you?

Sam: Actually, I'm not really interested in **doing** any water sports.

Chris: You aren't afraid of **getting** wet, are you?

Sam: No, it's not that. I don't mind that.

Chris: Well, what's the problem?

Sam: Um, I'm not very good at **swimming**, and the thought of **going** under …

Chris: Is that your only reason for **not wanting** to go?

Sam: Um, yes.

Chris: Well, don't worry about **falling** in the water. If you wear a life-jacket, nothing will happen. You'll be fine.

1. Schau dir den Dialog oben genau an. Welche Verben/Adjektive/Nomen + Präposition stehen unmittelbar vor dem *gerund*?

2. Welche weiteren Beispiele kennst du? Fertige eine Liste an.

REGEL

1. **Verben**, die **auf Verb/Adjektiv/Nomen + Präposition-Verbindungen** folgen, **stehen** immer **als Gerundium**.

   a) Das Gerundium steht nach folgenden **Verben mit Präposition**:
   believe in, care about, dream of/about, feel like, look forward to, talk of/about, think of/about, worry about.

Subjekt	Verb + Präposition	*gerund*
Tom	**is thinking of**	**writing** a book about the Scouts.
	Tom überlegt sich, ob er ein Buch über die Pfadfinder schreiben soll.	
I	**don't feel like**	**doing** anything this evening.
	Ich habe keine Lust, heute Abend etwas zu machen.	

TIPP

Nach „chance" ist auch eine Infinitiv-konstruktion mit „to" möglich:
The river trip will give us all a chance **to learn/of** learning new skills.

b) Das Gerundium steht nach folgenden **Adjektiven mit Präposition**:
afraid of, bad at, crazy about, famous for, good at, interested in, tired of, used to („etwas gewohnt sein") und *worried about.*

	Adjektiv + Präposition	*gerund*
Sam isn't	**crazy about**	**doing** water sports.
	Sam ist nicht erpicht darauf, Wassersport zu machen.	
He isn't	**good at**	**swimming**.
	Er kann nicht gut schwimmen.	

c) Das Gerundium steht nach folgenden **Nomen mit Präposition**:
the chance of, the idea of, the reason for, the thought of und *in danger of.*

	Nomen + Präposition	*gerund*
Sam doesn't like	**the thought of**	**going** under.
	Sam mag den Gedanken nicht, unterzugehen.	
That is his	**reason for**	**not wanting** to go.
	Das ist sein Grund dafür, dass er nicht mitfahren will.	

■ **Achtung!**

– **Bei** den Verben *look forward to* („sich freuen **auf**") und *be/get used to* („sich gewöhnen **an**") **ist** das *to* nicht Teil des Infinitivs, sondern eine **Präposition, auf die das Gerundium folgt**:
  • *I'm* **looking forward to going** *on the trip.*
  • *I'm* **used to working** *hard.*

English summary

How it works	Examples
The gerund can be used after a number of verbs/adjectives/nouns + prepositions.	– I'm **looking forward to going** on the canoe trip. – I'm not **worried about getting** wet but I don't like **the idea of falling** into the water.

Check-out

1. Vervollständige diese Sätze mit der richtigen Präposition.

   a) *Sam and Chris always look forward … sitting around the campfire in the evening.*

   b) *Sam is good … singing and Chris is good … playing the guitar.*

   c) *They are both members of the school drama club, so they are used … acting on stage.*

   d) *The thought … performing to an audience does not worry them.*

2. Übertrage die folgenden Sätze ins Englische. Verwende dabei die Angaben in Klammern und ein *gerund*.

   a) Sam ist nicht erpicht darauf, auf eine Kanutour zu gehen. *(not crazy about)*

   b) Er hat Angst davor, in den Fluss zu fallen. *(afraid of)*

   c) Er kann nicht gut schwimmen. *(not good at)*

   d) Er hat sich noch nie fürs Schwimmen interessiert. *(not interested in)*

G92 Die „Objekt + Gerundium"-Konstruktion
The 'object + gerund' construction

> I'm really looking forward to **Sam coming** home tomorrow.

Check-in

Sam has spent the last week at Scout camp. He is coming home tomorrow. Read his parents' conversation.

Dad: I'm really looking forward to **Sam coming** home tomorrow.

Mum: Yes, but I hope he won't find the rest of the holidays too boring now.

Dad: Oh, you worry too much. First you were worried about **him going** to camp, now you're worrying about **him being** bored when he gets home!

Mum: You know that's not true. I didn't mind **him going away** with the Scouts. I just didn't like the idea of **them sleeping** in a field, that's all. I mean, anything could happen, couldn't it?

1. Beantworte die beiden Fragen auf Deutsch.

   a) Worauf freut sich Sams Vater?

   b) Worüber macht sich seine Mutter jetzt Sorgen?

1. Vergleiche die beiden Sätze:
- *Dad can imagine having lots of fun with the Scouts.*
- *Dad can imagine Sam having lots of fun with the Scouts.*

Im ersten Satz ist *Dad* sowohl **Subjekt des ersten Verbs** (*can imagine*) als **auch Subjekt des *gerunds*** (*having*): *Dad* kann sich vorstellen, viel Spaß bei den Pfadfindern zu haben.

Im zweiten Satz dagegen ist *Dad* **nur Subjekt des ersten Verbs** (*can imagine*), während **Sam Subjekt des *gerunds* ist**: *Dad* kann sich vorstellen, dass Sam viel Spaß bei den Pfadfindern hat.

2. Wenn das **Subjekt** des Hauptsatzes (hier: *Dad*) und das Subjekt des *gerund*-Satzes (hier: *Sam*) **nicht identisch** sind, verwendest du im Englischen eine **Subjekt – Verb – Objekt + *gerund*-Konstruktion**. Im Deutschen wird sie meist mit einem „dass"-Satz wiedergegeben.

Subjekt	Verb/Nomen (+ Präposition)	Objekt + *gerund*	
Mum	**doesn't mind**	**Sam** going away	with the Scouts.
		… **dass** Sam mit den Pfadfindern wegfährt.	
She	**is worried about**	**him not getting**	enough sleep.
		… **dass** er nicht genug Schlaf bekommt.	
Mum	doesn't like **the idea of**	**the boys** (them) **sleeping**	outside.
		… **dass** die Jungs (sie) draußen übernachten.	

3. Das Objekt kann als Nomen (*Sam, the boys*) oder als Personalpronomen in der Objektform (*me, you, him, her, it, us, them*) stehen.

4. Auch bei „wenn"-Sätzen nach (*not*) *mind* ist im Englischen eine Objekt + Gerundium-Konstruktion möglich, jedoch nicht zwingend. Vergleiche:
- *Sam won't mind **us borrowing** his map.*
  = *Sam won't mind **if we borrow** his map.*
  Sam wird nichts dagegen haben, wenn wir uns seine Karte ausleihen.

English summary

How it works	Examples
In English it is possible to use a direct object before the gerund. The object can be a noun (e.g. *Sam*) or a pronoun in its object form (*me, you, him, her, it, us, them*).	– Sam's parents are not worried about **him being** away from home. – They are looking forward to **Sam coming** home.

Check-out

1. Formuliere die Sätze um, indem du den zweiten Satz mit einer „Objekt + Gerundium"-Konstruktion vervollständigst.

   a) *Do you mind if I use your compass?*
      Do you mind …
   b) *Mum hates it when we are late.*
      Mum hates …

2. Übertrage diese beiden Sätze ins Englische. Verwende dabei eine „Objekt + Gerundium"-Konstruktion.

   a) Meine Mutter hat nichts dagegen, wenn mein Bruder und ich mit den Pfadfindern wegfahren.   (*not mind/go away*)
   b) Sie macht sich aber Sorgen, dass wir das Essen nicht mögen werden. (*be worried about/not like*)

G93 Gerundium oder Infinitiv nach bestimmten Verben
Gerund or infinitive after certain verbs

> We were playing cricket on the beach when it started **raining**.

Check-in

Read what Sam and Tom have written in their albums next to the photos.

*We were playing cricket on the beach when it started **to rain**.*

We were playing cricket on the beach when it started **raining**.

1. Übertrage die Bildunterschriften ins Deutsche. Gibt es einen Unterschied?

REGEL

1. **Bei** den Verben *begin*, *continue* und *start* **kannst du den Infinitiv oder das Gerundium verwenden**. Es macht **keinen Unterschied**, ob du sagst:
   - *It started to rain.* oder *It started raining.*

2. Auch nach *hate*, *like* und *love* kannst du oft das **Gerundium oder den Infinitiv** praktisch **ohne Bedeutungsunterschied** verwenden:
   - *I like skiing.* ist das gleiche wie *I like to ski.*

3. Nach anderen Verben, die eine Vorliebe oder Neigung ausdrücken wie *enjoy*, *mind* und *can't stand*, kann jedoch **nur** das **Gerundium** stehen:
   - *You'll **enjoy spending** a week at Scout camp.*

4. Nach *would hate*, *would like* und *would love* und deren Zusammenziehungen (*I'd like …*) ist aber **nur** der **Infinitiv** möglich:
   - ***Would** you **like to go** to the beach with me? –Yes, but I**'d hate to meet** Tom there.*

■ **Achtung!**
   – Vor allem im britischen Englisch gibt es manchmal einen Unterschied zwischen *like doing sth* and *like to do sth*. Vergleiche:
   - *I like swimming.* (= ich habe Spaß daran)
   - *I like to go to bed early on schooldays.*
     (= ich halte es für eine gute Idee, ich habe nicht unbedingt Spaß daran)

English summary

How it works	Examples
The verbs *begin, continue, hate, like, love* and *start* can be followed by an infinitive or a gerund.	– Tom **started laughing/to laugh.** – Tom **loves climbing/to climb** mountains.

Check-out

1. Vervollständige die folgenden beiden Fragen mit der richtigen Form des Verbs.

   a) *Do you enjoy (hike)?*
   b) *Would you like (climb) the mountain with me today?*
      – Yes, I'd love to. Would you mind (wait) five minutes for me?

2. Übertrage die Sätze aus Aufgabe 1 ins Deutsche.

G94 **Gerundium oder Infinitiv mit Bedeutungsunterschied**
The difference in meaning between the gerund and the infinitive

> Please stop **talking** now and listen carefully.

Check-in

Look at the two scenes from Scout camp.

> **1** OK, boys. Please **stop talking** now and listen carefully.

> **2** Look there's Charlie. Let's **stop to talk** to him.

1. Übertrage die beiden Sprechblasen ins Deutsche.

REGEL

1. **Nach** einigen **wenigen Verben** – z. B. *forget, go on, mean, regret, remember, stop* und *try* – **bedeutet das Gerundium etwas anderes als der Infinitiv mit** *to*:

   a) Nach *go on, mean, stop* und *try* hängt die **Bedeutung des Verbs** davon ab, ob ihm ein Gerundium oder ein Infinitiv folgt.

Verb + *gerund*	Verb + Infinitiv mit *to*
go on doing sth (etw. weiter/immer wieder machen): Ben **went on talking**.	go on to do sth (etw. anschließend machen): Ben **went on to talk about** the Scouts.
… redete immer weiter.	Anschließend redete Ben über …
mean doing sth (bedeuten): If I join the Scouts, does that **mean having to** wear a uniform?	mean to do sth (die Absicht haben, wollen): I don't **mean to be** rude, but I think you should buy a new uniform. That one's a bit small for you now.
…, bedeutet das, dass ich eine Uniform tragen muss?	Ich will nicht … sein, aber …

Verb + *gerund*	Verb + Infinitiv mit *to*
stop doing sth (aufhören): Tom **stopped talking**.	stop to do sth (stehen bleiben / anhalten, um etw. Neues zu tun): Tom **stopped to talk** to me.
… hörte auf zu reden.	… blieb stehen, um … zu reden.
try doing sth (probieren, ausprobieren): If I'm not at home, **try calling** my mobile.	try to do sth (versuchen): I **tried to call** you yesterday.
… probier's mal …	… habe versucht, … anzurufen.

b) Bei *forget*, *regret* und *remember* steht das **Gerundium für eine Handlung**, **die bereits stattgefunden hat** und an die man sich erinnert, während der **Infinitiv** auf eine **Handlung** weist, **die beabsichtigt ist und noch bevorsteht**.

Verb + *gerund*	Verb + Infinitiv mit *to*
forget (vergessen): I'll never **forget buying** my first Scout uniform.	forget (vergessen): Don't **forget to buy** the sausages for the camping trip.
Ich werde nie vergessen, wie ich … kaufte.	Vergiss nicht, … zu kaufen.
regret (bedauern): I **regret telling** him the truth.	regret (bedauern): I **regret to inform** you that you did not pass the test.
Ich bedauere es, ihm … erzählt zu haben.	Ich bedauere dir mitteilen zu müssen, dass …
remember doing sth (sich erinnern an): I don't **remember packing** my compass.	remember to do sth (daran denken, etw. zu tun): I must **remember to pack** my compass.
Ich kann mich nicht erinnern, … gepackt zu haben.	… daran denken, … zu packen.

English summary

How it works	Examples
Some English verbs such as *forget, go on, mean, regret, remember, stop* and *try* are followed by a gerund or an infinitive with *to*, but the meaning is different.	– Has it stopped **raining**? – We stopped **to buy** some food.

Check-out

1. Vervollständige die folgenden Sätze mit dem Gerundium oder dem Infinitiv mit *to*.

   a) *Please stop (tell) scary stories.*
   b) *On our way home we stopped (take) a photo of the bridge.*
   c) *Tom joined the Scouts at the age of 10. Later he went on (become) a leader.*
   d) *The boys went on (sing) until well into the night.*
   e) *I meant (ask) Sam if I could borrow his compass, but I forgot.*
   f) *If we want to climb the mountain, that will mean (get up) early.*
   g) *We tried (start) the fire but the wood was too wet.*
   h) *If you can't sleep, try (drink) a glass of warm milk.*
   i) *Tom's dad remembers (go) to Scout camp when he was young.*
   j) *We mustn't forget (collect) the wood for the fire.*
   k) *I'll never forget (walk) down the mountain in the fog.*

G95 Das Gerundium nach Präpositionen
The gerund after prepositions

We drove up and down narrow country roads **without knowing** where we were going.

Check-in

When Sam got back from Scout camp, he was asked to write a short report for the newsletter. This is what he wrote.

Subject: | Newsletter from Scout camp

The Big Surprise

On Saturday morning we got up early and left the camp in two cars. **Apart from telling** us that we could expect a big surprise, the group leaders gave us no other information. For the next two hours we drove up and down narrow country roads **without knowing** where we were going. Finally, we stopped at a little café. After breakfast the leaders told us their big surprise: **instead of going** back to the camp with them, we would have to find our own way back!

I won't tell you exactly how we did it. All I will say is that, **in spite of having** no idea where we were, **by using** our compass (and our own initiative), we managed to get back long before lunch!

So, just who got the bigger surprise in the end I really can't say! I'll only say that they were so surprised that they gave us a prize **for being** so clever.

---

1. Nach welchen Präpositionen wird das *gerund* in dem Bericht oben verwendet? Fertige eine Liste an.

1. Zusammen mit den Präpositionen **apart from** („abgesehen von"), **by** („indem"), **for** („dafür, dass"), **in spite of** („trotz", „obwohl"), **instead of** („anstatt") und **without** („ohne") kann das Gerundium Teil einer adverbialen Bestimmung sein.
2. Im Deutschen wird für diese Konstruktionen meist ein adverbialer Nebensatz oder eine Infinitiv-Konstruktion mit „zu" verwendet.

Beispiel	Deutsch
Apart from being thirsty, the boys felt fine.	Abgesehen davon, dass sie Durst hatten, …
By using their initiative, the boys managed to get back quickly.	Indem sie … ergriffen, …
In spite of not knowing where they were, they were not worried.	Obwohl sie nicht wussten, …
Instead of going back in the car, they had to walk.	Anstatt … zu fahren, …
When they got back to the camp, they walked past the leaders **without saying** a word.	… ohne ein Wort zu sagen.
Will they get a prize **for** finding their way back so quickly?	… dafür bekommen, dass …

English summary

How it works	Example
You can use the gerund after prepositions such as *apart from, by, in spite of, instead of* and *without*.	– Can you guess the time **without looking** at your watch?

Check-out

1. Vervollständige die folgenden Sätze mit *in spite of, instead of, apart from, by, for* oder *without* und den richtigen Verbformen.

   a) *In the evening the boys thanked the leaders … (give) them a great day.*
   b) *… (sing) happy songs around the fire, the boys tried to frighten each other … (tell) scary ghost stories.*
   c) *At 10 pm Sam went to bed … (say) goodnight.*
   d) *… (feel) tired, he was very pleased with his day.*
   e) *… (be) very tired, he did not fall asleep at once.*

2. Schreibe die folgenden Sätze um. Verwende dabei die Angaben in Klammern.

   a) *The boys didn't catch the steam train. They walked down the mountain instead.   (instead of)*
   b) *It was cold, but it was a nice day.   (apart from)*
   c) *They followed a path but didn't know where they were going.   (without)*
   d) *Although they got lost, they did not panic.   (in spite of)*
   e) *They used their compasses and finally managed to find their way back.   (by)*

16 Die Partizipien

G96 Partizipien als Adjektive
Participles as adjectives

It was a **disappointing** result for the Wildcats.

Check-in

Andrea is reading an article in the school magazine about a basketball match the week before.

PANTHERS DEFEAT *WILDCATS* IN A FANTASTIC MATCH

On Friday afternoon, our own *Scarborough Panthers* defeated the *Wildcats* of Smith High 106–96. The **cheering** fans helped their team to this **unexpected** success. During the first quarter of the match, the *Wildcats* were well on top but the *Panthers* fans became more and more **excited** as their team started to turn the match. The *Panthers* forgot about their **lost** chances and improved in each quarter. The result was **disappointing** for the *Wildcats*. After the match they admitted that the *Panthers* had been truly **amazing**, especially their best player, Brad Henderson!

---

1. Woran erkennst du die Partizipien im Englischen? Sortiere die im Text hervorgehobenen Partizipien nach *present participles* und *past participles*.

2. Auf welche Wortart beziehen sich die Partizipien?

REGEL

1. In dem Zeitungsbericht werden **Partizipien als Adjektiv** verwendet. Sie können direkt **vor einem Nomen** stehen (*cheering fans*) **oder als Ergänzung zu bestimmten Verben** (z. B. *be, become, seem, look*) mit dem Subjekt des Satzes verknüpft sein: *The result was disappointing…*

2. Zur Bildung des ***present participle*** hängst du die Endung ***-ing* an den Infinitiv** an (*amazing, cheering, disappointing*). Diese Form des Partizips hat aktive Bedeutung und wird verwendet, um etwas oder jemanden zu beschreiben.

3. Zur Bildung des ***past participle*** hängst du die Endung ***-ed* an den Infinitiv** an (*excited, unexpected*). Ausnahmen sind die unregelmäßigen Verbformen wie *broken, lost, stolen*. Diese Form des Partizips hat passive Bedeutung und wird verwendet, um ein Ergebnis auszudrücken.

> **TIPP**
> Beachte die Bildung des present participle bei Verben, die auf -e enden, z. B.: los**e** – losing, amaz**e** – amazing

present participle	Deutsch
The **cheering** fans helped their team.	Die **jubelnden** Fans haben ihrem Team geholfen.
After the match the *Wildcats* had to admit that the *Panthers* had been truly **amazing**.	Nach dem Spiel mussten die *Wildcats* zugeben, dass die *Panthers* wirklich **unglaublich** gewesen waren.

past participle	Deutsch
The fans helped their team to this **unexpected** success.	Die Fans halfen ihrem Team zu diesem **unerwarteten** Erfolg.
The fans became more and more **excited**.	Die Fans wurden immer **aufgeregter**.

English summary

How it works	Examples
You can use participles as adjectives. They can come before the noun that they describe or they can be linked to the subject of the sentence by a linking verb, e.g. *be, seem, look*.	– I saw an **exciting basketball match** last Friday. – The result **was unexpected**.
You can use present participles to describe something or someone.	– The penalties in the last quarter of the match were really **annoying**.
You can use past participles to describe the result of something.	– The *Wildcats* fans were so **annoyed** that they went home immediately after the match.

Check-out

1. In einer Sportzeitschrift findet Andrea einen Artikel über ihren Lieblingssportler Dirk Nowitzki, einen deutschen Basketballer der *Dallas Mavericks*. Vervollständige den Artikel mit dem *present* bzw. *past participle*.

   Dirk and the Mavericks
   Dirk Nowitzki is one of the most (interested / interesting) basketball players of all time. He was born in Germany in 1978 and in 1998 he went to the United States, where he became a star player for the Dallas Mavericks. When his team defeated the Miami Heat in the 2011 NBA finals, the fans were all (thrilled / thrilling). The team's success was (surprised / surprising) because the Mavericks had never won the NBA championship before. Everybody is now looking forward to the (come / coming) season.

G97 Das Partizip anstelle eines Relativsatzes
Participles in place of relative clauses

The points **scored** by the other team from those penalties almost made us lose.

Check-in

Andrea and her classmate Jill saw the match that their school's basketball team won. Now they are talking to the best player of the match, Brad Henderson, about it.

Jill: Oh, Brad! The team was great! So all those hours **spent** on team practice made all the difference in the end!

Andrea: The crowd was really excited, Brad. The people **standing** near us were screaming so much that I couldn't even understand the people **sitting** next to me!

Brad: Well, we weren't too happy about some of the penalties in the fourth quarter. The points **scored** by the other team from those penalties were really annoying.

1. Auf welche Wortart beziehen sich die hervorgehobenen Partizipien?

2. Übertrage die drei Sätze, die Partizipien enthalten, ins Deutsche.

REGEL

1. **Partizipien** können **nach einem Substantiv** (dem Bezugswort) verwendet werden, **um einen Relativsatz zu ersetzen**. Diese Struktur bezeichnet man auch als verkürzten Relativsatz.
2. Während das *present participle* einem **Relativsatz im Aktiv** (*The people standing near us …*) entspricht, steht das *past participle* für einen **Relativsatz im Passiv** (*So all those hours spent …*).
3. In verneinten Relativsätzen setzt du *not* vor das *present* bzw. *past participle*:
   • *Sam was the only player **not informed** about our next team practice.*
     (= … *who was not informed* …)

Bezugswort	verkürzter Relativsatz	
The people	**standing** near us (= who/that **were standing** …)	were really screaming.
Die Leute,	**die** neben uns **standen**,	haben richtig geschrien.
All those hours	**spent** on team practice (= which/that **were spent** …)	made all the difference.
All die Stunden,	**die** auf das Training **verwendet wurden**,	machten den Unterschied.

Achtung!

– Das *present participle* kann sowohl die *progressive form* als auch die *simple form* der verschiedenen Zeitstufen ersetzen.
  • *I know the man **sitting** in front of us.*
    = … *the man **who sits** / **is sitting** in front of us.*
  • *I knew the man **sitting** in front of us.*
    = … *the man **who sat** / **was sitting** in front of us.*

– Das *present participle* kann auch von Zustandsverben gebildet werden, die nie oder nur selten in der *progressive form* auftreten, z.B. *agree, believe, belong to, consist, disagree, hate, hear, hope, know, like, look, love, mean, need, notice, own, prefer, remember, see, seem, sound, understand, want, wish.*
  • *These are the shirts **belonging to** our team.*

English summary

How it works	Examples
With the help of a present or a past participle you can shorten relative clauses.	– All the guys **playing** on the team have gone out to celebrate. (= All the guys who / that play / played …) – In the interviews **given** after the match the *Panthers* explained their success. (= In the interviews which / that were given …)

Check-out

1. Verwende Partizipialkonstruktionen, um die Relativsätze in den folgenden Sätzen zu verkürzen.

   a) *The player who scores the most points will be given a prize.*
   b) *Did you see the girl who was wearing the medals?*
   c) *I've seen all the Mavericks matches that have been shown on TV.*
   d) *John was the only one who wasn't cheering.*
   e) *Some of the things that were reported about the match were wrong.*

You mean you didn't come to **watch them play**?

G98 Das Partizip Präsens und der Infinitiv ohne *to* nach Verben der Wahrnehmung und einem Objekt *The participle and the infinitive after verbs of perception and an object*

Check-in

Jill meets her friend Meg on the way home from school. They talk about the match that their school's basketball team won.

Jill: What? You missed the game against the *Wildcats*? You mean you didn't come to **watch the *Panthers* play**?

Meg: No, I got there very late. Crazy, I know. Well, before I even got into the gym, I **heard everyone cheering**!

Jill: So did you watch the last part at least?

Meg: Not much of it! As soon as I got in, I **saw the referee look** at his watch and **stop** the match.

Jill: Why didn't you join us after the match?

Meg: Well, I **noticed you and Andrea leaving** the gym with Stan and Jeff, but you were too far away.

1. Welche beiden Verbformen stehen nach den Verben der Wahrnehmung und dem dazugehörigen direkten Objekt?

2. Überlege, welche dieser beiden Verbformen den Ablauf einer Handlung betont, und welche Verbform die Handlung als Ganzes beschreibt.

REGEL

1. Nach einem **Verb der Wahrnehmung** (z. B. *feel, hear, listen to, notice, see, watch*) **mit einem direkten Objekt** kannst du entweder das *present participle* oder den **Infinitiv ohne *to*** verwenden.

2. Das *present participle* beschreibt wie die *progressive form* eine **Handlung, die gerade abläuft** (… *I heard everyone cheering*). Es wird besonders dann verwendet, wenn der Beobachter nur einen **Teil der Handlung** wahrnimmt.

3. Der **Infinitiv** drückt aus, dass eine **Handlung als Ganzes** wahrgenommen wird (… *you didn't come to watch them play?*). Häufig handelt es sich hierbei um **Handlungen von kurzer Dauer** (*I saw the referee look at his watch* …) oder um eine **Folge von Handlungen** (… *look at his watch and stop the match*). Der Infinitiv **entspricht** hier der *simple form*.

> **TIPP**
> In Sätzen mit Adverbien wie *always, never, often,* etc. ist es besser, die Konstruktion mit dem Infinitiv zu verwenden, z. B.: I've **never** seen anyone **play** better than him.

Present participle: **Teil einer Handlung**

Beginn			Ende
	Verb der Wahrnehmung	**direktes Objekt**	***present participle***
I	**heard**	**you all**	**cheering!**
Ich	hörte hörte,	euch alle jubeln. wie ihr alle gejubelt habt.	
I	**noticed**	**Andrea**	**leaving** the gym.
Ich	bemerkte,	wie Andrea aus der Turnhalle gegangen ist.	

Infinitiv ohne *to*: Handlung als Ganzes

Beginn Ende			
	Verb der Wahrnehmung	**direktes Objekt**	**Infinitiv ohne *to***
Jill came	**to watch**	**the *Panthers***	**play**.
Jill ist gekommen	um zu sehen,	wie die *Panthers* spielen.	
I	**saw**	**the referee**	**look** at his watch and **stop** the match.
Ich	sah sah,	den Schiedsrichter auf seine Uhr schauen und das Spiel beenden. wie der Schiedsrichter auf seine Uhr schaute und das Spiel beendete.	

English summary

How it works	Examples
You can use the present participle after verbs of perception (*hear, see, watch,* etc.) and an object to describe an action that is in progress. Only part of the action is seen or heard.	– After the match we **listened to Brad Henderson giving** an interview to one of the reporters.
You can use the infinitive without *to* after verbs of perception and an object to describe a completed action. This action is often short. The infinitive is also used when one action after another is described.	– I **noticed one of the** *Wildcats* **kick** our best player. – After the match Andrea and Jill **saw the** *Wildcats* **trainer shout** at his team, **grab** his bag and **leave** the gym.

Check-out

1. Verbinde die beiden Sätze und schreibe einen Satz mit der gleichen Bedeutung. Verwende das Partizip Präsens oder den Infinitiv ohne *to*.

   a) *A player from the other team shouted at the referee. I heard him.*
   b) *Two players dropped the ball. The trainer noticed them.*
   c) *The other team was practising. Meg watched them.*
   d) *Sarah came home very late after team practice. Her mother saw her.*
   e) *Andrea and Jill were discussing the rules of the game. I heard them.*
   f) *The trainer talked to the players during time-out. We listened to him.*

Das Verb und seine Ergänzungen

G99 **Verben mit und ohne Objekt**
Verbs with and without an object

> Ms Garcia **corrected** our Spanish tests at the weekend.

Check-in

Jamie is writing an e-mail to his friend Pete about what happened at school that day. Pete was sick and couldn't go to school.

Subject:	Spanish test

Hi Pete,
I hope you're feeling better. You're lucky you weren't at school today.
Ms Garcia **corrected** our Spanish tests at the weekend. I was so nervous
that I couldn't **sleep** last night and I **went** to school with a really bad
feeling. I was lucky because my test was okay, but some of us **got** very
bad marks. Ms Garcia said we should concentrate more when we **write** in
Spanish. That's easy for her to say!
See you,
Jamie

1. Welche der hervorgehobenen Verben in Jamies E-Mail haben ein Objekt
   (Frage: Wen oder was?) und welche stehen allein?

REGEL

1. Einige Verben werden ohne ein Objekt (intransitiv) und andere mit einem
   Objekt (transitiv) verwendet. Dieses Objekt entspricht dem Akkusativobjekt
   im Deutschen (Frage: Wen oder was?) und wird auch als direktes Objekt bezeichnet.
2. Du kannst **drei Arten von Verben** unterscheiden:
   a) Verben, die du entweder **mit oder ohne Objekt** verwenden kannst
      (transitiv oder intransitiv; das sind die meisten der englischen Verben).

Subjekt	Verb	Objekt	
Ms Garcia	sings		in Spanish.
She	is singing	a Spanish song	right know.
Our teacher	writes		very clearly.
Jamie	wrote	an e-mail	yesterday.

b) transitive Verben, d.h. Verben, die **immer mit einem Objekt** stehen, z.B. *bring, broke, buy, catch, correct, found, get, like, make, spend, risk*.

Subjekt	Verb	Objekt	
Ms Garcia	corrected	our Spanish tests	at the weekend.
Some of us	got	very bad grades.	

c) intransitive Verben, d.h. Verben, die **immer ohne ein Objekt** stehen, z.B. *arrive, come, fall, go, happen, laugh, lie, sleep, wait, work*.

Subjekt	Verb	Objekt	
I	couldn't sleep		last night.
I	went		to school with a bad feeling.

English summary

How it works	Examples
Most verbs can be used with or without an object (transitive and intransitive).	– Maths is a mystery to me. When I **read** the rules, I don't understand anything. – Pete **is reading**.
Some verbs always take an object (transitive verbs).	– At the beginning of the school year we **bought** books for English and Spanish.
Some verbs never take an object (intransitive verbs).	– The school basketball team **went** to the gym to practise for their next match.

Check-out

1. Entscheide, ob die Verben in den folgenden Sätzen transitiv oder intransitiv verwendet werden.

   a) *I usually go home directly after school.*
   b) *You should buy a good Spanish dictionary.*
   c) *We have to write a text about our favourite pop star for homework.*
   d) *Please don't eat during the lesson.*
   e) *When the teacher arrived, the students were already there.*
   f) *You can bring your exchange partner with you to school.*

G100 Verben mit zwei Objekten
Verbs with two objects

> Ms Garcia **didn't explain the grammar to us** very well.

Check-in

Pete and Jamie are talking about the Spanish test that they'll take the next day. Pete doesn't feel prepared.

Pete: Ms Garcia **didn't explain** the grammar to us very well.
Jamie: That's not fair. She **gave** extra exercises to students who had problems.
Pete: Yeah, you're right. But I had problems last time and she **didn't give** me anything.
Jamie: But did you ask her? She usually **makes** an extra worksheet for everyone.

1. Schau dir die hervorgehobenen Verben und ihre Objekte an. Bestimme jeweils das direkte Objekt („Wen oder was?") und das indirekte Objekt („Wem?"). Welches bezeichnet eine Sache und welches eine Person?

REGEL

1. Es gibt **Verben**, die **mit zwei Objekten** verwendet werden können: einem **direkten Objekt** (meist eine **Sache**) und einem **indirekten Objekt** (meist eine **Person**). Das direkte Objekt entspricht dem Akkusativobjekt im Deutschen („Wen oder was?"), das indirekte Objekt entspricht dem Dativobjekt („Wem?").
2. Die beiden Objekte können auf unterschiedliche Weise an das Verb angeschlossen werden:

    a) Verb – indirektes Objekt – direktes Objekt

Subjekt	Verb	indirektes Objekt	direktes Objekt
She	didn't give	me	anything.

> **TIPP**
> Die folgenden Verben stehen oft mit zwei Objekten: bring („herbringen"), give, hand („reichen"), lend, offer, pass („reichen"), promise, sell, send, show, take („hinbringen"), tell, wish, write.

    b) Verb – direktes Objekt – indirektes Objekt mit *to*

Subjekt	Verb	direktes Objekt	indirektes Objekt mit *to*
She	gave	extra exercises	to everyone who had problems.

3. Konstruktion **a)** ist die gebräuchlichere. Nur wenn eines der beiden Objekte stärker betont werden soll – weil es einen Gegensatz ausdrückt, ungewöhnlich oder überraschend oder aber besonders lang ist –, steht es am Satzende.
4. Es gibt einige Verben, bei denen nur die Konstruktion mit *to* möglich ist, z. B.: *announce, deliver, describe, explain, introduce* („vorstellen"), *mention, report, say, suggest.*

Subjekt	Verb	direktes Objekt	indirektes Objekt mit *to*	
Ms Garcia	didn't explain	the grammar	to us	very well.

> **TIPP**
> Bei „tell" sagst du: Ms Garcia **told us** something about the test.
> Bei „say" ist nur die Konstruktion mit „to" möglich: Ms Garcia **said** something **to us** about the test.

5. Bei den Verben *buy*, *get* („holen", „bringen"), *make* und *order* kann das **indirekte Objekt** vor oder **nach** dem **direkten Objekt** stehen. Wenn es dahinter steht, wird es jedoch nicht mit *to*, sondern **mit *for* angeschlossen.**

Subjekt	Verb	direktes Objekt	indirektes Objekt mit *for*
She	makes	an extra worksheet	for everyone.

■ **Achtung!**
  – Wenn das direkte Objekt durch die Objektform eines Personalpronomens ersetzt wird (→ **G10**), steht das indirekte Objekt gewöhnlich mit *to* hinter diesem Pronomen.

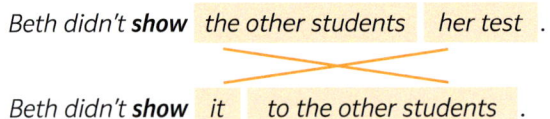

Beth didn't **show** *the other students* *her test* .

Beth didn't **show** *it* *to the other students* .

English summary

How it works	Examples
Some verbs can take an indirect object and a direct object. The indirect object can go before or after the direct object.	– The teacher **gave** the students some homework.
If the direct object comes first, *to* is used before the indirect object.	– The teacher **gave** some homework **to** the students that weren't at school last week.
With verbs like *describe, explain, say*, etc., the indirect object always follows the direct object.	– My brother **explained** the new maths rules to me.

Check-out

1. Neben Klassenarbeiten beschäftigen sich die Schüler in Jamies und Petes Klasse auch mit ganz anderen Dingen. Entscheide, welche Stellung der Objekte jeweils die richtige ist.

   a) *Why did you tell …?*
      Susan my secret • to Susan my secret • my secret Susan
   b) *I've … this birthday card for Jane. Do you like it?*
      made • given • lent
   c) *We're invited to Pete's birthday party. Can you buy …?*
      for him a present • a present to him • a present for him
   d) *Can you send …?*
      the photos for everyone who was at my party • the photos to everyone who was at my party • everyone who was at my party the photos
   e) *Do you remember? I lent … last week.*
      $5 you • to you $5 • you $5

G101 Verben mit Objekt und Ergänzung
Verbs with an object and object complement

> The others **elected** me student representative.

Check-in

Read what Jamie posted on a social networking site:

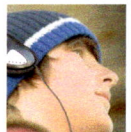

Jamie

What an awful day! I thought this school year was going to be great. When I went to school on the first day, the others **elected** me student representative for our class. Well, of course that **made** me happy. And everything went fine! But today a student from another class **called** Susan an idiot when she hit his arm accidentally. All the girls looked at me and they said that I had to do something. Next time, they can choose somebody else!

1. Vervollständige die Sätze:

   The class elected Jamie …
   That made him …
   Someone called Susan …

2. Mit welchen Wortarten hast du die Sätze in Aufgabe 1 beantwortet?

   a) Adjektiv **b)** Nomen **c)** Verb **d)** Adverb

REGEL

1. Manche Verben werden häufig mit einer Ergänzung nach dem direkten Objekt verwendet. Diese **Ergänzung kann ein Nomen oder ein Adjektiv sein**.
2. Bei einigen Verben wird die **Objektergänzung ohne Präposition** angeschlossen, z. B.: *call sb a star, elect sb president, find sth annoying, make sb sad, paint sth red*.
3. Bei anderen Verben wird die **Objektergänzung mit der Präposition *as*** angeschlossen, z. B.: *accept sth as a fact, choose sb as team captain, describe sb as a good friend, look upon sb as a hero, recognize sth as a risk, see sb as a nice person*.

   a) ohne Präposition

Subjekt	Verb	direktes Objekt	Objektergänzung
The others	elected	me	student representative for our class
This	made	me	happy.
A student from another class	called	Susan	an idiot.

   b) mit Präposition

Subjekt	Verb	direktes Objekt	Objektergänzung mit *as*
They	can choose	somebody else	as their representative.

English summary

How it works	Examples
Some verbs take an object complement after the direct object. The object complement gives more information about the direct object. It can be a noun or an adjective.	– At the end of the debating competition the teachers **declared our team the winners**. – Some people **find** classroom debates **boring**.
With a number of verbs the preposition *as* is placed before the complement.	– Jamie thinks of Pete **as** one of his best friends.

Check-out

1. Vervollständige die Sätze mit den Satzgliedern in Klammern.
   Tipp: In einigen Fällen musst du die Präposition *as* ergänzen.

   a) *When I came home from school, I … . (empty – found – the house)*
   b) *Our teacher says that we … . (our classroom – green – can paint)*
   c) *Susan … . (a good-looking guy – her boyfriend – describes)*
   d) *After our team won the debating competition, the others … .*
      (champions – called – us)
   e) *I … . (Jamie – a very close friend – don't see)*
   f) *There are a lot of things at school that … . (me – angry – make)*

G102 Die Wortstellung in bejahten und verneinten Aussagesätzen *Word order in positive and negative statements*

The day began badly.

Check-in

Last month Mrs Day's 15-year-old daughter did not come home from school.
Read what Mrs Day later told a reporter.

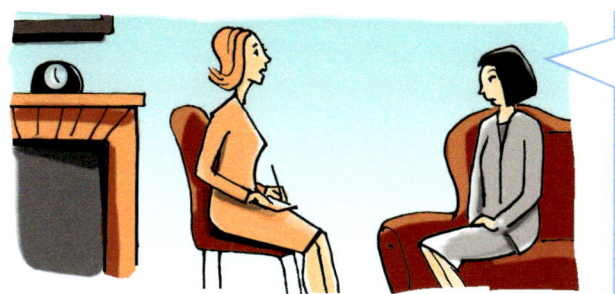

> **The day** began badly. **Julia** wasn't hungry and **she** didn't eat any breakfast. **She** was in a hurry, too, and **she** had to run to the bus stop. When **she** left the house, **I** had a strange feeling. **I** don't know why. **She** wanted to meet her friend Helen in town after school that day so **we** didn't expect her home before 6 pm. At 7 pm, when **there** was still no sign of her, **we** started to worry.

1. Schau dir die hervorgehobenen Wörter an und vervollständige die Regel:
   Im englischen Aussagesatz steht das Subjekt immer … dem Verb.

2. Welche Aussage trifft zu? Jeder Satz enthält …

   a) ein Verb und ein Objekt.
   b) eine Orts- und eine Zeitangabe.
   c) ein Subjekt und ein Verb.

REGEL

1. Die übliche Wortstellung im englischen Aussagesatz ist **Subjekt + Verb**. Danach können Objekt – Ort – Zeit folgen.

   TIPP
   Die Regeln zur Stellung der Adverbien im Satz findest du in **→ G35** und **→ G36**.

   a) Das **Subjekt** („Wer oder was?") steht immer **vor dem Verb**.

Subjekt	Verb	restlicher Satz
The day	began	badly.
Julia	wasn't	hungry.

   b) **Hinter dem Verb** steht oft ein **Objekt** („Wen oder was?").

Subjekt	Verb	Objekt
Julia	didn't eat	any breakfast.
She	wanted to meet	a friend.

c) Wenn das Verb kein Objekt hat, kann eine **Orts-** („Wo?") **oder Richtungs-angabe** („Wohin?") direkt folgen.

Subjekt	Verb	Ort/Richtung
They	met	at the bus stop.
They	wanted to go	to the new shopping centre.

d) **Zeitangaben** stehen meist am Satzende.

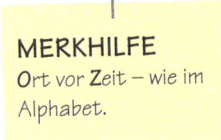

MERKHILFE
Ort vor Zeit – wie im Alphabet.

Subjekt	Verb	Objekt	Ort	Zeit
She	wanted to meet	a friend	in town	after school.
We	didn't expect	her	home	before 6 pm.

Zeitangaben können zur Betonung auch am Satzanfang stehen. Dies ändert aber nichts an der Subjekt-Verb-Regel.

Zeit	Subjekt	Verb
At 7 pm	we	started to worry.

Um 19 Uhr fingen wir an, uns Sorgen zu machen.

■ **Achtung!**
– Anders als im Deutschen darfst du nichts zwischen Verb und Objekt stellen. Vergleiche:
  • *She **left the house** at eight.*
    Sie **verließ** um acht **das Haus**.

– **Auch in Nebensätzen** steht das **Subjekt** immer **vor dem Verb**. Vergleiche:
  • *Julia was in a hurry because **she was** late.*
    Julia war in Eile, weil **sie** spät dran **war**.
  Diese Regel gilt auch für Hauptsätze, die nach einem Nebensatz stehen. Vergleiche:
  • *When she left the house, **I had** a strange feeling.*
    Als sie das Haus verließ, **hatte ich** ein merkwürdiges Gefühl.

– Hauptsätze und Nebensätze werden nur durch Kommas getrennt, wenn der Nebensatz vor dem Hauptsatz steht. Vergleiche:
  • *When she left the house**,** I had a strange feeling.*
  • *I had a strange feeling when she left the house.*

English summary

How it works	Examples
The subject always comes before the verb. The word order is subject + verb – (object) – (place) – (time).	– **I got up** late. – **I didn't eat** anything because **I was** in a hurry. – When **I left** the house, **everything seemed** normal.

How it works	Examples
The verb can be followed by an object.	– I caught **the bus** to school.
If the verb does not have an object, it can be followed by an adverbial of place or direction.	– I walked **to school**.
Adverbials of time usually go at the end of the sentence, sometimes after an adverbial of place or direction.	– I met a friend in town **after school**.
If the adverbial of time goes at the beginning of the sentence, it is always followed by the subject, never by the verb.	– **After school** I met a friend in town.

Check-out

1. Bringe die Satzteile in die richtigen Reihenfolge.

   a) *after breakfast • the house • left • Julia*
   b) *at the bus stop • met • her friend • she*
   c) *home • her parents • before six o'clock • her • didn't expect*
   d) *to the cinema • went • in the evening • she*

2. In dieser Geschichte ist die Wortstellung an drei Stellen durcheinander geraten. Finde die Fehler und korrigiere sie.

   Julia was a few weeks ago on the Internet when she found a teen chatroom. Just a few minutes after she had logged in, got she a private message from a boy called Paul. He was 16 years old and lived in the same town. They started to chat about music, school and friends. He was really sweet and funny, so when he asked her to meet him in town a month later, she said at once 'yes'.

Is Julia with you?
– **No**, she **isn't**.

G103 Entscheidungsfragen und Kurzantworten
Yes/No questions and short answers

Check-in

When 15-year-old Julia Day did not come home from a shopping trip, her mother phoned her daughter's best friend Helen. Read their conversation.

Mrs Day: Hello, Helen. It's Mrs Day here. I'm looking for Julia. **Is** she with you?

Helen: No, she **isn't**, Mrs Day. I'm afraid I don't know where she is.

Mrs Day: **Didn't** you **meet** her in town this afternoon?

Helen: No, I **didn't**. I had hockey practice after school today.

Mrs Day: Well, she met somebody. **Do** you **know** who?

Helen: No, I'm sorry. I **don't**.

Mrs Day: **Has** she ever **mentioned** a boy called Paul to you?

Helen: Um … Yes, she **has.** She chats to him on the Internet a lot, but I don't know him.

1. Vergleiche das Verb in der Entscheidungsfrage mit der dazugehörigen Kurzantwort. Was stellst du fest?

REGEL

1. Entscheidungsfragen sind Fragen, die du im Deutschen mit „ja" oder „nein" beantwortest. Im Englischen klingen 'yes' und 'no' allein etwas unhöflich. Deshalb antwortet man meistens mit einem verkürzten Satz, einer sogenannten Kurzantwort.
2. Im Englischen beginnt jede **Entscheidungsfrage mit einem Hilfsverb** wie *can, have/has, do/does, did* **oder mit einer Form von *be*** (*am/is/are, was/were*). Danach bleibt die übliche Wortstellung Subjekt – Vollverb – Objekt – Ort – Zeit immer erhalten.
3. Bei der Kurzantwort erscheint das Subjekt als Personalpronomen. Das Hilfsverb, das in der Frage verwendet wird, wird in der Antwort wieder aufgegriffen.

Frage				Kurzantwort		
Hilfsverb	**Subjekt**	**Vollverb**	**Objekt/Ort/Zeit**	*Yes/No*	**Subjekt**	**Hilfsverb (+ *n't*)**
Does	Mrs Day	phone	Helen in the evening?	Yes,	she	**does.**
Can	she	help	Mrs Day?	No,	she	**can't.**
Did	the girls	go	into town together?	No,	they	**didn't.**
Has	Helen	met	Paul?	No,	she	**hasn't.**
Is	Mrs Day	talking	on the phone?	Yes,	she	**is.**

■ Achtung!

– Kurzantworten mit *yes* stehen immer in der Langform:
  • *Yes, I **am**./Yes, we **are**./Yes, they **have**.*
  Kurzantworten mit *no* stehen meist in der Kurzform:
  • *No, I**'m** not./No, we **aren't**./No, we **haven't**.*

– Das Pronomen *you* in der Frage wird zu *I* oder *we* in der Kurzantwort. Vergleiche:
  • *Are **you** online? – Yes, **I** am./No, **I**'m not.*
  • *Do **you** use the Internet at home? – Yes, **we** do./No, **we** don't.*

English summary

How it works	Examples
Yes/No questions begin with an auxiliary verb (*can, have, do, …*) or a form of *be* (*am, is, are, …*).	– **Does** Julia use Internet chatrooms? – **Is** Mrs Day too strict?
It is possible to answer this type of question with '*Yes.*' or '*No.*', but if you use *yes* or *no* and a short sentence, it sounds more polite. Use long forms of the verb in positive answers, and short forms in negative answers.	– Have you used the Internet today? – Yes, I **have**./No, I **haven't**.

Check-out

1. Bilde Entscheidungsfragen für die folgenden Sätze. Gib auch die passende Kurzantwort an.

    a) *Helen and Julia are best friends.*
    b) *Julia is at Helen's house.*
    c) *Helen plays hockey after school on Thursdays.*
    d) *Paul met Helen in a chatroom.*
    e) *Julia has already met Paul a few times.*

Where is Julia?

G104 Der Fragesatz mit Fragewort
Questions with question words

Check-in

Mrs Day is worried because her daughter Julia has not arrived home and her mobile has been turned off.

> **Where** is Julia?
> **Who** did she meet in town after school?
> **Why** didn't she tell us about Paul?
> **How often** have we warned her about chatrooms?
> **What** happened to her?

1. Mrs Day verwendet fünf verschiedene Fragewörter. Welche weiteren kennst du?

2. Welche der Fragen fragt nach einem Subjekt („Wer oder Was")? Versuche den Unterschied zu den Objektfragen zu erkennen.

REGEL

1. **Fragen** können **mit den Fragewörtern** *what, when, where, why, who, how, how often, how much/many, whose* oder *which* eingeleitet werden.

2. Danach folgt dieselbe **Wortstellung wie bei Entscheidungsfragen**.

Fragewort	Hilfsverb	Subjekt	Vollverb	restlicher Satz
Where	can	Julia	be?	
Who	did	she	meet	in town after school?
How often	have	they	spoken	about the dangers of the Internet?

3. Beachte, dass du bei Fragen mit einer Form von *be* im *simple present* kein Hilfsverb benötigst:
   - *Why **is** Mrs Day worried?*
   - *Where **is** Julia?*

TIPP
Vergleiche:
– Who phoned Helen? – Wer hat Helen angerufen?
– Who **did** Helen **phone**? – Wen hat Helen angerufen?

🟧 **Achtung!**

– Wenn *who* oder *what* Subjekt des Fragesatzes ist, wird das Hilfsverb *do/does, did* nicht verwendet. Diese Fragesätze haben dieselbe Wortstellung wie Aussagesätze (➔ **G102**).

Wer oder was als Subjekt des Fragesatzes	
Who phoned Helen?	**Wer** hat Helen angerufen?
What made Mrs Day angry?	**Was** hat Mrs Day wütend gemacht?

– Wenn Verb und Präposition eine Einheit bilden, z. B. *talk to, wait for, look at, laugh at,* dann steht die Präposition auch im Fragesatz hinter dem Vollverb.

Fragen mit Fragewort + Verb + Präposition	
What are we **waiting for**?	**Worauf** warten wir?
What are you **laughing at**?	**Worüber** lachst du?
Who were you **talking to** on the phone just now?	**Mit wem** hast du gerade telefoniert?
What are the boys **talking about**?	**Wovon** reden die Jungs?

English summary

How it works	Examples
In questions with question words *what, why, where* … are put before the auxiliary verb or the form of *be*.	– **What did** Julia do after school? – **Where has** she gone? – **Why is** her mobile turned off?
If *who* or *what* is the subject of the sentence, you don't use the auxiliary verb *do/does/did*.	– **Who** saw her in town? – **What** happened?
In questions with verb + preposition, the preposition always goes after the verb.	– **What** are you **looking at**? – **Who** does this mobile **belong to**?

Check-out

1. Schau dir die Antworten an. Setze das fehlende Fragewort ein.

   a) … *is Paul?*   – *He's an online friend of Julia's.*
   b) … *did they meet?*   – *In a chatroom.*
   c) … *do they chat to each other?*   – *In the evenings.*
   d) … *do they do when they meet?*   – *They go to the cinema.*

2. Bilde Fragen mit Fragewörtern. Erfrage die hervorgehobenen Informationen.

   a) *Julia went **into town** after school.*
   b) *Her friend Helen didn't go with her **because she had hockey practice after school**.*
   c) *Julia met **Paul** outside the cinema.*
   d) *They **watched a film** together.*

3. Übertrage diese Fragen ins Englische.

   a) Mit wem spricht Julia jeden Tag im Internet?
   b) Worüber sprechen sie?

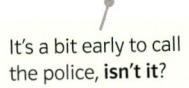

It's a bit early to call the police, **isn't it**?

G105 Bestätigungsfragen
Question tags

Check-in

Mr and Mrs Day are very worried. It is 8 pm and their daughter Julia has still not come home. They are talking about what they should do.

Mrs Day: I'm going to phone the police.

Mr Day: It**'s** a bit early to call the police, **isn't it**? I mean, it's only 8 pm. Let's wait a bit longer. I'm sure she'll be home soon. Sometimes she just **forgets** the time, **doesn't she**?

Mrs Day: Yes, but she**'s** never **been** more than half an hour late, **has she**?

Mr Day: You know what she's like when she meets up with her friends.

Mrs Day: But she **didn't meet** any of her friends this afternoon, **did she**? That's the point. She met some guy from the Internet.

Mr Day: Well, we **don't know** that for sure, **do we**? Let's wait until 9. We **can call** the police then, **can't we**?

1. Schau dir die Sätze mit Bestätigungsfragen an. Übertrage sie ins Deutsche.

> **REGEL**

1. **Bestätigungsfragen** sind kurze Fragen **am Ende eines Aussagesatzes**. Sie **entsprechen** dem deutschen „**nicht wahr?**", „**oder?**", „**gell?**" oder „**stimmt's?**"
2. Im Englischen bildest du sie, indem du das **Hilfsverb des Hauptsatzes wiederholst**. Steht im Hauptsatz kein Hilfsverb, sondern nur ein Vollverb (*forgets, met*), verwendest du *do/does* oder *did*.
3. **Bejahte Hauptsätze** werden in der Bestätigungsfrage **verneint**; verneinte Hauptsätze werden **bejaht**.
4. Das Subjekt des Hauptsatzes wird in der Bestätigungsfrage zum Personalpronomen, z. B. *Julia – she, Her parents – they.*

MERKHILFE
(+) wird zu (-),
(-) wird zu (+)

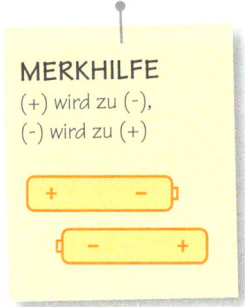

Hauptsatz			Bestätigungsfrage
Subjekt	**Verb**	**restlicher Satz**	**Hilfsverb + Pronomen**
It	**is**	a bit early to call the police,	**isn't it?**
We	**can**	call the police later,	**can't we?**
She	sometimes **forgets**	the time,	**doesn't she?**
Julia	**met**	her friend Helen in town,	**didn't she?**
Her parents	**will call**	the police later,	**won't they?**
We	**don't know**	that for sure,	**do we?**
Julia	**has never been**	two hours late before,	**has she?**

■ **Achtung!**
- **Apostroph + s** kann für *is* oder *has* stehen! Vergleiche:
  - *It's too early to call the police, **isn't** it?*
  - *She's never been more than half an hour late, **has** she?*
- Beachte die Bestätigungsfragen bei *have*:

simple present	The Days **have** tea at 6 pm,	**don't** they?
simple past	The Days **had** tea at 6 pm,	**didn't** they?
present perfect	The Days **have** just **had** tea,	**haven't** they?

■ **Schriftlicher/mündlicher Sprachgebrauch**
- Bestätigungsfragen kommen häufig in der mündlichen Sprache vor. In der schriftlichen Sprache solltest du sie vermeiden.

English summary

How it works	Examples
Question tags are short questions that are often put at the end of a sentence in spoken English. They begin with the auxiliary verb and are followed by the pronoun form of the sentence subject.	- The Days **are** very worried about their daughter, **aren't** they? - They **can't** contact her, **can** they?
If the sentence has no auxiliary verb, *do/ does, did* is used.	- Teenagers often **forget** the time, **don't** they?
Negative tags are used after positive sentences.	- Julia **will come** home, **won't** she?
Positive tags are used after negative sentences.	- You **don't often** get home late, **do** you?

Check-out

1. Um 21 Uhr klingelt das Telefon. Mr Day geht dran. Danach erzählt er seiner Frau die Neuigkeiten. Vervollständige den Dialog mit den richtigen Bestätigungsfragen.

Mr Day: *That was the police. They've found Julia.*

Mrs Day: *The police? She is okay, …?*

Mr Day: *Yes, she's fine, but she's had a nasty experience. She's at the police station now.*

Mrs Day: *I knew it! I just knew it! I told you, …? She met that guy from the Internet, …?*

Mr Day: *Yes, she did.*

Mrs Day: *And he wasn't a 16-year-old schoolboy, …?*

Mr Day: *No, it seems he was a lot older than that.*

Mrs Day: *And his real name wasn't Paul, …?*

Mr Day: *I don't know. Look, let's go to the police station.*
                Then we'll find out more, …?

Mrs Day: *I just don't understand her. We've warned her so many times, …?*
                But she never listens to us, …?

Mr Day: *Listen, let's not get too angry with her. It won't do any good, …?*
                I'm sure she's learned her lesson now.

Mrs Day: *Yes, I guess you're right.*

> **Don't use** your real name.

G106 Der Imperativ
The imperative

Check-in

Social networks can be a great way to chat to your friends or to people who share your interests, but remember there are risks. This flyer gives you some basic rules which will help you to stay safe.

How to stay safe on the Internet

① **Don't use** your real name.

② **Don't give** anyone your phone number, address, the name of your school.

③ **Don't tell** anyone how old you are.

④ **Be** careful about any photos you post of yourself online.

!

---

1. Im Text oben findest du eine Reihe von Warnungen.

    a) Welche davon sind positiv, welche negativ?

    b) Worin unterscheiden sie sich?

REGEL

1. **Mit dem Imperativ**, auch Befehlsform genannt, kannst du **jemanden auffordern, etwas (nicht) zu tun**.

2. Im Englischen gibt es nur eine Form: den **Infinitiv des Verbs** (ohne *to*), z. B. *be, remember*.

3. Um die **Befehlsform** zu **verneinen**, setzt du *don't* **vor den Infinitiv** des Verbs, z. B.: *Don't use … , Don't give … .*

bejahte Befehlsform		verneinte Befehlsform	
Be careful.	Sei vorsichtig! Seid vorsichtig! Seien Sie vorsichtig!	**Don't go**.	Geh nicht! Geht nicht! Gehen Sie nicht!

■ **Achtung!**
– Wörter wie *always* und *never* stehen immer **vor dem Infinitiv**:
  • ***Always*** *be careful.*
  • ***Never*** *send pictures of yourself to people you don't know.*

■ **Schriftlicher/mündlicher Sprachgebrauch**
– Beim Schreiben musst du nicht alle Aufforderungssätze mit einem Ausrufezeichen abschließen. Im Englischen dient das Ausrufezeichen nur dazu, Aufregung auszudrücken oder um etwas stark zu betonen.
  • *Watch out! The train's coming in!*

English summary

How it works	Examples
You can use commands (the imperative) to tell people what they should, must or mustn't do. Use the infinitive for positive commands and *don't* + infinitive for negative commands.	– **Use** an online name. – **Don't tell** anyone your real name.

Check-out

1. Gib einem Freund weitere hilfreiche Tipps zum Umgang mit dem Internet. Verwende dabei den Imperativ (positiv oder negativ) der Verben *go, remember, tell* und *believe*.

   a) *... that some people on the Internet may not be who they say they are, so ... everything that people tell you.*
   b) *If you want to meet somebody you have only spoken to online, ... your parents first.*
   c) *... alone.*

My friends are all people **who** normally prefer action films.

G107 Die Relativpronomen als Subjekt von notwendigen Relativsätzen *Relative pronouns as the subject of defining relative clauses*

Check-in

Read the film review Phil has posted on the Internet.

Phil

Witchcraft reloaded is a new fantasy film. I saw it last week with some friends. Although my friends are all people **who** normally prefer action films, they all enjoyed *Witchcraft reloaded* very much. The main characters are two witches. They decide to leave their underground home in the mountains and start scaring the people **that** live in the nearby city. They want to take control of the city themselves. But will they manage to do this? Find out for yourselves! Emilia Roberts and Jill Clark make frightening and sometimes funny witches. Of course, some people don't like films about things **which** can't happen in the real world. But I've never seen a film **that** thrilled me so much!

1. Auf welche Wörter beziehen sich die Relativpronomen *who, which* und *that* in der Filmkritik oben?

2. Ordne die Relativpronomen ihrer Verwendung nach zu.

who	Personen und Sachen
which ✚	Personen
that	Sachen

MERKHILFE

1. Relativsätze **bestimmen oder definieren Personen oder Sachen näher**, z. B. … *things which can't happen in the real world*. Ohne diese Information im Relativsatz wäre der Hauptsatz unvollständig oder nicht verständlich. Man spricht deshalb von **notwendigen Relativsätzen**.
2. Sie werden **von einem Relativpronomen eingeleitet, das** meist unmittelbar **nach dem Bezugswort steht**, d. h. der Person oder der Sache, auf die es sich bezieht.
3. Die Relativpronomen sind …
   - *who* für **Personen**,
   - *which* für **Sachen**,
   - *that* für **Personen, Tiere** oder **Sachen**
   für Bezugswörter im **Singular** (*film*) und **Plural** (*things, people*).

4. Wenn du dir die Filmkritik genau anschaust, stellst du fest, dass die Relativpronomen *who, which* und *that* **Subjekt** des Relativsatzes sind. Deshalb darfst
du die **Relativpronomen** hier im Gegensatz zu den *contact clauses* (➜ **G108**)
nie weglassen.

Hauptsatz		Nebensatz (= notwendiger Relativsatz)	
	Bezugs-wort	**Relativ-pronomen (= Subjekt)**	
My friends are all	**people**	**who/that**	normally prefer action films.
	... Leute,	**die**	normalerweise Actionfilme bevorzugen.
Some people don't like films about	**things**	**which/that**	can't happen in the real world.
	... Dinge,	**die**	nicht in Wirklichkeit passieren können.

■ **Achtung!**
 – Im Gegensatz zum Deutschen darfst du notwendige Relativsätze nicht durch
 Komma(s) vom Hauptsatz abtrennen.

■ **Mündlicher/schriftlicher Sprachgebrauch**
 – Im informellen Sprachgebrauch wird eher *that* als *who* oder *which* verwendet.

English summary

How it works	Examples
Defining relative clauses give important information about people or things. Without this information the sentence is incomplete. In defining relative clauses, *who*, *which* and *that* are used as the subject of the relative clause.	– Phil is the boy **who** likes fantasy films.
You use *who* for people.	– *Witchcraft reloaded* is the perfect film for **people who** like adventure stories.
You use *which* for things.	– Fantasy films sometimes have **storylines which** don't make much sense.
You use *that* for people, animals or things. *That* is used more often in spoken English.	– Have you seen *Witchcraft reloaded*? – Yes, but I prefer **films that** are about real life.

Check-out

1. Mike arbeitet für eine Produktionsfirma. Was braucht er für den nächsten Film noch? Verbinde die Satzteile mit *who* oder *which*.

They want boys and girls	*can take six people.*
Mike is looking for an assistant	*are between six and eight years old.*
They are trying to find costumes	*look like clothes from the 18th century.*
The company needs old carriages	*has worked with children before.*

Is there an actor **who** you especially like?

G108 Die Relativpronomen als Objekt von notwendigen Relativsätzen; *contact clauses* *Relative pronouns as the object of defining relative clauses; contact clauses*

Check-in

Julia meets Phil, her classmate. Find out what they are talking about.

Hi! I read the film review **that** you posted on the Internet yesterday. Is there an actor **who** you especially like?

Sure. My favourite actor is Johnny Depp. He's the kind of actor I really admire! All the roles he has played are just awesome!

1. Bestimme für die beiden Relativsätze in Julias Äußerung das Bezugswort, das Objekt und das Subjekt.

Bezugswort	Objekt	Subjekt
film review	…	…
…	…	…

2. Auch Phil verwendet zwei Relativsätze. Welche sind es und worin unterscheiden sie sich im Vergleich zu Julias Relativsätzen?

1. Die **Relativpronomen** *who, which* oder *that* (**→ G107**) **können** auch **Objekt des Relativsatzes sein**:
- *Is there an **actor who you** especially like?*
  Gibt es **einen Schauspieler, den du** besonders magst?

2. Die **Relativpronomen** *who, which* und *that* kannst du häufig einfach **weglassen**, **wenn sie Objekt im Relativsatz sind**. Solche Sätze nennt man ***contact clauses***, weil der Relativsatz ohne Relativpronomen in direktem Kontakt zum Hauptsatz steht:
- *Johnny Depp is the kind of actor I really admire.*

> **TIPP**
> Wenn direkt nach dem Relativ-pronomen ein neues Subjekt steht, ist das ein Zeichen dafür, dass du das Relativpronomen auslassen kannst.

Hauptsatz		Nebensatz (= notwendiger Relativsatz)	
	Bezugswort	**(Relativpronomen = Objekt) + Subjekt + Verb**	
I read	**the film review**	**(that) you** posted	on the Internet yesterday.
	... Filmkritik,	**die du** gestern ins Internet gestellt hast.	
Johnny Depp is	**the kind of actor**	**(who) I** really admire.	
	... der Typ von Schauspieler,	**den ich** wirklich bewundere.	
	The roles	**(which) Johnny Depp** has played	are just awesome.
	... Rollen,	**die Johnny Depp** gespielt hat, sind einfach toll.	

■ Achtung!
- Im Gegensatz zum Deutschen darfst du notwendige Relativsätze nicht durch Komma(s) vom Hauptsatz abtrennen.

- Viele **Verben** treten in Verbindung **mit Präpositionen** auf. Im Gegensatz zum Deutschen stehen die Präpositionen im Englischen in notwendigen Relativsätzen bzw. *contact clauses* **hinter dem Verb**:
  - *Many actors have a personal trainer **(who)** they **train with**.*
    Viele Schaupieler haben einen Personal Trainer, **mit dem** sie **trainieren**.
  - *Scriptwriters create the worlds **(which)** film characters **live in**.*
    Drehbuchautoren erfinden die Welten, **in denen** ihre Charaktere **leben**.
  - *This is the film **(that)** we **were talking about**.*
    Das ist der Film, **über den** wir **gesprochen haben**.

English summary

How it works	Examples
If the relative pronoun is the object of the relative clause, you can leave it out. A relative clause without a relative pronoun is called a contact clause.	– Steven Spielberg is a film director **(who)** you can really admire.

How it works	Examples
If the verb in the defining relative clause has a preposition, you put the preposition after the verb.	– Is this the DVD (**that**) you're looking **for**?

Check-out

1. Julia und Phil haben ein Internetforum zum Thema Film und Schauspieler eröffnet. Sie machen im Chatroom darauf aufmerksam. Schreibe den Eintrag mit Hilfe von *contact clauses* um.

   New forum on films and actors
   Are you interested in films? Then come and join our forum Cinemania. *Please write about all the films that you've seen recently or comment on the actors and the roles which they play. Who is the actor that you like most?*

> Johnny Depp, **who was born in 1963**, is one of the most popular actors in the world.

G109 Nicht notwendige Relativsätze
Non-defining relative clauses

Check-in

Read this encyclopedia entry on Johnny Depp.

Johnny Depp

Johnny Depp, **who was born on 9th June 1963**, is one of the most popular actors in the world. He first became famous in the 1980s as the main character in the TV series *21 Jump Street*. Since 1990, he has been the star in many blockbusters. The film *Edward Scissorhands*, **which was Johnny's first real success**, was seen by millions of people all round the world. It was made by Tim Burton, **who has since become one of Depp's best friends**.

1. Sind die hervorgehobenen Satzteile für die Verständlichkeit des Hauptsatzes unbedingt nötig oder verstehst du den Hauptsatz auch ohne diese Information?

2. Welche beiden Relativpronomen werden in den hervorgehobenen Relativsätzen verwendet? Wann wird welches benutzt?

REGEL

1. **Nicht notwendige Relativsätze enthalten zusätzliche, interessante Informationen**: *who was born on 9th June 1963*. Die Aussage des **Hauptsatzes**, dass Johnny Depp einer der berühmtesten Schauspieler der Welt ist, bleibt auch **ohne den Relativsatz verständlich**.
2. Als Relativpronomen verwendest du *who* für **Personen** und *which* für **Sachen** (jeweils im Singular und Plural).
3. Nicht notwendige Relativsätze musst du immer **durch Komma(s)** vom Hauptsatz **abtrennen**. Beim Sprechen solltest du eine kurze **Pause** einlegen und zwar genau da, wo die Kommas stehen.

> **TIPP**
> „Who" wird oft für Haustiere verwendet, da sie wie Familienmitglieder sind, z.B.: Sally, **who** is a big dog, needs a lot of exercise.

Hauptsatz		Nebensatz	Hauptsatz
	Bezugswort	nicht notwendiger Relativsatz	
	Johnny Depp	, **who** was born on 9th June 1963,	is one of the most popular actors in the world.
	Johnny Depp	, **der** am 9. Juni 1963 geboren wurde,	ist einer der beliebtesten Schauspieler weltweit.
	The film *Edward Scissorhands*	, **which** was Johnny Depp's first real success,	was seen by millions of people.
Der Film Edward Scissorhands		, **der** Johnny Depps erster wirklicher Erfolg war,	wurde von Millionen gesehen.
The film was made by	Tim Burton	, **who** has since become one of Depp's best friends.	
Der Film wurde von Tim Burton produziert		, **der** seitdem einer von Depps engsten Freunden ist.	

■ **Achtung!**
- Im Gegensatz zu notwendigen Relativsätzen (→ G107) darfst du das Relativpronomen *that* **in nicht notwendigen Relativsätzen nie verwenden**.
- Die **Relativpronomen** darfst du **in nicht notwendigen Relativsätzen nie weglassen**.
- Bei **Verben mit einer Präposition** kann diese am Ende des Relativsatzes stehen:
  - *Our trip to the Hollywood movie studios, which we had already heard a lot **about**, was great fun.*

■ **Mündlicher/schriftlicher Sprachgebrauch**
- Nicht notwendige Relativsätze gehören eher der Schriftsprache an. Sie helfen z.B. die Wiederholung von Namen, Nomen und Pronomen zu vermeiden. Im mündlichen Sprachgebrauch bildet man häufig zwei kürzere Sätze. Vergleiche:
  - *Johnny Depp, who has a brother and two sisters, was born in Kentucky.*
  - *Johnny Depp was born in Kentucky. He has a brother and two sisters.*

English summary

How it works	Examples
Non-defining relative clauses give extra information. They can help to make your texts more interesting. In non-defining clauses you use *who* for people and *which* for things. Always remember to put a comma between the non-defining relative clause and the main clause.	– *E.T.* was made by Steven Spielberg, **who** is also known for the *Indiana Jones* films. – *E.T.,* **which** was filmed in 61 days, was seen by millions of people around the world.

Check-out

1. In die Relativsätze haben sich drei Fehler eingeschlichen. Lies, was im Kino geschah und korrigiere die Fehler.

a) *Yesterday I went to the new cinema in Leicester Square which only opened last week. Two women, that were talking to each other loudly, were sitting in the row in front of me. I couldn't hear the dialogue in the movie clearly. So I said to them quietly, 'Excuse me, but I can't hear.' 'I hope not,' replied one woman. 'This is a private conversation.'*

b) *A friend and I were watching* Bend it like Beckham *at the MAX CINEMA, who was full of people inside. We played a game. We tried to guess what would happen next. My friend, who guessed the plot right, laughed so loud that people around us left to find new seats.*

> Tourists can see the famous cities **whose** towers shine with gold.

G110 Das Relativpronomen *whose*
The relative pronoun whose

Check-in

Read the article about the *Lord of the Rings* films and tourism that Julie has found on the Internet.

---

www.middle-earth-tours.com

New Zealand, **whose** landscape can be seen in the *Lord of the Rings* films, has attracted many more tourists since the films came out. Tourists are now staying longer in the country to visit the places where the films were made. A few companies are now offering trips to Middle-earth. There, tourists can see the famous cities **whose** towers shine with gold. And what's more, some of the tour guides are *Lord of the Rings* actors, **whose** faces you will recognize from the films.

---

1. Schau dir den Artikel einmal genau an. In welchen Relativsätzen kann man das Relativpronomen *whose* verwenden?

   a) nur in notwendigen Relativsätzen
   b) nur in nicht notwendigen Relativsätzen
   c) in notwendigen und nicht notwendigen Relativsätzen

2. Welche Wortart folgt immer nach dem Relativpronomen *whose*?

REGEL

1. Das Relativpronomen ***whose*** („deren", „dessen") kannst du sowohl in **notwendigen** (→ **G107**) als auch **nicht notwendigen Relativsätzen** (→ **G109**) verwenden, um Zugehörigkeit oder Besitz auszudrücken.
2. ***Whose* steht meist für Personen** im Singular oder Plural, aber gelegentlich auch für **Sachen**.

Hauptsatz			Nebensatz (= notwendiger Relativsatz)	
	Bezugswort		**Relativ-pronomen**	
Tourists can see	**some of the actors**		**whose**	faces they know from the films.

Hauptsatz		Nebensatz	Hauptsatz
	Bezugswort	**(= nicht notwendiger Relativsatz)**	
	New Zealand	**, whose** landscape can be seen in the *Lord of the Rings* films,	has attracted many more tourists.

■ **Achtung!**
 – Vermeide Verwechslungen von ***whose*** (Anzeige von Besitz oder Zugehörigkeit) mit ***who's*** (Kurzform von: ***who is*** bzw. ***who has***):
   • ***whose + noun:*** *I've met a girl **whose** father is a Hollywood star.*
   • ***who + is:*** *The film is about a girl **who's** in love with an alien.*
   • ***who + has:*** *The director is looking for an actress **who's** acted in science fiction films before.*

English summary

How it works	Examples
You use the relative pronoun *whose* to show that people or things belong together.	– That's the actor **whose** daughter goes to school with me.
You can use *whose* in defining clauses where the information is needed to make the meaning clear. Don't put a comma between the main clause and the defining relative clause.	– *Lord of the Rings* is about a hobbit **whose** mission is to throw a magic ring into a mountain of fire.

How it works	Examples
You can use *whose* in non-defining clauses to give extra information. Remember to put a comma between the main clause and the non-defining relative clause.	– Film writer and director Peter Jackson, **whose** *Lord of the Rings* films won 17 Oscars, was born in New Zealand in 1961.

Check-out

1. Lies den folgenden Text. Verknüpfe die Sätze mit *whose*, bei denen es sinnvoll ist. Handelt es sich um notwendige oder nicht notwendige Relativsätze? Setze ein Komma, wo du es für nötig hälst.

   Stephenie Meyer is a writer. Her vampire novels have been turned into films. They are about a 17-year-old girl. Her name is Bella Swan. She moves from Phoenix to Forks to live with her dad. There she falls in love with Edward Cullen. His family are all vampires. Stephenie Meyer has won the hearts of many teenagers. Her novels are often described as 'dark romance'.

Witchcraft reloaded won three Oscars, **which** made it the most successful fantasy film of the year.

G111 Das Relativpronomen *which* mit Bezug auf einen Hauptsatz *The relative pronoun* which *to comment on the main clause*

Check-in

Read the extract from a newspaper article.

And the winner is …

Yesterday *Witchcraft reloaded* won three Oscars, **which** made it the most successful fantasy film of the year. In his speech director Jonathan Peacock thanked his team. He also said that he was already planning a sequel, **which** came as a surprise to a lot of people.

1. Schau dir die beiden nicht notwendigen Relativsätze mit *which* an. Worauf bezieht sich *which*?

2. Wie übersetzt du *which* in diesen beiden Fällen ins Deutsche?

REGEL

1. Im Zeitungsartikel über *Witchcraft reloaded* ist davon die Rede, dass es der erfolgreichste Fantasyfilm des Jahres war. Der **Relativsatz** *which made it the most successful fantasy film of the year* **kommentiert den Hauptsatz**.
2. In diesem Fall hat *which* kein Bezugswort im Hauptsatz, sondern **bezieht sich auf den gesamten Hauptsatz.** Es entspricht im Deutschen dem Wort „was".
3. Da es sich um einen **nachgestellten Kommentar in Form eines nicht notwendigen Relativsatzes** handelt, musst du diesen **durch Komma(s) vom Hauptsatz abtrennen**.

Hauptsatz	Nebensatz (= nicht notwendiger Relativsatz)	
	Relativ-pronomen	
Witchcraft reloaded **won three Oscars,**	which	made it the most successful fantasy film of the year.
Jonathan Peacock is already planning a sequel,	which	came as a surprise to a lot of people.

English summary

How it works	Example
A non-defining relative clause with *which* can be used as a comment on the main clause.	– Julia has lent me the DVD of *Edward Scissorhands*, **which** is very kind of her.

Check-out

1. Vervollständige die Sätze mit einem passenden Kommentar.

   which was a pity • which was great for his fans • which his fans hadn't expected at all

   a) *Although Orlando Bloom wasn't feeling very well, he came to the film festival, …*
   b) *He even gave autographs while he was walking along the red carpet, …*
   c) *He only gave a short interview for a TV station, …*

20 Die Bedingungssätze

> If she **doesn't love** me back, **I'll** never **be** happy again.

G112 Bedingungssatz Typ I: Erfüllbare Bedingungen
Conditional sentence type I: Realistic conditions

Check-in

Tom has fallen in love with a girl at his school, but he doesn't know how to tell her. He is talking to his older brother about it.

Tom: Sarah is so sweet. If she **doesn't love** me back, **I'll** never **be** happy again.
Brother: She **won't know** how you feel about her if you **don't do** anything.
Tom: But what? If I **send** her a card on Valentine's Day, she **may not like** it.
I can tell you, if she **goes** to the school dance with someone else,
I'll go crazy.
Brother: If you **want** to be happy again, **don't** just **sit** there, **do** something!

1. Lies dir noch einmal die ersten beiden Beispielsätze mit *if* durch und bestimme die Zeiten im *if*-Satz und im Hauptsatz.

2. Schreibe den Satz *She won't know how you feel …* so um, dass der *if*-Satz am Anfang steht, also wie im ersten Beispielsatz.

> **REGEL**

1. Bedingungssätze bestehen im Englischen, wie auch im Deutschen, aus einem **Nebensatz (*if*-Satz)** und einem **Hauptsatz**.
2. Wenn du ausdrücken willst, dass sich **eine Bedingung erfüllen kann**, verwendest du den Bedingungssatz Typ I. In der Tabelle siehst du, welche Zeiten dabei normalerweise verwendet werden.

> **MERKHILFE**
> After if, no will or would! For English people that's no good.

if-Satz: *simple present*	Hauptsatz: *will-future*
If she **doesn't love** me back,	**I'll** never **be** happy again.
Wenn sie nicht auch in mich verliebt ist,	werde ich nie wieder glücklich sein.

3. Im Hauptsatz kann statt des *will-future* auch ein **Modalverb + Infinitiv** oder der **Imperativ** stehen.

> **TIPP**
> Steht der Hauptsatz am Satzanfang, darfst du zwischen Haupt- und Nebensatz kein Komma setzen.

if-Satz: *simple present*	Hauptsatz: Modalverb + Infinitiv / Imperativ
If I **send** her a card,	she **may not like** it.
Wenn ich ihr eine Karte schicke,	mag sie sie vielleicht nicht.
If you **want** to be happy again,	**don't** just **sit** there, **do** something!
Wenn du wieder glücklich sein willst,	sitz nicht einfach rum, tu etwas!

■ **Achtung!**
- Das deutsche Wort „wenn" hat im Englischen zwei Bedeutungen:
  - „wenn" im Sinne von „falls" = *if*
    ***If** she goes to the school dance with someone else, I'll go crazy.*
    Wenn (= falls) sie mit jemand anderem zum Schulball geht, werde ich verrückt.
    (Es ist nicht sicher, dass sie mit jemand anderem zum Schulball geht.)
  - „wenn" im Sinne von „dann", „wenn" = *when*
    ***When** Valentine's Day comes, I'll send her a card.*
    Wenn (= dann, wenn) Valentinstag ist, werde ich ihr eine Karte schicken.
    (Valentinstag kommt sicher. Es ist nur eine Frage der Zeit.)

- Bei den Bedingungssätzen Typ I kann im *if*-Satz statt des *simple present* auch das *present perfect* stehen:
  - *If you **haven't sent** her a card yet, she won't get it in time.*
    Wenn du ihr noch keine Karte **geschickt hast,** wird sie sie nicht rechtzeitig bekommen.

English summary

How it works	Examples
A conditional sentence has two parts, the if-clause and the main clause. You use a conditional sentence type I if you think the condition may be fulfilled.	– If you **don't tell** her, she **will** never **know** how much she means to you. – She **won't know** how you feel about her if you **don't do** anything.
In the if-clause you usually use the simple present, in the main clause you use … – the will-future, – a modal verb + infinitive, – the imperative.	 – If I **see** her on the bus tomorrow, I'**ll speak** to her. – If she **likes** you, you **can ask** her to go out with you. – If you **get** the chance, **talk** to her.

Check-out

1. Während Tom darüber nachdenkt, wie er Sarah auf sich aufmerksam machen könnte, haben seine Freunde ganz andere Dinge im Kopf. Formuliere Sätze mit *If I …* und den vorgegebenen Elementen.

   a) Sue: *pass driving test • get a car from my parents*
   b) Steve: *save enough money • buy a new computer*
   c) Ian: *work hard at school • go to university*
   d) Chloe: *go to the party • meet John*
   e) Noah: *get a well-paid job soon • go to Spain on holiday*
   f) Emily: *parents allow it • invite all my friends to a party*

> If I **had** wings, I **would fly** up to heaven.

G113 Bedingungssatz Typ II: Unerfüllbare Bedingungen
Conditional sentence type II: Unrealistic conditions

Check-in

Tom, who has fallen in love with a girl at his school, hears the following song on the radio and sings along:

> If I **had** wings, I **would fly** up to heaven and I **could see** everything.
> I **would fly** to you if I **had** wings.
> If you **loved** me back, I **would be** the happiest man in the world.

1. Warum kann man sagen *if I had wings* („wenn ich Flügel hätte"), aber nicht *if I have wings* („wenn ich Flügel habe")?

2. Übertrage den Satz *If you loved me back* … ins Deutsche. Vergleiche dann die Zeitformen im *if*-Satz. Was fällt dir auf?

REGEL

1. Mit einem Bedingungssatz kannst du auch **Bedingungen ausdrücken, die nicht oder nur theoretisch erfüllbar sind**, weil …
   a) sie unmöglich sind.
   b) der Sprecher sie für unmöglich hält.
   c) der Sprecher sie (zur Zeit) für unwahrscheinlich hält.

2. Für diese Bedingungssätze vom Typ II benutzt du die folgenden Zeiten:

> **TIPP**
> Das conditional bildest du aus „would (not)" + Infinitiv.

if-Satz: *simple past*	Hauptsatz: *conditional*
If I **had** wings,	I **would fly** up to heaven.
Wenn ich Flügel hätte,	würde ich zum Himmel fliegen.
If you **loved** me back,	I **would be** the happiest man in the world.
Wenn du mich auch lieben würdest,	wäre ich der glücklichste Mann der Welt.

3. Im Hauptsatz können statt des *conditional* auch die **Modalverben** *could* („könnte") oder *might* („würde … vielleicht") **+ Infinitiv** stehen.

if-Satz: *simple past*	Hauptsatz: *could / might* + Infinitiv
If you **had** wings, too,	we **could / might meet** in heaven.
Wenn du auch Flügel hättest,	könnten/würden wir uns vielleicht im Himmel treffen.

■ **Achtung!**
– Manchmal findest du auch die Ausdrücke *as if* und *what if*. Mit *as if* („als ob")
kannst du einen **Vergleich** anstellen, **der** aber **nicht wirklich zutrifft**. Mit *what if*
(„was wenn", „was wäre wenn") stellst du dir eine **Situation** vor, **die wahrscheinlich nicht eintreten wird**. Du verwendest in diesen Sätzen ebenfalls das *simple
past*, auch wenn im Deutschen der Konjunktiv stehen muss. Vergleiche:
  • *I feel **as if** I **was** in heaven.*
    Ich habe das Gefühl, **als ob** ich im Himmel **wäre**.
  • ***What if** we **broke up**?*
    Was wenn wir uns **trennen würden/trennten**?

■ **Mündlicher/schriftlicher Sprachgebrauch**
– Im formalen schriftlichen Sprachgebrauch verwendet man bei dem Verb *be* im
if-Satz in der 1. und 3. Person Singular *were* statt *was*. Das ist die korrekte Form
des Konjunktivs.
  • schriftlich: *If I were in heaven … / If he were in heaven …*
  • mündlich: *If I was in heaven … / If he was in heaven …*

– Im mündlichen Sprachgebrauch verwendest du *If I were you* („An deiner Stelle",
„Wenn ich du wäre"), um einen Vorschlag zu machen oder eine Empfehlung zu
geben.
  • ***If I were you**, I would ask her for a date.*

English summary

How it works	Examples
You use a conditional sentence type II in situations that cannot be fulfilled or that you think cannot be fulfilled. In the if-clause you use the simple past, in the main clause you use …	
– the conditional,	– If we **lived** nearer, I **would see** her more often.
– the modal verbs *could* or *might* + infinitive.	– If I **was** two years older, she **might notice** me.

Check-out

1. Vervollständige die folgenden Bedingungssätze mit dem *simple past* und dem
conditional.

   a) *I (have) lots of friends if people (know) how nice I am.*
   b) *My ex-girlfriend (still like) me if I (be) a completely different person.*
   c) *My mum and I (not fight) so much if she (try) to understand me.*
   d) *I (buy) all the coolest clothes if my parents (give) me more pocket money.*
   e) *I (not always yell) at my little brother if he (act) more like a normal kid!*

If only we **hadn't been** in such a hurry, we **would have said** 'I love you' one more time.

G114 Bedingungssatz Typ III: Unerfüllbare Bedingungen mit Vergangenheitsbezug *Conditional sentence type III: Conditions that can no longer be fulfilled*

Check-in

On September 11, Tom finds a poem in the newspaper. It was written after the terrorist attacks on the World Trade Center in 2001:

If only …

If only we **hadn't been** in such a hurry, we **would have said** 'I love you' one more time.
If only we **had said** 'I love you' one more time, we **might have stayed** together longer that morning.
If only we **had stayed** together longer, they **couldn't have taken** you from me forever.
(…)

1. Lies dir noch einmal das Gedicht durch und bestimme die Zeiten im ersten *if*-Satz und dem dazugehörigen Hauptsatz.

2. Übertrage den Satz mit *If only we hadn't been* … ins Deutsche. Was fällt dir an der Verwendung der Zeiten im *if*-Satz und im Hauptsatz auf?

REGEL

1. In dem Gedicht überlegt ein Mensch, was er anders gemacht hätte, wenn er von den Terroranschlägen des 11. September 2001 vorher gewusst hätte. Mit dem Bedingungssatz Typ III drückst du aus, **wie eine Situation oder ein Ereignis** unter bestimmten Bedingungen **hätte anders verlaufen können**. Da man aber die Vergangenheit nicht ändern kann, ist die **Bedingung unerfüllbar**.

2. Für diese Bedingungssätze vom Typ III benutzt du die folgenden Zeiten:

TIPP
Das conditional perfect bildest du aus „would (not) have" + past participle.

if-Satz: *past perfect*	Hauptsatz: *conditional perfect*
If we **hadn't been** in such a hurry,	we **would have said** 'I love you' one more time.
Wenn wir nicht so in Eile gewesen wären,	hätten wir noch einmal „Ich liebe dich" gesagt.

3. Im Hauptsatz können statt des *conditional perfect* auch die **Modalverben** *could/might* + ***have*** + ***past participle*** stehen.

if-Satz: *past perfect*	Hauptsatz: *could / might + have + past participle*
If we **had said** 'I love you' one more time,	we **might have stayed** together longer that morning.
Wenn wir noch einmal „Ich liebe dich" gesagt hätten,	wären wir vielleicht an jenem Morgen länger zusammen geblieben.

if-Satz: *past perfect*	Hauptsatz: *could / might + have + past participle*
If we **had stayed** together longer,	they **couldn't have taken** you from me forever.
Wenn wir länger zusammen geblieben wären,	hätten sie dich mir nicht für immer wegnehmen können.

■ Achtung!

- Im Deutschen wird „**hätte(n)**" bzw. „**wäre(n)**" sowohl im Bedingungssatz als auch im Hauptsatz verwendet. Im Englischen brauchst du jedoch unterschiedliche Zeiten:
  - Wenn wir ein Taxi **genommen hätten**, **hätten** wir viel Zeit **gespart**.
    *If we **had taken** a taxi, we **would have** saved a lot of time.*

- Wenn die Folge einer Bedingung in der Gegenwart wirksam ist, steht im Hauptsatz das *conditional*:
  - *If we **had taken** a taxi, we **would be** at home by now.*
    Wenn wir ein Taxi **genommen hätten**, **wären** wir jetzt zu Hause.

  Auch die Kombination *simple past – conditional perfect* ist möglich:
  - *If you **knew** New York better, we **wouldn't have needed** a taxi.*
    Wenn du New York besser **kennen würdest**, **hätten** wir kein Taxi **gebraucht**.

■ Mündlicher/schriftlicher Sprachgebrauch

- Im formellen schriftlichen Sprachgebrauch werden die Langformen verwendet. Im mündlichen Sprachgebrauch hörst du dagegen sehr oft die Kurzformen:
  - *If we'd known, we'd have loved more.*

- Das verkürzte *'d* hat allerdings zwei Bedeutungen:
  - *If we**'d** known … = If we **had** known …*
    *we**'d** have loved … = we **would** have loved …*

English summary

How it works	Examples
You use a conditional sentence type III to talk about the past and how things would/could/might have been different if something had or hadn't happened. These conditions cannot be fulfilled because it is impossible to change the past.	– If he **hadn't been** at a meeting in the World Trade Center, he **would have survived**.
In the if-clause you use the past perfect, in the main clause you use … – the conditional perfect, – the modal verbs *could/might + have + past participle*	– If we **had known**, we **would have loved** more. – If you **had told** me earlier, I **could have helped** you.

Check-out

1. Schreibe die Langform des folgenden Satzes auf.
   If you'd told me, I'd have tried to help you.

2. Tom denkt darüber nach, was wäre, wenn einige Dinge in der Vergangenheit nicht passiert wären. Schreibe seine Gedanken auf.

   a) *my dad • not find a new job* → *we • not move to this town*
      If my dad hadn't …
   b) *we • not move to this town* → *I • not come to this school*
   c) *I • not come to this school* → *Sarah and I • not meet*
   d) *Sarah and I • not meet* → *I • not fall in love with her*
   e) *I • not fall in love with her* → *I • spend more time with friends*

If someone you love **doesn't love** you back, it really **hurts**.

G115 Bedingungssatz Typ 0: Gesetzmäßigkeiten oder Regelmäßigkeiten ausdrücken *Conditional sentences type 0: Expressing facts or regular activities*

Check-in

Sarah and her best friend Carolyn are reading a teenage magazine. They have found this answer from an agony aunt for a teenager with a broken heart.

> If someone you love **doesn't love** you back, it really **hurts**. But if you **sit** at home and **think** about him or her all the time, it just **makes** you unhappy. So what can you do? If you **go out** and **enjoy** yourself, you normally **forget** about your troubles.

1. Die Sätze in der Antwort der Kummerkastentante verstoßen eigentlich gegen die Regeln der Bedingungssätze Typ I. Warum?

2. Erkläre den Unterschied zwischen den folgenden beiden Sätzen:

   a) *If she doesn't love me back, I'll be unhappy.*
   b) *If someone you love doesn't love you back, it makes you unhappy.*

1. Wenn du **Aussagen von allgemeiner Gültigkeit machen willst** oder **ausdrücken** möchtest, **dass Dinge mit einer gewissen Regelmäßigkeit eintreten**, verwendest du sowohl im Haupt- als auch im Nebensatz das *simple present*.

if-Satz: *simple present*	Hauptsatz: *simple present*
If someone **doesn't love** you back,	it really **hurts**.
Wenn jemand dich nicht auch liebt,	tut das wirklich weh.
If you only **sit** at home and **think** about him or her,	you **become** unhappy.
Wenn du nur zu Hause sitzt und an ihn oder sie denkst,	wirst du unglücklich.

English summary

How it works	Example
You use the simple present in the if-clause and in the main clause to say that things usually happen in a certain way in life or if you want to express facts.	– If you **go out** and **meet** other people, you always **feel** better.

Check-out

1. Ein Paar ist erst seit wenigen Monaten zusammen. Jetzt streiten sie sich zum ersten Mal. Entscheide jeweils, welches der passendere Satz ist und erkläre den Bedeutungsunterschied zwischen den beiden Sätzen.

She says:
a) *If you talk this way, it hurts me.*
b) *If you talk this way, it will hurt me.*

A day later, he talks to his best friend. His friend says:
a) *Don't worry. It's not the end of the world if you fight sometimes.*
b) *Don't worry. It won't be the end of the world if you fight sometimes.*

> I wish I had met you earlier.

G116 Wunschsätze mit dem *simple past* und dem *past perfect*
Simple past and past perfect to express wishes

Check-in

Tom decides to send a valentine's card to the girl he likes. On the Internet he finds some examples:

1. Welche der Wünsche auf den Valentinskarten beziehen sich auf die Gegenwart und welche auf die Vergangenheit?

2. Bestimme die hervorgehobenen Zeitformen, die in den Wunschsätzen jeweils verwendet werden.

REGEL

1. Wunschsätze können sich auf die Gegenwart oder auf die Vergangenheit beziehen.
2. Mit *I wish … / I'd rather … / If (only) … / It's (high) time …* und dem *simple past* drückst du **Wünsche** aus, **die du in der Gegenwart für nicht oder nur kaum erfüllbar hältst**.
3. *I wish … / If only …* und das *past perfect* verwendest du für **Wünsche, die nicht mehr erfüllbar sind, da** die entsprechenden **Handlungen in der Vergangenheit** geschahen oder versäumt wurden.
4. Im Deutschen verwendest du in beiden Fällen den Konjunktiv:

Wünsche für die Gegenwart: *simple past*	**I wish** you **were** here.
	Ich wünschte, du wärst hier.
	If only you **were** here.
	Wenn du nur hier wärst.
Wünsche für die Vergangenheit: *past perfect*	**I wish** I **had met** you earlier.
	Ich wünschte, ich hätte dich früher kennen gelernt.
	If only I **had met** you earlier.
	Wenn ich dich nur früher kennen gelernt hätte.

English summary

How it works	Examples
With *I wish …/I'd rather …/If only …/ It's (high) time …* and the simple past you express wishes that relate to the present and that you know cannot come true.	– **I wish** you **knew** how much I think of you.
With *I wish …/If only …* and the past perfect you express wishes that relate to the past and therefore cannot come true.	– **If only** I **hadn't waited** so long.

Check-out

1. Schreibe die folgenden Satzanfänge aus Songtexten um, sodass sie zu Wunschsätzen werden.

   a) *If I were a boy …*
      I wish I were a boy.
   b) *If you'd called yesterday …*
   c) *If you want to be my lover …*

21 Satzverknüpfungen

I'm interested in the Native Americans, **and** I'd definitely like to find out more about them.

G117 Die Verknüpfung von Hauptsätzen durch Konjunktionen und Adverbien *Using conjunctions and adverbs to link main clauses*

Check-in

Katie and her class are doing a project on America. She is working in a group with three others, Mark, Adam and Jonathan. The topic they have chosen is 'The American West'. Read their conversation.

Katie: Well, how are we going to start? The American West is a big subject, **so** we'll have to make a plan. Who wants to do what?

Mark: I'm interested in the Native Americans, **and** I'd definitely like to find out more about their traditions.

Adam: OK. I could look for information on the early settlers, **or** Jonathan and I could work on that together. What do you think, Jonathan?

Jonathan: Normally I'd say 'yes', **but** actually I'd prefer to do 'the Wild West'. You know, the difference between Hollywood films and reality, that kind of thing.

Katie: Right. Well, I'm quite interested in the early settlers, like you, Adam, **so** maybe I can help you with that. OK then, let's see what we can all find on the Internet **and** then we can go on from there.

1. Welche der hervorgehobenen Konjunktionen drückt …
   a) aus, dass auch etwas anderes möglich ist?
   b) einen Gegensatz aus?

2. Übertrage die beiden Sätze mit der Konjuktion *so* ins Deutsche.

TIPP

Mit „and", „but", „so" etc. kannst du auch einzelne Wörter oder Satzteile verbinden:
- There is a difference between Hollywood films **and** reality.
- Jonathan is interested in old cowboy films **but** Katie isn't.

REGEL

1. Du verwendest Verknüpfungen, um Texte interessanter zu machen. Außerdem lassen sie sich so besser lesen.
2. Du kannst **Hauptsätze durch** die **Konjunktionen** *and*, *but*, *or* oder *so* miteinander **verbinden**.

Verknüpfung durch Konjunktionen	
Mark is interested in the Native Americans, **and** he wants to find out more about them.	… und …
Have we got enough material on the early settlers, **or** should we look on the Internet again?	… oder …

Verknüpfung durch Konjunktionen	
We were in California last summer, **but** we didn't meet any Native Americans.	… aber …
There's a lot to do on this project, **so** we must start right away.	… also/deshalb/ darum …

3. Auch mit Hilfe des **Adverbs** *however* kannst du Hauptsätze miteinander verknüpfen.

Verknüpfung durch Adverb	
Some people decide to drive all the way from Chicago to Los Angeles along Route 66; **however** most people prefer to fly.	… jedoch/ aber …

◼ **Schriftlicher/mündlicher Sprachgebrauch**
 – Während im **umgangssprachlichen** Englisch normalerweise *but* verwendet wird, um einen Gegensatz auszudrücken, wird **in förmlicheren Texten** oft das Adverb *however* gebraucht.

English summary

How it works	Examples
You can use conjunctions and adverbs (*and, but, so* etc.) to link main clauses. In this way you can make texts more interesting.	– Jonathan has been watching some old Hollywood films about the Wild West, **and** he's putting a few ideas together. – I can collect information about national parks, **or** I could just concentrate on the Grand Canyon. – Adam's mother teaches History, **so** she can give him a few tips.

Check-out

1. Verbinde zwei passende Hauptsätze mit Hilfe von *and, but, or* oder *so*.

You can find a lot of information in history books.

We can make a poster with interesting texts and pictures.

We must finish the project by the end of the month.

The Wild West seems to be all about cowboys and Indians.

Hollywood Westerns can be very exciting.

I'm interested in the 'first Americans'.

Often they haven't got much to do with reality.

Would you prefer to look on the Internet?

We can also give a presentation to the class.

The important part that women played is often forgotten.

I want to find out more about them.

Let's start as soon as possible.

It was not possible to cross the continent quickly **until** the first transcontinental railroad opened in 1869.

G118 Adverbiale Nebensätze der Zeit
Adverbial clauses of time

Check-in

Read what Katie and Adam have found on the Internet.

www.morehistory.com/transcontinentalrailroad

When people want to travel from the East Coast to the Pacific, distance is no problem. They just hop on a plane.
It wasn't always that easy. In fact, it was not possible to cross the continent quickly **until** the first transcontinental railroad opened in 1869.

Before this railroad was built, the journey had taken months. Earlier in the 19th century, **when** the first groups of white settlers began to move west in their covered wagons, travelling was difficult. It was also dangerous, especially **while** they were making their way through Indian territory. And it was very slow. But **after** the railroad was finally completed, people could get from New York to California in only 83 hours.

1. Übertrage die beiden Sätze ins Deutsche. Wie übersetzt du jeweils *when*?

   a) *When people want to travel from the East Coast to the Pacific, distance is no problem.*
   b) *When the first groups of white settlers began to move west in their covered wagons, travelling was difficult.*

2. Übertrage den folgenden Satz ins Deutsche. Wie unterscheidet sich die Wortstellung im Englischen von der im Deutschen?
   Before the railroad was built, the journey had taken months.

1. Wenn du einer Aussage noch **zusätzliche Informationen** (z. B. Zeitbestimmungen) hinzufügen möchtest, kannst du einen **adverbialen Nebensatz an** deine **Hauptaussage anschließen**.
2. **Mit** den **Konjunktionen** *after, as soon as, before, since, until, when* und *while* kannst du so **einen Hauptsatz mit einem Nebensatz verbinden**. Dabei entsteht ein Satzgefüge:

Hauptsatz	Nebensatz
The journey had taken months	**before** the first transcontinental railroad was built.

3. **Nebensätze** können **sowohl nach** dem Hauptsatz **als auch vor dem Hauptsatz** stehen:

* *Before the first transcontinental railroad was built,* the journey had taken months.

Nebensätze der Zeit *after* (nachdem), *as soon as* (sobald), *before* (bevor/ehe), *since* (seit), *until* (bis), *when* (wenn/als), *while* (während)	
Before the Europeans arrived in North America, between one and two million Indians lived there.	**Bevor** die Europäer in Nordamerika ankamen, lebten dort zwischen ein und zwei Millionen Indianer.
As soon as white settlers started to move west, trouble began for the Indians.	**Sobald** weiße Siedler anfingen, gen Westen zu ziehen, begannen die Probleme für die Indianer.
Some tribes decided to fight for their land **when** the US government wanted to move them away to reservations.	Einige Stämme beschlossen, um ihr Land zu kämpfen, **als** die US-Regierung sie in Reservationen umsiedeln wollte.
Many people were killed **while** the railroad was being built.	Viele Menschen wurden getötet, **während** die Eisenbahnstrecke gebaut wurde.
Adam and Katie have discovered a lot of interesting facts **since** they started work on the project.	Adam und Katie haben viele interessante Fakten entdeckt, **seit** sie mit der Arbeit an ihrem Projekt begonnen haben.
Yesterday they worked at Katie's house **until** Adam had to go home.	Gestern arbeiteten sie bei Katie, **bis** Adam nach Hause gehen musste.
Katie did another hour on her own **after** Adam had left.	Katie machte noch eine Stunde lang weiter, **nachdem** Adam gegangen war.

🟧 **Achtung!**

– Die Satzstellung im Deutschen ist anders als im Englischen. Im Englischen bleibt die Reihenfolge **Subjekt – Verb – Objekt** im Hauptsatz und im Nebensatz immer erhalten. Vergleiche:

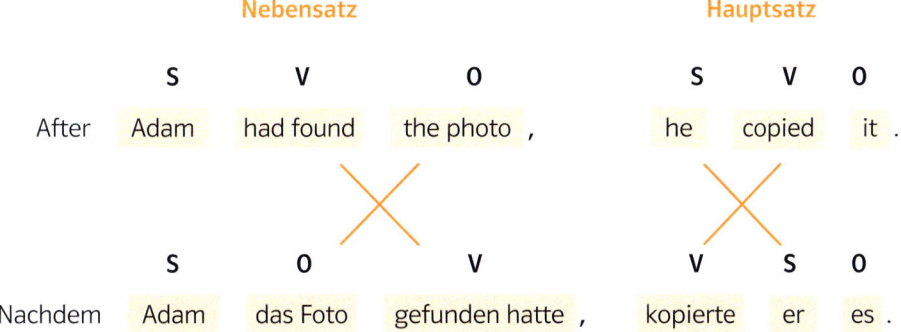

English summary

How it works	Examples
Adverbial clauses of time are often used to add information. You can introduce them with *after, as soon as, before, until, since, when, while*.	– **When** the first settlers travelled west in their covered wagons, the journey to California took months.
You can start your sentence either with the main clause or the adverbial clause.	– It was especially dangerous **while** they were moving through Indian territory.
If you put the adverbial clause first, then you must use a comma.	– **After** the railroad was finished, the journey west became easier and much safer.

Check-out

1. Vervollständige die folgenden Sätze mit der passenden Konjunktion.

   after • as soon as • before • when • while • until

   a) … *you travel from the East Coast to the Pacific, you cross the Mississippi.*
   b) … *the Transcontinental Railroad was built, the journey had taken months.*
   c) … *it was finished, the trip took 'only' 83 hours.*
   d) … *the railroad opened, more and more white settlers started to move into Indian territory.*
   e) *In those days people sometimes saw large numbers of buffalo … they were travelling west.*
   f) *Sometimes the train had to stop … a group of buffalo had left the track.*

2. Übertrage die folgenden Sätze ins Englische.

   a) Katie hört gerne Musik, während sie ihre Hausaufgaben macht.
   b) Sobald Jonathan einen guten Text gefunden hat, können wir weitermachen.
   c) Wir müssen warten, bis er anruft.
   d) Nachdem sie genügend Texte gefunden hatten, fingen sie an gute Bilder zu suchen.

G119 Adverbiale Nebensätze des Grundes
Adverbial clauses of reason

> The buffalo were very important for the Sioux Indians **because** they needed the animals for their daily lives.

Check-in

Read the texts Mark has written for a poster on Indian traditions.

THE IMPORTANCE OF THE BUFFALO

The buffalo on the Great Plains were very important for the Sioux Indians **because** they needed the animals for their daily lives.

    Since the Sioux ate the meat of the buffalo, life without them was not possible. They also needed buffalo skins and bones **because** they used them for their clothes, their homes and other equipment.

In the second half of the 19th century, the whites killed most of the buffalo. **As** they realized the Sioux would die without the buffalo for food, this was a sure way to bring their numbers down. White settlers often said: 'The only good Indian is a dead Indian.'

---

1. a) Übertrage den folgenden Satz ins Deutsche.
   Since the Sioux ate the meat of the buffalo, life without them was not possible.
   b) Welche andere Konjunktion in dem Text hat die gleiche Verwendungsweise wie *since*?

2. Schreibe den Satz *Since the Sioux ate the meat …* um. Beginne mit dem Hauptsatz und leite den Nebensatz mit *because* ein.

1. Während Nebensätze der **Zeit** (→ G118) verdeutlichen, **wann** etwas geschieht, sagen Nebensätze des **Grundes** aus, **warum** etwas geschieht.
2. **Nebensätze mit *because* stehen normalerweise hinter dem Hauptsatz. Nebensätze mit *as* oder *since* stehen meist vor dem Hauptsatz.**

Nebensätze des Grundes *because* (weil), *as* (da), *since* (da)	
The buffalo on the Great Plains were important for the Sioux Indians **because** they couldn't survive without them.	Die Büffel in der Prärie waren wichtig für die Sioux, **weil** sie ohne sie nicht überleben konnten.
Since the Indians had a simpler lifestyle, the whites had no respect for them.	**Da** die Indianer eine einfachere Lebensweise hatten, hatten die Weißen keinen Respekt vor ihnen.
As they wanted the best land for themselves, the whites forced a lot of Indian tribes to move to reservations.	**Da** sie das beste Land für sich selbst wollten, zwangen die Weißen viele Indianerstämme in Reservationen zu ziehen.

■ **Achtung!**
  – Die Konjunktion *since* kann sowohl einen **Nebensatz der Zeit** als auch einen **Nebensatz des Grundes** einleiten. Vergleiche:
    • *Katie and the others have found out a lot about the Native Americans **since** they started work on the project last week.* (… seit …)
    • ***Since** Adam is going to be away at the weekend, they won't be able to discuss things before Monday.* (Da …)

English summary

How it works	Examples
Adverbial clauses of reason say why something is done. An adverbial clause with *because* normally follows the main clause.	– Some Indian tribes fought against the whites **because** they didn't want to give up their land.
Clauses with *as* and *since* usually come before the main clause.	– **As** so many of them died in the 19th century, the US Indian population was down to 250,000 by 1900. – **Since** more and more settlers wanted land, the Native Americans had no chance in the end.

Check-out

1. Bilde Sätze mit *as*, *since* oder *because*. Wähle dazu eine logische Begründung.
   Tipp: Überlege gut, welcher Satzteil den Haupt- bzw. Nebensatz darstellt.
   Manchmal muss die Konjunktion am Satzanfang stehen.

   a) *The buffalo were important for the Indians. (because)*
      - *Their children could ride them.*
      - *They kept them as pets.*
      - *They ate their meat.*
   b) *The whites didn't respect them. (since)*
      - *The Indians lived in better houses.*
      - *The Indians couldn't speak English.*
      - *The Indians had a simpler lifestyle.*
   c) *The whites killed most of the buffalo. (as)*
      - *They were afraid of the huge animals.*
      - *The animals stopped the trains.*
      - *They realized that the Indians couldn't survive without buffalo meat.*
   d) *The whites moved a lot of Indians to reservations. (because)*
      - *They wanted to give them a better life.*
      - *They wanted the land for themselves.*
      - *The land on the reservations was much better.*
   e) *Some Indian tribes fought against the whites. (since)*
      - *They wanted the reservations for themselves.*
      - *They didn't like the colour of their skins.*
      - *They didn't want to give up their land.*
   f) *The Indian population in the US was down to 250,000 by the end of the 19th century. (as)*
      - *Many Indians had moved to Europe.*
      - *It was too cold in their simple houses.*
      - *Lots of them had been killed by the whites or died on the way to reservations.*

> In old Westerns all American Indians are played by white actors, **although** Native Americans could have taken those parts.

G120 Weitere adverbiale Nebensätze
Other adverbial clauses

Check-in

Read the ideas Jonathan has put together for a presentation.

The Wild West: Myth and reality

- Have you noticed? In old Hollywood films about the Wild West, all the American Indians are played by white actors, **although** lots of Native Americans could have taken these parts!
- Cowboys in these old films all seem to be white men, **as if** that was a true picture of reality. In fact, many of the cowboys in the Wild West were African-Americans, **while** others were Mexicans or – yes! – American Indians!
- The mythical idea of cowboys in fights against 'wild' Indians was created **so that** films would offer top entertainment. Films about life out west **as** it really was would not have been exciting enough for 20th-century audiences.

---

1. Welche der adverbialen Nebensätze in dem Text drücken aus, dass ein anderer oder gegensätzlicher Gesichtspunkt eingeräumt wird?

2. Welche Sätze drücken einen Vergleich aus? Und welcher Satz beschreibt eine logische Folge ?

REGEL

1. Außer den Nebensätzen der Zeit (➔ **G118**) und des Grundes (➔ **G119**) gibt es noch eine Reihe weiterer adverbialer Nebensätze, die durch Konjunktionen eingeleitet werden. Zu ihnen gehören:

Nebensätze, die einen Gegensatz beschreiben oder etwas einräumen (*although, while*)	A lot of people still enjoy the old Wild West films **although** they aren't very realistic.
	Viele Leute genießen immer noch die alten Westernfilme, **obwohl** sie nicht sehr realistisch sind.
	In reality, a lot of cowboys were African-Americans **while** some were Mexicans or even Indians!
	In Wirklichkeit waren viele Cowboys Afro-Amerikaner, es gab **aber auch** einige, die Mexikaner oder sogar Indianer waren.

Nebensätze, die etwas mit der Aussage im Hauptsatz vergleichen (*as, as if*)	Even in films, the whites continued to treat the Indians unfairly **as** they had always done.
	Sogar in Filmen behandelten die Weißen die Indianer weiterhin unfair, **so wie** sie es immer getan hatten.
	The old films were full of clichés about 'good guys' and 'bad guys', **as if** that was the true story of the West.
	Die alten Filme waren voller Klischees über ‚gute Jungs' und ‚böse Jungs', **als ob** das die wahre Geschichte des Westens wäre.
Nebensätze, die einen Zweck oder eine logische Folge beschreiben (*so that*)	Jonathan wants to show the others some photos **so that** they can help him to choose the best one.
	Jonathan möchte den anderen einige Fotos zeigen, **damit** sie ihm dabei helfen können, das beste auszusuchen.

> **TIPP**
> Wenn du mehr zu den Nebensätzen der Bedingung wissen möchtest, schau dir Kapitel 20 an.

English summary

How it works	Examples
Apart from the adverbial clauses of time and reason there are a few other types of adverbial clauses. These can describe a contrast (*although, while*), express a comparison (*as, as if*) or state that something is the result of something else (*so that*).	– Jonathan's father still likes the old Westerns **although** some of them are in black and white. – *The Good, the Bad and the Ugly* is on TV again tonight! Dad's planning to watch it, of course, **as** I'd expected. – Let's go round to Jonathan's house this evening **so that** we can all watch the film together.

Check-out

1. Verwende die Konjuktionen in Klammern und verbinde einen Hauptsatz mit einem Nebensatz zu einem Satzgefüge. Tipp: An manchen Stellen musst du die englischen Sätze leicht verändern.

   a) *They had planned everything very carefully. But still a lot of things went wrong.* (although)

   b) *Adam wanted to ask his mother for help. The others preferred to do everything themselves.* (while)

   c) *Jonathan talked about cowboy films for ages. But they didn't have all the time in the world.* (as if)

   d) *We can all watch an old Western together. Then we can understand things better.* (so that)

   e) *Could you do something on Yellowstone? You know far more about national parks than we do.* (as)

Anhang

Zahlen, Uhrzeit, Datum

Die Kardinalzahlen *Cardinal numbers*

0 = zero	10 = ten	20 = twenty	30 = thirty
1 = one	11 = eleven	21 = twenty-one	40 = forty
2 = two	12 = twelve	22 = twenty-two	50 = fifty
3 = three	13 = thirteen	23 = twenty-three	60 = sixty
4 = four	14 = fourteen	24 = twenty-four	70 = seventy
5 = five	15 = fifteen	25 = twenty-five	80 = eighty
6 = six	16 = sixteen	26 = twenty-six	90 = ninety
7 = seven	17 = seventeen	27 = twenty-seven	100 = one hundred
8 = eight	18 = eighteen	28 = twenty-eight	200 = two hundred
9 = nine	19 = nineteen	29 = twenty-nine	1,000 = one thousand

■ **Achtung!**
- Für die Zahl Null gibt es im Englischen verschiedene Ausdrücke. Du sagst:
  - **zero** beim Zählen: 0, 1, 2, … (*zero, one, two, …*)
    bei Temperaturangaben: 0° (*zero degrees*)
  - **oh** beim Telefonieren: *My number is 82044.* (*eight two oh double four*)
    bei Jahreszahlen: 1905 (*nineteen oh five*)
    bei der Uhrzeit: 7:05 (*seven oh five*)
  - **nil** bei Fußballergebnissen: *We won 1:0.* (*one nil*)
  - **love** beim Tennis: 15:0 (*fifteen love*)

Die Ordnungszahlen *Ordinal numbers*

MERKHILFE
„First", „second" und „third" sind unregelmäßige Formen, die nicht wie die anderen Ordnungszahlen auf „-th" enden.

1st first	11th eleventh	21st twenty-first
2nd second	12th twelfth	22nd twenty-second
3rd third	13th thirteenth	23rd twenty-third
4th fourth	14th fourteenth	24th twenty-fourth
5th fifth	15th fifteenth	…
6th sixth	16th sixteenth	30th thirtieth
7th seventh	17th seventeenth	40th fortieth
8th eighth	18th eighteenth	50th fiftieth
9th ninth	19th nineteenth	60th sixtieth
10th tenth	20th twentieth	100th (one) hundredth

Die Uhrzeit *The time*

Bei Zeitangaben verwendest du für die ersten 30 Minuten nach der vollen Stunde *past*, z. B.:

8:05 five past eight	8:15 quarter past eight	8:30 half past eight
(oder: eight oh five)	(oder: eight fifteen)	(oder: eight thirty)

Nach *half past* zählst du mit **to** zur nächsten vollen Stunde hin, z. B.:

8:40 twenty to nine	8:45 quarter to nine	8:55 five to nine
(oder: eight forty)	(oder: eight forty-five)	(oder: eight fifty-five)

Bei vollen Stunden benutzt du *o'clock*, z. B.: 9 *o'clock*, 11 *o'clock*.
- **am** bedeutet **in the morning**
- **pm** bedeutet **in the afternoon** bzw. **in the evening**

Das Datum *The date*

Im *British English* setzt sich das Datum aus der Ordnungszahl und dem Monat zusammen, z. B.:
- *23rd May* (gesprochen: *the twenty-third of May*)
- *9th June* (gesprochen: *the ninth of June*)

Die Jahreszahlen *The year*

- 1998 kann eine normale Zahl (*number*) oder eine Jahreszahl (*year*) sein.
  Du sagst:
  - 1,998: *one thousand nine hundred and ninety-eight* (*number*)
  - 1998: *nineteen ninety-eight* (*year*)

- Ab 2000 werden Zahlen und Jahreszahlen gleich gesprochen:
  - 2000: *two thousand*
  - 2001: *two thousand and one*
  - 2014: *two thousand and fourteen;*
         Bei Jahreszahlen kannst du auch *twenty fourteen* sagen.

◼ Achtung!

- Zahlen und Jahreszahlen über Tausend schreibt man unterschiedlich. Vergleiche:
  - 2,014 (*number*)
  - 2014 (*year*)

> **TIPP**
> Im American English schreibt man erst den Monat und dann die Ordnungszahl, z. B.: May 23rd – gesprochen: May (the) twenty-third. Man schreibt: 5.23.2020.

> **TIPP**
> Im Gegensatz zum British English lässt du „and" bei Zahlen im American English weg, z. B.:
> 1,998: one thousand nine hundred ninety-eight
> 2,014: two thousand fourteen

Die Dezimalzahlen *Decimal numbers*

Bei Zahlen mit Stellen hinter dem Komma musst du im Englischen einen Punkt setzen, z. B.:
12,46 Sekunden = 12.46 *seconds* (gesprochen: *twelve point four six*)
17,8 Kilo = 17.8 *kilos*

Die Bruchzahlen   *Fractions*

Bei den Bruchzahlen sprichst du im Englischen den Nenner (unter dem Bruch stehend) als Ordnungszahl. Ist der Zähler (über dem Bruch stehend) größer als eins, steht der Nenner im Plural.

1/3 = one/a **third** 1/5 = one/a **fifth** 1/10 = one/a **tenth** 1/100 = one/a **hundredth** 1/1000 = one/a **thousandth** 2/3 = two **thirds** 3/5 = three **fifths** 5/10 = five **tenths** 5 3/8 = five and three **eighths**	**Es gibt folgende Ausnahmen:** 1/2 = one/a half 1/4 = one/a quarter 3/4 = three quarters 1 1/2 = one and a half

Unregelmäßige Verben

■ ■ ■   *infinitive*, *simple past* und *past participle* sind identisch
■ ● ●   *infinitive* unterscheidet sich vom *simple past* und *past participle*
■ ● ■   *infinitive* und *past participle* sind identisch; nur das *simple past* hat eine andere Form
■ ● ▲   *infinitive*, *simple past* und *past participle* haben alle eine andere Form

■ *infinitive*	■ *simple past*	■ *past participle*	Deutsch
to **cost** [kɒst]	**cost** [kɒst]	**cost** [kɒst]	kosten
to **cut** [kʌt]	**cut** [kʌt]	**cut** [kʌt]	schneiden
to **hit** [hɪt]	**hit** [hɪt]	**hit** [hɪt]	schlagen, treffen
to **hurt** [hɜːt]	**hurt** [hɜːt]	**hurt** [hɜːt]	verletzen, (sich) weh tun
to **let** [let]	**let** [let]	**let** [let]	lassen
to **put** [pʊt]	**put** [pʊt]	**put** [pʊt]	setzen, stellen, legen

■ *infinitive*	● *simple past*	● *past participle*	Deutsch
to **bleed** [bliːd]	**bled** [bled]	**bled** [bled]	bluten
to **bring** [brɪŋ]	**brought** [brɔːt]	**brought** [brɔːt]	(mit)bringen
to **build** [bɪld]	**built** [bɪlt]	**built** [bɪlt]	bauen
to **burn** [bɜːn]	**burned/burnt** [bɜːnd, bɜːnt]	**burned/burnt** [bɜːnd, bɜːnt]	(ver)brennen
to **buy** [baɪ]	**bought** [bɔːt]	**bought** [bɔːt]	kaufen
to **catch** [kætʃ]	**caught** [kɔːt]	**caught** [kɔːt]	fangen
to **deal** (with) [diːl]	**dealt** (with) [delt]	**dealt** (with) [delt]	(be)handeln
to **feed** [fiːd]	**fed** [fed]	**fed** [fed]	füttern
to **feel** [fiːl]	**felt** [felt]	**felt** [felt]	(sich) fühlen
to **fight** [faɪt]	**fought** [fɔːt]	**fought** [fɔːt]	kämpfen, (sich) streiten
to **find** [faɪnd]	**found** [faʊnd]	**found** [faʊnd]	finden
to **get** [get]	**got** [gɒt]	**got** [gɒt] **gotten** [gɒtn] (AE)	holen, bringen, (be)kommen, werden
to **hang** [hæŋ]	**hung** [hʌŋ]	**hung** [hʌŋ]	hängen
to **have** [hæv]	**had** [hæd]	**had** [hæd]	haben
to **hear** [hɪə]	**heard** [hɜːd]	**heard** [hɜːd]	hören
to **hold** [həʊld]	**held** [held]	**held** [held]	halten
to **keep** [kiːp]	**kept** [kept]	**kept** [kept]	behalten
to **lay** [leɪ]	**laid** [leɪd]	**laid** [leɪd]	legen
to **learn** [lɜːn]	**learned/learnt** [lɜːnd, lɜːnt]	**learned/learnt** [lɜːnd, lɜːnt]	lernen
to **leave** [liːv]	**left** [left]	**left** [left]	(ver)lassen, abfahren
to **lend** [lend]	**lent** [lent]	**lent** [lent]	leihen
to **lose** [luːz]	**lost** [lɒst]	**lost** [lɒst]	verlieren
to **make** [meɪk]	**made** [meɪd]	**made** [meɪd]	machen, tun

to **mean** [miːn]	**meant** [ment]	**meant** [ment]	bedeuten, meinen
to **meet** [miːt]	**met** [met]	**met** [met]	(sich) treffen
to **pay** [peɪ]	**paid** [peɪd]	**paid** [peɪd]	bezahlen
to **read** [riːd]	**read** [red]	**read** [red]	lesen
to **say** [seɪ]	**said** [sed]	**said** [sed]	sagen
to **sell** [sel]	**sold** [səʊld]	**sold** [səʊld]	verkaufen
to **send** [send]	**sent** [sent]	**sent** [sent]	schicken
to **shine** [ʃaɪn]	**shone** [ʃɒn]	**shone** [ʃɒn]	scheinen, glänzen
to **shoot** [ʃuːt]	**shot** [ʃɒt]	**shot** [ʃɒt]	schießen
to **sit** [sɪt]	**sat** [sæt]	**sat** [sæt]	sitzen
to **sleep** [sliːp]	**slept** [slept]	**slept** [slept]	schlafen
to **slide** [slaɪd]	**slid** [slɪd]	**slid** [slɪd]	rutschen, gleiten
to **smell** [smel]	**smelled/smelt** [smeld, smelt]	**smelled/smelt** [smeld, smelt]	riechen
to **spend** [spend]	**spent** [spent]	**spent** [spent]	ausgeben, verbringen
to **stand** [stænd]	**stood** [stʊd]	**stood** [stʊd]	stehen
to **teach** [tiːtʃ]	**taught** [tɔːt]	**taught** [tɔːt]	unterrichten, lehren
to **tell** [tel]	**told** [təʊld]	**told** [təʊld]	erzählen, sagen
to **think** [θɪŋk]	**thought** [θɔːt]	**thought** [θɔːt]	denken, glauben
to **understand** [ˌʌndəˈstænd]	**understood** [ˌʌndəˈstʊd]	**understood** [ˌʌndəˈstʊd]	verstehen
to **win** [wɪn]	**won** [wʌn]	**won** [wʌn]	gewinnen, siegen

■ *infinitive*	● *simple past*	■ *past participle*	**Deutsch**
to **become** [bɪˈkʌm]	**became** [bɪˈkeɪm]	**become** [bɪˈkʌm]	werden
to **come** [kʌm]	**came** [keɪm]	**come** [kʌm]	kommen
to **run** [rʌn]	**ran** [ræn]	**run** [rʌn]	laufen, rennen

■ *infinitive*	● *simple past*	▲ *past participle*	**Deutsch**
to **be** [biː]	**was/were** [wɒz, wɜː]	**been** [biːn]	sein
to **break** [breɪk]	**broke** [brəʊk]	**broken** [ˈbrəʊkn]	(zer)brechen, kaputtmachen
to **choose** [tʃuːz]	**chose** [tʃəʊz]	**chosen** [ˈtʃəʊzn]	(aus)wählen
to **do** [duː]	**did** [dɪd]	**done** [dʌn]	machen, tun
to **draw** [drɔː]	**drew** [druː]	**drawn** [drɔːn]	zeichnen
to **drink** [drɪŋk]	**drank** [dræŋk]	**drunk** [drʌŋk]	trinken
to **drive** [draɪv]	**drove** [drəʊv]	**driven** [ˈdrɪvn]	fahren
to **eat** [iːt]	**ate** [et]	**eaten** [iːtn]	essen
to **fall** [fɔːl]	**fell** [fel]	**fallen** [ˈfɔːlən]	(herunter)fallen, hinfallen

to **fly** [flaɪ]	**flew** [fluː]	**flown** [fləʊn]	fliegen
to **forget** [fəˈget]	**forgot** [fəˈgɒt]	**forgotten** [fəˈgɒtn]	vergessen
to **give** [gɪv]	**gave** [geɪv]	**given** [ˈgɪvn]	geben
to **go** [gəʊ]	**went** [went]	**gone** [gɒn]	gehen
to **grow** [grəʊ]	**grew** [gruː]	**grown** [grəʊn]	wachsen
to **hide** [haɪd]	**hid** [hɪd]	**hidden** [ˈhɪdn]	(sich) verstecken
to **know** [nəʊ]	**knew** [njuː]	**known** [nəʊn]	kennen, wissen
to **ride** [raɪd]	**rode** [rəʊd]	**ridden** [ˈrɪdn]	fahren, reiten
to **ring** [rɪŋ]	**rang** [ræŋ]	**rung** [rʌŋ]	klingeln, läuten
to **see** [siː]	**saw** [sɔː]	**seen** [siːn]	sehen
to **shake** [ʃeɪk]	**shook** [ʃʊk]	**shaken** [ˈʃeɪkn]	schütteln
to **show** [ʃəʊ]	**showed** [ʃəʊd]	**shown** [ʃəʊn]	zeigen
to **sing** [sɪŋ]	**sang** [sæŋ]	**sung** [sʌŋ]	singen
to **sink** [sɪŋk]	**sank** [sæŋk]	**sunk** [sʌŋk]	sinken
to **speak** [spiːk]	**spoke** [spəʊk]	**spoken** [ˈspəʊkn]	sprechen
to **steal** [stiːl]	**stole** [stəʊl]	**stolen** [ˈstəʊlən]	stehlen
to **swim** [swɪm]	**swam** [swæm]	**swum** [swʌm]	schwimmen
to **take** [teɪk]	**took** [tʊk]	**taken** [ˈteɪkn]	(mit)nehmen, bringen
to **throw** [θrəʊ]	**threw** [θruː]	**thrown** [θrəʊn]	werfen
to **wake** (up) [weɪk]	**woke** (up) [wəʊk]	**woken** (up) [ˈwəʊkn]	(auf)wecken, (auf)wachen
to **wear** [weə]	**wore** [wɔː]	**worn** [wɔːn]	anhaben, tragen
to **write** [raɪt]	**wrote** [rəʊt]	**written** [ˈrɪtn]	schreiben

Welcher Lernertyp bist du?

Warum solltest du wissen, welcher Lernertyp du bist?

Verstehen und Behalten

Sicherlich kennst du das Gefühl im Unterricht etwas verstanden zu haben und mit Zufriedenheit, Stolz und Begeisterung aus dem Klassenzimmer bzw. am Ende eines Schultags nach Hause gegangen zu sein. Vielleicht hast du auch schon die Erfahrung gemacht, im Unterricht alles bestens verstanden zu haben, doch als du später Hausaufgaben erledigen solltest, war alles nicht mehr so leicht wie in der Schule. Du wurdest unsicher, hast vielleicht Fehler gemacht und wurdest unzufrieden. Warum war das so?

Kurz- und Langzeitgedächtnis

Verstehen und Behalten sind zwei unterschiedliche Vorgänge:

1. Im Unterricht sorgt deine Lehrerin bzw. dein Lehrer dafür, dass du und deine Klassenkameraden den Lernstoff verstehen, d.h. neues Wissen im Kurzzeitgedächtnis gespeichert wird.

   Wie aber kommt gerade erworbenes Wissen aus dem Kurzzeitgedächtnis in das Langzeitgedächtnis, sodass du es auch bei Hausaufgaben, in der nächsten Stunde, in der Klassenarbeit und in realen Lebenssituationen nicht nur abrufen, sondern auch erfolgreich anwenden kannst?

Effektiver Lernen

2. Dein Gehirn ist immer aktiv – es will lernen; und mit stetigem Üben und Wiederholen kannst du die Behaltensleistung deines Gehirns sogar noch steigern. (Besonders gut funktioniert das übrigens, wenn verschiedene Sinne – Hören, Sehen, Riechen, Schmecken, Fühlen – angesprochen werden.) Da jeder Mensch einzigartig ist und deshalb anders lernt, eigene Lernwege und Interessen hat, benötigst du das für dich passende Übungsmaterial. Indem du Übungen bzw. Tätigkeiten machst, die dich ansprechen und zu deinem Lernertyp passen, lernst du schneller, effektiver und erfolgreicher.

Im Nachfolgenden haben wir für dich einen Test zusammengestellt, mit dem du ermitteln kannst, welcher Lernertyp du bist und wo deine Stärken liegen. Wie du wahrscheinlich feststellen wirst, gehörst auch du nicht nur einem Lernertyp an, denn die meisten Menschen sind Mischtypen.

Passende Lernertyp-Aufgaben findest du im Anschluss an den Test. Diese kannst du im Unterricht oder Zuhause bearbeiten. Wichtig ist, dass die Lösungen z.B. von deiner Lehrerin/deinem Lehrer kontrolliert werden.

Der Test

Um deine Stärken und damit deinen Lernertyp herauszufinden, wird dir der nachfolgende Test – bestehend aus vier Teilen – eine Reihe von Aktivitäten vorstellen. Kreuze diejenigen an, die dir zusagen und die du erfahrungsgemäß am besten kannst. Mache auch ein Kreuz, wenn es sich dabei nicht um alle Aktivitäten einer Auswahlmöglichkeit handelt. Am Ende können in den Tabellen nur ganz wenige, oder aber auch sehr viele Kreuze stehen.

Dein Lernertyp

Los geht's!

PS: Solltest du dieses Buch nur ausgeliehen haben und deshalb nicht hineinschreiben dürfen, findest du diesen Test auch als Download unter dem **Online-Link 560012-0001** auf www.klett.de

Teil 1

Aktivitäten	Lernertyp	Kreuz
Aus Buchstaben Wörter zusammensetzen (z. B. Scrabble), Wortspiele spielen (z. B. Wörter-Domino, aus Wörtern Sätze bilden)	1	
Gedichte, Reime, Lieder, Raps hören, schreiben, auswendig lernen	3	
Zahlenspiele spielen – im Kopf oder schriftlich	2	
Suchbilder erkunden, Puzzle machen	4	
Bewegungsspiele spielen	7	
Ein Grammatikheft und/oder Vokabelheft anlegen	6	
Mit einem Partner und/oder in einer Gruppe arbeiten, an Projektarbeit und Projektwochen teilnehmen	5	
An Unterricht außerhalb des Klassenzimmers teilnehmen (z. B. Exkursionen in einen Wald, auf einen Flughafen)	8	

Teil 2

Aktivitäten	Lernertyp	Kreuz
Über Haustiere sprechen, Tiergeschichten und Fabeln lesen und erzählen	8	
Geschichten (zu vorgegebenen Wörtern) erfinden	1	
Ein Tagebuch mit persönlichen Einträgen schreiben	6	
Mind-maps erstellen	2	
Mit einem Partner und/oder in einer Gruppe Regeln aufstellen, Probleme und Denkspiele lösen	5	
Eselsbrücken, Merksätze rhythmisch sprechen, Silben klatschen	3	
Tanzen, Geschichten pantomimisch darstellen	7	
Pläne zeichnen, Geheimschriften entwerfen und verwenden	4	

Teil 3

Aktivitäten	Lernertyp	Kreuz
Körpersprache bei anderen deuten oder ein Mimikquiz gestalten	7	
Freunde, Mitschüler beschreiben	5	
Ein Stimmungsbarometer für mich selbst erstellen	6	
Bildergeschichten erzählen, Fantasiereisen zu unbekannten Orten machen	4	
Naturcollagen anfertigen	8	
Texte schreiben und vorlesen	1	
Ein Hörspiel gestalten	3	
Denksportaufgaben und Detektivgeschichten lösen	2	

Teil 4

Aktivitäten	Lernertyp	Kreuz
Tabellen, Statistiken, Diagramme erstellen und auswerten	2	
Poster oder Plakate erstellen	4	
Gedanken formulieren, aufschreiben, warum mir etwas gut gefallen hat oder warum mir etwas gut gelungen ist	6	
Auf dem Rücken von Mitschülern schreiben	7	
Eigene Sinneseindrücke beschreiben	8	
Etwas pantomimisch darstellen	5	
Gefühle zu Musik beschreiben	3	
Eine Rede halten und meine Aussagen begründen, aktiv an Diskussionen teilnehmen	1	

Die Testauswertung

In der linken Spalte der Tabelle findest du die Nummern wieder, die du aus den Teilen 1–4 kennst. Sie stehen für verschiedene Lernertypen. Zähle nun die Kreuze zusammen, die du in den Tabellen oben bei den verschiedenen Nummern gesetzt hast und finde dann heraus, welcher Lernertyp du bist. Es kann gut sein, dass du bei mehreren Lernertypen eine ähnliche Anzahl von Kreuzen gesetzt hast. Dies bedeutet einfach, dass deine Stärken in verschiedenen Bereichen liegen.

Lernertyp	Das sind deine Stärken	Anzahl der Kreuze
1 wortklug	Du kannst gut mit Sprache umgehen.	
2 logikklug	Logisches Denken und das Erkennen und Lösen von mathematischen Problemen fallen dir leicht.	
3 musikklug	Klänge, Rhythmen und Melodien spielen für dich eine große Rolle. Du kannst spielerisch und leicht mit ihnen umgehen.	
4 bildklug	Du kannst geschickt mit Farben und Formen umgehen und besitzt die Gabe, dich gut orientieren zu können.	
5 menschenklug	Du kannst dich gut in andere hineinversetzen, arbeitest gern in der Gruppe und bist hilfsbereit.	
6 selbstklug	Du handelst selbstständig und kannst deine Stärken und Schwächen realistisch einschätzen.	
7 körperklug	Du bewegst dich gern und hast gute motorische Fähigkeiten.	
8 naturklug	Du magst Tiere und Pflanzen und kannst schnell Gesetzmäßig-keiten erkennen.	

So sieht nun dein „Profil" aus. Doch was bedeutet es für das Üben?

Erledige im Folgenden die Aufgaben, die mit dem von dir am häufigsten gewählten Lernertyp(en) ausgezeichnet sind und lass deine Lösungen z. B. von deiner Lehrerin/deinem Lehrer kontrollieren. So kannst du sicher sein, dass sie dir helfen werden, dein erworbenes Wissen leicht zu behalten. Gehörst du beispielsweise dem Lernertyp „bildklug" an, so kannst du dir Grammatikphänomene besser einprägen, wenn du die Regel oder einige Beispielsätze selbst einmal grafisch darstellst.

Manche Aufgaben sind mit mehreren Lernertypen gekennzeichnet, lass dich davon nicht irritieren! Es genügt, wenn einer der in der Randspalte genannten Lernertypen auf dich zutrifft.

Natürlich darfst du auch andere Aufgaben lösen. Dies ist sogar hilfreich, denn oft eröffnen neue Lernwege neue Einsichten, oft führt der Mut, Neues zu erkunden, zu neuen Einblicken und ganz überraschenden Lernerfolgen.

Lernertypaufgaben

G11 Die Reflexivpronomen und *each other*

logikklug, bildklug

1. Machst du manchmal Fehler bei der Unterscheidung zwischen *themselves* und *each other*? Denke dir zwei Beispielsätze aus und zeichne Bilder dazu.
Beispiel: *They looked at themselves / each other.*

wortklug, musikklug

2. Suche im Internet drei Songtexte, die eines oder mehrere Reflexivpronomen beinhalten.
TIPP: Bei der Internetrecherche hilft es dir, in die Suchmaschine das entsprechende Reflexivpronomen zusammen mit dem Stichwort *lyrics* einzugeben.
Übertrage dann die Sätze mit den Reflexivpronomen ins Deutsche und ordne sie danach, ob das Reflexivpronomen rückbezüglich (mich, dich, sich, …) oder als verstärkendes Pronomen („selbst") verwendet wird.

G24 Die Verwendung von Adjektiven

wortklug, menschenklug, naturklug

1. Wähle drei Tiere aus, die drei Personen aus deiner Klasse positiv (!) beschreiben und notiere dir, warum du dieser Meinung bist, z. B. … *is like a fox because he/she is clever and has red hair*. Lies deine Sätze anschließend in der Klasse vor und lasse die anderen raten, um welche Person es sich handelt.

G30 Die Adverbien der Art und Weise

wortklug, logikklug, menschenklug

1. Finde sechs Adverbien, die beschreiben, wie dein bester Freund/deine beste Freundin etwas tut. Schreibe dann sechs Sätze und verwende darin jeweils eines deiner Adverbien. Verwende dabei die folgenden Verben: *run, laugh, jump, learn, sing, write.*

G31 Die Steigerung der Adverbien

wortklug, selbstklug

1. Überlege dir, was du wann wie gut konntest, z. B. *When I was six years old, I was already good at sports and could run very* **fast***. When I was nine, I could run even* **faster***. When I was 14, however, I could run* **fastest***, and I won every competiton.* Schreibe nun drei Beispiele aus deinem Leben auf. Verwende dabei drei verschiedene Adverbien mit den entsprechenden Steigerungsformen.

logikklug, bildklug

2. Zeichne ein *word web* mit sieben Linien, die von der Mitte ausgehen. An die Enden der Linien schreibst du die sieben für dich am schwersten zu merkenden Adverbien mit ihren Steigerungsformen und zeichnest ein inhaltlich passendes Bild dazu. In die Mitte könntest du z. B. schreiben *The adverbs I love to forget* oder *My adverbs.*

musikklug

Variante: Du kannst dir auch einen Rap mit den sieben Adverbien und ihren Steigerungsformen überlegen.

G31 Die Steigerung der Adverbien + G32 Vergleiche mit Adverbien

1. Schreibe Sätze über deine beste Freundin oder deinen besten Freund auf. Du kannst dabei die Steigerungsformen der Adverbien (z. B. *better, louder, brighter*) und Vergleiche mit den Adverbien (z. B. *runs as fast as the wind*) verwenden.

logikklug, menschenklug

G33 Gradadverbien

1. Beim ersten Besuch eines neuen Cafés schickst du deinem englischen Freund/ deiner englischen Freundin überschwängliche SMS-Nachrichten zur Qualität der Musik, des Essens, der Getränke und der Atmosphäre. Was schreibst du ihm/ihr?
   Beispiel: *The music is absolutely fantastic here.*

wortklug

G35 Adverbien und adverbiale Bestimmungen der bestimmten Zeit und Häufigkeit

1. Übertrage die Wörter aus der Tabelle auf zwei Würfel:

wortklug, selbstklug

Würfel 1		Würfel 2	
1	yesterday	1	feel
2	early this morning	2	hear
3	today	3	see
4	tonight	4	smell
5	tomorrow	5	taste
6	next week	6	"verb joker"

Werfe die beiden Würfel und bilde sinnvolle Sätze mit der Zeitangabe und dem dazugehörigen Verb.
Beispiel: ***Early this morning** I **smelled** fresh coffee.*
TIPP: Achte auf die richtige Zeitform!

Variante: Du spielst mit einem/einer Partner/in oder in einer größeren Gruppe. Dieses Mal geht es darum, positive (!) Aussagen über die Mitspieler/innen zu treffen. Verwende dabei für den zweiten Würfel die folgenden Verben: *look, wear, have, learn, sleep* + verb joker.

wortklug, menschenklug

G36 Adverbien der unbestimmten Zeit und Häufigkeit

1. Schreibe in die linke Spalte einer Tabelle die folgenden Adverbien von oben nach unten:
   1. *always,* 2. *often,* 3. *usually,* 4. *sometimes,* 5. *hardly ever,* 6. *never.*
   Dann schreibe in die rechte Spalte Sätze mit diesen Adverbien, die auf dich und dein Leben zutreffen.
   Beispiel: *I **usually** walk the dog./I **often** feed the cat.*

wortklug, logikklug, selbstklug,

2. Schreibe mit dem Finger eines der folgenden Adverbien auf den Rücken deines Partners/deiner Partnerin: *already, almost, just, now, soon.* Er/Sie muss herausfinden, um welches Wort es sich handelt, und dann mit diesem Wort einen englischen Satz zu bilden.

körperklug

G37 Adverbien des Orts und der Richtung

wortklug, bildklug

1. Du hast Besuch von einem Freund/einer Freundin aus England, und er/sie hat nur einen Tag Zeit, sich deinen Heimatort anzuschauen. Da du ihn/sie nicht begleiten kannst, bittet er/sie um eine Liste mit interessanten Sehenswürdigkeiten und Hinweisen, wie er/sie dorthin gelangen kann. Wähle 3–4 Sehenswürdigkeiten aus und beschreibe den Weg dorthin. Verwende dabei Ortsadverbien und Adverbien der Richtung.
   Beispiel: *Take the bus to the town centre. Turn left at the theatre. The castle is around the corner.*

G49 Die einfache Vergangenheit

wortklug, bildklug, menschenklug

1. Deine Lieblingsband wird in Kürze in deiner Nähe ein Konzert geben. Im Englischunterricht bittet dich deine Lehrerin/dein Lehrer deshalb, deine Band im Unterricht vorzustellen. Suche auf der Homepage der Band oder über eine Suchmaschine wichtige Ereignisse rund um die Band und sammle sie in chronologischer Reihenfolge.
   Beispiel: *In 2002 the band members met at an audition.*
   Wähle anschließend geeignete Bilder für deinen Kurzvortrag aus.

G57 Das Futur mit *will*

wortklug, selbstklug

1. Stelle dir vor, du planst mit Mitschülern/Mitschülerinnen ein Videoprojekt wie auf S. 133. Entscheide dich spontan, welche Aufgaben du übernehmen würdest. Formuliere deine Antwort mit dem *will-future*.

G107 Die Relativpronomen als Subjekt von notwendigen Relativsätzen

wortklug, logikklug, bildklug

1. Schau dir noch einmal die Merkhilfe auf S. 228 an und erstelle dann deine eigene Merkhilfe: Zeichne ein Dreieck und ordne jeder Ecke ein Relativpronomen zu. Finde dann für jedes Relativpronomen fünf mögliche Bezugswörter. Diese kannst du entweder aufschreiben oder zeichnen.

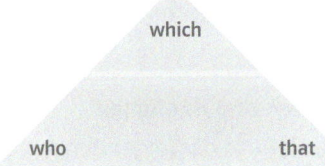

G108 Die Relativpronomen als Objekt von notwendigen Relativsätzen; *contact clauses*

wortklug, selbstklug

1. Beschreibe mit Hilfe von *contact clauses* drei Dinge, die dir heute gut gelungen sind, z. B. *The story I wrote was exciting.*

Lösungen

1 Das Nomen

G1 Nomen zur Bezeichnung von Personen
Check-in:

1. weiblich: *aunt*
   männlich: *uncle*
   männlich oder weiblich: *cousin*
2. Von *cousin* gibt es keine weibliche Form, es könnte sich also um beide Geschlechter handeln. Auf den ersten Blick würden die meisten Deutsch-Muttersprachler an die männliche Form des Nomens denken.

Check-out:

1. männlich: *Ben, brother, Mr Turner, uncle*
   weiblich: *aunt, Emma, grandmother, Caroline, sister, waitress*
   männlich oder weiblich: *author, baby, bus driver, cousin, dancer, doctor, film star, footballer, lawyer, model, police officer, tennis player*

G2 Nomen zur Bezeichnung von Gruppen
Check-in:

1. people: *So many people are waiting for **their** flights.*
   team: ***They**'re so angry – **they**'re afraid, **they**'ll miss **their** match.*
   police: ***They**'re just coming in …*
2. Die Verbform steht im Plural.

Check-out:

1. b) *The police have stopped the fighting.*
2. a) *The police try to help people.*
   b) *Do you see the two police officers over there?*

G3 Regelmäßige und unregelmäßige Pluralformen
Check-in:

1. *child, woman, foot*
2. *family, baby*

Check-out:

1. a) *men; women*   b) *mice*   c) *teeth*   d) *families; children; babies*   e) *photos; sheep*

G4 Nomen, die nur im Singular stehen und Nomen, die nur im Plural stehen
Check-in:

1. Die beiden Nomen werden im Plural gebraucht, da sie aus zwei Teilen (in diesem Fall zwei Hosenbeinen) bestehen.
2. a) Die Informationen, die wir bekommen haben, waren nicht gut genug.
   b) Die gute Nachricht ist, dass die Konferenz morgen sein wird.

Check-out:

1. nur Singular: *advice, baggage, butter, bread, coal, furniture, homework, information, milk*
   Singular und Plural: *book • books, child • children, foot • feet, glass • glasses, job • jobs, mouse • mice, tomato • tomatoes, tree • trees, wife • wives*
2. a) *The homework was too difficult.*
   b) *Thanks for the good advice. It will help me very much.*
   c) *I've bought a new pair of trousers.*
   d) *The news is not very interesting today.*

2 Der Artikel

G5 Der bestimmte Artikel
Check-in:

1. *Life* meint das Leben im Allgemeinen. Deshalb verwendet er es ohne Artikel.
2. *Food* ist zunächst ganz allgemein gemeint. Danach wird es näher bestimmt *The food I'm getting* (= Das Essen, das ich bekomme …).

Check-out:

1. *Jack, Ben's cousin, is a vegetarian and he doesn't eat – meat. He only eats – cereals, – vegetables and **the** bread his mother bakes herself. But he enjoys – life just as much as everyone else. He says that – people often have no idea about **the** hard life of – animals. He likes – coffee, and especially **the** coffee his mother makes. Jack still goes to – school. He goes to – school by – bus. He always catches **the** 8:30 bus. Every day he has – lunch in the school cafeteria. But this isn't always easy because Jack likes – healthy food, and **the** food they offer at the cafeteria is not very good.*

G6 Der bestimmte Artikel bei Namen
Check-in

1. *Jack; Uncle David; the Tower of London; the Thames*
2. *Poor Aunt Chrissie* (= Die arme Tante Chrissie); *Buckingham Palace* (= den Buckingham Palast); *Oxford Street* (= in der Oxford Street); *Big Ben* (= dem Big Ben)

Check-out:

1. a) *The Spencers and the Carters are neighbours./ The Carters and the Spencers are neighbours.*
   b) *Mount Whitney isn't the highest mountain in the United States./The highest mountain in the United States isn't Mount Whitney.*
   c) *Poor Uncle David almost fell into the Thames on the way to the Tower of London.*
   d) *Is Central Park bigger than Hyde Park?/Is Hyde Park bigger than Central Park?*

e) *Lake Michigan is on the border to Canada.*

f) *Is Oxford Street more famous than Fifth Avenue?/ Is Fifth Avenue more famous than Oxford Street?*

G7 Der unbestimmte Artikel
Check-in:

1. a) *A* benutzt man bei Nomen, die mit einem Konsonanten beginnen; *an* bei Nomen, die mit einem Vokal beginnen.

   b) wegen der Aussprache [jʊːnɪ...]

2. Du bist Polizistin. (Im Gegensatz zum Englischen steht im Deutschen bei Berufsbezeichnungen kein Artikel.)

Check-out:

1. *My dad/father is (an) American. He works as a journalist in Los Angeles./ He's a journalist in Los Angeles. He works five days a week and he's always in a hurry. He always tries to be perfect. I'll give you an example: he never leaves (the house) without a shopping list. But last week he missed a press conference and thought 'I'm an idiot!'*

G8 Die Stellung der Artikel
Check-in:

1. a) *All the people Ben has met.* b) *Quite a large part of California is desert.* c) *A lot of water is used for all the golf courses, green gardens and swimming pools.*

Check-out:

1. *Ben had **a great/wonderful time** here. **All the people** who met him liked him a lot. Yesterday we were in (the) town. **Both the boys** bought the same T-shirt. After that we went to the Bristol Kite Festival and watched the kites for **half an hour**. We had **quite a strong wind**. What a **wonderful/nice/great day**!*

3 Pronomen und Begleiter

G9 Die Personalpronomen als Subjekt im Satz
Check-in:

1. she, it, they

2. a) **Sie** sind im Zentrum unserer berühmten Stadt!

   b) Weißt **du** es, Papa?

Check-out:

1. *Yesterday my dad and I went to Macduff. **We** wanted to visit the aquarium, but **it** was closed. Then **we** went into a café. A woman there told us about the ships in the harbour. **She** said that **they** were very famous. Dad said, "Let's go there," so **we** went to find the harbour. But **we** got lost. There was a large street map, but **it** was full of graffiti. So **we** asked two boys for help and **they** pointed to the right street.*

G10 Die Objektformen der Personalpronomen
Check-in:

1. „Bist du sicher, dass dieses Foto von uns ist? Für mich sieht es aus wie zwei Bäume im Wasser!"

2. *you; it* (Personalpronomen als Subjekt)

Check-out:

1. David: *You saw the monster? I don't believe you. Show me a picture of it!*

   Jake: *The monster was bigger than me. It looked at us, but it didn't follow us.*

2. *it; them; us; him; them*

G11 Die Reflexivpronomen und *each other*
Check-in:

1. a) Machen Sie sich auf eine große Überraschung gefasst!

   b) Besucher können sich in einem Luxushotel amüsieren.

2. *myself, himself, herself, ourselves, yourselves*

Check-out:

1. *himself; myself; themselves; each other; –; me; each other; yourself*

G12 Die Demonstrativbegleiter und -pronomen
Check-in:

1. Die hervorgehobenen Wörter stehen mit einem Nomen. Ausnahme: In dem Satz *That's a good idea.* steht *that* für sich alleine.

2. *This/these* werden verwendet, um auf etwas hinzuweisen, das in der Nähe ist. *That/those* werden verwendet, um auf etwas hinzuweisen, das weiter entfernt ist.

Check-out:

1. a) *This* b) *Those* c) *this* d) *that* e) *These* f) *that*

2. Martin: *Hello, Steve! Look at this T-shirt!*

   Steve: *It's great! Did you buy it in that shop over there?*

   Martin: *No, my brother gave it to me this morning.*

   Steve: *That's a surprise! Why?*

   Martin: *He bought it in of those little shops at the market. And it's too small for him.*

G13 Die Possessivbegleiter
Check-in:

1. Er hat sich seinen Arm verletzt./ Er hat sich den Arm verletzt.

Check-out:

1. *your; our; its; my; their; our; My; her; your*

G14 Die Possessivpronomen
Check-in:

1. *Is this your dog?/ No, it's not our dog./ Because my camera is better than her camera.*

Check-out:

1. a) *me; hers*   b) *his*   c) *his*   d) *mine; theirs*
   e) *ours*

G15 Der *s*-Genitiv
Check-in:

1. a) Der Apostroph steht vor dem *s*, wenn das Nomen im Singular steht oder bei Pluralformen, die nicht auf -*s* enden.
   b) Der Apostroph steht nach dem *s*, wenn das Nomen im Plural steht und auf -*s* endet.
2. Das *s* von *She's* zeigt nicht den Genitiv an, sondern steht für die Kurzform *is*: *She is too old.*

Check-out:

1. a) *My uncle's hotel*   b) *My friend's dog at the beach*   c) *The teenagers' favourite café*   d) *Alex's bike after the accident*   e) *Charlotte at the doctor's*

G16 Der Genitiv mit *of*
Check-in:

1. a) Sie beziehen sich eher auf Sachen.
   b) *the second husband of Mary Queen of Scots*

Check-out:

1. a) *of the school holidays.*   b) *of the Scottish coast.*   c) *of all the people in her group.*   d) *of the dark sea at night.*
2. a) *Marcus's trip*   b) *the flat of a friend*   c) *a model of a Roman soldier*   d) *a postcard of the royal family*   e) *the most famous city in the world*

4   Die Mengenwörter

G17 Die Mengenwörter *much/many, a lot of/ lots of*
Check-in

1. Zählbar sind a) *vegetables,* b) *bananas,* d) *kiwis.* Erkennen kann man zählbare Nomen am Plural ‚s'.

Check-out

1. a) *much*   b) *many*   c) *lots of/a lot of*   d) *much*
   e) *lots of/a lot of*

G18 Mengenangaben mit *of*
Check-in

1. Obstsalat: 6 Bananen, 8 Kiwis
   Pommes: 3 Pfund Kartoffeln, eine Flasche Ketchup
   Pizza: 600g Käse, eine Tüte Mehl
   Getränke: 4 Packungen Eistee
   Das Wörtchen *of* braucht man bei der Wiedergabe im Deutschen nicht.

Check-out

1. a) *five bottles of water*   b) *three pounds of apples*
   c) *a packet of tea*   d) *two boxes of eggs*

G19 Die Mengenwörter *a little* und *a few*
Check-in

1. *A few* wird vor zählbaren und *a little* vor nicht zählbaren Nomen verwendet.
   zählbar: *a few friends, a few people*
   nicht zählbar: *a little help, a little water*

Check-out

1. a little: *milk, tea, coffee, coke*
   a few: *bagels, noodles, apples, kiwis*

G20 Die Verwendung von *some* und *any*
Check-in

1. a) einen bejahten Aussagesatz: *Nick's just making some more in the kitchen./I can get you some.*
   b) einen verneinten Aussagesatz: *I never eat any salads./We don't need any.*
   c) einen Satz, in dem eine höfliche Bitte oder Frage gestellt wird: *Could I have some more chips?/Would you like to try some Indian salad?/Would you like some more?*
   d) einen einfachen Fragesatz: *Is there any more iced tea, Jill?*
2. *Is there any more iced tea, Jill?* – Gibt es noch (etwas) Eistee?
   Any muss im Deutschen nicht zwingend wiedergegeben werden.

Check-out

1. a) *Have we got any candles for the birthday cake?*
   b) *Would you like some chips?*
   c) *There isn't any milk (left) in the bottle.*
   d) *Are there any plates on the table?*

G21 Die Verwendung von *no* und *none*
Check-in

1. no: *no reason, no curry* – steht direkt vor einem Nomen
   none: *none* – nachfolgendes Nomen wird nicht wiederholt
   none of: *none of our friends* – Pronomen

Check-out

1. a) *None of*   b) *no*   c) *none*

G22 Zusammensetzungen mit *some* und *any*
Check-in

1. 1) *someone, something, somewhere*
      c) bejahte Aussagen   d) höfliche Bitten, Vorschläge
   2) *anyone, anything, anywhere*
      a) Fragen   b) verneinte Aussagen

Check-out

1. *something; anybody; someone; anything; anybody*

G23 Zusammensetzungen mit *every* und *no*
Check-in:
1. a) jeder (*everybody*) – niemand (*nobody*)
   b) alles (*everything*) – nichts (*nothing*)
   c) überall (*everywhere*) – nirgendwo (*nowhere*)

Check-out:
1. a) *everywhere* b) *nobody* c) *nothing*
   d) *everybody*
   Lösung: *rule*

5 Das Adjektiv

G24 Die Verwendung von Adjektiven
Check-in:
1. a) Nomen   b) unveränderlich
2. a) Das Adjektiv steht vor einem Nomen.
   b) Das Adjektiv steht nach einer Form von *be*.

Check-out:
1. *pink; white; blue; dark; attractive; strict*
2. a) *Wendy is a happy young American teenager.*
   b) *She likes to wear her nice yellow jacket.*

G25 Das Adjektiv nach bestimmten Verben
Check-in:
1. c) nach dem Verb
2. a) *keep (quiet); are (lazy); stay (calm); seems (fine)*
   b) *get (fit); turn (nasty)*
   c) *feel (great)*
   d) *make (you happy); finds (you attractive)*

Check-out:
1. – *Horoscopes can be helpful.*
   – *Many boys and girls / A lot of teens get nervous without advice.*
   – *A lot of teens / Many boys and girls seem glad to have them.*
   – *Readers feel safe when they read them.*
2. a) *My mother finds horoscopes embarrassing.*
   b) *Paul doesn't make his parents happy.*

G26 Die Steigerung der Adjektive
Check-in:
1. a) *nice • nicer • the nicest* b) *sweet • sweeter • the sweetest* c) *attractive • more attractive • the most attractive* d) *heartless • more heartless • the most heartless*
2. Einsilbige Adjektive (*nice, sweet*) werden auf *-er/-est* gesteigert. Mehrsilbige Adjektive (*attractive, heartless*) werden mit *more/most* gesteigert.

Check-out:
1. *dirty, dirtier, the dirtiest • disappointing, more disappointing, the most disappointing • clean, cleaner, the cleanest • silly, sillier, the silliest • realistic, more realistic, the most realistic • wet, wetter, the wettest • dry, drier, the driest • shocking, more shocking, the most shocking*
2. a) *friendlier; more ambitious* b) *the biggest; the most expensive* c) *funnier; more polite; more helpful; the best; the easiest*

G27 Vergleiche mit Adjektiven
Check-in:
1. Ungleichheit: *… they are richer than teens five years ago! / … e-mails are not as important as social networks and text messages today.*
   Gleichheit: *… they are as old as five years ago.*

Check-out:
1. a) *A cheeseburger is cheaper than a giant doubleburger.*
   b) *A green salad is healthier than a doughnut.*
   c) *A giant doubleburger is bigger than a cheeseburger.*
   d) *A small coke is as expensive as a doughnut.*
   e) *A cheeseburger is tastier / not as tasty as a green salad.*

G28 Das Stützwort *one/ones* nach Adjektiven
Check-in:
1. c) *dress*
2. *earrings*

Check-out:
1. *black ones; white ones; white ones; new one; old one*

G29 Adjektive als Nomen
Check-in:
1. bezieht sich auf eine Gesamtgruppe von Personen: *the rich, the famous, the young*
   bezieht sich auf eine bestimmte Person: *a young girl, a talented performer*

Check-out:
1. a) *A homeless man; the rich; the poor*
   b) *an old woman*

6 Das Adverb

G30 Die Adverbien der Art und Weise
Check-in
1. *talk, answer, take, give, think, react*
   Es handelt sich jeweils um ein Verb.
2. *open – openly; honest – honestly; serious – seriously; gentle – gently; realistic – realistically; emotional – emotionally*
   Fragen 1-3: an das Adjektiv wird zur Bildung des Adverbs die Endung *-ly* angehängt;

Frage 4: beim Adjektiv entfällt *-le*; zur Bildung des Adverbs wird *-ly* angehängt

Fragen 5: Adjektiv auf *-ic*; zur Bildung des Adverbs wird + *-ally* angehängt

Frage 6: Adjektiv auf *-al*; das Adverb endet auf *-ally*

Check-out
1. *helpful; carefully; seriously; in a friendly way; True; openly*

G31 Die Steigerung der Adverbien
Check-in
1. *sooner; more closely; most openly; better – best; nearest*
2. a) Freunde bleiben deinem Herzen am nächsten.
   b) Ich spreche am offensten mit dir.

Check-out
1. a) *quickly* b) *easily* c) *more carefully* d) *more seriously* e) *fastest*

G32 Vergleiche mit Adverbien
Check-in
1. a) 1. Steigerung b) Grundform
2. Je mehr ihr schreit, desto besser können wir eure Stimmen aufnehmen.

Check-out
1. a) Ich kehre so oft wie ich kann in den Park zurück.
   b) Ich fahre mehr als einmal mit dem Riesenrad, wenn ich den Park besuche/im Park bin.
   c) Ich bevorzuge Tiershows. Sie gefallen mir besser als andere Attraktionen.
2. individuelle Antwort
3. *as loud as; quicker/more quickly; more often; the higher; the faster*

G33 Gradadverbien
Check-in
1. *very important, really want to; absolutely necessary, truly open*
2. vor Adjektiven, Adverbien und Verben

Check-out
1. a) *My friend absolutely drives me crazy / My friend drives me absolutely crazy*
   b) *They completely ignore me*
   c) *My mate really treats others badly / My mate treats others really badly*
   d) *I don't get enough pocket money*
   e) *She almost forgot my birthday*

G34 Adverbien mit der gleichen Form wie Adjektive und Adverbien mit und ohne *-ly*
Check-in
1. *nearly* – fast; *daily* – täglich; *lately* – in letzter Zeit; *fairly* – ziemlich; *late* – spät; *fast* – schnell; *well* – gut; *near* – nahe; *deeply* – zutiefst; *fair* – fair; *highly* – höchst

Check-out
1. a) *daily* b) *nearly* c) *lately; fairly/pretty* d) *fairly/pretty* e) *long* f) *hardly* g) *well* h) *highly*

G35 Adverbien und adverbiale Bestimmungen der bestimmten Zeit und Häufigkeit
Check-in
1. **bestimmte Zeit:** *yesterday, this evening, today, this afternoon, between 5 and 7, last month, tonight*
   bestimmte Häufigkeit: *every second Friday, once a month, twice*
2. Im Englischen steht die Angabe der bestimmten Zeit am Satzanfang oder am Satzende. Im Deutschen steht die Angabe der bestimmten Zeit meist in der Binnenstellung.
   – *Sorry I missed you yesterday.* – Tut mir leid, dass ich dich gestern verpasst habe.
   – *Have you got any plans for this evening?* – Hast du für heute Abend irgendwelche Pläne?
   – *I'm pretty busy today.* – Ich habe heute ziemlich viel zu tun.
   – *Later this afternoon I'm meeting Kelly and Mike.* – Heute Nachmittag treffe ich mich mit Kelly und Mike. / Ich treffe mich heute Nachmittag mit Kelly und Mike.
   – *Are you going to that dance tonight, too?* – Gehst du heute Abend auch auf den Ball?

Check-out
1. – *She's heard Jenny and Brenda do something together almost/nearly every day.*
   – Das stimmt, aber sie sehen sich nicht jedes Wochenende.
   – Er glaubt, dass Jenny dieses Wochenende zu Hause bleibt.
   – *Jenny is not going out so much right now because her aunt is visiting this week.*
   – *But as far as Jenny's aunt knows, Jenny is going to come/go (is coming/is going) to your house tonight/ this evening.*
   – Vielleicht sehen sie sich (dann) später noch.

G36 Adverbien der unbestimmten Zeit und Häufigkeit
Check-in
1. a) **mit dem Verb** *be*: *LAN parties with friends* **are always** *great fun.* / *… so it's* **usually** *every player for him or herself.*
   b) **mit Modalverb + Vollverb:** *You* **can sometimes go** *up one or even two levels …*
   c) **mit Vollverb:** *Multiplayer games* **normally get** *you to play …* / *The game* **regularly asks** *friends …*
   d) **mit Hilfsverb + Vollverb:** *… you'll* **often find** *that …* / *We've* **never played** *a game …*

2. a) Das Adverb steht nach dem Verb *be*.
   b) Das Adverb steht zwischen Modal- und Vollverb.
   c) Das Adverb steht vor dem Vollverb.
   d) Das Adverb steht zwischen Hilfs- und Vollverb.

Check-out

1. a) *have never played*   b) *usually order*
   c) *sometimes don't*   d) *soon became*   e) *should always play*   f) *is hardly ever*

G37 Adverbien des Orts und der Richtung
Check-in

1. a) *Tina and Jenny are at home.*
   b) *They can go to a dance party/to the New City Palace/to the forum.*
   c) *They can park the car around the corner (from the disco).*
   d) *They're going to walk to the disco/to the dance party.*
2. Adverbien des Orts und der Richtung stehen am Satzende.

Check-out

1. a) *to a dance* (2. Richtung)   b) *upstairs in the bathroom* (2. Ort); *everywhere* (2. Ort); *somewhere* (2. Ort)   c) *behind the sofa* (2. Richtung); *anywhere* (2. Ort)

G38 Die Reihenfolge mehrerer adverbialier Bestimmungen
Check-in

1. Die Reihenfolge adverbialer Bestimmungen ist Art und Weise, Ort/Richtung, Mittel, Zeit.

Art und Weise (Wie?)	Ort (Wo?)/ Richtung (Wohin?)	Mittel (Womit?)	Zeit (Wann?)
wildly	near the DJ	–	all evening
–	home	by train	quite early
enthusiastically	–	–	for hours
hard	at college	–	this year
–	–	–	at weekends
–	in school	–	tomorrow

Check-out

1. a) *She talked to him happily at the youth club yesterday evening.*
   b) *They will chat about the disco online tomorrow.*
   c) *Did you miss your friend at the party last night?*
   d) *They go to school by bus at 8 every morning.*
   e) *I enjoyed the weekend at my friend's house last month.*

2. a) *On the stage Tariq and Rhona were dancing happily all the time./All the time Tariq and Rhona were dancing happily on the stage.*
   b) *In the college canteen her cousin talked excitedly the next day./The next day her cousin talked excitedly in the college canteen.*
   c) *At school the girls discuss their plans every morning./Every morning the girls discuss their plans at school.*

G39 Satzverknüpfende und kommentierende Adverbien
Check-in

1. a) Anfangsstellung
2. *actually* – Betonung
   in fact – Erläuterung
   hopefully – Hoffnung
   unfortunately – Bedauern

Check-out

1. a) *Obviously, our winner wasn't experienced in writing songs.*
   b) *Therefore, she didn't think/believe that she would win.*
   c) *When she won, she was happy, of course.*
   d) *We'll probably see her again here next year.*

7 *Be, have* und *do* als Voll- und Hilfsverben

G40 *Be* als Voll- und Hilfsverb
Check-in:

1. ohne ein anderes Verb: *It's OK, thanks. • These blue ones are nice. • You're right. • But they're expensive, Ben. • Aren't those little teddies sweet? • That pink one is cool • I'm sure she'll like it.*
   mit einem anderen Verb: *We're just looking. • You're joking! • They're made in China. • It can be from both of us.*
2. *simple present* (alle Formen in der Spalte „ohne ein anderes Verb") • *present progressive* (We're just looking./You're joking.) • Passiv (They're made in China.) • Infinitiv (It can be from both of us.)

Check-out:

1. a) Vollverb   b) Hilfsverb   c) Hilfsverb   d) Hilfsverb
2. a) *Are Kim and Ben both invited to Sue's house?*
   b) *Were the T-shirts hanging in the shop window?*

G41 *Have* als Voll- und Hilfsverb
Check-in:

1. ohne ein anderes Verb: *Have a drink. • We had no idea what to get. • It has beautiful blue eyes.*
   mit einem anderen Verb: *I'm so glad you've come. • We've brought you … • But Fiona has given me …*
2. *present perfect (simple)*

Check-out:
1. a) *Has Ben been invited to Sue's party?*
   b) *Did Kim have a good time at the party last Saturday?*
2. a) *The house doesn't have a large garden.*
   b) *The Brooks haven't bought a new house.*

G42 *Do* als Voll- und Hilfsverb
Check-in:
1. ohne ein anderes Verb: *No, I* **don't**. • *Well, actually I* **did** *the cooking yesterday!* • *My mum always* **does** *everything in the kitchen.*
   mit einem anderen Verb: **Do** *you* **help** *at home?* • **Do** *you* **sit down** *with your family for meals?* • *No, I* **don't** *often* **help** *at home.* • **Do** *you* **do** *much, Sue?* • *What* **did** *you* **cook**? • *It* **didn't taste** *too bad.* • *I've never* **done** *anything like that.*
2. **Do** *you* **do** *much, Sue?*

Check-out:
1. a) Vollverb b) Vollverb c) Hilfsverb d) Hilfsverb
2. a) *Do you often meet your friends?*
   b) *Does Sue like their new house?*
   c) *Did Kim and Ben do their homework yesterday?*

8 Die Zeitformen der Gegenwart

G43 Die einfache Gegenwart
Check-in:
1. Das *simple present* wird mit dem Infinitiv (= Grundform) des Verbs gebildet.
2. Bei der 3. Person Singular muss im *simple present* ein -s angehängt werden.

Check-out:
1. a) *I don't enjoy TV shows about fashion.*
   b) *Josie doesn't work in a clothes shop.*
   c) *Models don't earn too much money.*
2. a) *Do you like jewellery?*
   b) *Where does Tony get his T-shirts?*
   c) *When do most people go shopping for clothes?*

G44 Die Verlaufsform der Gegenwart
Check-in:
1. Das *present progressive* wird mit einer Form von *be* und dem *present participle* gebildet.
2. Sie sagt *She's wearing a long green dress*, weil Lena es jetzt gerade trägt.

Check-out:
1. a) *Lisa is talking to a journalist.*
   b) *We aren't wearing our winter clothes today.*
   c) *Is Tom watching his favourite TV programme?*
   d) *I'm reading a fashion magazine.*
   e) *Are you enjoying the show?*

G45 Gegenüberstellung von *simple present* und *present progressive*
Check-in:
1. a) normalerweise b) zur Zeit
2. Gewohnheiten: *simple present*
   Handlungen, die momentan passieren oder sich über einen längeren Zeitraum erstrecken: *present progressive*

Check-out:
1. *loves; travels; goes; isn't travelling; is writing; meets; don't talk; forget*

G46 Die einfache Form des Perfekts
Check-in:
1. Das *present perfect simple* wird mit *have* oder *has* und dem *past participle* gebildet.
2. a)

Check-out:
1. *has been; has just landed; has already sold; have won; have given; have had: Has your success changed; Have you ever wished*

G47 Die Verlaufsform des Perfekts
Check-in:
1. Das *present perfect progressive* wird mit *have* oder *has + been* und dem *present participle* gebildet.
2. *Since* gibt den Zeitpunkt an, an dem die Handlung begann; *for* den Zeitraum, wie lange die Handlung schon andauert.

Check-out:
1. *for*: weeks, ages, a long time, half an hour, a few months
   since: 2011, last week, yesterday, the beginning of the year, August
2. a) *The boys have been chatting with fans for two hours.*
   b) *They have been answering their fans' questions since 11 am.*
   c) *Jason has been playing the drums for as long as he can remember.*
   d) *The boys have been making music together since they met on a TV talent show.*
3. b) *They have been touring France all month/all May.*
   c) *Harry has been signing autographs for one and a half hours.*
   d) *Jason has been answering fan mail for four hours.*
   e) *They have been working hard all year.*

G48 Gegenüberstellung von *present perfect simple* und *present perfect progressive*
Check-in:
1. a) Sie haben in den letzten zwei Jahren kein Mal/gar nicht in Birmingham gespielt.
   b) Sie machen schon seit sechs Jahren zusammen Musik.

Check-out:

1. a) *How long have you been working on your new album?*
   b) *How long have you known each other?*
   c) *The band hasn't/haven't played in Germany yet.*
   d) *I have been trying to get tickets for their concert since last week.*

9 Die Zeitformen der Vergangenheit

G49 Die einfache Vergangenheit

Check-in:

1.

Infinitiv	Aussagesatz	Verneinung	Frage
join	joined	didn't join	did (he) join
have	had	didn't have	did (he) have
get	got	didn't get	did (it) get
steal	stole	didn't steal	did (they) steal
paint	painted	didn't paint	did (they) paint
carry	carried	didn't carry	did (they) carry
hurt	hurt	didn't hurt	did (they) hurt
stop	stopped	didn't stop	did (they) stop

2. Die Handlungen liegen in der Vergangenheit und sind abgeschlossen.

Check-out:

1. *make – made; build – built; see – saw; eat – ate; teach – taught; do – did; fly – flew; go – went; be – were*
2. *was; joined; painted; stole, didn't do; were; picked; put; had; was; stopped; found; didn't believe; called; wasn't allowed to*
3. a) *When did you join the gang? / How old were you when you joined the gang?*
   b) *Did you steal from shops?*
   c) *Why did the store manager call the police? / Why weren't you allowed to enter his shop again?*

G50 Die Verlaufsform der Vergangenheit

Check-in:

1. Das *past progressive* wird mit *was* oder *were* und dem *present participle* gebildet. (*was/were = simple past* von *be; present participle = -ing*-Form)
2. Die Handlungen liefen gerade ab. Die Dauer der Handlungen soll betont werden.

Check-out:

1. *The boy was about 15 years old. He had dark hair. He was carrying a bat. He was wearing jeans, a dark blue T-shirt and large black sunglasses.*
2. *I was watching TV. • We were listening to some music. • We were doing (our) homework. • I was sleeping.*

G51 Gegenüberstellung von *simple past* und *past progressive*

Check-in:

1. kurze, abgeschlossene Handlung: *got on and sat down, began, fell, apologized, moved away, discovered* länger andauernde Handlung: *was sitting, were pushing and pulling, was unpacking*
2. *simple past: when, (almost) at once, suddenly, after that, later* *past progressive: while, when*

Check-out:

1. *was waiting; saw; were kicking; was watching; noticed; shouted; arrived; got on; were closing; jumped; were, was; were standing; came; saw; moved*
2. a) *They were kicking a plastic bottle around the platform.*
   b) *They shouted something at him angrily.*
   Unterschied:
   a) Sie kickten gerade mit einer Plastikflasche auf dem Bahnsteig herum.
      Die Handlung ist im Verlauf und erstreckt sich über einen Zeitraum.
   b) Sie schrien ihn verärgert/wütend an.
      Die Handlung ist kurz und abgeschlossen.

G52 Gegenüberstellung von *simple past* und *present perfect*

Check-in:

1. *simple past (were, picked up, put, walked, was, asked, said, didn't have, happened)*
2. *present perfect ('ve known, has done, have given, 've told)*

Check-out:

1. *have read; have seen; was; stole; gave; ever really lived*

G53 Die Verwendung von *used to* (früher)

Check-in:

1. – *You never used to mind.* • Es hat dir (doch) früher nichts ausgemacht. / Es hat dich doch früher nicht/ nie gestört.
   – *They just don't seem to be as safe as they used to be.* • Sie scheinen nicht mehr so sicher wie früher zu sein.
   – *Did your parents use to pick you up from parties when you were my age?* • Haben dich deine Eltern früher von Partys abgeholt? / Haben dich deine Eltern von Partys abgeholt als du in meinem Alter warst?
   – *I didn't use to stay out as late as you do.* • Ich war (früher) nicht so spät unterwegs wie du.
   – *I always used to be home by ten.* • Ich war (früher) immer vor 22 Uhr zu Hause.
2. im Infinitiv (= Grundform)

Check-out:

1. a) *This used to be a safe neighbourhood (but it isn't now).*
   b) *There never used to be much crime in the area when I was a kid. / There didn't use to be much crime in the area when I was a kid.*
   c) *It certainly didn't use to be as bad as it is today.*
   d) *We always used to leave our doors open (but you can't do that now).*
2. a) *We always used to take/catch the bus into town. / We always used to go into town by bus.*
   b) *Our parents didn't use to drive us anywhere. / Our parents never used to drive us anywhere.*
   c) *Itneverusedtobeaproblem./Itdidn'tusetobea problem.*
   d) *Did your parents use to pick you up from the disco?*

G54 Das Plusquamperfekt
Check-in:

1. Das *past perfect simple* wird mit *had* und dem *past participle* (= 3. Verbform) gebildet.
2. a) *simple past*
   b) *past perfect simple*

Check-out:

1. a) *had already started*   b) *didn't like; was*
   c) *sat down*   d) *remembered; had left*
2. *stayed; had already come; became; left; had changed; had built; had also introduced*

G55 Die Verlaufsform des Plusquamperfekts
Check-in:

1. Das *past perfect progressive* wird mit *had been* und dem *present participle* (= -ing Form) gebildet.
2. *They had already been living there for hundreds of years.*

Check-out:

1. a) *have only been learning*   b) *had only been learning*
2. a) Aber wir lernen erst seit zwei Wochen etwas über die Römer in Großbritannien.
   b) Die Schüler hatten vor dem Test am letzten Montag erst zwei Wochen (lang) etwas über die Römer in Großbritannien gelernt.
3. *had been working; had forgotten; had left; had eaten; had only been watching*

10 Die Zeitformen der Zukunft

G56 Das Futur mit *going to*
Check-in:

1.

Subjekt	Form von *be*	*going to*	Infinitiv	restlicher Satz
I	*'m*	*going to*	*give*	*you some information.*
You	*'re*	*going to*	*find*	*a topic.*
We	*'re*	*going to*	*make*	*videos.*
We	*'re*	*going to*	*show*	*each other our videos.*
We	*aren't*	*going to*	*have*	*live presentations.*
The next few weeks	*are*	*going to*	*be*	*hard enough.*

2. Am Ende des Monats werden wir uns unsere Videos zeigen. (am Ende des Monats, werden … zeigen)
   Am Ende des Monats zeigen wir uns unsere Videos. (am Ende des Monats, zeigen)

Check-out:

1. a) *I'm going to do my project with Chris and Sarah.*
   b) *My/Our project is going to be about cars.*
   c) *My/Our video is going to be five minutes.*
   d) *We are going to make our video in a car factory. / I'm going to make my video in a car factory.*

G57 Das Futur mit *will*
Check-in:

1. a) eine Frage: *What kind of cars will we have 50 years from now? / Will you write an introduction for the interview?*
   b) die Kurzform von *will: 'll*
   c) eine Aussage: *I'll interview a British car maker. / I think that will be interesting for Australians. / Great, and I'll be the cameraman!*
   d) eine verneinte Aussage: *But promise me that you won't play around with the camera!*
2. b) eine Vorhersage, wie das Projekt (wahrscheinlich) bei den Australiern ankommen wird

Check-out:

1. Chris: *I phoned Royal Cars yesterday. They'll have time for an interview on Monday.*
   Jay: *I'll come with you.*
   Chris: *Good idea, we'll both ask them questions.*
2. a) *I think a project about cars will be interesting for students.*
   b) *In 80 years' time the world won't have (will not have) cars.*

G58 Gegenüberstellung des Futurs mit *will* und *going to*

Check-in:

1. a) Zukünftiges, das sich schon in der Gegenwart abzeichnet)
   b) feststehender Plan
   c) Vorhersage über die wahrscheiniche Zukunft
   d) spontane Entscheidung
2. Das *going to-future* verwendet man für Zukünftiges, das sich schon in der Gegenwart abzeichnet und für feststehende Pläne.
   Das *will-future* verwendet man für Vorhersagen über die wahrscheinliche Zukunft oder um eine spontane Entscheidung auszudrücken.

Check-out:

1. a) *I hope my maths test won't be too difficult.*
   b) *Sarah is a clever girl. With my help I'm sure she'll get a good mark in her maths test.*
   c) *I'm going to prepare the questions now and then I'm going to send them to the people.*

G59 Die einfache Gegenwart mit Futurbedeutung

Check-in:

1. *simple present*
2. *My guitar lesson finishes at five.*

Check-out:

1. Jay: *Can we meet on Wednesday? Football practice finishes at five.*
   Chris: *That's difficult. My basketball training doesn't finish until 5:30 / starts at four and finishes at 5:30.*
   Jay: *I can catch the bus to the town centre. There is a bus that leaves/goes at 5:15. So I'll arrive in the town centre shortly after 5:30.*
   Chris: *I hope our trainer will finish on time.*

G60 Die Verlaufsform der Gegenwart mit Futurbedeutung

Check-in:

1. durch die Zeitangabe *at 7 pm on Friday*
2. *present progressive*

Check-out:

1. *On Monday morning I'm interviewing someone from Royal Cars. We are meeting in his office. Jay is coming with me as our cameraman.*

G61 Das Futur Perfekt

Check-in:

1. Bis 2060 werden wir die Ölvorkommen aufgebraucht haben.
2. *will + have + past participle*

Check-out:

1. a) *Professor Cole expects that oil companies will have discovered new oil fields by 2060.*
   b) *He is sure that scientists will have invented new ways to produce energy in 30 years' time.*
   c) *He hopes that people will have saved a lot of energy by 2050.*
   d) *He thinks that the world will have understood the importance of energy within the next 25 years.*

11 Die Modalverben

G62 Die Merkmale von Modalverben

Check-in:

1. a) Infinitiv (ohne *to*) b) Bei der Verneinung wird *not* bzw. *n't* hinter das Modalverb gestellt bzw. an das Modalverb angehängt, z. B. *needn't, mustn't.*

Check-out:

1. *I can play football but I can't play rugby.*
   Sports club members must pay at the beginning of each month.
   My back hurts. Maybe I should see a doctor before I start rugby training.
   The trainer wants to know if you can swim.
   I wasn't allowed to join the club because I was too young.
   The doctor will be able to see you tomorrow morning.

G63 Eine Fähigkeit mit *can, could* und *be able to* ausdrücken

Check-in:

1. a) *Yes, he can.* b) *No, he can't.*
2. Nach dem Verb *can* folgt immer der Infinitiv ohne *to.*

Check-out:

1. *can't / 'm not able to; can / 'm able to; could / was able to; couldn't / wasn't able to; will be able to*

G64 Eine Erlaubnis oder ein Verbot mit *can, may, mustn't* und *be allowed to* ausdrücken

Check-in:

1. a) Den Hockeyschläger über Schulterhöhe zu halten ist nicht erlaubt.
   b) Einen durch die Luft fliegenden Hockeyball zu schlagen ist nicht erlaubt.

Check-out:

1. a) *can / 'm allowed to* b) *was allowed to* c) *will be allowed to* d) *can / are allowed to*

G65 Mit *must*, *needn't* und *have to* ausdrücken, was (nicht) notwendig ist
Check-in:
1. Ja, beide Sätze sind möglich.
2. *Needn't* bedeutet „nicht müssen" oder „nicht brauchen". Du musst keinen eigenen Schläger mitbringen. / Du brauchst keinen eigenen Schläger mitzubringen.

Check-out:
1. a) Ich muss ein paar gute Fußballschuhe/-stiefel kaufen.
   b) Wir müssen/brauchen die Umkleidekabinen nicht putzen/sauber (zu) machen.
   c) Frank ist müde. Er muss/braucht nicht zum Training (zu) gehen.
   d) Musstest du teure Tennisschuhe kaufen?
   e) Sie mussten/brauchten für den Schwimmunterricht nicht (zu) bezahlen.

G66 Mit *shall* und *should* etwas vorschlagen oder raten
Check-in:
1. a) Soll/Sollte ich mehr essen?
   b) Soll ich am Samstag zu dir kommen?
2. *Should I eat more?* – bittet allgemein um Rat
   Shall I come to your house on Saturday? – bezieht sich auf eine einmalige Situation

Check-out:
1. Shall/Should; should; shouldn't; shall/should; Shall

G67 Mit *could*, *may* und *might* sagen, was möglich ist
Check-in:
1. a) vielleicht b) vielleicht

Check-out:
1. a) Carl könnte nächsten Monat Mitglied in unserem Sportverein werden.
   b) Vielleicht lerne ich Rugby zu spielen.
   c) Lisa wird vielleicht die beste Spielerin im Team.
   d) *Could we play next Sunday?*
   e) *I may/might watch the game on TV.*
   f) *The team might/could lose the game.*

G68 Modalverben mit dem Infinitiv Perfekt
Check-in:
1. a) Nein, er kann es sich nur ungefähr vorstellen.
   b) Nein, Paul ist zum Hockey gegangen.
2. Um über Dinge zu reden, die in der Vergangenheit hätten geschehen können, sollen oder müssen, verwendest du ein Modalverb + *have* + *past participle*.

Check-out:
1. a) *She must have won the tennis match.*
   b) *Serkan shouldn't have worn his glasses while he was playing volleyball.*
   c) *You should have been more careful!*
   d) *I needn't/shouldn't have worried about winning this race.*

12 Das Passiv

G69 Die Bildung und Verwendung des Passivs
Check-in:
1. a) 2 b) 1

Check-out:
1. a) *Tickets are sold.*
   b) *Musicals are performed.*
   c) *Backstage tours are offered.*
   d) *Costumes are made.*
2. a) *were made* b) *were thanked* c) *were invited*
   d) *were interviewed*

G70 Der *by*-agent
Check-in:
1. von Stephen Sondheim
2. nein (nur, dass es in andere Sprachen übersetzt wurde)

Check-out:
1. is loved by children and adults; was first performed; has been enjoyed by audiences; was designed by architects from Florida; was built; was attended by 1,740 people; was presented; was discovered by Alan Smith; was enjoyed by the party guests

G71 Das Passiv in den verschiedenen Zeiten
Check-in:
1. a) *present progressive* b) *past progressive*
   c) *future perfect*

Check-out:
1. a) *will be informed* b) *have been sent* c) *would be asked* d) *is going to be used*

G72 Der Infinitiv des Passivs
Check-in:
1. a) *They expect to be chosen for a big role right away.*
   b) *He hoped to be welcomed with open arms.*
2. a) bei Modalverben (*should*, *can*, *must*) steht der Infinitiv ohne *to*.
   b) bei den Verben *expect* und *hope* wird der Infinitiv mit *to* verwendet

Check-out:
1. Mobile/Cell phones mustn't be used (during the show). • Costumes should be washed once a week. • Snacks must be prepared (for the audience). • Souvenirs can be bought (in the shop).
2. a) to be served   b) to be treated   c) be cleaned   d) be put

G73 Das Passiv bei Verben mit zwei Objekten
Check-in:
1. Jemand hat ihm einen Job angeboten. • Man bat ihm einen Job an. • Ihm wurde ein Job angeboten.
2. Somebody gave him a job.

Check-out:
1. a) A map of New York was given to them in the hotel.
   b) The city was shown to them.
   c) She was sent a postcard from New York.
   d) Tino was taught words in American English.

G74 Die Verwendung von *have something done*
Check-in:
1. ArtExperts
2. Nichts. Er sitzt nur da uns lässt sich malen.

Check-out:
1. a) He has his letters taken to the post office.
   b) He has his/the door answered.
   c) He has his/the swimming pool cleaned.
   d) He has his clothes washed.

G75 Passivsätze mit Verben des Sagens und Meinens
Check-in:
1. Man sagt, dass New York die Stadt ist, die nie schläft.

Check-out:
1. a) Len Marconi is said to earn millions of dollars a month.
   b) He is believed to spend his vacations on his own private island.
   c) He is thought to have a holiday home in Dubai.

13 Die indirekte Rede

G76 Die indirekte Rede mit Einführungssatz im Präsens
Check-in:
1. simple present
2. "Greg, you shouldn't go surfing in stormy weather."

Check-out:
1. a) My girlfriend says (that) she worries about me when the weather is bad.
   b) My older sister says (that) we should be more careful.

   c) My dad says (that) he always listened to his father when he was younger.
2. a) The sign says (that) the beach is closed in winter.
   b) The sign says (that) dogs are not allowed on the beach.
   c) The sign says (that) you mustn't go surfing when the red flag is up.

G77 Die indirekte Rede mit Zeitverschiebung
Check-in:
1. simple past
2. b) Sie sagten, Australien sei toll für hohe Wellen.

Check-out:
1. a) She said (that) she felt excited when she was riding on top of a wave.
   b) He said (that) one day he'd (= would) be the best surfer in the world.
   c) A man mentioned (that) you could hurt yourself very badly if you went out in stormy weather.
   d) A boy told the reporter/journalist (that) he had learnt a lot from his father.

G78 Zeit- und Ortsangaben in der indirekte Rede
Check-in
1. b) "I am going surfing tomorrow."
2. b) im selben Monat, in dem Keith auf den hohen Wellen gesurft ist

Check-out
1. a) Keith told me that he didn't have time for an interview that evening.
   b) Keith said that there would be a lot of big waves the following week.
   c) Keith told me that he had ridden a 10m wave on that beach (in Los Angeles) two weeks before.
   d) Keith told me that someone else had asked him for an interview the next day.

G79 Indirekte Fragen
Check-in:
1. b) "How high were the waves?"
2. Er fragte mich, ob wir die Sturmwarnungen nachgeschaut/angesehen/angehört hätten. (whether = „ob")

Check-out:
1. a) My mom wanted to know if/whether I was OK.
   b) My girlfriend asked if/whether my hand hurt badly.
   c) My older sister wondered if/whether I had seen a doctor.
   d) My dad wanted to know who had been with me.
   e) My best friend wondered why I hadn't asked him for help.

G80 Indirekte Aufforderungssätze
Check-in:
1. a) Befehl
2. b) Ratschlag

Check-out:
1. a) *The weather bureau advised people to park their car in the garage.*
   b) *The weather bureau advised people to buy enough food for two days.*
   c) *The weather bureau warned people not to go near the beaches.*
2. a) *Greg's dad advised him not to leave the house.*
   b) *Greg's dad told him to close all the windows.*
   c) *Greg's dad told him to bring his bike inside.*
   d) *Greg's dad warned him not to let the cat out.*

14 Der Infinitiv

G81 Der Infinitiv mit *to* nach bestimmten Verben
Check-in:
1. *try*, *want*, *'d love*, *would like*

Check-out:
1. a) *would like to join*   b) *offered to introduce*
   c) *wants to meet*   d) *hopes to be able to*

G82 Der Infinitiv mit *to* nach Verb + Objekt
Check-in:
1. Objekt(pronomen)
2. Die Sekretärin hat Frau/Ms. Carter gebeten, Jonas diese Formulare zu geben.

Check-out:
1. a) *Jonas wanted Lynn to go to the fall dance with him.*
   b) *Lynn had not expected him to invite her.*
   c) *She asked him to meet her at/in school at 7 pm.*
   d) *Lynn's parents told her not to be/come home too late.*

G83 Der Infinitiv mit *to* nach Adjektiven und Nomen
Check-in:
1. a) *There are so many interesting things to do here / in Florida.*
   b) *It's easy to drive down to the Everglades. But right now isn't really the best time to visit. It's better to go when it's a bit cooler and there aren't so many mosquitos about.*

Check-out:
1. a) *place to spend*   b) *things to do*   c) *happy to take*
   d) *chance to see*

G84 Der Infinitiv mit *to* nach Fragewörtern
Check-in:
1. *I didn't really know (= (not) know); I wasn't sure (= (not) be sure); she showed me (= show); she told me (= tell); I'm wondering (= wonder)*

Check-out:
1. a) *who to phone*   b) *whether to walk there; whether to catch/to catch/catch*   c) *how to get*

G85 Der Infinitiv mit *to* zum Ausdruck einer Absicht
Check-in:
1. um sein Englisch zu verbessern; um mehr über amerikanische Schulen zu erfahren; um die amerikanische Kultur zu erleben

Check-out:
1. a) *to watch*   b) *to get*   c) *to tell*   d) *to listen to*
   e) *to ask*

G86 Der Infinitiv mit *to* nach *the first*, *the last*, *the only one*
Check-in:
1. Jonas hat gewonnen, weil er als Erster im Wasser war.
2. Jonas war der Einzige, der den Hai nicht gesehen hat.

Check-out:
1. a) *Jonas was the first German student to go to Miami High School.*
   b) *But he won't be the last German to spend a year there.*
   c) *Jonas is not the only person to write an Internet blog about her/his experiences.*

G87 Der Infinitiv ohne *to* nach *make* und *let* und einem Objekt
Check-in:
1. *let:* Erlaubnis; *make:* Zwang

Check-out:
1. a) *makes; lets*   b) *lets; makes*

G88 Der Infinitiv ohne *to* nach Verben der Wahrnehmung und einem Objekt
Check-in:
1. eine Wahrnehmung
2. komplette Handlung

Check-out:
1. a) *He didn't hear the dog bark.*
   b) *He didn't hear anybody open the window and climb in.*
   c) *He didn't notice the man pick up his wallet.*
   d) *He didn't see him take his money.*
   e) *He didn't see him leave.*

15 Das Gerundium

G89 Das Gerundium als Subjekt des Satzes

Check-in:

1. Das *gerund* wird aus dem Infinitiv des Verbs ohne *to* + *-ing* gebildet.
2. Subjekt

Check-out:

1. a) *working*   b) *sitting*   c) *giving*   d) *lying*
2. a) Zelten mit den Pfadfindern macht immer Spaß. / Es macht immer Spaß mit den Pfadfindern zu zelten.
   b) Das Sammeln von Geld für Wohltätigkeitsorganisationen ist nur eine von vielen Aktivitäten, die die Pfadfinder machen. / Geld für Wohltätigkeitsorganisationen zu sammeln, ist nur eine von vielen Aktivitäten, die die Pfadfinder machen.

G90 Das Gerundium als Objekt nach bestimmten Verben

Check-in:

1. *like, enjoy, imagine*
2. *hate, love, can't stand, begin, continue, finish, keep, (not) mind, practise, risk, start, stop*

Check-out:

1. b) *My dad loved being a scout when he was a boy.*
   c) *What do you enjoy doing in your free time?*
   d) *The boys didn't want to risk climbing the mountain in the fog.*
2. a) Würde es dir/Ihnen etwas ausmachen, auf mich zu warten?
   b) Mein Vater war als Junge gern Pfadfinder. / Mein Vater mochte es, als Junge Pfadfinder zu sein.
   c) Was machst du gern in deiner Freizeit?
   d) Die Jungs wollten es nicht riskieren, den Berg im Nebel zu besteigen.

G91 Das Gerundium nach Verben, Adjektiven oder Nomen + Präposition

Check-in:

1. *look forward to, interested in, afraid of, good at, the thought of, reason for, worry about*
2. **Verben mit Präposition:** *believe in, care about, dream of/about, feel like, talk of/about, think of/about*
   Adjektive mit Präposition: *bad at, crazy about, famous for, tired of, used to*
   Nomen mit Präposition: *the chance of, the idea of, in danger of*

Check-out:

1. a) *to*   b) *at; at*   c) *to*   d) *of*
2. a) *Sam isn't crazy about going on a canoe trip.*
   b) *He's afraid of falling in the river.*
   c) *He isn't good at swimming.*
   d) *He has never been interested in swimming.*

G92 Die „Objekt + Gerundium"-Konstruktion

Check-in:

1. a) Er freut sich darauf, dass Sam morgen nach Hause kommt.
   b) Sie macht sich Sorgen, dass er sich langweilt, wenn er nach Hause kommt.

Check-out:

1. a) *Do you mind me using your compass?*
   b) *Mum hates us being late.*
2. a) *My mum doesn't mind us (me and my brother) going away with the Scouts.*
   b) *But she is worried about us not liking the food.*

G93 Gerundium oder Infinitiv nach bestimmten Verben

Check-in:

1. Beide Bildunterschriften haben die gleiche Bedeutung: Wir spielten gerade Kricket am Strand, als es anfing zu regnen.

Check-out:

1. a) *Do you enjoy hiking?*
   b) *Would you like to climb the mountain with me today? – Yes, I'd love to. Would you mind waiting five minutes for me?*
2. a) Gehst du gern wandern? / Wanderst du gern?
   b) Möchtest du heute mit mir den Berg besteigen? – Ja, gern. Würde es dir etwas ausmachen, fünf Minuten auf mich zu warten?

G94 Gerundium oder Infinitiv mit Bedeutungsunterschied

Check-in:

1. **Abbildung 1:** Okay, Jungs. Hört jetzt bitte auf zu reden und hört aufmerksam zu.
   Abbildung 2: Guck mal! Da ist Charlie. Lass uns stehen bleiben, um mit ihm zu reden.

Check-out:

1. a) *telling*   b) *to take*   c) *to become*   d) *singing*
   e) *to ask*   f) *getting up*   g) *to start*   h) *drinking*
   i) *going*   j) *to collect*   k) *walking*

G95 Das Gerundium nach Präpositionen

Check-in:

1. *apart from, without, instead of, in spite of, by, for*

Check-out:

1. a) *In the evening the boys thanked the leaders for giving them a great day.*
   b) *Instead of singing happy songs around the fire, the boys tried to frighten each other by telling scary ghost stories.*
   c) *At 10 pm Sam went to bed without saying goodnight.*

d) *Apart from feeling tired, he was very pleased with his day.*

e) *In spite of being very tired, he did not fall asleep at once.*

2. a) *Instead of catching the steam train, the boys walked down the mountain.*

b) *Apart from being cold, it was a nice day.*

c) *They followed a path without knowing where they were going.*

d) *In spite of getting lost, they did not panic.*

e) *Finally they managed to find their way back by using their compasses.*

16 Die Partizipien

G96 Partizipien als Adjektive
Check-in:

1. *Present participles* erkennt man an der Endung *-ing*, z. B. *cheering, disappointing, amazing.* Die *past participles* der regelmäßigen Verben haben die Endung *-ed* (*unexpected, excited*); die *past participles* der unregelmäßigen Verben haben verschiedene Formen (*lost*).

2. auf Nomen

Check-out:

1. *interesting; thrilled; surprised; coming*

G97 Das Partizip anstelle eines Relativsatzes
Check-in:

1. auf Nomen

2. – All die Stunden, die auf das Training verwendet wurden, haben am Ende den Unterschied gemacht! / … haben es ausgemacht.

– Die Leute, die in der Nähe von uns standen, schrien so laut, dass ich noch nicht einmal die Leute verstehen konnte, die neben mir saßen.

– Die Punkte, die von dem anderen Team durch diese Freiwürfe gemacht / erzielt wurden, waren wirklich ärgerlich.

Check-out:

1 a) *The player scoring the most points will be given a prize.*

b) *Did you see the girl wearing the medals?*

c) *I've seen all the Mavericks matches shown on TV.*

d) *John was the only one not cheering.*

e) *Some of the things reported about the match were wrong.*

G98 Das Partizip Präsens und der Infinitiv ohne *to* nach Verben der Wahrnehmung und einem Objekt
Check-in:

1. Infinitiv (ohne *to*): *watch the Panthers* **play**; *saw the referee* **look**, *saw the referee* **stop**

Partizip Präsens (= *present participle*): *heard everyone* **cheering**, *noticed you and Andrea* **leaving**

2. Während der Infinitiv (ohne *to*) die Handlung als Ganzes beschreibt, betont das Partizip Präsens (= *present participle*) den Ablauf der Handlung.

Check-out:

1. a) *I heard a player from the other team shout at the referee.*

b) *The trainer noticed two players drop the ball.*

c) *Meg watched the other team practising.*

d) *Sarah's mother saw her come home very late after team practice.*

e) *I heard Andrea and Jill discussing the rules of the game.*

f) *We listened to the trainer talking/talk to the players during time-out.*

17 Das Verb und seine Ergänzungen

G99 Verben mit und ohne Objekt
Check-in:

1. mit Objekt: *corrected our Spanish tests; got very bad marks*
   allein: *sleep; went; write*

Check-out:

1. a) *go*: intransitiv   b) *buy*: transitiv   c) (*have to*) *write*: transitiv   d) (*Don't*) *eat*: intransitiv   e) *arrived*: intransitiv; *were*: intransitiv   f) *bring*: transitiv

G100 Verben mit zwei Objekten
Check-in:

1. direktes Objekt: Sache
   indirektes Objekt: Person
   didn't explain the grammar (direktes Objekt = Sache)
   to us (indirektes Objekt = Person)
   gave extra exercises (direktes Objekt = Sache)
   to students (indirektes Objekt = Person)
   didn't give me (indirektes Objekt = Person)
   anything (direktes Objekt = Sache)
   makes an extra worksheet (direktes Objekt = Sache)
   for everyone (indirektes Objekt = Person)

Check-out:

1. a) *Susan my secret*   b) *made*   c) *a present for him*   d) *the photos to everyone who was at my party*   e) *you $5*

G101 Verben mit Objekt und Ergänzung
Check-in:

1. *The class elected Jamie student representative.*
   That made him happy.
   Someone called Susan an idiot.

2. a) + b)

Check-out:

1. a) *When I came home from school I found the house empty.*
   b) *Our teacher said that we can paint our classroom green.*
   c) *Susan describes her boyfriend as a good-looking guy.*
   d) *After our team won the debating competition, the others called us champions.*
   e) *I don't see Jamie as a very close friend.*
   f) *There are a lot of things at school that make me angry.*

18 Die Satzarten

G102 Die Wortstellung in bejahten und verneinten Aussagesätzen
Check-in:

1. Im englischen Aussagesatz steht das Subjekt immer vor dem Verb.
2. c)

Check-out:

1. a) *Julia left the house after breakfast. / After breakfast Julia left the house.*
   b) *She met her friend at the bus stop.*
   c) *Her parents didn't expect her home before six o'clock.*
   d) *She went to the cinema in the evening. / In the evening she went to the cinema.*
2. ***A few weeks ago*** *Julia was on the Internet (**a few weeks ago**) when she found a teen chatroom. Just a few minutes after she had logged in, **she got** a private message from a boy called Paul. He was 16 years old and lived in the same town. They started to chat about music, school and friends. He was really sweet and funny, so when he asked her to meet him in town a few weeks later, she said 'yes' **at once**.*

G103 Entscheidungsfragen und Kurzantworten
Check-in:

1. Sie sind gleich.

Check-out:

1. a) *Are Helen and Julia best friends? –Yes, they are.*
   b) *Is Julia at Helen's house. – No, she isn't.*
   c) *Does Helen play hockey after school on Thursdays? – Yes, she does.*
   d) *Did Paul meet Helen in a chatroom? – Yes, he did.*
   e) *Has Julia already met Paul? – Yes, she has. (She has met Paul online.)*

G104 Der Fragesatz mit Fragewort
Check-in:

1. *when, whose, how, how much, how many, which*
2. What happened to her? (Nach dem Fragewort folgt kein Hilfsverb und kein Subjekt. Die Satzstellung ist wie im Aussagesatz.)

Check-out:

1. a) *Who*   b) *Where*   c) *When*   d) *What*
2. a) *Where did Julia go after school?*
   b) *Why didn't her friend Helen go with her?*
   c) *Who did Julia meet outside the cinema?*
   d) *What did they do together?*
3. a) *Who does Julia talk to on the Internet every day?*
   b) *What do they talk about?*

G105 Bestätigungsfragen
Check-in:

1. – Es ist ein bisschen früh, die Polizei anzurufen, oder?
   – Manchmal vergisst sie einfach die Zeit, nicht wahr?
   – Ja, aber sie war noch nie mehr als eine halbe Stunde zu spät, oder?
   – Aber sie hat heute Nachmittag keinen von ihren Freunden getroffen, stimmt's?
   – Nun, das wissen wir nicht genau, oder? Wir können später die Polizei rufen, nicht wahr?

Check-out:

1. *She is okay, isn't she?*
   I told you, didn't I?
   She met that guy from the Internet, didn't she?
   And he wasn't a 16-year-old schoolboy, was he?
   And his real name wasn't Paul, was it?
   Then we'll find out more, won't we?
   We've warned her so many times, haven't we?
   But she never listens to us, does she?
   It won't do any good, will it?

G106 Der Imperativ
Check-in:

1. a) positiv: 4; negativ: 1, 2, 3
   b) Die bejahte Form des Imperativs wird mit dem Infinitiv des Verbs ohne *to* gebildet, bei der verneinten Form setzt du *don't* davor.

Check-out:

1. a) *Remember; don't believe*   b) *tell*   c) *Don't go*

19 Die Relativsätze

G107 Die Relativpronomen als Subjekt von notwendigen Relativsätzen
Check-in:

1. *which*: things; *who*: people; *that*: people, film
2. *who*: Personen; *which*: Sachen; *that*: Personen und Sachen

Check-out:

1. – *They want boys and girls who are between six and eight years old.*
   – *Mike is looking for an assistant who has worked with children before.*
   – *They are trying to find costumes which look like clothes from the 18th century.*
   – *The company needs old carriages which can take six people.*

G108 Die Relativpronomen als Objekt von not-wendigen Relativsätzen; *contact clauses*

Check-in:

1.

Bezugswort	Objekt	Subjekt
film review	*that*	*you*
an actor	*who*	*you*

2. Phil lässt jeweils das Relativpronomen weg.
   He's the kind of actor (who) I really admire!
   All the roles (that) he has played are just awesome!

Check-out:

1. *New forum on films and actors*
   Are you interested in films? Then come and join our forum Cinemania. Please write about all the films you've seen recently or comment on the actors and the roles they play. Who is the actor you like most?

G109 Nicht notwendige Relativsätze

Check-in:

1. Der Hauptsatz bleibt auch ohne die hervorgehobenen Satzteile (= Zusatzinformation) verständlich.
2. In nicht notwendigen Relativsätzen wird *who* für Personen und *which* für Sachen verwendet.

Check-out:

1. a) *Yesterday I went to the cinema in Leicester Square,* **which** *only opened last week. Two women,* **who** *were talking to each other loudly, were sitting in the row in front of me. …*
   b) *A friend and I were watching* Bend it like Beckham *at the MAX CINEMA,* **which** *was full of people inside. …*

G110 Das Relativpronomen *whose*

Check-in:

1. c)
2. ein Nomen (= Substantiv)

Check-out:

1. *Stephenie Meyer is a writer whose vampire novels have been turned into films. They are about a seventeen-year old girl whose name is Bella Swan. She moves from Phoenix to Forks to live with her dad. There she falls in love with Edward Cullen, whose family are all vampires. Stephanie Meyer, whose novels are often described as 'dark romance', has won the hearts of many teenagers.*

G111 Das Relativpronomen *which* mit Bezug auf einen Hauptsatz

Check-in:

1. *Which* bezieht sich auf den gesamten vorhergehenden Hauptsatz.
2. was

Check-out:

1. a) *Although Orlando Bloom wasn't feeling very well, he came to the film festival, which his fans hadn't expected at all.*
   b) *He even gave autographs while he was walking along the red carpet, which was great for his fans.*
   c) *He only gave a short interview for a TV station, which was a pity.*

20 Die Bedingungssätze

G112 Der Bedingungssatz Typ I: Erfüllbare Bedingungen

Check-in:

1. *if*-Satz: *simple present*; Hauptsatz: *will-future*
2. *If you don't do anything, she won't know how you feel about her.*

Check-out:

1. a) *If I pass my driving test, I'll get a car from my parents.*
   b) *If I save enough money, I'll buy a new computer.*
   c) *If I work hard at school, I'll go / I might go to university.*
   d) *If I go to the party, I'll meet / I may meet John.*
   e) *If I get a well-paid job soon, I'll go to Spain on holiday.*
   f) *If my parents allow it, I'll invite all my friends to a party.*

G113 Der Bedingungssatz Typ II: Unerfüllbare Bedingungen

Check-in:

1. Man kann nicht sagen *if I have wings*, weil dies eine erfüllbare Bedingung ausdrückt, Menschen aber keine Flügel haben können.
2. *Wenn du mich auch lieben würdest/liebtest, wäre ich der glücklichste Mann auf der Welt.*
   Im Deutschen verwendet man im Nebensatz den Konjunktiv und im Englischen das *simple past*.

Check-out:

1. a) *I would have lots of friends if people knew how nice I am.*
   b) *My ex-girlfriend would still like me if I were/was a completely different person.*
   c) *My mum and I wouldn't fight so much if she tried to understand me.*

d) *I would buy all the coolest clothes if my parents gave me more pocket money.*

e) *I wouldn't always yell at my little brother if he acted more like a normal kid.*

G114 Der Bedingungssatz Typ III: Unerfüllbare Bedingungen mit Vergangenheitsbezug

Check-in:

1. *if*-Satz: *past perfect (simple)*; Hauptsatz: *conditional perfect*

2. Wenn wir nicht so in Eile gewesen wären, hätten wir noch einmal „Ich liebe dich" gesagt.
   Im Deutschen wird im Nebensatz und im Hauptsatz der Konjunktiv verwendet, im Englischen steht im Nebensatz das *past perfect*.

Check-out:

1. *If you had told me, I would have tried to help you.*

2. a) *If my dad hadn't found a new job, we wouldn't have moved to this town.*
   b) *If we hadn't moved to this town, I wouldn't have come to this school.*
   c) *If I hadn't come to this school, Sarah and I wouldn't have met.*
   d) *If Sarah and I hadn't met, I wouldn't have fallen in love with her.*
   e) *If I hadn't fallen in love with her, I would have spent more time with friends.*

G115 Bedingungssatz Typ 0: Gesetzmäßigkeiten oder Regelmäßigkeiten ausdrücken

Check-in:

1. Im *if*-Satz und im Hauptsatz steht jeweils das *simple present*. Eigentlich müsste im Hauptsatz das *will-future* stehen.

2. Während sich der erste Satz sich auf eine konkrete Situation bezieht, trifft der zweite Satz eine allgemeingültige Aussage.

Check-out:

1. a) *If you talk this way, it hurts me.* (allgemeingültige Aussage)
   b) *Don't worry. It won't be the end of the world if you fight sometimes.* (bezieht sich auf die Zukunft)
   Don't worry. That's not the end of the world if … (allgemeingültige Aussage)

G116 Wunschsätze mit *simple past* und *past perfect*

Check-in:

1. Gegenwart: *I wish you were here!* • *If only you knew how much I think of you.* • *It's time we moved together, isn't it?*
   Vergangenheit: *If only you had talked to me!* • *I wish I had met you earlier.*

2. *past perfect* und *simple past*

Check-out:

1. b) *If only you had called yesterday. / I wish you had called yesterday.*
   c) *I wish you wanted to be my lover. / If only you wanted to be my lover.*

21 Satzverknüpfungen

G117 Die Verknüpfung von Hauptsätzen durch Konjunktionen und Adverbien

Check-in:

1. a) *or*   b) *but*

2. Der amerikanische Westen ist ein breites Thema, deshalb/darum werden wir einen Plan erstellen müssen.
   Ich interessiere mich auch (wie du, Adam,) für die ersten Siedler, also/deshalb kann ich dir vielleicht dabei helfen.

Check-out:

1. – *You can find a lot of information in history books, or would you prefer to look on the Internet?*
   – *We can make a poster with interesting texts and pictures, and (but) we can (also) give a presentation to the class.*
   – *We must finish the project by the end of the month, so let's start as soon as possible.*
   – *The Wild West seems to be all about cowboys and Indians, but the important part that women played is often forgotten.*
   – *Hollywood Westerns can be very exciting, but often they haven't got much to do with reality.*
   – *I'm interested in the 'first Americans', and/so I want to find out more about them.*

G118 Adverbiale Nebensätze der Zeit

Check-in:

1. a) Wenn Menschen von der Ostküste zum Pazifik reisen wollen, ist die Entfernung kein Problem.
   b) Als sich die ersten weißen Siedler in Planwagen auf den Weg gen Westen machten, war Reisen beschwerlich.

2. Bevor die Bahnstrecke gebaut wurde, hatte die Reise monatelang gedauert.
   Im Englischen ist die Wortstellung sowohl im Haupt- als auch Nebensatz Subjekt – Verb (– Objekt). Im Deutschen steht im Nebensatz Subjekt – (Objekt) – Verb; im Hauptsatz Verb – Subjekt (– Objekt), wenn der Nebensatz an erster Stelle steht.

Check-out:

1. a) *When* b) *Before* c) *After* d) *As soon as*
   e) *while* f) *until*
2. a) *Katie likes listening to music while she's doing her homework. / … while she does her homework.*
   b) *As soon as Jonathan has found a good text, we can carry on / continue with our project.*
   c) *We must / have to wait until he phones / calls.*
   d) *After they (had) found enough texts, they started looking / to look for good pictures.*

G119 Adverbiale Nebensätze des Grundes
Check-in:

1. a) Da/Weil sich die Sioux von Büffelfleisch ernährten, war ein Leben ohne Büffel/sie nicht möglich.
   b) *as*
2. Life without the buffalo was not possible because the Sioux ate their meat.

Check-out:

1. a) *The buffalo were important for the Indians because they ate their meat.*
   b) *Since the Indians had a simpler lifestyle, the whites didn't respect them.*
   c) *As they realized that the Indians couldn't survive without buffalo meat, the whites killed most of the buffalo.*
   d) *The whites moved a lot of Indians to reservations because they wanted the land for themselves.*
   e) *Since they didn't want to give up their land, some Indian tribes fought against the whites.*
   f) *As lots of them had been killed by the whites or died on the way to reservations, the Indian population in the US was down to 250,000 by the end of the 19th century.*

G120 Weitere adverbiale Nebensätze
Check-in:

1. *… although lots of Native Americans could have taken these parts.*
   … while others were Mexicans or – yes! – American Indians.
2. Vergleich: *Cowboys in these old films all seem to be white men, **as if** that was a true picture of reality. Films about life out west **as** it really was would not have been exciting enough for 20-century audiences.*
   logische Folge: *The mythical idea of cowboys in fights against 'wild' Indians was created **so that** films would offer top entertainment.*

Check-out:

1. a) *Although they had planned everything very carefully, a lot of things still went wrong.*
   b) *While Adam wanted to ask his mother for help, the others preferred to do everything themselves. / While the others preferred to do everything themselves, Adam wanted to ask his mother for help. / Adam wanted to ask his mother for help while the others preferred to do everything themselves.*
   c) *Jonathan talked about cowboy films for ages as if they had all the time in the world. / As if they had all the time in the world, Jonathan talked about cowboy films for ages.*
   d) *We can all watch an old Western together so that we can understand things better.*
   e) *Could you do something on Yellowstone as you know far more about national parks than we do? / As you know far more about national parks than we do, could you do something on Yellowstone?*

Grammatikbegriffe

Englisch	Deutsch	Erklärung/Beispiel
active (voice)	Aktiv	⟺ **passive (voice)** Aktiv: *Emma Perry **drove** to the opening of the new Broadway show.* Passiv: *Emma Perry **was driven** to the opening of the new Broadway show.*
adjective	Adjektiv, Eigenschaftswort	*I've got a **nice** family.*
adverb	Adverb, Umstandswort	Es gibt verschiedene Arten von Adverbien: *adverbs of degree, frequency, manner.*
adverbial	adverbiale Bestimmung	*He smiles in **a friendly way**.*
adverbial clause	adverbialer Nebensatz (der Zeit, des Grundes, des Gegensatzes, des Vergleichs, des Zwecks, der Folge)	Adverbiale Nebensätze werden z. B. eingeleitet durch Wörter wie *before, because, although, as, so that.*
article	Artikel	Es gibt den bestimmten (*definite*) und den unbestimmten (*indefinite*) Artikel.
auxiliary (verb)	Hilfsverb	Formen von *be, have* und *do*, die du z. B. für die Bildung einiger Zeitformen, für Fragen und zur Verneinung benötigst.
clause	Teilsatz	Es gibt verschiedene Arten von Teilsätzen: *contact clause, main clause, if-clause, relative clause.*
collective noun	Sammelbegriff	*I missed my **baggage**.*
comparative (form)	Komparativ, 1. Steigerung	*I can't believe there's anyone with a **bigger** problem.*
conditional	Konditional	*would + infinitive* *If I had wings, I **would fly** up to heaven.*
conditional perfect	Konditional II, Konditional Perfekt	*would + have + past participle* *If we had known, we **would have** loved more.*
conjunction	Konjunktion	*and, or, but* *Mark is interested in the Native Americans, **and** he wants to find out more about them.*
contact clause	Relativsatz ohne Relativpronomen	*Johnny Depp is the kind of actor ~~who~~ I really admire.*
countable noun	zählbares Nomen	⟺ **uncountable noun** *I've just bought **two magazines** in the shop over there.*
defining relative clause	notwendiger Relativsatz	⟺ **non-defining relative clause** *My friends are all people **who normally prefer action films**.*
definite article	bestimmter Artikel	***The** flight was OK.*
demonstrative determiner	Demonstrativbegleiter	*Let's go to **that** café over there.*

demonstrative pronoun	Demonstrativpronomen	*Chris: There's a big festival party here at 10 o'clock.* *Emma: Really? I didn't know **that**.*
direct object	direktes Objekt, Akkusativobjekt	⇔ **indirect object** *Ms Garcia **gave extra exercises** to everyone who had problems.*
direct speech	direkte Rede	⇔ **indirect speech**, ⇔ **reported speech** *"You can't go surfing in stormy weather."*
dynamic verb	Tätigkeitsverb, Vorgangsverb	⇔ **stative verb** Verb, das in der Verlaufsform vorkommen kann, z. B.: *eat, drink, play, sing, speak, walk.*
emphasis	Betonung, Hervorhebung	z. B. mit Reflexivpronomen, durch Umstellung z. B. von Orts- oder Zeitangaben.
future (tense)	Zukunft, Futur	Die wichtigstens Zeitformen der Zunkunft sind: *will-future, going to-future, simple present with future meaning, present progressive with future meaning.*
future perfect	Futur II, vollendetes Futur, Futur Perfekt	*We**'ll have run out** of oil by 2060.*
genitive	Genitiv	Es gibt zwei Genitivformen: *genitive with of, s-genitive.*
gerund	Gerundium, Verb als Nomen	***Hiking**, **singing** songs and **telling** ghost stories around the campfire is always fantastic fun.*
going to-future	Zukunft/Futur mit *going to*	*I**'m going to** give you some information about our video project now.*
if-clause	Bedingungssatz	***If I send her a card**, she may not like it.*
imperative	Imperativ, Befehlsform, Aufforderungssatz	***Don't use** your real name.*
indefinite article	unbestimmter Artikel (ein/eine/ein)	*Ben's aunt works as **a** detective.*
indirect object	indirektes Objekt, Dativobjekt	⇔ **direct object** *Ms Garcia didn't give **me** anything.*
indirect speech	indirekte Rede	= **reported speech**, ⇔ **direct speech** *One surfer said **he would risk anything for a big wave**.*
infinitive	Infinitiv, Grundform des Verbs	mit *to:* *Lynn offered **to help** him.* ohne *to: I noticed a black car **stop** outside a jeweller's shop.*
intransitive verb	intransitives Verb	⇔ **transitive verb** Verb, das kein direktes Objekt nach sich zieht. *I **went** to school with a bad feeling.*
irregular verb	unregelmäßiges Verb	⇔ **regular verb** *write – wrote – written*

long form	Langform	⇔ **short form** vorwiegend schriftlicher Sprachgebrauch, z. B. *had not* (statt *hadn't*)
main clause	Hauptsatz	Satz mit Subjekt und Verb, der für sich allein stehen kann.
modal verb/ auxiliary	Modalverb, modales Hilfsverb	*can, may, might, must, mustn't, needn't, should* etc. *How **can** I join the club?*
negative form	Verneinung, Negation	*Julia **wasn't** hungry.*
negative statement	verneinte Aussage	⇔ **positive statement** *Julia didn't eat any breakfast.*
non-defining relative clause	ergänzender/nicht notwendiger Relativsatz	⇔ **defining relative clause** *Johnny Depp, **who was born in 1963**, is one of the most popular actors in the world.*
noun	Nomen, Substantiv, Hauptwort	Es gibt verschiedene Arten von Nomen: *collective noun, countable noun, uncountable noun, adjectives as nouns.* *My **aunt** and **uncle** have got a **hotel** in Malaga.*
number	Zahl, Numerus	Mehrzahl/Plural (*plural*) Einzahl/ Singular (*singular*)
object	Objekt	Es gibt zwei Arten von Objekten: direktes Objekt = Akkusativobjekt (*direct object*); indirektes Objekt = Dativobjekt (*indirect object*).
of-genitive	Genitiv mit *of*, präpositionaler Genitiv	*You'll get to know the old quarter **of** the city.*
participle construction	Partizipialkonstruktion	*The people **standing** near us were screaming so much.*
passive (voice)	Passiv	⇔ **active (voice)** Aktiv: *Emma Perry **drove** to the opening of the new Broadway show.* Passiv: *Emma Perry **was driven** to the opening of the new Broadway show.*
past (tense)	Vergangenheit, Präteritum	Dazu gehören Zeitformen wie z. B. das *simple past* oder *past progressive*.
past participle	Partizip Perfekt; auch dritte Verbform genannt	Du benutzt es, um z. B. das *present perfect* zu bilden, als Adjektiv oder um einen Relativsatz zu verkürzen.
past perfect (simple)	Plusquamperfekt, Vorvergangenheit	*In 43 AD the Romans arrived in Britain. But, of course, they **had been** here before.*
past perfect progressive	Verlaufsform des Plusquamperfekts, Verlaufsform der Vorvergangenheit	*When the Romans arrived in Britain in 43 AD, the Celts **had** already **been living** there for hundreds of years.*
past progressive	Verlaufsform der Vergangenheit	*Just as I **was going** past house number 20, a woman stopped me.*

person	Person	1st person sg: *I am* 2nd person sg: *You are* etc.
personal passive	persönliches Passiv	Aktiv: *He gave me a book.* Passiv: *I was given a book.*
personal pronoun	Personalpronomen	als Subjekt: *I, you, he, she, it, we, you they* als Objekt: *me, you, him, her, it, us, you, them*
phrase	Phrase, Wendung	Einheit aus mehreren zusammengehörigen Wörtern, z.B. *a bottle of milk, early in the morning.*
plural	Plural, Mehrzahl	⇔ **singular** *I've spoken to two **women** who are travelling with their **babies**.*
positive	Grundform des Adjektivs/ Adverbs, Positiv	*I've seen a **trendy** skirt.*
positive statement	bejahte/positive Aussage	⇔ **negative statement** *Julia wanted to meet a friend.*
possessive determiner	Possessivbegleiter, besitzanzeigender Begleiter	*my, your, his* etc.
possessive pronoun	Possessivpronomen, besitzanzeigendes Pronomen	*mine, yours, his* etc.
preposition	Präposition, Verhältniswort	*at, behind, between, in, next to* etc.
present (tense)	Gegenwart, Präsens	Dazu gehören die Zeitformen *simple present* und *present progressive.*
present participle	Partizip Präsens	Du benutzt es, um z.B. das *present progressive* oder *past progressive* zu bilden, als Adjektiv oder um einen Relativsatz zu verkürzen.
present perfect (simple)	Perfekt	*I**'ve known** Holly for years.*
present perfect progressive	Verlaufsform des Perfekts	*We**'ve been touring** the UK for the past ten months.*
progressive (form)	Verlaufsform	Auch *continuous* genannt. Dazu gehören z.B. die Zeitformen *present progressive* und *past progressive.*
pronoun	Pronomen	Es gibt verschiedene Arten von Pronomen: *demonstrative pronoun, personal pronoun, possessive pronoun, reciprocal pronoun, reflexive pronoun, relative pronoun.*
prop word	Stützwort	*one/ones* *Which dress should I wear? The black **one** or the red **one**?*
quantifier	Mengenwort	*some, any, a few, a little, a lot of, much, many* etc.

question	Frage	Es gibt Fragen ohne Fragewort = Entscheidungsfrage (*yes/no question*) und Fragen mit Fragewort (*question with question word*).
question tag	Frageanhängsel, Bestätigungsfrage	*We can phone the police later, **can't we?***
question word	Fragewort	*who, what, where, when, why, how* etc.
reciprocal pronoun	reziprokes Pronomen	Das Pronomen drückt eine gegenseitige Handlung aus. *They are looking at each other.*
reflexive pronoun	Reflexivpronomen	*myself, yourself, himself, herself, itself, ourselves, yourselves, themselves*
regular verb	regelmäßiges Verb	⇔ **irregular verb** *join – join**ed** – join**ed***
relative clause	Relativsatz	Es gibt verschiedene Arten von Relativsätzen: *contact clause, defining relative clause, non-defining relative clause.*
relative pronoun	Relativpronomen	*who, which, that, whose*
reported speech	indirekte Rede	= **indirect speech**, ⇔ **direct speech** *One surfer said he would risk anything for a big wave.*
reporting verb	einleitendes Verb; Verb, das die indirekte Rede einleitet	*One surfer **said** he would risk anything for a big wave.*
s-genitive	Genitiv mit ‚s'	*I came in my **parents'** car.*
sentence	Satz	*Sue has moved house.*
short answer	Kurzantwort	*Did you meet Julia in town this afternoon? – **Yes**, **I did.**/ **No**, **I didn't.***
short form	Kurzform	⇔ **long form** durch Auslassung oder Zusammenziehung entstandene Verbform; vorwiegend mündlicher Sprachgebrauch, z.B. *is* ⇒ *'s, had not* ⇒ *hadn't*
simple (form)	einfache Form	⇔ **progressive form** Dazu gehörten z.B. das *simple present* und das *simple past.*
simple past	einfache Vergangenheit	= **past simple** *Three years ago, when I **was** 14 years old, I **joined** a gang.*
singular	Einzahl, Singular	⇔ **plural** *Amy is reading a **book** at the moment.*
statement	Aussagesatz	⇔ **question** Es gibt positive/bejahte Aussagesätze (*positive statement*) und negative/verneinte Aussagesätze (*negative statement*).

stative verb	Zustandsverb	⇔ **dynamic verb** Verb, das normalerweise nicht in der Verlaufsform vorkommt: *be, know, seem, have* etc.
subject	Subjekt (Wer?)	**She** *was in a hurry.*
superlative	Superlativ, 2. Steigerung	*Jason can't decide which of the two girls **is the nicest**. He finds himself in **a most embarrassing** situation.*
syllable	Silbe	einsilbig: *mouse*; zweisilbig: *trend-y*; mehrsilbig: *beau-ti-ful*
tense	Zeitform, Tempus	*simple present, present progressive, present perfect, simple past, will-future* etc.
transitive verb	transitives Verb	⇔ **intransitive verb** Verb, das ein direktes Objekt nach sich ziehen kann. *Ms Garcia **corrected our Spanish tests** at the weekend.*
uncountable noun	nicht zählbares Nomen	⇔ **countable noun** *advice, baggage, water* etc.
verb	(Voll)Verb	Es gibt verschiedene Arten von Verben: *auxiliary verb, dynamic verb, intransitive verb, irregular verb, modal verb/auxiliary, regular verb, stative verb, transitive verb, verb of perception.*
verb of perception	Verb der Wahrnehmung	*feel, hear, listen to, notice, see, watch*
will-future	Futur/Zukunft mit *will*, Futur I	*I hope we**'ll find** enough information.*
word order	Satzstellung, Wortstellung	Subjekt – Verb – Objekt – Ort/Richtung – Zeit
yes/no question	Entscheidungsfrage, Ja-/Nein-Frage, Frage ohne Fragewort	***Did you meet Julia in town this afternoon**? – Yes, I did./ No, I didn't.*

Register